# THE DYNAMICS OF AGGRESSION
## Biological and Social Processes in Dyads and Groups

# THE DYNAMICS OF AGGRESSION
## Biological and Social Processes in Dyads and Groups

Edited by

## Michael Potegal
Walter Reed Army Institute of Research

## John F. Knutson
University of Iowa

**LEA** LAWRENCE ERLBAUM ASSOCIATES, PUBLISHERS

1994  Hillsdale, New Jersey                     Hove, UK

Lawrence Erlbaum Associates, Inc., Publishers
365 Broadway
Hillsdale, New Jersey 07642

**Library of Congress Cataloging-in-Publication Data**

The Dynamics of aggression : biological and social processes in dyads
and groups / edited by Michael Potegal, John F. Knutson.
    p.  cm.
  Includes bibliographical references and indexes.
  ISBN 0-8058-0729-2
  1. Aggressiveness (Psychology)  2. Escalation (Military science)
3. Psychology, Comparative.  I. Potegal, Michael.  II. Knutson,
John F.
  BF575.A3D8  1994
  302.5'4 – dc20               94-442
                                  CIP

Printed in the United States of America
10  9  8  7  6  5  4  3  2  1

To our families and friends,
who gave us their unstinting support
during the long period when this book
was more a possibility than a certainty.

# Contents

# Preface

THREE INTERPRETATIONS OF ESCALATION
AND FROM WHENCE THEY COME

The point of origin of this book was a symposium on the temporal aspects of aggression organized by the editors at a meeting of The International Society for Research on Aggression in Swansea, Wales, in 1988. A common denominator of the work presented at that symposium was that when aggression was analyzed over time, escalations in the form or intensity of aggression often appeared. It seemed to us that a focus on such escalations, and the dynamics of aggression more generally, could provide a context in which social and biological research on the aggressive behaviors of human and nonhuman subjects, interacting in dyads or groups, could be compared and integrated.

A diversity of chapters on aggression and its vicissitudes has been assembled between the covers of this book. Aggressive behavior is described at different levels of analysis in a variety of animal species, including Siamese fighting fish, laboratory strains of house mouse, Syrian golden hamsters, and humans. A major question being addressed by this juxtaposition is whether it is possible to discern general principles controlling the dynamics of aggression. We see three basic interpretations of escalation being delineated by the contributors of this book. The first of these is essentially an economic one: Aggression will be escalated when it pays one of the combatants to do so or, more generally, when the potential benefits outweigh the risks. Although escalated combat may involve emotional arousal and stress, the crucial aspect of escalation in this interpretation is that the decision to escalate is part of a calculated "strategy," in one or another sense. This interpretation is presented in historical perspective by Bohstedt, who reminds us that riots are not as chaotic as they may appear but that the behavior of rioters involves the evaluation of payoffs and risks. For example, the historical record supports the intuitive hypothesis that the larger the crowd, the greater the likelihood of success. This intuition is as least as likely to occur to riot participants before the fact as it is to riot scholars afterwards. The economic interpretation is formalized within game theoretic models like those found in Archer and Huntingford's chapter, which describes some successful applications of these models to conflict between individual nonhuman animals. Leng's chapter on international conflict describes applications to conflict between large political organizations of humans. Empirical tests of these models applied to the behavior of individual humans have also been conducted; Daly and Wilson (1988) have identified patterns of homicide predicted by inclusive fitness analysis (e.g., around the world, children are more likely to be murdered by their stepfathers than by their fathers).

The second interpretation of escalation places emphasis on processes within the individual. Berkowitz stresses the importance of acute emotional states of anger and aggressive arousal in the escalation of impulsive aggression. Zillmann argues for the role of peripheral sympathetic activation in these emotional processes in humans, while Potegal proposes a central neural mechanism based on observations of other animals. There is no necessary contradiction between these latter views, insofar as each has been shaped by the limits of the available experimental evidence; physiological observations of central processes in humans have not been possible until recently, and hamsters have yet to offer a verbal report on their feelings of anger. Several chapters take cognizance of chronic factors affecting the likelihood of escalation. Caprara and his colleagues have attempted to identify factors in the adult personality that would influence susceptibility to escalation. Einon and Potegal's chapter on tantrums in young children describes some new evidence suggesting that aggressiveness is a consistent cross-situational trait in very young children. They also review the data, to which Cairns and his colleagues add, showing that aggressiveness in humans remains stable during development from middle childhood to adulthood. Bronstein's report that, under fixed conditions, different fish consistently choose to attack or escape and similar findings by Cairns and his colleagues of consistency in mice are in the same spirit.

The third interpretation is that the most important process in escalation is the interaction between antagonists; that it is an emergent event. Knutson and Bower cite the work of Patterson and others showing that child abuse can emerge from the escalating interaction between parent and child. In the same vein, the Einon and Potegal chapter suggests that the feelings and behaviors of mothers of aggressive, highly tantrum-prone children differ from those of other mothers; these authors also present evidence suggesting that some of the mothers' behaviors may exacerbate the children's tantrums. Orford's (1986) review of findings that hostile/dominant behavior elicits equivalent counterhostility in clinical interview and therapeutic situations is noteworthy, in part because it refers to a literature rarely cited in the present context, but also because these observations contradicted the theoretical expectations of some of the investigators who were looking for complementarity in social interactions. The term *interaction* in this context readily conjures up images of unbounded escalation (e.g., Leng's "conflict spiral"), but interactions can also be guided by rules that lead to other outcomes. The strategy of "tit for tat" has been shown by computer simulations to minimize the cost of conflict and encourage cooperation in the long run (Axelrod, 1984; cf. the discussion of "reciprocity" in the chapter by Cairns and colleagues). In the context of riots, Bohstedt suggests that underresponse by police encourages the rioters, but overresponse can induce a persisting anger that will kindle the next riot. These latter formulations mirror a point made in greater detail by Knutson and Bower and by Cairns and his colleagues. There are both acute and chronic aspects to aggressive interactions in humans and other animals. Thus, when the window of analysis truncates the representation of interactions, it can obscure the full temporal course of behavior. Investigations of naturally occurring groups or dyads must consider the rapidity of escalation in relative terms. For example, a growing literature on the prevalence of physical coercion in dating relationships has established that there are few pure users or recipients of violence in these couples. To some extent, coercion is reciprocal (e.g., Cate, Henton, Koval, Christopher, & Lloyd, 1982; Knutson & Mehm, 1988; Lane & Gwartney-Gibbs, 1985; Makepeace, 1981; Marshall & Rose, 1988; Matthews, 1984; Roscoe & Callahan, 1985). Because the more extreme forms of coercion do not emerge initially in these relationships, there must be an escalation across episodes of interaction. Moreover, not all the dating relationships described in this literature terminate on the occurrence of physical violence, making it clear that the more injurious interactions are embedded within an extended series of episodes. Similarly, most physical abuse of children is not a single-episode affair. Thus, a considerable corpus of research suggests that escalation across episodes needs to be considered in studies of human aggression. The same theme appears in the Einon and Potegal tantrum chapter.

## FINDING LINKS AMONG THE THREE INTERPRETATIONS

Is there any possibility of integration among the foregoing interpretations? In the most typical game thoretical analyses, aggression is about the capture and holding of resources. In species and circumstances where successful aggression leads directly to territory, access to mates, or other resources, the goals of aggression and its instrumentality are obvious. The logical connection between aggressiveness and inclusive fitness is less obvious in many other conflict situations, however. Teasing, harassment, and other hostile behaviors by bullies in the school yard, young men on the street corner, or corporate executives in the board room may appear gratuitous. They are not. They are about establishing and displaying status. Among the young of many species, play fighting is important in establishing dominance; Neill (1985) has implied that at least some rough-and-tumble bouts between children which even the children themselves would describe as playful may function as tests of strength that help establish dominance. Moving to behaviors with more serious consequences, arguments and disputes over apparently trivial causes are a source of a large fraction of reported homicides, at least in industrialized countries where such statistics are kept (e.g., Curtis, 1974). At first glance these latter instances of aggression seem to be more appropriately explicable in terms of the short-term motivational stages and/or long-term personality factors favored by the second interpretation of escalation. These concepts lie securely within the classical domains of psychology; what could game theory have to say about these conflicts? The link may be that the control of tangible resources is only one aspect of maintaining or increasing inclusive fitness. In the context of group living, increasing one's dominance status in general increases mating success and the survival of one's own young. Chagnon (1988) found that the patterns of homicide and warfare in a Yanomamö tribal population were consistent with game theoretic expectation; men who had killed, and thereby earned a reputation for fierceness, had more progeny than those who had not killed. By continually reasserting their own status, dominant animals may also impose a degree of stress on their subordinates, which reduces the latter's level of function (Eberhart, Yodyingyuad, & Keverne, 1985).

Reducing subordinates' inclusive fitness indirectly increases their own. The benefits of dominance also extend into future generations; among social mammals as diverse as rabbits, wolves, and monkeys, the progeny of dominant animals are often themselves dominant (e.g., Koyama, 1967).

But aggression is not the exclusive province of the dominants in a group. A very recent report indicates that encounters between subordinate swordtail fish escalate even more quickly than encounters between dominants (Ribowski & Franck, 1993). In many groups, subdominants intermittently probe the fitness of the dominant, ready to take advantage of momentary situational weakness or the more gradually debilitating effects of sickness or age. Subdominant animals may also form alliances and together take over control of the group (de Waal, 1989). Similarly, under some laboratory conditions, dominance status can be associated with increased likelihood of being the target of attack, whereas subordinate status can be associated with a lowered probability of being the target of attack. In a recent study, Meyerson (1988) selected dominant and subordinate rats living in small social groups and tested them later in the resident–intruder paradigm. Regardless of the dominance status of the resident, when dominant animals were placed in an intruder role, they were attacked more quickly and frequently than subordinate rats serving as intruders. Thus, although there are transituational consequences of dominance status, dominance in one situation is not necessarily associated with agonistic success in other settings. Momentary social role and the interactive aspects of an exchange can influence the outcome of an aggressive sequence. Based on these findings, Meyerson (1988) speculated that subordinate status in some circumstances can be adaptive in that it can reduce the frequency and intensity of agonistic encounters.

In the course of the evolution of social animals, the dominance route to inclusive fitness appears to have assumed primary importance. The common coins of this struggle are short, low-cost encounters; nonescalated forays that occur much more frequently than prolonged fights (see chapters by Potegal and by Cairns et al.). An important but little cited observation is that even within stable, long established rat colonies, a few minutes of fighting occurs daily (Blanchard, Flannelly, & Blanchard; 1988). This fighting was discovered by 24-hr/day videotaping using cameras invisible to the subjects so that even the slight disturbance introduced by the coming and going of human observers was eliminated. Thus, fighting occurs in circumstances where there are no *apparent* sources of aversiveness (pain, frustration, etc.) or social disorganization which have been alleged to be necessary for aggression. Such fighting can function to reconfirm the dominant/subordinate heirarchy.

Rhesus monkeys, for example, are notorious for their continual challenges to one another. Escalation by one combatant can signal the detection of weakness in his opponent, a *realpolitik* among the monkeys, in Leng's terms. Probably the best known nonhuman example is the chimpanzee politics described by de Waal (1989). This interpretation can be applied to some intergenerational conflicts between child and parent; Einon and Potegal report that most tantrums flare up and subside quickly as children briefly probe the limits of parental acquiesence.

It has been demonstrated in the laboratory that prior interactions between animals can determine the probability and the form of their subsequent agonistic encounters (e.g., Knutson & Viken, 1984; Viken & Knutson, 1983). More generally, animals have memory, and social animals remember what other members of their group have done or not done. Thus, threats and other displays of dominance must be backed up by occasional action to be believable. Individuals may attack to preclude future challenges. On the group level, Chagnon (1988) has reported that a tribal village with a reputation for not fighting is likely to be raided by its neighbors. Leng notes that for nation states, too, making threats automatically raises the political stakes. National leaders must be willing to back up bluffs; their opponents have historical memory. In this view, escalation to overt aggression is the inevitable concomitant, sooner or later, of the continual displays and probings that are a large part of daily politics. In von Clauzewitz's (1968) famous dictum, "War is the conduct of politics by other means." Indeed, there is generally a positive correlation between threat and attack in animals (see reviews by Bronstein and by Potegal). Similarly, Leng notes that shows of military force are associated with actual attack. The relationship between threat and attack has been explored within the game theory context. As reviewed by Archer and Huntingford in their section on deception, some early, simple models (e.g., the War of Attrition) suggested that aggressive threat should be uncorrelated with the actual willingness to attack and that bluffing should be common because giving away one's intentions provides information that would be advantageous to one's opponents. However, a number of empirical studies have shown that threat can, in fact, predict attack (e.g., Dabelsteen & Pedersen, 1990). Subsequent models, which take into account additional factors such as the costs of concealing intent, the immediate reactions of the opponent, or the recognition of individual opponents and the concomitant memory of how that opponent behaved in the past, indicate that the expected relationship between threat and attack depends on the particular circumstances being modeled. These models predict that, in many situations, displays should be more or less accurate indicators of the probability of subsequent attack.

The foregoing arguments notwithstanding, the spectacle of animals snapping and snarling at each other, a child having a tantrum, parents maltreating their children, or men engaged in a bloody fight seems hardly reconcilable with the deployment of rational strategies. On a psychological level, furthermore, children escalating their tantrums, adult humans and animals of other species intensifying their interpersonal conflicts, and national leaders going to a war footing all appear to suffer a narrowing of attention and progressive failure of cognitive abilities under the intensifying stress of conflict. Of course, this fits the psychologist's standard U-shaped function of arousal and performance, but this sort of explanation masks the important point that distal evolutionary ends are subserved by proximal neurobehavioral mechanisms that have logic and limitations of their own. Perhaps some of these changes in attention, pain threshold, cognitive function in general, and risk taking in particular reflect a "commitment to aggression," in Bronstein's felicitous phrase, which is necessary to allow organisms to engage in dangerous and painful encounters for a possible major payoff.

## PATTERNS IN THE TIME COURSE OF ESCALATION

Theories, like other bargains with the devil, are a trade-off. They provide a certain sort of tunnel vision, allowing one look deeply along particular lines of sight. The price for such insight is the loss of other perspectives. If game theoretic analyses reveal similarities between conflict among humans and that among other animals, is it simply because the data are being fitted to the same theory? Post facto explanations of behavioral phenomena according to evolutionary theory can easily become just-so stories. An alternative to deductive, theory based research and its concomitant tunnel vision is the empirical search for patterns in the data. Aggressive episodes, from tantrums to riots, begin, escalate, reach a peak, and are resolved. This similarity of temporal pattern across scales of minutes to days is the necessary consequence of the fatigue, defeat, withdrawal, injury, or death that ends the conflict. As described by Archer and Huntingford, game theoretic models strongly predict that all but the briefest agonistic encounters should have an asymmetrical structure: A relatively long period of escalation during which combatants evaluate their relative fighting abilities should be followed by a rapid de-escalation when one combatant, having decided that he cannot win or that winning would be too costly, escapes or submits. Many encounters do follow this pattern. However, several contributors to this volume have identified another pattern. Cairns and his colleagues relate their counterintuitive discovery that encounters between adolescents escalate rapidly and de-escalate slowly. This kind of asymmetry also appears to be true of episodes of spouse abuse as reported in the surveys reviewed by Einon and Potegal. If one considers escalation across a series of episodes, the epidemiologic data on recidivism and the chronicity of child abuse suggests that progressively more rapid escalations of aggression occur in the homes of maltreated children (Knutson & Schartz, in press). These particular situations may be uniquely characterized by the fact that the individuals involved know each other, and it is quite clear to all parties who is dominant in strength, fighting ability, and willingness to fight. A pattern of rapid rise and slow descent has also been observed in the attack priming effect in dyadic agonistic encounters between animals (Potegal). Leng comments that " . . . crises ranking highest on escalation . . . were the cases most likely to end in war." Leng's rankings of escalation included a measure of the rate of escalation, suggesting that rapid escalation is associated with greater risk of war. As a strategy, either consciously planned or genetically programmed, rapid escalation has the advantage of surprise. However, Bohstedt notes that riots also tend to build quickly and wind down more slowly. Riots do not have strategies. An explanation on a different level of analysis is that a positive feedback is involved; the more an individual (or a group) invests in a conflict, the more they are likely to invest (cf. Pruitt & Rubin, 1986, for descriptions of such processes). In the case of riots, risks go down and the probability of success increases as numbers rise, so individuals may be recruited to the riot at an accelerated rate. Events like these, in which the rate of growth is proportional to magnitude already attained, grow exponentially. Perhaps the dynamics by which individuals become involved in conflict are governed by similar principles. Certainly Zillmann's theorizing about progressive sympathetic involvement would lend itself to such models. It would be most useful to define the range of conditions under which each kind of asymmetry occurs. In looking for similarities and continuities in the dynamics of aggression across scales, we add the caveat that it is important to remember that groups are not individuals. Until similarities in the dynamics of individuals and groups are formally demonstrated and/or empirically discovered, individual emotion and behavior can, at best, be only a metaphor for group action (see, e.g., some of the arguments in Harris, Fried, & Murphy, 1967).

## AN ORGANIZATIONAL COMMENT

Finally, a comment on the order of chapters. The chapters by Archer and Huntingford and by Berkowitz were placed first and second, respectively, to introduce two different orientations to aggression dynamics which the reader could keep in mind as he or she peruses the remainder of the book. The first chapter is a game theoretic account of conflicts among animals, and the last chapter is a similarly based account of human arms races. In part, we have chosen to so bracket this volume to illustrate some of the commonalities which we believe to exist between humans and other animals. Some will question whether animals who torture, have blood feuds with, and make war on fellow species members and who, in the pursuit of those wars, have invented poison gas, nuclear weapons, and Rambo can be plausibly compared with animals of species that merely butt, claw, and bite each other. But humans are, after all, biological organisms, and some of the processes central to their aggression surely must be shared with other vertebrates. Young males of many species engage in dominance contests in which aggression may be escalated to great intensity without regard to personal injury. In evolutionary context, the payoffs presumably outweighed the risks. The current homicide rate among young men in the United States, a testimony to the lethality of guns, suggests that a trade-off that may have been adaptive for individuals in the original evolutionary context has been rendered devastating for society by the technology of weaponry. Insofar as weapons are unlikely to disappear, the development of an understanding of the factors leading to their use is an important route to the eventual control of these factors. We hope that this volume contributes to such understanding.

## REFERENCES

Axelrod, R. (1984). *The evolution of cooperation.* New York: Basic Books.

Blanchard, R. J., Flannelly, K. J., & Blanchard, D. C. (1988). Life-span studies of dominance and aggression in established colonies of laboratory rats. *Physiology and Behavior, 43,* 1-7.

Cate, R. M., Henton, J. M., Koval, J., Christopher, F. S., & Lloyd, S. (1982). Premarital abuse: A sociological perspective. *Journal of Family Issues, 3,* 79-90.

Chagnon, N. (1988). Life histories, blood revenge, and warfare in a tribal population. *Science, 239,* 985-992.

Curtis, L. (1974). *Criminal violence.* Lexington, MA: Lexington Books, D. C. Heath & Co.

Dabelsteen, T., & Pedersen, S. B. (1990). Song and information about aggressive responses of blackbirds, *Turdus merula,* evidence from interactive playback experiments with territory owners. *Animal Behaviour, 40,* 1158-1168.

Daly, M., & Wilson, M. (1988). Evolutionary social psychology and family homicide. *Science, 242,* 519-524.

de Waal, F. (1989). *Peacemaking among primates.* Cambridge, MA: Harvard University Press.

Eberhart, J. A., Yodyingyuad, U., & Keverne, E. B. (1985). Subordination in male species Talapoin monkeys lowers sexual behavior in the absence of dominants. *Physiology and Behavior, 35,* 673–677.

Harris, M., Fried, M., & Murphy, R. (Eds.). (1967). *War, the anthropology of armed conflict and aggression.* Garden City, NY: The Natural History Press.

Knutson, J. F., & Mehm, J. G. (1988). Transgenerational patterns of coercion in families and intimate relationships. In G. W. Russell (Ed.), *Violence in intimate relationships.* New York: PMA Publishing.

Knutson, J. F., & Schartz, H. A. (in press). Evidence pertaining to physical abuse and neglect of children as a parent–child relational diagnosis. In T. A. Widiger, A. J. Frances, & H. A. Pincus (Eds.), *DSM–IV sourcebook.* Washington, DC: American Psychiatric Association.

Knutson, J. F., & Viken, R. J. (1984). Animal analogs of human aggression: Studies of social experience and escalation. In K. J. Flannelly, R. J. Blanchard & D. C. Blanchard (Eds.), *Biological perspectives on aggression* (pp. 75–94). New York: Alan Liss.

Koyama, N. (1967). On dominance rank and kinship of a wild Japanese monkey troop in Arashiyama. *Primates, 8,* 189–216.

Lane, K. E., & Gwartney-Gibbs, P. A. (1985). Violence in the context of dating and sex. *Journal of Family Issues, 6,* 45–49.

Makepeace, J. M. (1981). Courtship violence among college students. *Family Relations, 32,* 101–109.

Marshall, L. L., & Rose, P. (1988). Family of origin violence and courtship abuse. *Journal of Counseling and Development, 66,* 494–498.

Matthews, W. J. (1984). Violence in college couples. *College Student Journal, 18,* 150–158.

Meyerson, D. (1988). *Effects of prior social experience upon rat aggression in the resident intruder paradigm.* Unpublished masters thesis, University of Iowa, Iowa City.

Neill, S. R. St. J. (1985). Rough-and-tumble and aggression in schoolchildren: Serious play? *Animal Behaviour, 33,* 1380–1381.

Orford, J. (1986). The rules of interpersonal complementarity: Does hostility beget hostility and dominance, submission? *Psychological Review, 93,* 1–10.

Pruitt, D. G., & Rubin, J. Z. (1986). *Social conflict.* New York: Random House.

Ribowski, A., & Franck, D. (1993). Subordinate swordtails males escalate faster than dominants. *Aggressive Behavior, 19,* 223–229.

Roscoe, B., & Callahan, J. E. (1985). Adolescents' self-reports of violence in families and dating relationships. *Adolesence, 79,* 545–553.

Viken, R. J., & Knutson, J. F. (1983). Effects of reactivity to dorsal stimulation and social role on aggressive behavior in laboratory rats. *Aggressive Behavior, 9,* 287–301.

von Clauzewitz, K. (1968). *On war.* New York: Penguin.

# PART I

# Differing Perspectives on Aggression Dynamics: Introduction to Game Theoretical Analyses and Arousal Hypotheses

# CHAPTER 1

# Game Theory Models and Escalation of Animal Fights

John Archer
*University of Central Lanchashire, United Kingdom*

Felicity Huntingford
*University of Glasgow, United Kingdom*

## ESCALATION IN ANIMAL FIGHTS

Fighting is widespread in the animal kingdom (Archer, 1988; Huntingford & Turner, 1987), occurring most commonly over access to valuable but limited resources, such as food or mates. The exact form of the behavior is very variable; anemones club each other with specialized tentacles, crickets kick each other and lash out with their antennae, frogs wrestle, gulls peck, and gorillas beat their chests. There are, however, some features that are common to the great majority of animal fights, one of these being the occurrence of escalation.

Most species have a number of different aggressive actions in their repertoire, and these are deployed in a characteristic sequence. Fights often begin when the opponents are at a distance from one another, exchanging movements or displays that are of relatively low intensity and therefore low cost both in terms of energy consumption and the likelihood of damage. If these low-intensity actions do not cause one or the other contestant to withdraw, then patterns of behavior that are progressively more energetic and more risky come into play, culminating in the most intense and damaging acts in the animals' repertoire. These are the most effective in inducing withdrawal or submission in the opponent. This progressive increase in the intensity and cost of behavior as a fight proceeds is referred to as *escalation*.

Escalation has been described in detail in many ethological studies of animal fights. One example is a laboratory study of the cichlid fish (*Nannacara anomala*) by Jakobsson, Radesater, and Jarvi (1979), which fight over status within a social group. In the initial phases of the fight, the fish commonly engage in actions such as lateral display and tail beats that are performed at a distance and involve a low risk of injury. As the fight progresses, these actions drop out in favor of mouth wrestling and biting, which involve direct physical contact and are more intense; in this species escalated fighting carries a greater risk of injury, in the form of lost scales and damaged fins.

A second example comes from a field study of iguanas carried out on an islet near Panama by Rand and Rand (1976). Iguanas (*Iguana iguana*) come here to breed, and the females dig burrows in which they lay their eggs; digging burrows is hard work and occurs over several days, interspersed with resting periods away from the burrow. Disputes arise when a female returning from resting tries to take over a burrow that currently has a resident. Here again, fights involve an escalating series of displays that can be characterized in terms of increasing cost, cost for these ectothermic animals being mainly in terms of energy expenditure. Thus, fights progress from open mouth display to head swing, to huff, lunge, and bite, each one bringing the opponents nearer together, as well as being more energetic and more effective in intimidating a rival.

As a last example, red deer stags (*Cervus elephas*) fight during the rut over access to females (Clutton-Brock, Guinness, & Albon, 1982). Initially, they simply roar at each other from a distance (Fig 1.1a), and the male with the slowest roar often retires at this point. However, some fights progress to the more intense stage of parallel walking (Fig. 1.1b), and of these a proportion proceed to antler wrestling (Fig. 1.1c), which is energetically costly and may result in injury.

In all three species, fights stop when one animal, the loser, gives up, thus leaving its opponent victorious. The behavior shown by the winner and loser are similar and indicative of aggressive motivation until near the end of the fight; the eventual loser then reverts rapidly to low-cost actions (de-escalation) and withdraws from the encounter. For example, early on in fights between cichlid fish (*Nannacara anomala*), both the eventual winner and the eventual loser tend to respond to a bite (a high-cost, escalated action) by retaliating in kind. However, just before the end one animal starts responding to a bite with tail beating and frontal displays, and this is the eventual loser (Jakobsson et al., 1979).

FIG. 1.1. Fight between red deer stags during the rut over access to females: (a) roaring from a distance, (b) parallel walking, (c) antler wrestling (after Clutton-Brock et al., 1982).

**5**

## GAME THEORY AND ANIMAL FIGHTS

Such ethological studies provide detailed descriptions of the process of escalation but do not explain why escalation occurs, either in terms of its evolution or the behavioral mechanisms responsible for it. Recent attempts to explain the evolution of animal fighting make extensive use of a branch of applied mathematics called *game theory*. These analyses investigate the evolutionary consequences of using different patterns of fighting by depicting animals fighting in these different ways as players in a game. The earliest game theory models of animal fights were used to explain why, given the great rewards for winning, animals do not always fight as fiercely as possible; in other words, they set out to explain the existence of both low-intensity and high-intensity forms of fighting. Later models dealt with, among other things, the question of why animal fights so often take the form of a sucession of increasingly intense and costly actions; in other words, these models explain the occurrence of escalation.

## EXPLAINING THE EXISTENCE OF HIGH- AND
## LOW-INTENSITY FIGHTING

The simplest game theory model of animal fighting is the hawk–dove model (Maynard Smith, 1976, 1982). This model considers two individuals competing for some resource to which one gains exclusive access if its opponent retreats or is injured. The players are identical except that doves use only low-cost displays and continue until one withdraws, whereas hawks always launch straight into fierce, high-cost fighting, stopping only when one animal is injured. In the game theory literature, hawks are sometimes described as showing escalated (as opposed to conventional) fighting, which is different from the ethological use of the term (see Caryl, 1981).

The costs and benefits gained by hawks and doves in fights against opponents using these same two strategies are calculated (based on preset rules that determine the outcome of each kind of fight) to give the payoff matrix shown in Table 1.1. The analysis works out the overall fitness of individuals pursuing each strategy and from this the relative frequency of the strategies in successive generations. In particular, it works out if either strategy is *evolutionarily stable*, meaning that when it is common it cannot be bettered by any other strategy in the game under the cost–benefit conditions defined by the game's rules. Evolutionarily

TABLE 1.1
Payoff Matrix for the Hawk–Dove Game

| Payoff to: | When Fighting: | |
| | Hawk | Dove |
| --- | --- | --- |
| Hawk | 1/2 (V-I) | V |
| Dove | 0 | 1/2 V |

Note. V = Benefit accruing to victor. I = Cost of injury.

stable strategies (ESSs) are how we would expect real animals to behave if the game has defined correctly the costs and benefits of high-risk and low-risk fighting. In this game, hawk is an ESS when the benefits of victory outweigh the costs of injury; when the converse is true, even though hawks always defeat doves, because costs are high they lose out, so that neither is an ESS; there is, however, a certain (evolutionarily stable) proportion of doves and hawks at which the two strategies gain equal payoffs.

## PREDICTING THE OCCURRENCE OF ESCALATION

By showing that, because of the costs of injury, hawk is not always an ESS, the hawk–dove model explains the co-existence of high- and low-intensity forms of fighting. However, the simple hawk–dove dichotomy was set up to investigate the fitness-related consequences of using displays rather than overtly aggressive actions and so does not depict the progressive increase in intensity described in the ethological studies of animal fights (Caryl, 1981). Later we show other game theory models that *can* help us to understand certain features of the process of escalation.

### The Importance of Risk of Injury

So far, we have described the process of escalation as if all fights in a particular species proceed in an identical way. There is, however, great variability in whether and to what extent animal conflicts become escalated. In some cases, one animal may flee relatively quickly without engaging in intense, costly fighting; in other encounters involving the same species, and perhaps even the same individuals on a different occasion, fights may be long and fierce. Game theory models can help us to predict the circumstances in which we would expect fights to escalate to high-cost actions by specifying in functional terms when it will no longer be advantageous for an animal to continue fighting. To anticipate and oversimplify, escalated fights are to be expected when the animals concerned are equally matched in fighting ability and when both place a high value on the disputed resource.

The game theory model most relevant to predicting the occurrence of escalated fights is Parker's (1974) assessment strategy model. Building on Maynard Smith's earliest analyses (Maynard Smith, 1972; Maynard Smith & Price, 1973), Parker set out the following simple but compelling argument: Any individual that is able to assess how its own fighting ability (designated as *resource holding power* or RHP) compares with that of its opponent will be at a selective advantage, because it could withdraw without damage when its own RHP was lower but attack (with a good chance of winning) when its own RHP was higher.

The simple concept of RHP enables us broadly to predict the circumstances when escalated fights will occur. These exist when the opponents' RHPs are reasonably well matched; when they are not, the one with the lower RHP will withdraw after an initial assessment or "sizing up" phase (Parker, 1974). These principles have been incorporated into formal game theory models (Maynard Smith, 1982, Maynard Smith & Parker, 1976), which extend the original hawk–dove game. The additional feature is a strategy called *assessor* that attacks (plays hawk strategy) if its RHP is higher and displays (plays dove strategy) if it is lower. Where escalation proves to be costly, as in the case of animals with dangerous weapons, the assessor strategy is shown to be an ESS (Table 1.2). More precisely, assessor will be an ESS when the cost of losing an escalated fight is greater than the cost of the assessment phase. Under the opposite conditions, where assessment is costly yet escalation is less dangerous, the hawk strategy of unconditional attack is the ESS.

Assessment may be more costly than escalated fighting in ectothermic animals (i.e., where energy resources can be problematic) without dangerous weapons, for example, in toads and newts (Davies &

**TABLE 1.2**
**Payoff Matrix for the Hawk–Dove–Assessor Game**

| | When Fighting: | | |
|---|---|---|---|
| Payoff to: | Hawk | Dove | Assessor |
| Hawk | 1/2 (V-I) | V | 1/2 (V-I) |
| Dove | 0 | 1/2 V | 1/4 V |
| Assessor | 1/2 V | 3/4 A | 1/2 V |

Notes. V = Benefit accruing to victor. I = Cost of injury. A = Cost of assessment.

Halliday, 1978; Smith & Ivins, 1986). However, many kinds of animal have weapons (teeth, claws, hoofs, or horns) that are capable of wounding a rival, and in these cases losing an escalated fight is likely to involve a relatively high cost. Here, therefore, the hawk–dove–assessor model predicts that the assessor strategy is an ESS. In other words, we should expect that such animals will adapt the intensity of their aggressive responses to the relative RHP of a potential opponent. Many studies of animal fights have shown that this is, indeed, the case (Archer, 1988, Table 9.1).

This raises the question of how an animal is able to assess its opponent's resource holding power—or fighting ability—relative to its own. In practice, a number of cues may be used, but because bigger animals are usually stronger perhaps the most widespread one is the opponent's size. The sensory channels through which size is assessed must be variable, because the larger of two opponents is more likely to initiate a fight in animals as varied as the sea anemone (Brace & Pavey, 1978), a Gastropod mollusc (Zack, 1975), hermit crabs (Mitchell, 1976), field crickets (Dixon & Cade, 1986), and a wide variety of vertebrates (see Archer, 1988, Table 9.1). Tail beating in male cichlid fish (*Nannacara anomala*, see earlier) may perhaps create pressure waves whose size depends on the size of the performer; certainly, in red deer only strong males can roar fast (see before), and stags can use this to identify large differences in RHP at an early stage in an encounter.

Knowledge gained about fighting ability from previous encounters will also provide a powerful cue for animals that live in social groups and are able to recognize one another individually (Van Rhijn & Vodegel, 1980). Such learning will form the basis of dominance hierarchies. It has often been noted that recognition of the superior fighting ability of a more dominant animal by a subordinate is crucial for maintaining dominance relationships (Gartlan, 1968; Rowell, 1966; Tinbergen, 1953). In primate societies, where individuals may gang together to defeat a high-ranking opponent, assessment of the probability of winning an encounter will depend not just on the individual RHP and past experience of the main contestants but also on the presence and RHP of potential allies (Datta, 1983).

The Importance of Resource Value

There are, therefore, a wide range of cues an animal might use to assess its opponent's fighting ability. The empirical evidence generally supports the prediction that animals assess relative RHP and that longer, fiercer fights (escalated fights in game theory terminology) occur between opponents whose fighting abilities are similar. Nevertheless, as

Parker (1974) recognized, a model based only on relative RHP is a naive one. Even though the concept of RHP has proved one of the most important insights to come from game theory analyses of animal fights, it is not the whole story. Several other factors must be considered. All game theory models are based on calculations of the payoffs to the participants, given that certain costs and benefits are involved. RHP involves one very important aspect of the costs of fighting, but we have not yet considered the benefits to be obtained from winning a fight.

Most cases of animal fights to which game theory analyses have been applied are competitive in the sense that the protagonists are competing for a resource such as food, a territory, a nest site, or a potential mate (Archer, 1988). When considering the benefits of winning a fight, complications arise if the resource is not of equal value to the two individuals; for example, the same piece of food may be of more value to a starving animal than to a better fed one and, to give a more complicated example, a male that has invested a certain amount of time and energy in fertilizing a female's eggs has more to gain by winning a fight over access to the female than does a challenger. Theory predicts that animals will be more likely to escalate to high-cost actions when fighting over a resource that is of high value. This is the case for newts (*Notophthalmus viridescens*), in which fights over larger, more fecund, females are particularly fierce (Verrell, 1986). It has also been found in *Gammarus pulex*: Fights between males over a precopula female become longer and more persistent where the female is larger and nearer to the moult, the time when copulations can occur (Dick & Elwood, 1990).

In social species, the advantages associated with group living may be such that animals have evolved forms of affiliative and tolerant behavior that serve to counter competitive tendencies (de Waal, 1986). Although this consideration has not been included in game theory models, disruption of social relations (which indirectly benefit group-living individuals) could be regarded as another cost of fighting in these circumstances. It would account for social animals tolerating the sharing of resources rather than competing for them (e.g., Senar, 1990), and for the occurrence of affiliative behavior in conditions likely to lead to conflict among social primates (de Waal, 1989).

Interaction of RHP and Resource Value

It will often be the case that opponents differ both in RHP and in the value that they place on a disputed resource; these considerations have been introduced into game theory models representing contests that are "asymmtrical" in terms of both resource value and RHP. The most satisfactory model to consider these complexities was developed by Parker and Rubenstein (1981). Essentially, they were concerned within-teractions between RHP and resource value. Such interactions could be either mutually reinforcing, when the animal with the most to gain also has the highest RHP, or contradictory, when the one with the highest RHP has the least to gain. The first case is straightforward and will follow the rules of the simple assessor model. Contradictory interactions were considered in terms of whether an opponent occupies a particular "assessment role." If both animals have full information about the value of the resource, and about RHP, the one with the lesser value of V/K (V = resource value; K = rate of incurring costs) should retreat first; a convention based on this assessment rule was shown to be the only ESS. Even if opponents were not able to assess their "roles" with perfect accuracy before the fight (as is likely to be the case), an assessor strategy that made the best estimate of relative values of V/K and modified its behavior accordingly was still an ESS.

To test Parker and Rubenstein's model, it is necessary to measure the value of a resource to the two combatants. Several studies have gone some way toward achieving this (e.g., Ewald, 1985, for hummingbirds), but it has been achieved most successfully in a study of mate guarding in spiders (Austad, 1983). Two males will fight over a female with whom one of them has not finished mating. The resident could potentially lose the fertilizations not yet achieved. Because there is no sperm displacement in this species, and males cannot assess the number of eggs a female contains, there are relatively few additional complications. Austad manipulated the value of the resource by introducing the second male at different times throughout the mating sequence, from the beginning to after 21 minutes (when practically all the eggs will have been fertilized). RHP was manipulated by varying the relative sizes of the two males. In the simple case when both males were introduced together, the outcome followed what was expected from Parker's assessment strategy model, that is, if one spider was smaller, it withdrew prior to a fight starting, but if they were of approximately equal size, an escalated fight occurred.

When an intruder was introduced after the resident had begun copulation, V/K assessment becomes relevant. Intruders cannot tell the reproductive value of the female; for them, the value of V will be the same irrespective of when they are introduced. For the resident, on the other hand, the female will be of less value at successive points during the course of the copulation, as the number of fertilizations remaining decline. Austad calculated the values of V/K for the various combinations of opponents that had been set up, to test the predictions of Parker and Rubenstein's model. A summary of his findings is that, the closer the estimates of V/K in the two opponents, the longer the contests lasted. There were some exceptions to this, which Austad explained in terms of both contestants perceiving the other's V/K value to be larger than it in fact was, hence shortening the contest time.


ASSESSING ASYMMETRIES


Thus, game theory predicts, and empirical studies show, that animals will base decisions about whether to escalate to fierce fighting on the potential cost incurred (in the form of relative RHP) and on the potential value of winning. The models often assume that information about any asymmetries is accurate and that it is available to the animals at the start of the encounter, although Parker and Rubenstein (1981) showed that the assessment strategy in their model is evolutionarily stable even when animals have only inaccurate information about asymmetries in RHP and resource value. The assumption that even inaccurate information about asymmetries is available from the start of an encounter is unlikely to be the case if differences in RHP or resource value are small or where they depend on properties that cannot be assessed by distance cues. In such cases, after an exchange of displays performed at a distance, animals may engage in trials of strength, usually some form of pushing and pulling contest, before escalating to more damaging forms of fighting. For example, when opponents are evenly matched so that assessing relative size is difficult, stags escalate from roaring and parallel walking to antler-locked pushing (Clutton-Brock et al., 1982), and cichlids escalate from tail beating to ramming displays and mouth wrestling (Jakobsson et al., 1979).

More recent game theory models not only assume initially imperfect information but also include the effects of gradually accumulating information during an encounter.

The sequential assessment model of Enquist and Leimar (1983), and Enquist, Leimar, Ljungberg, Mallner, and Segerdahl (1990) explains the occurrence of escalation, in functional terms, as the result of a process of gradual acquisition of information about RHP. In this model, two opponents with different fighting abilities come into conflict. At the start of the encounter, the opponents have little or no information about their relative fighting ability, but during successive aggressive exchanges they accumulate this information. The animals have available to them several different behavior patterns, and at any point in the fight the two contestants tend to perform the same kinds of action. Low-intensity actions give only inaccurate information about RHP (any cichlid can perform an impressive tail beat) but are cheap to perform. On the other hand, high-intensity actions provide reliable information about RHP (only strong fish can mouth wrestle effectively) but are costly both in terms of energy and in terms of risk of injury. The "aim" of a fight is to acquire sufficiently accurate information about RHP at the lowest possible cost.

What happens during a fight is similar to a process of statistical sampling, in that there is a random error in an animal's assessment of its relative RHP. This error is reduced as more exchanges occur and assessments are based on a larger sample size. At any point in the fight an animal bases its decisions about whether to continue a fight or to withdraw on its current assessment of relative RHP and on the precision of that estimate (Fig. 1.2) The choice of what action to use if it does continue (e.g., whether to escalate to a more intense level of fighting) is based on how much information has been acquired up to this point; if the animal is still uncertain in spite of extensive low-level display, it will switch to actions that are more effective at gaining information, even though these are more costly.

The model makes several predictions about how animals should behave. For example, the number of different behavioral elements used during a fight should increase as the difference in RHP decreases. Figure 1.3 shows that this is indeed the case for cichlid fish. Another more complex prediction is that, when animals enter the final round of a fight, regardless of the level of cost to which the fight has escalated, the length of time spent fighting up to the switch to the final phase should be independent of relative RHP. Intuitively, this is because combatants

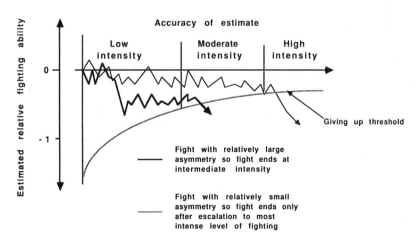

FIG. 1.2. Changes in estimated relative fighting ability and giving up threshold during progressive increases in fight intensity in the sequential assessment model (modified from Enquist et al., 1990).

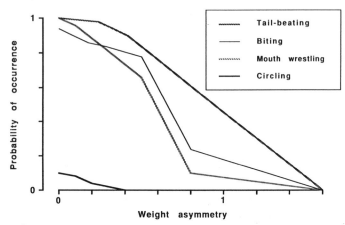

FIG. 1.3. Number of different behavioral elements in a fight between cichlid fish as a function of the asymmetry of combatants' weights (after Enquist et al., 1990).

switch to an escalated level only when they have failed to acquire an accurate estimation of relative fighting ability (so this cannot influence their behavior); by the rules of the game (only escalate if you do not have an accurate assessment of relative RHP), this is the case for all rounds except the final one in which the fight is resolved. In contrast, the model predicts that the length of this final round will be negatively related to the difference in RHP, because if the animals are nearly equally matched they need to exchange many actions of the highest, most informative, level before their estimates are sufficiently accurate to allow one to give up. Table 1.3 shows that this also is the case for cichlid fights (Enquist et al., 1988), indicating that, for this species at least, the central point of the sequential assessment game (namely, that escalation during fights reflects the gradual acquisition of information about asymmetries) is correct.

**TABLE 1.3**
**Spearman Rank-Order Correlations Between Weight Asymmetry
and Length of Fights up to and Following the Switch to the
Most Escalated Phase in Three Categories of Fights Between
Male Chichlids (from Enquist et al., 1988).**

|  | Correlation Coefficient | |
|---|---|---|
|  | *Up to Final Phase* | *After Final Phase* |
| Fights with tail beating | 0.08 (NS) | −0.46 (***) |
| Fights with bites | −0.05 (NS) | −0.34 (**) |
| Fights with mouth wrestling | 0.03 (NS) | −0.25 (**) |

*Note.* NS = Nonsignificant.
**p < .01. ***p < .001.

## THE BEHAVIORAL MECHANISMS UNDERLYING
## ESCALATION

Game theory models have demonstrated the importance of information about relative RHP and resource value in strategic decision making during fights, including decisions about whether and how much to escalate. However, they are all functional in focus and do not address the mechanisms by which information about asymmetries is converted into behavior. On the other hand, existing theories about the internal mechanisms of escalation (whether psychological or ethological) do not take account of the kind of functionally relevant variables identified by game theory models.

For example, there is some comparative psychological research on "warm-up" or sensitization at the start of animal fights (i.e., the gradual increase in intensity of behavior and mood; e.g., Peeke, 1982; Potegal & tenBrink, 1984). This is similar to escalation in that an increase in the level and rate of attack occurs as the fight progresses, but the proposed mechanism does not allow for input of information about RHP and resource value. Ethological studies of the causes of animal fights explain what happens during fights as the result of simultaneously activated, incompatible, motivational tendencies designated aggression and fear (Baerends, 1975; Groothius, 1989a, 1989b; Tinbergen, 1952). For example, Moynihan (1955) studied the postures of the black-headed gull and concluded that their threat displays could be explained in terms of different strengths of activation of the tendency to escape and to attack. Another study analyzed the postures and facial expressions of cats in terms of their being influenced by different combinations of levels of aggression and fear motivation (Leyhausen, 1956, 1979). However, to explain in causal terms what is now known about the strategic importance of RHP and resource value in fights, such explanations must be extended to provide a mechanism whereby these factors can influence aggression and fear.

Maynard Smith and Riechert (1984) developed a model of fights over feeding territories in spiders (*Agelena asperta*) that does exactly this. The spiders use several different aggressive behavior patterns during fights and go through a process of escalation from locating movements performed at a distance, through threats performed closer together, to intense contact fighting. A previous study within the functional framework of game theory (Riechert, 1979, 1982, 1984) had shown that, all other things being equal, the owner of a territory will win a fight, but that if there is a size discrepancy of more than 10% a larger intruder can take over the territory. The more closely matched the opponents are, the more fiercely they fight, and the more valuable the territory, the more intensely the owner will defend it. These findings were used in constructing the model.

The model itself has two main features: First, what a spider does during a fight depends on the level of two independently varying motivational systems, which for convenience are labeled *attack* and *fear*. The rules that relate internal state to behavioral action are shown in simplified form in Table 1.4. Briefly, if the strength of the fear tendency (F) is greater than that of the attack tendency (A), the spider retreats; if A > F it engages in a fight, the actual behavior chosen depending on the absolute strength of the attack tendency. The owner starts with a higher attack tendency than the intruder, the size of this advantage depending on the value to the territory.

Second, the model envisages a fight as consisting of a series of behavioral exchanges in each of which one animal is the performer and the other is the observer, whose attack and fear levels are altered by seeing a rival perform an agonistic action; the nature of these changes depends on the relative size of the performer and the action it performs according to the rules shown (again in simplified form) in Table 1.4. After one spider has performed a given action, the two animals switch roles and the next performer chooses its next action on the basis of its new, reset values of A and F. If A increases enough to cross one of the thresholds in attack/flight space shown in Fig. 1.4, then the fight will escalate; if the new value of A is less than the new value of F, the spider withdraws and the fight ends. The model was used to simulate many hypothetical fights, whose nature and outcome were found to be very similar to those of real fights (with one exception). This suggests that the critical features of the mechanisms that determine how fighting spiders behave are correctly envisaged in the model.

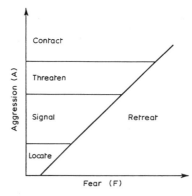

FIG. 1.4. Agonistic behaviors in the spider *Agelena asperta* as a function of the strengths of the tendencies for fear (F) and aggression (A) (redrawn from Huntingford & Turner, 1987).

TABLE 1.4
The Rules of How Aggression and Fear Change During Spider
Fights (simplified from Maynard Smith & Riechert, 1984).

$$A_{after} = A_{before} + X + (G \times D) + E$$
$$F_{after} = F_{before} + (G \times B)$$

where A = aggression before and after observing opponent

F = fear before and after observing opponent

D = weight difference between the spiders

E = a random variable from $-1$ to $+1$

X and B = constants representing rate of change of aggression and fear; both greater
in grassland spiders

G = 1 if opponent locates

2 if opponent signals

3 if opponent threatens

4 if opponent makes contact

With this model, studies originating in the essentially functional framework of game theory have generated causal explanations of the process of escalation during fights. In this respect, they converge on recent studies in a very different field of aggression research, namely, behavioral endocrinology. More particularly, the rapid, experience-mediated hormonal changes that are now known to occur during conflicts potentially provide a physiological mechanism for the strategic patterns of escalation identified by game theory (see Huntingford & Turner, 1987). To give just a few examples, in males of many species androgen levels rise in the presence of fertile females (rats: Kamel, Mock, Wright, & Frankel, 1975; sheep: Illius, Haynes, & Lamming, 1978; white-crowned sparrows: Moore, 1984). In those species in which males fight over females and in which androgens facilitate aggression (see Archer, 1988; Huntingford & Turner, 1987, for examples), this would provide a mechanism whereby aggressiveness is tuned to resource value. During fights between males of various species, including swordtail fish (Hannes, Franck, & Liemann, 1984), redwing blackbirds (Harding, 1983), and song sparrows (Wingfield, 1985), levels of testosterone increase rapidly *during* agonistic encounters (Fig. 1.5), especially in the eventual winner. Because androgen facilitates aggression in at least some of these species, we have here a possible mechanism for allowing good fighters to escalate during successful fights.

## THE RESOLUTION OF FIGHTS

Fights often end abruptly, in contrast to their slow buildup. Until the final stages of the fight, the behavior of the eventual winner and the eventual loser is very similar. In functional terms, this is as predicted by

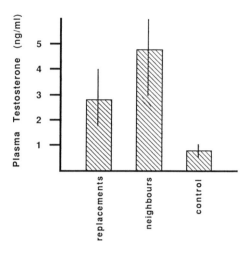

FIG. 1.5. Levels of plasma testosterone in wild male song sparrows caught while engaged in fighting for a recently vacated territory (replacements), in their new neighbors and in undisturbed controls (after Wingfield, 1985).

another early game theory model, namely, Maynard Smith's (1974) war of attrition model. Here two equally matched opponents, neither of whom would attack the other, display simultaneously, and victory goes to the one that displays for the longest. Later models (Caryl, 1979; Norman, Taylor, & Robertson, 1977) replaced duration of display by a more generalized cost function, enabling the model to be applied to cases where different levels of escalation are involved.

The model predicts that the cost an animal is prepared to pay is set in advance but is not communicated to the opponent through signals indicating motivation or intentions. There would be selection for a sharp switch in motivation from attack to flee at the point where one animal has reached the highest point to which it is prepared to go. This implies that, as long as the motivational balance between attack and escape favors attack, this will be maintained at full intensity. However, once escape becomes the dominant motivation, there will be a sudden shift from attack to escape. Therefore the resolution of a fight occurs as a consequence of rapid de-escalation by one of the protagonists.

Once again, some findings from behavioral endocrinology may suggest a possible mechanism underlying the rapid de-escalation of fights. Circulating glucocorticoid levels increase during fights, especially in the eventual loser (fish: Hannes et al., 1984; rats: Schuurman, 1980, see Fig. 1.6; humans: Elias, 1981). In mice, it is known that glucocorticoids promote submission (Leshner, 1983), so its release during fights may be involved in the mechanism for the resolution of contests.

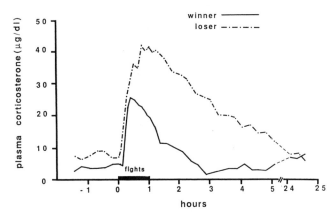

FIG. 1.6. Levels of plasma corticosterone in the winning and the losing rat before, during, and after a protracted fight (after Schuurman, 1980).

## THE QUESTION OF DECEPTION

The prediction from the modified war of attrition model that information about the cost that an animal is prepared to pay, or its motivation to fight, should not be signaled during a fight has prompted much argument. This is partly because it initially appeared to be incompatible with traditional ethological theories about the causation of threat displays but also because it introduces the possibility of deception.

In ethological studies, animal displays were often explained as the outcome of different combinations of underlying motivational tendencies — aggression and fear in the case of threat displays (see section on behavioral mechanisms underlying escalation). This view implies that information about the animal's motivational state should be available to the opponent. It is, however, complicated by the ritualization of displays during the course of evolution, that is, their alteration to provide a species-typical signal. Such signals will have become "emancipated" (Tinbergen, 1952) from their original causal factors and subject to causal influences concerned with their signaling function (Blest, 1961). They will also tend to be performed in a constant manner and intensity over a range of stimulus strengths, a process known as *typical intensity* (Morris, 1957).

In ethological studies of displays, therefore, there has been the assumption that these either directly reflect the animal's motivational state, or else they had become emancipated from this simple relationship as a result of evolutionary changes reflecting a signaling function (see also Groothius, 1989b).

The original war of attrition model (Maynard Smith, 1974) predicted that accurate signaling of display-length intentions would not be an ESS and therefore would be subject to replacement by individuals who exaggerated their intended display lengths. In the modified, more general, version of the model (Caryl, 1979, 1981; Norman et al., 1977), this was replaced by the conclusion that displays would not transmit the cost the individual is prepared to pay (i.e., the intended degree of escalation will not be signaled in advance to the other animal). This prediction has been regarded as incompatible with the traditional ethological conflict hypothesis, that threat displays reflect the animal's motivational balance of aggression and fear (Caryl, 1979, 1982; see Hinde, 1981).

Caryl (1979) analyzed four earlier ethological studies of bird displays to test whether predictions from the conflict hypothesis or the extended war of attrition model fitted the results. He found that the type of display shown in an encounter could broadly predict whether the animal subsequently stayed, attacked, or took flight; however, although subsequent escape was readily predicted, the probability of attack was not. Because escape is the one type of action that game theory does predict will be signaled (to avoid further damage; Maynard Smith, 1982), these results can be regarded as broadly supporting the extended model (Caryl, 1981). A similar conclusion about animal signals was reached in a more general discussion of functional considerations by Dawkins and Krebs (1978) and Krebs and Dawkins (1984). Briefly, they predicted that signals would not have evolved to provide accurate information transfer but to manipulate the actions of another animal in the interests of the signaller. Of course, there may be cases where the interests of two animals coincide, and there will also be coevolution to counter such manipulative effects.

Hinde (1981) argued that these functional analyses have characterized the ethological position in oversimplified terms. By concentrating only on a broad prediction based on the conflict hypothesis, they have overlooked ethological contributions that are more consistent with functional predictions (e.g., ritualization; see earlier). Hinde also emphasized that ethological studies involve detailed descriptions of the changing and interactive nature of aggressive interactions. Some of the lack of predictability will follow from the uncertainty inherent in such an interaction. Hinde argued that Caryl's (1979) analysis did not take this into account, seeking to establish only whether winners and losers could be identified from the earlier parts of an aggressive exchange. This may in fact be different from the specific prediction of the extended war of attrition model, that animals will not signal the degree of escalation to which they are prepared to go in the course of the fight. The situation may also alter as a consequence of information obtained during the course of the contest, either about the opponent or about the value of the resource (see earlier section on sequential assessment games).

A study by Senar (1990) of displays within a group of social birds (siskins) found that the ability of a particular display to predict attack is often dependent on the response of the opponent. By examining the initial display, the reaction by the opponent and the response of the first bird, he showed that the probability of attack was a function of the dominance relations of the two birds, the type of display, and the response of the reactor. More dominant birds were less tolerant than subordinate ones, and some displays signaled intolerance whereas others signaled tolerance. In some cases, a nonaggressive response to an aggressive display could lead to a further nonaggressive response and to both birds sharing the resource.

Bond (1989a) proposed another possible solution to the apparent contradiction between ethological and game theory approaches to animal displays. His conclusion was a compromise between these two predictions, that there is an optimum level of deceit (or bluffing) in displays, but that this will be subject to stabilizing selection. This was derived from a form of game theory involving individual strategic choices of signaller and recipient, rather than the calculation of an ESS from a population model. Therefore the term *optimum* in this context was not necessarily an ESS. For this and other reasons there are doubts about the soundness of predictions from the model. Maynard Smith and Parker (1976) had in fact addressed the problem of bluff using an ESS model and reached a similar conclusion to that of Bond. They concluded that a stable strategy in which bluff is extensive could evolve, particularly in species where serious injury is possible. However, discrimination of bluff can also be an ESS (see Lazarus, 1982, for further discussion of this issue). Although similar to those of Bond, these conclusions have a sounder basis.

Bond (1989b) also proposed an alternative hypothesis for resolving the same issue. He suggested that it would be to any individual's advantage to be able to respond gradually in an aggressive exchange, rather than in a crude all-or-nothing manner. Positive feedback in the motivational mechanism underlying aggression (Archer, 1988; Toates & Archer, 1978) would achieve this. One by-product of such a mechanism would be to facilitate information exchange about possible future action. Bond argued that any disadvantages connected with this communication (as shown by war of attrition models) would be outweighed by the benefits of having a graded output.

As a test of Bond's hypothesis, Hazlett (1990) examined data from aggressive exchanges between hermit crabs, to determine whether they responded in a more aggressive way to an opponent's display when they had previously shown a more aggressive display themselves. This was found to be the case. However, these results only demonstrate that there is an internal mechanism underlying escalation (in addition to any influence from the partner's behavior). The existence of both internal and external mechanisms underlying escalation is already known from several studies (Archer, 1988, pp. 196–197). But it does not address Bond's evolutionary hypothesis, which would have to be tested by comparing the relative fitness of animals differing in the latency to reach high-level acts in response to a common stimulus. Game theory models would predict that this would depend on the costs and benefits involved in any specific case. Therefore, a general functional hypothesis of the type Bond proposed would appear to be misleading, again emphasizing the importance of using ESS thinking to derive functional hypotheses about social behavior.

Bond (1989b) posed the question of whether the need to avoid rapid high-level responding could provide the selective pressure underlying the escalation of displays. This was in fact answered by one of the game theory models described earlier. In a simple hawk–dove game, Maynard Smith (1982) predicted that the ESS would be a mixed strategy in which the likelihood of adopting a hawk strategy (i.e., rapid high-level responding) would be defined by $P(H) = V/C$, where V is the value of the resource and C is the cost of injury.

Individual recognition provides a further complicating influence on the conclusions reached about deception. Its influence was explored in a series of game theory models by van Rhijn and Vodegel (1980), based on the original model of Maynard Smith and Price (1973). Van Rhijn and Vodegel argued that such fights ware asymmetrical ones (i.e., the contestants will use the outcome of past experience to predict RHP). They will also use such information to predict *intentions* because it will be possible to predict these from past encounters. Under such circumstances, it is unlikely that deception would be successful.

This model concerns a special case of when RHP differs between combatants. In most of the models considered in this section, it was assumed that the animals show similar RHP values. In an earlier section, we discussed the importance of RHP for predicting when escalated fights would be expected and when they would not. In the assessor game, it was assumed that animals would signal their RHP, and that this would be relatively accurate because the features involved would be difficult to imitate and costly to produce in the first place (Maynard Smith, 1982). They include features such as size, possession of weapons, a deep voice, and strength. Thus, displays that involve signaling RHP will be relatively accurate whereas those signaling "intentions" (or more accurately maximum cost), which are the ones discussed in war of attrition and related models, will not. Maynard Smith (1982) emphasized the importance of separating the two types of display in game theory models. It may not, however, always be possible to separate the two in practice (Enquist, 1985; Turner & Huntingford, 1986), because perceived RHP will influence motivational state and hence perceived intentions. In practice, it is always difficult to tell whether two animals are equally matched for RHP.

## CONCLUSIONS ABOUT ESCALATION IN ANIMAL FIGHTS

As far as animal fights are concerned, game theory has highlighted the importance of low-cost acquisition of information about relative fighting ability. It has therefore provided an explanation for the fact that aggressive encounters frequently take the form of a gradual escalation (during which the information is acquired) followed by rapid de-escalation (when one animal establishes that it cannot win). By considering the potential costs and benefits of victory, this approach also explains the level of intensity to which animals are prepared to escalate in any particular encounter. By focusing on the way that costs and benefits influence decisions during fights, game theory has given a new impetus to studies of the behavioral mechanisms that determine how animals behave during fights. Because game theory leads to the theoretical issues being spelled out in detail, experiments designed to test its predictions tend to be focused on specific, theoretically important questions. One consequence of this approach is that the search for general principles is highlighted. Such a research strategy also coincides with recommendations to use fewer animals in behavioral research and thereby minimize animal suffering (e.g., Bateson, 1986; Huntingford, 1984; Still, 1982).

## HUMAN AGGRESSION

Game theory was initially used to analyze human conflict in disciplines such as economics and social psychology. It was later applied to animals to explain the existence of ritualized fighting. Having proved useful in this context, the approach was developed to analyze other problems about animal fights. Now the wheel has turned full circle: Insights from the models of animal fights are beginning to be applied to human behavior.

Escalation is well known in human aggressive exchanges, and it is likely that some of the conclusions derived from game theory models of animal fighting apply to aspects of human aggression at an individual level. There are, however, no precise tests of the applicability of the models to humans, so that the discussion of this issue must remain speculative. We first provide an example from a clinical investigation of a person who shows marked escalation in response to provocation. We then illustrate the applicability of Parker's (1974) assessment strategy model, and the V/K assessment rule (Parker & Rubenstein, 1981) to some human aggressive exchanges. These examples all concern conflicts between individuals. In the next and final section, we consider possible parallels between principles derived from game theory models of animal fights and those involved in interstate conflicts (which are discussed in this volume by Leng).

Physical aggression arising out of interpersonal conflicts rarely occurs suddenly, even in highly aggressive individuals. In discussing a violence-prone person who was receiving treatment within an anger-management program, Howells (1989) noted that "the violent act itself rarely occurred immediately but followed an escalating sequence of angry social exchanges" (p. 164). Microanalysis of the particular patient's behavior indicated a marked tendency to respond to lower level hostile acts in others by a much more hostile reply, thus repeatedly escalating what would otherwise be mildly critical comments or mild conflicts. For example, he would respond to mild criticism with counter criticism of a generally disparaging and abusive kind, such as "You ignorant bastard, what do you know about" He would readily swear at the other in disagreements and tended to issue physical threats, such as "Say that again, and I'll down you." He would also display a very loud volume in his voice early in the exchange, and others would perceive him as shouting angrily in disputes even when his subjective sense of anger was low. Angry facial expressions and voice tones were identified early on in the exchange. If the other person was seated, he would stand over him or her in a threatening way. Aggressive gesticulation such as hand waving and excessive eye contact were also present early in the exchange. The individual was himself largely unaware of his role in escalating his exchanges toward physical violence.

From this account it is apparent that there is some convergence between the way clinicians concerned with anger management have produced detailed descriptions of the behavior leading up to physically damaging acts and the observations of ethologists who have documented changes in behavioral elements over the course of a contest.

The first game theory model discussed in this chapter was the assessment strategy model of Parker (1974), which predicts that escalated fights will be restricted to animals of similar RHP, and that RHP assessment will be made prior to the fight. This simple prediction presumes, of course, that the resource value is the same for both of them, and that RHP information is available prior to the fight. In human terms, it can be said that the RHP rule is implicitly recognized in boxing contests, where there are clearly defined weight bands, whose boundaries conform to the relative weights within which animals will enter into fights with one another (Caryl, personal communication, 1988).

Real-life human fights are difficult to study by direct observation, but occasionally a researcher interested in the field of aggression witnesses one. The following description from Blanchard and Blanchard (1989) suggests an assessor phase in which relative RHP is signaled:

> Two young men obviously strangers to each other, collided in a doorway of a public bar. After (and while) words were exchanged, they postured, moved their upper bodies for maximum effect, pushed up sleeves to display biceps, and generally exchanged information relative to their fighting abilities, for some twenty-five minutes before actually exchanging the first blow. (p. 113)

One of the few specific attempts to carry out a functional analysis of human aggression was a study of conflicts over objects by schoolchildren by Weigel (1984). Although he viewed these conflicts in terms of maximizing benefits and minimizing costs, no quantitative calculations were offered. The predictions were broad ones, for example, that children who had previously won conflicts would be more likely to resist another child taking an object and would extend the duration and intensity of the dispute. Such a prediction could, however, have been made on the basis of psychological processes such as past reinforcement and frustration (although it should be emphasized that the two types of explanation—proximate and ultimate—are not incompatible).

Weigel found that both a higher level of previous aggression and current possession of an object were associated with increased likelihood of resisting an attacker, and hence of escalation, results that were in accordance with his broad predictions. These findings would also be predicted by the V/K assessor rule (Parker & Rubenstein, 1981), if we assume that the value of a resource is greater to the existing owner than to the challenger, and if we assume the cost of a conflict will be less for a child who has previously been successful in other conflicts. One finding that did not fit the authors' broad predictions was that defenders were observed to resist more than expected against aggressive opponents. This result would, however, fit the assessor rule in that possession of an object would make the value of V higher for the defendant. It is consistent with findings from several animal studies showing that owners are prepared to continue and escalate contests in proportion to the value of the resource they possess (Austad, 1983; Dowds & Elwood, 1983; Riechert, 1979, 1984).

Although it could be argued that such rules are likely to operate in most human conflicts over a wide range of resources, the choice of children's disputes over objects is perhaps not the best place to begin testing models derived from functional considerations. As Weigel (1984) pointed out, the relationship between such disputes and adult fitness is not clear. Conflicts between adults over resources important for fitness would provide the ideal test of functional predictions.


### INTERSTATE CONFLICTS


In this final section we consider whether game theory can illuminate any general principles applicable to both animal fights and to interstate conflicts (see Leng, this volume). We should begin by emphasizing that game theory applied to animal conflicts concerns rules that have arisen as a result of the process of natural selection. In discussing animal conflict, there was no implication that conscious processes direct these rules. In the case of interstate conflicts, we *are* dealing with conscious intentions rather than rules derived from natural selection. Nevertheless, because these conscious intentions occur in organisms that are the product of natural selection, they may follow similar principles to those involved in animal conflicts, at least when the circumstances are similar.

Assuming we are dealing with a conflict between two independent nations, their behavior will not be constrained by a centralized authority, as is the behavior of individual humans by the state (cf. Leng, this volume). They are therefore in the position of two animals or people facing one another without allies or external constraints. Certain general principles appear to operate in both cases. Just as animals will tend to escalate when the resource value (V) is higher, so too are international crises escalated much more rapidly when vital national interests such as political independence or territorial integrity are at stake (Gochman & Leng, 1983).

Another principle involves the overwhelming importance of basing a decision on the "costs and risks associated with provoking or attacking a powerful and highly motivated adversary" (Leng, this volume). This is a generalization that applies to statesmen dealing with a more powerfully armed national adversary, and to animals as diverse as sea anemones and chimpanzees when they face a larger opponent. It was incorporated into ESS game theory models early on in the form of using RHP to settle disputes during an assessment phase (Parker, 1974).

If this is such a general principle, we may ask why states do not always act on the basis of intelligence information about one another's military strength. As Leng explained in his chapter, this is indeed the most effective constraint on interstate crises. However, there are a number of other influences on the decision-making process that prevent it becoming a universal rule: first, the difficulty in estimating comparative military strength; second, the influence of motivation. In animal conflicts, game theory models predict that so-called "intentions" are not signaled, or, more precisely, that the maximum cost the animal is prepared to pay is not communicated early in the exchange. Again, there are general parallels with interstate conflicts. Unlike military strength, intentions are less straightforward to ascertain, are less stable over time, and can be concealed without difficulty. It is recognized that in many cases of human bargaining, it is advantageous to conceal one's intentions in order to seek to manipulate the opponent. In conflicts between states, this may take the form of concealing preparations for war on the one hand, and on the other of using deterrent threats in the absence of the intention to use force (cf. Kahn's competition in risk taking: Leng, this volume).

Although there are these parallels in the general principles governing animal and interstate conflicts, there are additional factors underlying human bargaining that complicate the resolution of interstate crises. These consist of psychological variables such as prestige and reputation for resolve, and the pressures of public opinion. In referring to them as "psychological," we mean that they arise from the perceptions of the individuals involved rather than from the logic of the conflict situation. They serve to increase the stakes (i.e., to make the apparent costs of losing and the benefits of winning higher than they really are). In this respect, they do not fit the *rational choice* model of analysts who have applied the logical principles of game theory to interstate conflicts. Rather, they fit more with the approach of those who emphasize the importance of psychological variables in crisis decision making (Leng, this volume). Even if the beginning of an interstate crisis can be seen in terms of the same logical rules as an animal conflict, the rules soon change to involve psychological variables as the conflict progresses.

In conclusion, the principles behind interstate crisis resolution show a number of parallels with the logic of animal conflicts, but it is clear that these parallels apply only when those involved carefully weigh the risks and assess the motivation of the opponent. As Leng indicates, this view is indeed limited because it does not include psychological variables that tend to "drive crises to escalate out of control."

## ACKNOWLEDGMENT

We thank John Lazarus for his helpful comments on this chapter.

## REFERENCES

Archer, J. (1988). *The behavioral biology of aggression.* Cambridge, UK: Cambridge University Press.

Austad, S. N. (1983). A game theoretical interpretation of male combat in the bowl and doily spider (*Frontinella pyramitela*). *Animal Behaviour, 31,* 59–73.

Baerends, G. P. (1975). An evaluation of the conflict hypothesis as an explanatory principle for the evolution of displays. In G. P. Baerends, C. Beer, & A. Manning (Eds.), *Function and evolution in behaviour* (pp. 187–227). Oxford: Clarendon Press.

Bateson, P. P. G. (1986). When to experiment on animals. *New Scientist, 109* (1496), 30–32.

Blanchard, D. C., & Blanchard, D. C. (1989). Experimental animal models of aggression: What do they say about human behaviour? In J. Archer & K. Browne (Eds.), *Human aggression: Naturalistic approaches* (pp. 102–124). London & New York: Routledge.

Blest, D. (1961). The concept of ritualization. In W. H. Thorpe & O. L. Zangwill (Eds.), *Current problems in animal behaviour* (pp. 102–124). London & New York: Cambridge University Press.

Bond, A. (1989a). Toward a resolution of the paradox of aggressive displays: I. Optimal deceit in the communication of fighting ability. *Ethology, 81,* 29–46.

Bond, A. (1989b). Toward a resolution of the paradox of aggressive displays: II. Behavioral efference and the communication of intentions. *Ethology, 81,* 235–249.

Brace, R. C., & Pavey, J. (1978). Size-dependent dominance hierarchy in the anemone *Actina acquina. Nature, 273,* 752–753.

Caryl, P. G. (1979). Communication by agonistic displays: What can games theory contribute to ethology? *Behaviour, 68,* 136–139.

Caryl, P. G. (1981). Escalated fighting and the war of nerves: Games theory and animal combat. In P.P.G. Bateson & P. Klopfer (Eds.), *Perspectives in ethology* (Vol. 4, pp. 199–224). New York & London: Plenum.

Caryl, P. G. (1982). Animal signals: A reply to Hinde. *Animal Behaviour, 30,* 240–244.

Clutton-Brock, T. H., Guinness, F. E., & Albon, S. D. (1982). *Red deer: Behaviour and ecology of two sexes.* Edinburgh: Edinburgh University Press.

Datta, S. (1983). Relative power and the acquisition of rank. In R. A. Hinde (Ed.), *Primate social relationships* (pp. 93–103). Oxford: Blackwell Scientific.

Davies, N. B., & Halliday, T. M. (1978). Deep croaks and fighting assessment in toads *Bufo bufo. Nature, 274,* 683–685.

Dawkins, R., & Krebs, J. R. (1978). Animal signals: Information or manipulation. In J. R. Krebs & N. B. Davies (Eds.), *Behavioural ecology: An evolutionary approach* (pp. 282–390). Oxford: Blackwell Scientific.

de Waal, F. B. M. (1986). The integration of dominance and social bonding in primates. *The Quarterly Review of Biology, 61,* 459–479.

de Waal, F. B. M. (1989). *Peacemaking among primates.* Cambridge, MA: Harvard University Press.

Dick, J. T. A., & Elwood, R. W. (1990). Symmetrical assessment of female quality by male *Gammarus pulex* (Amphipoda). *Animal Behaviour, 40,* 877–883.

Dixon, K. A., & Cade, W. H. (1986). Some factors influencing male–male aggression in the field cricket *Gryllus integer* (time of day, age, weight and sexual maturity). *Animal Behaviour, 34,* 340–346.

Dowds, B. M. & Elwood, R. W. (1983). Shell wars: Assessment strategies and the timing of decisions in hermit crab shell fights. *Behaviour, 85,* 1–24.

Elias, M. (1981). Serum cortisol, testosterone, and testosterone-binding globulin responses to competitive fighting in human males. *Aggressive Behavior, 7,* 215–224.

Enquist, M. (1985). Communication during aggressive interactions with particular reference to variation in choice of behaviour. *Animal Behaviour, 33,* 1152–1161.

Enquist, M., Leimar, O. (1983). Evolution of fighting behaviour: Decision rules and assessment of relative strength. *Journal of Theoretical Biology, 102,* 387–410.

Enquist, M., Leimar, O., Ljungberg, T., Mallner, Y., & Segerdahl, N. (1988). Test of the sequential assessment game I: Fighting in the cichlid fish *Nannacara anomala.* In O. Leimar, *Evolutionary analysis of animal fighting* (pp. 92–124). Ph.D. Thesis, University of Stockholm, Sweden.

Enquist, M., Leimar, O., Ljungberg, T., Mallner, Y., & Segerdahl, N. (1990). A test of the sequential assessment game: Fighting in the cichlid fish *Nannacara anomala. Animal Behaviour, 40,* 1–14.

Ewald, E. W. (1985). Influence of asymmetries in resource quality and age on aggression and dominance in black-chinned hummingbirds. *Animal Behaviour, 33,* 705–709.

Gartlan, J. S. (1968). Structure and function in primate society. *Folia primatologica, 8,* 89–120.

Gochman, C. S., & Leng, R. J. (1983). Realpolitik and the road to war: An analysis of attributes and behavior. *International Studies Quarterly, 27,* 97–120.

Groothius, A. G. G. (1989a). On the ontogeny of display behaviour in black-headed gulls I: The gradual emergence of adult forms. *Behaviour, 109,* 76–124.

Groothius, A. G. G. (1989b). On the ontogeny of display behaviour in black-headed gulls II: Causal links between the development of aggression, fear and display behavior: Emancipation reconsidered. *Behaviour, 110,* 161–204.

Hannes, R-P., Franck, D., & Liemann, F. (1984). Effects of rank-order fights on whole-body and blood concentrations of androgens and corticosteroids in the male swordtail (*Xiphophorus helleri*). *Zeitschrift fur Tierpsychologie, 65,* 53–65.

Harding, C. F. (1983). Hormonal influences on avian aggressive behavior. In B. B. Svare (Ed.), *Hormones and aggressive behavior* (pp. 435–467). New York: Plenum Press.

Hazlett, B. A. (1990). Evaluation of behavioural efference. *Animal Behaviour, 40,* 999–1001.

Hinde, R. A. (1981). Animal signals: Ethological and games-theory approaches are not incompatible. *Animal Behaviour, 29,* 535–542.

Howells, K. (1989). Anger-management methods in relation to the prevention of violent behaviour. In J. Archer & K. Browne (Eds.), *Human aggression: Naturalistic approaches* (pp. 153–181). London & New York: Routledge.

Huntingford, F. A. (1984). Some ethical issues raised by studies of predation and aggression. *Animal Behaviour, 32,* 210–215.

Huntingford, F. A., & Turner, A. (1987). *Animal conflict.* London & New York: Chapman & Hall.

Illius, A. W., Haynes, N. B., & Lamming, G. E. (1978). Effects of ewe proximity on peripheral testosterone levels and behaviour in the ram. *Journal of Reproduction and Fertility, 48,* 25–32.

Jakobsson, S., Radesater, T., & Jarvi, T. (1979). On the fighting behaviour of *Nannacara anomala* (Pisces, Cichlidae) males. *Zeifschrift fur Tierpsychologie, 49,* 210–220.

Kamel, F., Mock, E. J., Wright, W. W., & Frankel, A. I. (1975). Alterations in plasma concentrations of testosterone, LH and prolactin associated with mating in the male rat. *Hormones and Behavior, 6,* 277–288.

Krebs, J. R., & Dawkins, R. (1984). Animal signals: Mind reading and manipulation. In J. R. Krebs & N. B. Davies (Eds.), *Behavioural ecology: An evolutionary approach* (2nd ed., pp. 380–402). Oxford: Blackwell Scientific.

Lazarus, J. (1982). Competition and conflict in animals. In A. Colman (Ed.), *Cooperation and competition in humans and animals* (pp. 26–56). Wokingham: Van Nostrand Reinhold.

Leshner, A. I. (1983). Pituitary adrenocortical effects on inter male agonistic behavior. In B. B. Svare (Ed.), *Hormones and aggressive behavior* (pp. 27–83). New York: Plenum.

Leyhausen, P. (1956). Verhaltensstudien bei Katzen. *Zeifschrift fur Tierpsychologie, Beiheft, 2.*

Leyhausen, P. (1979). *Cat behavior.* New York: Garland STPM.

Maynard Smith, J. (1972). *On evolution.* Edinburgh: Edinburgh University Press.

Maynard Smith, J. (1974). The theory of games and the evolution of animal conflicts. *Journal of Theoretical Biology, 47,* 209–221.

Maynard Smith, J. (1976). Evolution and the theory of games. *American Scientist, 64,* 41–45.

Maynard Smith, J. (1982). *Evolution and the theory of games.* Cambridge & New York: Cambridge University Press.

Maynard Smith, J., & Parker, G. A. (1976). The logic of asymmetric contests. *Animal Behaviour, 24,* 159–175.

Maynard Smith, J., & Price, G. R. (1973). The logic of animal conflict. *Nature, 246,* 15–18.

Maynard Smith, J., & Riechert, S. E. (1984). A conflicting-tendency model of spider agonistic behaviour: Hybrid-pure population line comparisons. *Animal Behaviour, 32,* 564–578.

Mitchell, K. A. (1976). Competitive fighting for shells in the hermit crab, *Clibanarius vittatus. Aggressive Behavior, 2,* 31–37.

Moore, M. C. (1984). Changes in territorial defence produced by changes in circulatory testosterone: A possible hormonal basis for mate-guarding in white-crowned sparrows. *Behaviour, 88,* 215–226.

Morris, D. (1957). "Typical intensity" and its relation to the problem of ritualisation. *Behaviour, 11,* 1–12.

Moynihan, M. (1955). Some aspects of reproductive behaviour in the black-headed gull (*Larus ridibundus ridibundus L.*) and related species. *Behaviour, Supplement 4,* 1–201.

Norman, R. F., Taylor, P. D., & Robertson, R. J. (1977). Stable equilibrium strategies and penalty functions in a game of attrition. *Journal of Theoretical Biology, 65,* 571–578.

Parker, G. A. (1974). Assessment strategy and the evolution of fighting behavior. *Journal of Theoretical Biology, 47,* 223–243.

Parker, G. A., & Rubenstein, D. I. (1981). Role assessment, reserve strategy, and acquisition of information in asymetric animal conflicts. *Animal Behaviour, 29,* 221–240.

Peeke, H. V. S. (1982). Stimulus- and motivation-specific sensitization and redirection of aggression in the three-spined stickleback (*Gasterosteus aculeatus*). *Journal of Comparative and Physiological Psychology, 96,* 816–822.

Potegal, M., & tenBrink, L. (1984). Behavior of attack-primed and attack-satiated female golden hamsters (*Mesocricetus auratus*). *Journal of Comparative Psychology, 98,* 66–75.

Rand, W. M., & Rand, A. S. (1976). Agonistic behavior in resting iguanas: A stochastic analysis of dispute settlement dominated by minimization of energy cost. *Zeifschrift fur Tierpsychologie, 40,* 279–299.

Reichert, S. E. (1979). Games spiders play II: Resource assessment strategies. *Behavioral Ecology and Sociobiology, 6,* 121–128.

Riechert, S. E. (1982). Spider interaction strategies: Communication versus coercion. In P. N. Witt & J. Rovner (Eds.), *Spider communication: Mechanisms and ecological significance* (pp. 281–315). Princeton, NJ: Princeton University Press.

Reichert, S. E. (1984). Games spiders play III: Cues underlying context-associated changes in agonistic behaviour. *Animal Behaviour, 32,* 1–15.

Rowell, T. E. (1966). Hierarchy in the organization of a captive baboon group. *Animal Behaviour, 14,* 430–443.

Schuurman, T. (1980). Hormonal correlates of agonistic behavior in adult male rats. *Progress in Brain Research, 53*, 415–420.

Senar, J. C. (1990). Agonistic communication in social species: What is communicated? *Behaviour, 112*, 270–283.

Smith, A. T., & Ivins, B. L. (1986). Territorial intrusions by pikas (*Ochotona princeps*) as a function of occupant activity. *Animal Behaviour, 34*, 392–397.

Still, A. W. (1982). On the number of subjects used in animal behaviour experiments. *Animal Behaviour, 30*, 873–880.

Tinbergen, N. (1952). Derived activities, their causation, biological significance, origin, and emancipation during evolution. *Quarterly Review of Biology, 27*, 1–32.

Tinbergen, N. (1953). *Social behaviour in animals.* London: Methuen.

Toates, F. M., & Archer, J. (1978). A comparative review of motivational systems using classical control theory. *Animal Behaviour, 26*, 368–380.

Turner, G. F., & Huntingford, F. A. (1986). A problem for game theory analysis: Assessment and intention in male mouthbreeder contests. *Animal Behaviour, 34*, 961–970.

Van Rhijn, J. G., & Vodegel, R. (1980). Being honest about one's intentions: An evolutionary stable strategy for animal conflicts. *Journal of Theoretical Biology, 85*, 623–641.

Verrell, P. A. (1986). Wrestling in the red-spotted newt (*Notophthalmus viridescens*): Resource value and contestant asymmetry determine contest duration and outcome. *Animal Behaviour, 34*, 398–402.

Weigel, R. M. (1984). The application of evolutionary models to the study of decisions made by children during object possession conflicts. *Ethology and Sociobiology, 5*, 229–238.

Wingfield, J. C. (1985). Short-term changes in plasma levels of hormones during the establishment and defense of a breeding territory in male song sparrows, *Melospiza melodia. Hormones and Behavior, 19*, 174–187.

Zack, S. (1975). A description and analysis of agonistic behavior in an opisthobranch mollusc, *Hermissenda crassicornis. Behaviour, 53*, 238–267.

# CHAPTER 2

# On The Escalation of Aggression

Leonard Berkowitz

*University of Wisconsin—Madison*

On June 14, 1988, Edward Byrne, Jr., 28 years old, was executed in Louisiana for murdering a woman during the robbery of a gasoline station. This case was not especially notable, except for the people involved. Byrne was the 100th person executed in the United States since the Supreme Court reinstated the death penalty in 1977, and Louisiana is only one of 37 American states that now exercise capital punishment. Nor were the facts of the case particularly dramatic. Byrne had dated the woman he killed, planning to rob her because he knew she handled large sums of money on her job. He insisted, though, that he had not intended to murder her. When he carried out the robbery, he maintained, he had only wanted to knock her unconscious with his hammer.

But the fact is that he had killed her. Byrne's first blow did not achieve its purpose, and he kept hitting the woman again and again—until she died.

Of course, we do not know what had been in Ed Byrne's mind when he struck his victim. He might well have intended from the outset to murder the woman, as the district attorney argued. It is also conceivable, however, that the killing had not been premeditated, as Byrne claimed. In a great many homicides, the murderer does not start out consciously wanting to take the victim's life. Years ago, a police detective in Dallas, Texas, emphasized how, in many homicide cases, the initial acts of aggression had quickly escalated, became very intense, and a death resulted, unplanned. "Murders," he said, "result from little ol' arguments about nothing at all . . . Tempers flare. A fight starts, and somebody gets stabbed or shot" (Mulvihill & Tumin, 1969 p. 230).

The detective probably was referring to those killings, the majority of homicides, in which the offender and victim knew each other and were in conflict. But even murders occurring in the course of a felony in which the victim is a stranger to his or her slayer can be impulsive and unplanned in this way. On the basis of his analysis of police-reported robberies in Detroit from 1962 through 1974, Zimring (1979) estimated that a good fraction of whatever killings had occurred in these crimes were accidental rather than instrumental to the furtherance of the perpetrators' aims. Something might have happened during the encounter in these instances that stimulated the criminals to violence. Maybe the victims resisted or were slow to comply with the robbers' commands. Highly aroused emotionally—their nerves on edge, so to say—they might have then lashed out at their victims. Had they had guns, they would have shot. Those who did not have firearms, however, conceivably might have impulsively struck out at the victim several times, with their fists, a knife, or maybe, as in Byrne's case, a hammer.

## A THEORY OF EMOTIONAL AGGRESSION

I have long maintained that emotional (or hostile) aggression is different in important respects from instrumental aggression, and that emotional aggression generally, and many violent crimes in particular, should be regarded as relatively involuntary outbursts in which the aggressors mainly want to hurt (and sometimes destroy) their victim (e.g., Berkowitz, 1974, 1978, 1986, 1992). Block (1977) made a somewhat similar point when he distinguished between "two models of behavior" in his analysis of Chicago homicides. "The first model," he said, assumes that the victim and offender are both acting to maximize their benefits and minimize their costs in a dangerous situation" (p. 9). Block believed many robberies are instrumental actions in this sense. "The second model, impulsive action, assumes noninstrumental behavior. There is no weighing of costs and benefits, only the desire to injure or kill" (p. 9). I would qualify this latter statement by saying there can be *some* weighing of the costs and benefits but still would add that these considerations have a smaller role, because there is less controlled thought than in instrumental behavior. Nevertheless, the important point is that this kind of emotional aggression is relatively unaffected by anticipations of rewards and punishments. To a greater or lesser extent, the aroused aggressors are impelled by their strong internal agitation to assault their target, thinking little of their possible long-term gains and losses and conscious mainly of their desire to hurt or destroy (Berkowitz, 1992).

This distinction between emotional and instrumental aggression can also be applied to characteristically highly aggressive personalities (Berkowitz, 1992). Some people are primarily instrumental aggressors in that they habitually use force in a cool, calm, and collected manner to attain whatever objectives they might have in mind. Many robbers are instrumental aggressors, as are those school-yard bullies who want to assert their dominance and control over others. Other highly aggressive individuals, by contrast, tend to be much more emotionally reactive. They are often assaultive but mainly because they are quick to lose their temper and explode into a violent outburst. And then, of course, there are people who seem to be a mixture of both of these types, and it is my guess that Ed Byrne was one of these "mixed" aggressors.

Dodge and Coie (1987) showed that this distinction can help us understand some highly aggressive boys. Dividing youths into emotionally reactive, "proactive" (or instrumental) aggressors, and mixtures of both, on the basis of teacher ratings, Dodge and Coie found that the former boys were especially likely to see hostility in the world around them and then think that they had to react aggressively to these threats. I suspect that these reactive aggressors are also apt to escalate the intensity of their attacks once they start fighting because of their emotionality and their inability to restrain their violent urges.

Personality characteristics are not the only determinants of emotional aggression, however. Aggression can also be greatly affected by external stimulation (Berkowitz, 1974). People disposed to attack someone for one reason or another can be incited to stronger aggression than they otherwise would have displayed if they encounter a stimulus in the surrounding environment that has an aggressive meaning for them (or, more particularly, is associated in their minds with previously reinforced aggression). Even the sight of their victim's suffering can stimulate increased violence if they are strongly aroused at the time (Baron, 1977; Berkowitz, 1992). In a sense, the "pain cues" function much like a hungry person's first bite of food and tell the aggressors that they are approaching their goal; they are coming close to satisfying their appetite: getting an adequate meal or, in the latter case, hurting their victim sufficiently. As a consequence, their impetus to reach this goal is heightened. This internal spur to violence can be strengthened even further by the attackers' violent ideas. Thinking "I hate you" or "I'll smash you" or "I'll kill you," they arouse themselves even more, and their assault intensifies (Berkowitz, 1992).

## EMOTIONAL AGGRESSION AND THE ESCALATION OF VIOLENCE

This analysis of emotional aggression can tell us much about emotionally generated crimes of violence. More particularly, it can not only help us understand the escalation of the attackers' assault on their victims but also it suggests that such an escalation should not be uncommon. It is of some importance for the present formulation, then, to determine what factors influence this behavior, to the extent that it does take place. In the following subsections, I spell out some pertinent research with humans, leaving others the task of bringing in relevant animal studies.

### Aggressively Prone Personality

Although the formulation being advanced here is largely concerned with situational influences on involuntary emotional reactions, it does recognize the role played by personality dispositions. As I have just indicated, some people (who I have termed *emotionally reactive aggressors*) are especially apt to explode in violent outbursts when they see themselves threatened, and these persons are more likely than others to accelerate the intensity of their attacks when they do strike out at their targets.

Hans Toch's (1969) monograph on the personalities of violent criminals gives us one example of how the aggression displayed by violence-prone personalities can mount in fury. Toch related the story of Jimmy, a 23-year-old "minor league pimp" with a record of "many and diverse offenses, such as forcible rape . . . kidnapping, intoxication, grand theft, and disturbing the peace," as well as "several instances of battery and assaults with deadly weapons, and two attacks on police officers" (pp. 68–69).

More relevant to us here, though, was an incident that had occurred before Jimmy reached adolescence (and which was not entered into his police record). He had gone to a school dance but was barred from the hall because the policeman at the door knew of his reputation as a troublemaker. Jimmy became angry. He first threw a can at the officer's feet, then insulted him furiously, and when the officer tried to retaliate, actually attempted to shoot the man with the weapon Jimmy had with him. His aggression was halted only when other people in the hall joined to restrain him forcibly.

Jimmy's case is illustrative in several ways. It indicates, first of all, that highly violent personalities are inclined to be generally antisocial; they depart from our socially approved modes of conduct by being assaultive and are more likely than less aggressive people to be lawbreakers (Berkowitz, 1992; Eron, 1987; Farrington, 1982; Wilson & Herrnstein, 1985). Because of this connection between antisociality and aggressivity, it is quite possible that Edward Byrne was strongly disposed to violence as well as to other criminal modes of behavior.

Although I have no information about Byrne's childhood, this conjectured aggressive disposition could have been the product of harsh and inconsistent family experiences together with frequent rewards for aggressive action (Berkowitz, 1992; Patterson, DeBaryshe, & Ramsey, 1989). Moreover, as was true of Toch's Jimmy, Byrne might also have been quick to see threats in the world around him, threats that he believed he could overcome only by an attack (see Dodge & Coie, 1987).

More than being only emotionally reactive, however, according to the present reasoning, people with aggressive personalities, such as Jimmy, also tend to be deficient in self-restraints (see Berkowitz, 1992). Jimmy certainly had not "kept his cool" when the policeman blocked his entry into the dance. The frustration had enfuriated him. More than this, though, he did not hold back in attacking the policeman even though he could not possibly have believed he would gain his objective (admission to the hall) and was likely to be punished severely. If Byrne was the same kind of emotionally reactive aggressive personality, he too might have been relatively unable to restrain himself.

Situational Influences

As was indicated earlier, this analysis suggests that situational influences also contribute to the escalation of emotional aggression. Unfortunately, however, because investigators of human aggression have given surprisingly little systematic attention to this phenomenon, we can only speculate as to what some of these factors might be.

One of the very few laboratory studies concerning the escalation of aggression was conducted by Goldstein, Davis, and Herman (1975). Noting that such an escalation was seen in a number of experiments, these researchers gave their subjects repeated opportunities to punish a fellow student in the standard teacher–learner paradigm and found that the participants steadily increased the severity of the punishment that they administered over the blocks of trials. For Goldstein and his associates, these increasingly punitive reactions were primarily due to a disinhibitory process; the subjects' restraints against hurting the target had presumably weakened as the trials progressed, perhaps because they had not suffered any bad consequences for punishing the learner in the initial trials.

My own guess, however, is that whereas a lowering of inhibitions could have contributed to the heightened aggression, other factors might also have been at work. One possibility is that the subjects became more and more frustrated as the learning trials progressed. After all, they were trying to teach the learner something and found that the "other student" was unable to learn the concept they were trying to get across. They could have become increasingly vexed by the learner's apparent stupidity so that, in their growing impatience and rising emotional arousal, they punished the learnes ever more severely.

Their thoughts might have also played a part. A considerable body of research has demonstrated that words having a particular meaning can prime semantically related ideas and action tendencies (Wyer & Srull, 1981). People induced to use aggressive words tend to form hostile impressions of other persons and may even become aggressively inclined (see Loew, 1967, for an early demonstration), especially if they are subsequently reinforced for this word usage (Parke, Ewall, & Slaby, 1972). In essence, their aggressively related thoughts can stimulate them to increased aggression.

Not surprisingly, then, when angry persons think "hit" as they watch someone assault another individual, they become more punitive to their own tormentor afterward than they would have been if they had not had these aggressive ideas (Turner & Berkowitz, 1972). Byrne conceivably may have primed himself in this manner as he struck at his victim. The aggressive ideas that came to his mind as he saw himself hit the woman might have served to intensify his attacks—until he killed her.

Cognitive dissonance theory suggests that even more complicated thoughts might facilitate such continued attacks, at least under some circumstances. According to this theory, and some supporting research (Glass, 1964), those aggressors who want to think well of themselves tend to develop an increased dislike for their victim after they assault this person. It is as if they try to justify their attacks on the target by convincing themselves that the victim was detestable and deserved being beaten. If such a dissonance reduction process had taken place in Byrne's mind as he hit the woman, he too might have momentarily formed an intense hatred for her that lowered his restraints.

Even the woman's first cries of pain could have spurred Byrne on, as was mentioned earlier. An experiment by Baron (1977) testifies to how this could have happened and is worth summarizing in some detail.

In this study, male university students were first either deliberately angered or were treated in a neutral manner by the experimenter's confederate and then were provided with 10 opportunities to punish the offender with electric shocks for mistakes he supposedly made on a learning task. The subjects had to deliver a shock for each mistake but were free to select the intensity of the punishment. Moreover, half the men were given fictitious information about the level of pain supposedly being felt by the shock recipient.

If the subjects were not angry with the target person, the pain information served to lessen the intensity of the shocks that were delivered. These people had not wanted to hurt the target and reduced the severity of their punishment when they saw that they were inflicting pain. On the other hand, if the men had been provoked earlier by the target, the same pain information led to an increase in the intensity of the shocks given to him. The pain cues essentially told these angry persons that they were approaching their aggressive goal (hurting their tormentor sufficiently) and thus incited them to increased aggression.

Hartmann's (1969) study of juvenile delinquents' reactions to the sight of pain cues is also relevant here. He found that these youths were highly punitive to a peer (in the teacher–learner paradigm) if they had been angered by the target previously and then saw a film in which an aggression victim displayed clear signs of pain. Interestingly, the angry boys having the longest records of antisocial behavior were the ones who were most stimulated to greater aggression by the observed pain cues. Edward Byrne, presumably being highly antisocial himself, might have responded the same way to the woman's pain, an increase in the fury of his assault.

## CONCLUSION

With some notable exceptions, research-oriented behavioral scientists have not given sufficient attention to the emotional and impulsive aspects of aggression. Concentrating on the purposes to which aggression might be put, that is, the external objectives that could be served by an attack on other persons, they have not adequately recognized the degree to which this behavior is often carried out in the heat of passion, impelled by strong internal agitation and relatively oblivious to considerations of long-term costs and benefits. It is this type of emotional aggression that is especially likely to escalate in intensity at times.

This escalation is not the product of any one set of factors or any single psychological process. A variety of influences can operate to bring about this increased intensity as the attacks continue. Whereas this discussion has identified a number of factors that probably contribute to this escalation, I undoubtedly have omitted some other important influences. Whatever these might be, however, the central point of this chapter is that we should recognize how impulsive and involuntary an emotionally charged assault on another can be on occasion. All aggression is not cooly calculated action in pursuit of some subtle purpose. Edward Byrne's murder of his victim was not necessarily instrumental behavior intended solely to further his robbery. He, like other highly aroused persons, could well have gotten carried away, so to speak, by the mounting fury inside him as he hit his victim.

## REFERENCES

Baron, R. A. (1977). *Human aggression*. New York: Plenum.

Berkowitz, L. (1974). Some determinants of impulsive aggression: Role of mediated associations with reinforcements for aggression. *Psychological Review, 81,* 165–176.

Berkowitz, L. (1978). Is criminal violence normative behavior? Hostile and instrumental aggression in violent incidents. *Journal of Research in Crime and Delinquency, 15,* 148–161.

Berkowitz, L. (1986). Some varieties of human aggression: Criminal violence as coercion, impression management, and impulsive behavior. In A. Campbell & J. J. Gibbs (Eds.), *Violent transactions: The limits of personality* (pp. 87–103). Oxford and New York: Blackwell.

Berkowitz, L. (1992). *Aggression: Its causes, consequences, and control*. New York: McGraw-Hill.

Block, R. (1977). *Violent crime*. Lexington, MA: Lexington.

Dodge, K. A., & Coie, J. D. (1987). Social information-processing factors in reactive and proactive aggression in children's peer groups. *Journal of Personality and Social Psychology, 53,* 1146–1158.

Eron, L. D. (1987). The development of aggressive behavior from the perspective of a developing behaviorism. *American Psychologist, 42,* 435–442.

Farrington, D. P. (1982). Longitudinal analyses of criminal violence. In M. E. Wolfgang & N. A. Weiner (Eds.), *Criminal violence* (pp. 171–200). Beverly Hills, CA: Sage.

Glass, D. C. (1964). Changes in liking as a means of reducing cognitive discrepancies between self-esteem and aggression. *Journal of Personality, 32,* 531–549.

Goldstein, J. H., Davis, R. W., & Herman, D. (1975). Escalation of aggression: Experimental studies. *Journal of Personality and Social Psychology, 31,* 162–170.

Hartmann, D. P. (1969). Influence of symbolically modeled instrumental aggression and pain cues on aggressive behavior. *Journal of Personality and Social Psychology, 11,* 280–288.

Loew, C. A. (1967). Acquisition of a hostile attitude and its relation to aggressive behavior. *Journal of Personality and Social Psychology, 5,* 335–341.

Mulvihill, D. J., & Tumin, M. M. (1969). *Crimes of violence. Staff report to the National Commission on the Causes and Prevention of Violence* (Vol. 11). Washington, DC: U.S. Government Printing Office.

Parke, R. D., Ewall, W., & Slaby, R. (1972). Hostile and helpful verbalizations as regulators of nonverbal aggression. *Journal of Personality and Social Psychology, 23,* 243–248.

Patterson, G. R., DeBaryshe, B. D., & Ramsey, E. (1989). A developmental perspective on antisocial behavior. *American Psychologist, 44,* 329–335.

Toch, H. (1969). *Violent men.* Chicago: Aldine.

Turner, C. W., & Berkowitz, L. (1972). Identification with film aggressor (covert role taking) and reactions to film violence. *Journal of Personality and Social Psychology, 21,* 256–264.

Wilson, J. Q., & Herrnstein, R. J. (1985). *Crime and human nature.* New York: Simon & Schuster.

Wyer, R. S., Jr., & Srull, T. K. (1981). Category accessibility: Some theoretical and empirical issues concerning the processing of stimulus information. In E. T. Higgins, C. P. Herman, & M. P. Zanna (Eds.), *Social cognition: The Ontario Symposium* (Vol. 1 pp. 161–197). Hillsdale, NJ: Lawrence Erlbaum Associates.

Zimring, F. (1979). Determinants of the death rate from robbery: A Detroit time study. In H. M. Rose (Ed.), *Lethal aspects of urban violence* (pp. 31–50). Lexington, MA: Lexington.

# PART II

# Aggressive State and Trait: Behavioral and Physiological Processes Within Individuals

# CHAPTER 3

# Cognition-Excitation Interdependencies in the Escalation of Anger and Angry Aggression

Dolf Zillmann
*University of Alabama*

*Emotions are fleeting things, aren't they? They wear off, and then you have a conscience.*

—Mel Gibson, 1991

The literature on aggression among intimates (e.g., Finkelhor, 1986; Gelles, 1974; Gil, 1973; Pagelow, 1984; Straus, Gelles, & Steinmetz, 1980; Walker, 1979) abounds with descriptions of conflicts that start innocently enough with disagreements over rather trivial, nosubstantive matters, but that quickly grow to intensely emotional confrontations, and that end in violent eruptions in which involved parties, usually children and women, come to harm. Such outbursts and their destructive consequences seem incommensurate with the precipitating initial events. The perpetration of violent actions in these outbursts lacks social utility and tends to be highly counterproductive. Not only does the violence fail to resolve the initial disagreements, it further aggravates conflict and places new demands on its resolution. Those who perpetrate violence under the indicated conditions usually recognize the futility of their actions soon after committing them. In fact, they often respond with disbelief to their own actions. "I didn't mean to," and "How could I do this?" are typical responses. In expressing such disbelief, they insinuate a loss of rationality and of control over their own actions. Once reason and control return, they tend to be remorseful about what they did in their fit of rage.

The perpetrators of enraged violence are not alone in believing that they temporarily lost control over their behavior. In all cultures on earth it is recognized and in one form or another acknowledged that people occasionally perpetrate acts of violence "in the heat of passion," and that they usually regret their actions as soon as the extreme state of agitation that invariably accompanies these actions has subsided (Averill, 1982; Zillmann, 1979). Laws regulating violent, destructive behavior characteristically show leniency for persons who committed their transgressions when extremely agitated and excited. Compassion for those who maim and kill "in the heat of anger" can be so great that the temporary loss of reason, manifest in what seems to be a total disregard for consequences other than the accomplishment of the intended destruction, is deemed a form of insanity.

Regardless of the merits of such characterizations of violent rage, however, the knowledge manifest in folklore, common sense, and legal stipulations suggests (a) that conflict among humans can quickly grow from moderate to high levels and produce hostile feelings of extreme excitatory intensity, (b) that—in line with the blind-passion truism— rational control of these feelings is greatly compromised under conditions of extreme agitation and arousal, and (c) that such feelings fuel violent actions that seem involuntary and impulsive, if not automatic.

In the sociological literature on violence among intimates (e.g., Dobash & Dobash, 1978; Pagelow, 1984, Shupe, Stacey, & Hazlewood, 1987) such impulsive aggression tends to be explained as the result of stress and frustration as "external" factors. Gelles (1974), for instance, suggested that, because the immediate circumstances of conflicts rarely, if ever, warrant violent action, impulsive destructive outbursts are better "explained as arising out of the buildup of stress and frustration" (p. 74).

General references to stress and frustration do not provide an adequate or acceptable explanation of the escalation process and its destructive climax, however. Compelling evidence for the alleged effect of frustrating experiences on angry aggression is nonexistent (Bandura, 1973; Zillmann, 1979). In particular, the buildup of frustrations and its presumed consequences for aggression has not been demonstrated and remains popular conjecture. Stress, on the other hand, is a more likely contributor to impulsive, angry aggression. However, if the stress concept is not operationalized and expressed in measurable terms, it is bound to be used as the same patently post hoc explanation as is frustration. It should be possible, surely, to spot some frustration or stress in anybody who erupts violently. Virtually all acts of violence, therefore, could be retrospectively "explained" as the result of these omnipresent forces.

It is imperative, then, to complement the existing descriptive and occasionally speculative accounts of impulsive, angry aggression among intimates and between persons in other social settings with specific and, to the extent possible, validated explanations of the critical processes that lead to violent eruptions. The escalation of the experience of anger, because it so frequently creates the propensity for destructive violent action, may be considered the crucial process to be understood. We, consequently, concentrate on theory capable of explaining the escalation of anger and on research pertaining to this escalation. In addition, we focus attention on the characteristics and conditions that define the acute propensity for impulsive violence.

We start with the examination of anger and its escalation in psychophysiological terms. Thereafter, we investigate the implications of the physiological changes that are associated with anger on cognitive processes in perception and judgment; and we explore how effects on cognition feed back into anger, especially into its physiological manifestations. The focal point of this analysis is the interdependence of cognitive and excitatory reactivity and its immediate consequences for impulsive, angry aggression.

## ESCALATION OF ANGER

Disagreements, in which the parties in conflict perceive themselves to be treated unfairly, unjustly, dishonestly, demeaningly, rudely, or brutally, constitute provocations that tend to produce intense feelings of anger toward antagonists and tormentors. These feelings of anger are invariably accompanied by significant elevations of the level of sympathetic excitation in the autonomic nervous system. The magnitude of such excitatory changes is known to influence the intensity of experienced anger and to facilitate aggressive inclinations and actions (Averill, 1982; Zillmann, 1979, 1988).

### Excitatory Reactions to Endangerment

In general terms, it is the recognition of endangerment that gives rise to feelings of anger, aggressive dispositions, and alternative reactions (feelings of anxiety, flight dispositions) that are associated with increased sympathetic activity. Confronted with social or environmental conditions that threaten welfare and well-being, individuals respond in a fight-or-flight manner (Cannon, 1929). They act on these conditions, either by attacking them in hopes of defusing the threats they pose, or by escaping from them in hopes of eluding these threats. Individuals seem predisposed to resolve behavioral emergencies through vigorous actions of the specified kinds. This partiality for immediate action is the result of accelerated anabolic processes that generate the energy for a burst of vigorous action. The cited increase in sympathetic activity is a salient aspect of this behavior energization. It also is the critical factor determining the experiential intensity of anger (Averill, 1982; Schachter, 1964; Zillmann, 1978, 1983a).

The tendency to respond with vigorous action to endangerment undoubtedly has served humans well during the course of evolution. In addition, vigorous displays of emotional reactions and the performance of violent actions have retained some degree of the indicated utility. Temper tantrums, for instance, signal the strength of a reaction to endangerment and a readiness "to go to war" over an issue. Such signaling may intimidate opponents and prompt them to yield, potentially making the display of a fit of bad temper an effective coercive strategy. (See Archer and Huntingford, this volume, and Potegal, this volume, for discussions of threat displays in other species.) Moreover, beating someone into submission in a fit of violence, when this can be done with impunity or under conditions where the attainable benefits outweigh any repercussion, also constitutes an effective strategy—but apparently only as long as the stipulated conditions prevail. However, the utility of archaic vigorous action as a means of coping with endangerment and of conflict resolution has been lost for the most part. The social conditions of contemporary society have severely compromised the adaptive value of fight and flight reactions. Responding "emotionally" to threats to self-esteem, social status, social power, or economic standing not only tends to lack adaptive utility but can be counterproductive and maladaptive. It tends to have less utility than more controlled, cautions, thought-out reactions. For example, the burst of energy from the fight–flight reaction to an erroneous request for payment from the Internal Revenue System is likely to fuel irritation and anger but probably functions as an impediment to successful, clarifying negotiations with representatives of the institution. Similarly, such a burst of energy is neither useful in tackling global pollution hazzards nor helpful in eluding them. Upon recognition and comprehension of endangering conditions, the archaic agonistic reaction tendencies exert their influence nonetheless and people do get excited, when staying calm and collected in devising strategies for effective action would better serve their welfare and self-interest.

Phasic and Tonic Excitatory Reactions

In the analysis of the bodily conditions that favor conflict resolution by immediate vigorous action, it is useful to distinguish between excitation mediated by the adrenomedullary system and excitation mediated by the adrenocortical system (cf. Leshner, 1978; Turner & Bagnara, 1971).

Activity in the adrenomedullary system, through the release of catecholamines and their fast but short-lived hyperglycemic effect, provides energy for essentially one behavioral engagement. The energization is said to be *phasic* or *episodic*. It is energy for one course of vigorous action, such as in fight or flight.

Activity in the adrenocortical system, mainly through the release of glucocorticoids and their hyperglycemic effect, also generates energy but does so for extended periods of time. This energization is said to be *tonic*. Such tonic energization is part of the coping response to social and environmental stressors (cf. Appley & Trumbull, 1986; Selye, 1950).

In the production of their sympathomimetic effect, the two systems operate in an integrated fashion. Heightened activity in the adrenocortical system usually defines the undercurrent for acute emotions. It places the organism in a state of increased action readiness. It creates, among other things, superior conditions for anger and aggressive responsiveness, and it does so tonically. Emotional reactions build on this foundation. Phasic excitation from heightened activity in the adrenomedullary system combines with tonic excitation, and this combination creates emotional reactions of potentially great intensity.

The correspondence between the duration of tonic or phasic excitation, on the one hand, and the time course of the stimulation that induces the excitatory reactions under consideration, on the other, is usually very poor. This poorness of fit, which is mainly the result of the humoral nature of the mediating agents (Zillmann, 1983b), proves to have significant consequences for anger and angry aggression.

Stressful stimulation fosters heightened adrenocortical activity only after a considerable latency period. More importantly, the activity may persist for hours and days after the termination of the stressful stimulation. Individuals suffering from stress induced by conditions external to specific conflicts thus carry adrenocortical activity along into these conflicts, a circumstance that increases their vulnerability to anger escalation and to impulsive aggression.

Emotion-inducing stimulation fosters heightened activity in the adrenomedullary system also only after some latency. The latency is a matter of seconds, however, and has little practical significance. The period of time by which the excitatory reaction outlasts the emotional stimulation is again more important. The time beyond the cessation of emotional stimulation is a matter of minutes. These minutes may seem unimportant but turn out to be crucial in the escalation of anger and angry aggression.

## Excitatory Escalation

Escalating conflict can be conceptualized as a sequence of provocations, each triggering an excitatory reaction that materializes quickly and that dissipates slowly. If a second sympathetic reaction occurs before the first has dissipated, the second reaction combines with the tail end of the first. Moreover, if a third reaction occurs before the second and first reactions have dissipated, this third reaction combines with the tail ends of both earlier reactions. In general, *any excitatory reaction to provocation late in the escalation process rides the tails of all earlier excitatory reactions.* The specifics of this paradigm of excitation transfer are detailed elsewhere (Zillmann, 1983b, 1984).

The combination of residual sympathetic excitation from earlier provocations with the excitation in response to a subsequent provocation may, of course, be expected to produce anger and angry aggression that is incommensurate with that subsequent provocation. Sympathetic excitation is at "artificially" high levels, and these overly high levels should foster overly intense feelings of anger and a propensity for overly intense outbursts of violence.

Perception and judgment of disproportionality between provocations and angry aggression depend, of course, on the time interval between the outburst-triggering provocation and those preceding it. If provocations are contiguous, they are likely to be lumped together and seen as a unit. Under these perceptual conditions, provocation and angry aggression should be judged as commensurate. But generally speaking, the likelihood of perceptions of disproportionality between these events increases with the indicated time discrepancies. When initial provocations are followed by momentary or extended disengagements during which excitatory residues persist, the aggressive reaction to subsequent provocation should be judged as incommensurate with the provocation at hand. Judgments of disproportionality thus favor the involvement of lingering excitatory residues from sources that are not perceived as contributors to later reactions to provocation. This makes persisting activity in the adrenocortical system a prime contender. Stress- or distress reactions are known to increase sympathetic activity, mainly through the confounded release of cortisol and catecholamines (e.g., Frankenhaeuser, 1979, 1986; Levi, 1967), for extended periods of time. Apprehensions and anticipations of distressing experiences have very similar extended effects (cf. Rose, 1985). It may be expected, then, that residual excitation from stressful experiences facilitates anger reactions to substantially delayed provocations, and that such residues are capable of contributing to a propensity for violent outbursts in response to what appears to be insufficient provocation. The endocrinological analysis of excitatory reactivity may explain, therefore, what was conjecture in the sociological literature on violence among intimates (e.g., Gelles, 1974)—namely, that stress from various sources finds its way into impulsive, angry aggression.

Excitatory escalation has obvious limits, however. If it is accepted that residual excitation from earlier provocations combines additively and is part and parcel of prevailing levels of sympathetic activity, and if it were assumed that a particular provocation, regardless of prevailing activity levels, evokes a unique and invariable excitatory reaction, the prediction of excitatory reactivity would often exceed possible maxima. For instance, a particular provocation may trigger a substantial excitatory reaction in a calm person. It cannot produce a similarly strong reaction when that person is already highly excited. The additive combination of prevailing levels of excitation with the excitatory response to provocation under more normal excitatory circumstances would yield levels of excitation above human capacity.

The law of initial values (Sternbach, 1966; Wilder, 1957) prevents the indicated mispredictions. It presents the magnitude of excitatory reactions as a function of prevailing levels of excitation. Specifically, it states that excitatory reactions are likely to be inversely proportional to prestimulus levels of excitation. To rule out all maxima-violating predictions, a corrective formula has been offered (Zillmann, 1983b):

$$\alpha = 1 - \frac{p-b}{m-b},$$

where $p$ is the prestimulus, $b$ the basal, and $m$ the maximal level of excitation. The factor $\alpha$ modifies the normative intensity of subsequent excitatory reactions (i.e., their intensity assessed against basal or resting levels). Thus, intensity is not modified if $p = b$. If $p = m$, in contrast, it is reduced to zero.

This necessary correction of excitatory reactivity in provocation sequences has consequences that seem counterintuitive. The correction fosters the expectation that the excitatory contribution of provocations diminishes as their ordinal position in the escalation sequence increases. Or expressed in terms of time, their contribution is smaller, the later they occur in this sequence. This gives great excitatory starting power to minor disagreements but assigns a trivial effect to their placement late in the excitatory sequence.

Such predictions appear to be inconsistent with numerous descriptive accounts of anger escalating to violent action (e.g., Dobash & Dobash, 1978; Gelles, 1974; Pagelow, 1984). Disagreements late in the escalation sequence seem to have a powerful effect, especially with regard to their outburst-triggering capacity. Appearances may be deceptive, however. It certainly is not inconsistent with considerations of the function of sympathetic activity in emotion theory (e.g., Schachter, 1964; Zillmann, 1979, 1983a) to expect that disagreements that materialize when excitation is at extremely high levels are extremely intensely experienced. The magnitude of the excitatory contribution from such disagreements may be of little consequence here. It could, nonetheless, eventually be "the straw that breaks the camel's back." It may create conditions under which the experiential intensity of further provocation becomes noxious to a point where immediate relief through violent action is deemed feasible and is sought.

This proposal should not be construed as a threshold hypothesis predicting that, whenever a particular extreme level of sympathetic activity is reached, outbursts are likely or even unavoidable. Nor should it be construed as a threshold hypothesis applied to the duration of excessively high levels of sympathetic activity, which would predict that outbursts are likely or unavoidable after a particular period of extreme agitation. Instead, it is suggested that provocations late in an escalation sequence, although they may contribute little by way of heightening sympathetic activity, extend excessive levels of excitation in terms of time and thereby extend the propensity for violence. It is mainly this prolonging of acute agitation, a condition viewed as *readiness* for violent action (see Heiligenberg, 1974, for a discussion of the ecological significance of aggression readiness), that is expected to increase the likelihood of eruptions—because with time (a) it becomes apparent that nonviolent options fail to resolve the conflict, (b) the noxious experience grows, is deemed less bearable, and becomes increasingly partial to relief-providing actions, and (c) additional opportunities arise for acting with vigor toward conflict resolution and immediate relief.

In this discussion of excitatory escalation, it has been assumed that the perception and judgement of provocations is relatively independent of the level of excitatory activity. Such an assumption, as we see later, is untenable, however. If the cognitive assessment of provocations should change, such that the perception of any endangerment that they entail is enhanced at high levels of excitation, a better correspondence between theory and descriptive findings concerning the escalation sequence may be achieved. We consider shortly the indicated cognitive processes and their effects.

Pertinent Research

The intensification of anger and aggressive behavior by residual sympathetic excitation from reactions unrelated to the instigation of aggression has been demonstrated in numerous experiments. For instance, aggressively instigated men were subjected to strenuous physical exercise or not and then, while excitation from exercise was still in evidence, provided with an opportunity to retaliate. Retaliatory aggression was found to be greatly enhanced by residual arousal unrelated to provocation (Zillmann, Johnson, & Day, 1974; Zillmann, Katcher, & Milavsky, 1972). In similar research, provoked men and women were exposed to differently arousing, pleasant or unpleasant films and then given a chance to retaliate. The intensity of retaliatory aggression was consistently found to be proportional with the magnitude of residual excitation from ulterior sources (e.g., Bryant & Zillmann, 1977; Cantor, Zillmann, & Einsiedel, 1978; Ramirez, Bryant, & Zillmann, 1982; Zillmann, 1971; Zillmann, Hoyt, & Day, 1974). This research is presented more completely and in greater detail elsewhere (Baron, 1977; Zillmann, 1979, 1983a).

Whereas research on the intensification of anger and angry aggression by residual excitation from sources other than provocation exists in abundance, research on excitatory escalation and the corresponding escalation of anger in provocation sequences does not exist at all. However, the demonstration of anger intensification by residual excitation from effective experiences unrelated to anger, even from pleasurable experiences, may be considered conservatively biased evidence for the intensification of anger by residual excitation from preceding anger. The affinity of the sequenced affective reactions should invite the integration of excitatory components. If this reasoning is accepted, it may be considered established that residual excitation from a preceding provocation is capable of intensifying anger in response to a subsequent provocation. Excitation would have escalated from the first to the second provocation. However, demonstrations of excitatory escalation from more than one preceding affective reaction do not exist—not to mention such demonstrations in provocation sequences of more than two incidents. This circumstance renders the escalation of anger in provocation sequences theory in dire need of empirical validation.

Inspection of the aggression literature pertaining to the excitatory interplay of tonic adrenocortical activity from stress and adrenomedullary activity from phasic emotions leads to the same conclusion. Presumably because of the formidable difficulties in conducting investigations in which prolonged stress and acute anger are convincingly

manipulated and measured in physiological and cognitive manifestations, controlled experiments do not exist and theoretical proposals remain just that.

## COGNITIVE GUIDANCE

The primary function of cognition is to guide behavior. The immediate objective of such guidance is the avoidance of harm and the minimization of aversion. The maximization of gratification is, of course, a further objective.

Awake and alert individuals continually monitor their environment for conditions posing threats and for opportunities to attain gratifications. Based on their experience with the circumstances, they recognize prevailing action contingencies and *anticipate* aversion or gratification as the result of particular contemplated courses of action as well as of contemplated inaction. Table 3.1 summarizes anticipations that influence and control aggressive actions, whether motivated by anger or the attainment of incentives.

Under ordinary circumstances, the anticipation of costly consequences of contemplated aggressive actions fosters the inhibition of the actions. Probable social reproach, for instance, might be expected to produce unacceptable noxious experiences. Such reproach might be

**TABLE 3.1**
**Anticipations in the Cognitive Guidance of Aggressive Behavior**

| Appraisal of Circumstances | Appraisal of Consequences |
|---|---|
| (a) Contingencies of reward and punishment | Anticipation of gratification or aversion |
| (b) Coercive contingencies | Anticipation of success[a] or failure[b] |
| (c) Stable abilities and inabilities of self | Anticipation of success or failure |
| (d) Transitory abilities and inabilities of self | Anticipation of success or failure |
| (e) Opposing situational forces | Anticipation of cost[c] |
| (f) Punitive and retaliatory potentialities of others | Anticipation of cost |
| (g) Contingencies of social approval and reproach | Anticipation of gratification or aversion |

[a]Success ultimately translates into attainment of gratification or removal of aversion.
[b]Failure ultimately translates into removal of gratification or attainment of aversion.
[c]Cost ultimately translates into aversion. (Adapted from Zillmann, 1979. Reprinted with permission.)

deemed more noxious than inaction or the consequences of other nonaggressive reactions. Furthermore, attacking a tormentor might be feared to prompt retaliatory actions likely to increase present suffering. On the other hand, knowledge of superior strength and fighting skills, together with the belief that the victim is unlikely to resist or retaliate, would be most conducive to acting out aggressive inclinations.

## Appraisals, Reappraisals, and Preappraisals

Appraisals and repeated reappraisals of the circumstances in which individuals find themselves are capable of modifying excitatory activity. Threats and dangers produce excitedness. So do anticipations of threats and dangers. The excitedness, in this case, is part of a preparatory emotional reaction that is to facilitate vigorous coping reactions once their need materializes. However, as conditions change and threats and dangers are reappraised and deemed less severe or inconsequential, excitatory activity serves no cause and starts to dissipate. In accordance with theory and research evidence (Zillmann, 1979), it may be expected that this dissipation lowers the propensity for destructive behavior. Moreover, it may be expected that information that prevents individuals from appraising threats and dangers as deliberate acts against them personally will also prevent the strong, preparatory, excitatory reactions that direct attacks evoke. Noxious treatments that catch individuals by surprise, and for which they have not prepared coping reactions, are known to produce particularly intense excitatory and emotional reactions (Leventhal, 1974). However, noxious treatments that can be anticipated, and for which individuals are prepared or can prepare, especially when these treatments cannot be attributed to deliberate malevolence of others, are unlikely to instigate intense emotions.

## Pertinent Research

The indicated influence of cognition on excitatory activity, with its effect on the experience of anger and hostile behavior, has been demonstrated in an investigation by Zillmann and Cantor (1976). Male subjects were severely provoked by a rude male experimenter and later given an opportunity to harm him. In one condition, the subjects received no information about circumstances that could have made their tormentor's behavior appear less assaultive. His rudeness seemed deliberate, and the subjects had no alternative to appraising it as a personal attack. In the other conditions, information of mitigating circumstances was provided. The rude experimenter was said to be under a lot of stress from his preliminary doctoral examination. In one of these conditions, the subjects received the mitigating information prior to being mistreated. In the other, they received it after the mistreatment.

In the case of prior communication about mitigating circumstances, any seemingly hostile action on the part of the experimenter was *preappraised*. His actions could be attributed to stress and frustration deriving from conditions unrelated to the subjects' behavior. His rudeness did not have to be construed as a personal attack, and subjects did not have to ready themselves for such an attack. Compared with the control condition in which mitigating information had not been communicated, subjects should appraise the situation as less threatening. As a result, their excitatory reactions should be subdued, their experience of annoyance should be less severe, and they should be less inclined to take strong retaliatory measures.

In the case of the later communication of the same mitigating information, the subjects had suffered the full impact of the experimenter's rudeness. Excitatory reactions were comparatively strong, and experiences of annoyance were intense. The reception of the mitigating information eventually fostered a *reappraisal* of the circumstances. This reappraisal should remove the personal, deliberate, and arbitrary component from the mistreatment. Once such recognition materializes, excitation, now expendable, should start to dissipate, and the experience of annoyance should diminish. However, related research (Bryant & Zillmann, 1979) has shown that intensely felt anger may instigate retaliatory intentions, and that these intentions may be executed "in cold blood" long after recovery from acute anger. Reappraisal is thus unlikely to curtail retaliatory action as effectively as preappraisal.

In the experiment, excitatory activity was monitored at critical times between provocation and retaliation. Sympathetic excitation was ascertained in peripheral manifestations (blood pressure, heart rate). The findings, summarized in Fig. 3.1, show that subjects who had prior knowledge of mitigating circumstances were relatively unperturbed by the mistreatment they received. Sympathetic excitation never reached high levels, and it dissipated to particularly low levels. In contrast, the mistreatment prompted extreme excitatory reactions in subjects without such prior knowledge. The communication of mitigating information after the mistreatment apparently fostered a reappraisal that initiated and accelerated excitatory recovery. Excitation quickly fell below levels in the control condition in which subjects had not received mitigating information. But the reappraisal clearly failed to lower excitedness to levels comparable with those in subjects who had prior knowledge of the mitigating circumstances.

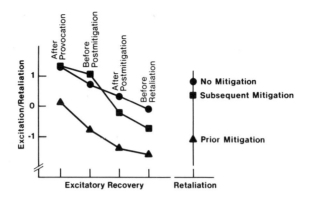

FIG. 3.1. The effect of mitigating information on excitatory reactions to provocation and on retaliatory hostility. The provision of mitigating information prior to provocation (labeled Prior Mitigation) prevented strong excitatory reactions and intense feelings of anger, and it kept retaliation to a minimum. The subsequent provision of mitigating information (labeled Subsequent Mitigation or Postmitigation) accelerated the decay of excitation, but it failed to reduce retaliation effectively. Excitation and retaliation are expressed in z scores for ease of comparison. (From Zillmann, 1979. Reprinted with permission.)

The severity of retaliatory actions proved to be proportional to levels of sympathetic excitation at the time these actions were taken. Persons who received mitigating information prior to being mistreated showed considerable compassion for their tormentor. On the other hand, persons who had received this information after having suffered the full blow of this treatment were almost as punitive with their tormentor as those who never learned of mitigating circumstances.

It has been pointed out that retaliatory intentions that are formed during acute anger may outlast the dissipation of excitation associated with the anger experience by a considerable period of time. In the investigation by Bryant and Zillmann (1979), retaliatory opportunities were delayed for 8 days. Identical provocations had been received at different levels of prevailing excitation. Subjects provoked at high levels of excitation had been expected to feel their anger more intensely than subjects provoked in the same manner but at lower levels of excitation. As a result, they should have committed themselves to retaliation more firmly and perhaps to stronger retaliatory measures. When finally provided with an opportunity to retaliate, subjects in the high-excitation condition did, as expected, retaliate more strongly than subjects in other conditions. This outcome is consistent with the proposal that retaliatory intentions are formed during acute anger, and that these intentions are comparatively stable over time. The research leaves open the possibility, however, that delayed retaliation is mediated, in part at least, by the more basic excitatory mechanics of affective memory (e.g., Clark & Williamson, 1989; Isen & Diamond, 1989). It is conceivable that the reconfrontation with an annoyer revives, to some degree, the initial experience of anger, especially its excitatory component. There can be little doubt that such a reconfrontation reinstates anger in cognitive terms. To the extent that this reinstatement is capable of instigating an excitatory reaction, earlier felt anger may be reactivated and then, depending on its excitatory intensity, lead to retaliatory decisions and actions. A commitment to retaliatory action, made during the initial experience of anger and sustained postemotionally, may thus not be necessary. However, the available evidence does not permit a determination of the degree to which the two outlined mechanisms are actually involved in the mediation of delayed retaliation. More research is needed to elucidate the reinstatement of anger and of the consequences of revived anger for aggression. (See Caprara, this volume, for a discussion of rumination.)

## COGNITIVE DEFICIT

The term *cognitive deficit* refers to the apparent inability of extremely agitated and aroused persons to conceive and execute rational, effective courses of action. Such deficit seems to manifest itself in all emotions associated with hypersympathetic activity. As a behavioral emergency develops and elevated sympathetic activity readies the body for fight or flight, but the social and environmental conditions are such that neither attack nor escape avenues are immediately apparent, the actions taken are often patently counterproductive. People in panic, for instance, are known to run where others are running; and they do so in the face of superior options (e.g., Kelley, Condry, Dahlke, & Hill, 1965; Mintz, 1951). In earthquakes and fires, crowds often come to harm at particular blocked exits without ever having tried others that were open (Quarantelli, 1954; Schultz, 1964). Phobic behavior is generally marked by nonproductive, if not maladaptive, action selections (Gray, 1971; Marks, 1969). But deficit is also to be found in emotions of positive valence. Extreme sexual excitedness, for example, may lead to action choices that would not be made under conditions more conducive of reflection and rational planning (Zillmann, 1984).

Despite a bounty of possible illustrations of the failure of cognition in guiding emergency behaviors efficiently, some caution in the use of the deficit concept is indicated. Most importantly, deficit should not be interpreted in absolute terms. It need not be assumed that the impairment of cognitive functioning is all encompassing. The impairment may be specific to the demands that the behavioral emergency places on cognitive assistance. If demands on higher cognitive operations are minimal, as in physical fighting or evasive actions, considerations of deficit are probably immaterial. On the other hand, if elaborate behavioral strategies are involved, and numerous consequences of possible actions are to be contemplated, persons seething with anger may be at a loss. Their cognitive apparatus may be so occupied with immediate threats and immediate hostile actions, as well as with their own impending counteractions, that less immediately relevant cognitions fail to be executed.

Predictions to this effect may be derived from various models of processing resources (e.g., Baddeley & Hitch, 1974; Johnston & Heinz, 1978; Navon & Gopher, 1979; Norman & Bobrow, 1975). In all these models it is assumed that processing capacity is limited. The capacity for the simultaneous processing of information, in particular, is viewed as severely restricted. As a result, the usage of processing capacity for one assignment is expected to reduce that for another and, hence, impair performance on this other assignment. This using-up of processing capacity by a primary assignment, at the expense of capacity for alternative assignments, becomes extreme as excitation reaches exceedingly high levels. (See Potegal's review, this volume, about a possibly analogous reduction of antipredator vigilance in animals involved in an agonistic encounter.)

The indicated correspondence between level of excitation and cognitive functioning is more generally specified in the inverted-U relationship between arousal and behavioral efficiency (e.g., Freeman, 1940; Malmo, 1959; Yerkes & Dodson, 1908). Easterbrook's (1959) reformulation in the cue-utilization model seems to have best withstood the test of time (cf. Eysenck, 1982). This model predicts an optimal level of arousal for the balanced and well-integrated processing of information pertinent to the assessment of an issue and to appropriate action. Such optimal conditions are provided, as a rule, by moderate levels of arousal. For extreme, especially for exceedingly high levels of arousal, the model predicts a concentration on immediately relevant information with a diminished sensitivity to less immediately relevant information. The model, then, does not so much predict a deficit of information processing as it predicts a reallocation of processing resources. What appears to be "blindness" at high levels of excitation is simply the result of a necessary overinvestment in attentional focus and information processing to deal with an emergency situation at hand.

The predicted effects of arousal on information processing are perhaps best demonstrated in an investigation by Bacon (1974). Subjects, whose arousal levels were manipulated by the administration of electric shock, performed a pursuit rotor-tracking task as their primary assignment and a simultaneously applied auditory signal-detection task as their secondary assignment. Performance on the primary task was not appreciably influenced by levels of excitation. Performance on the subsidiary task, in contrast, was significantly affected. It was, as predicted, poorer under conditions of high excitation than under conditions of moderate excitation. Because the performance impairment was most pronounced when the report of detection was delayed for a few seconds, the findings were thought to reveal difficulty in holding (rather than detecting) information. Such an interpretation would suggest that highly agitated, aroused persons engender a reduction of their working-memory capacity (cf. Baddeley & Hitch, 1974) for information that appears not to be useful in the pursuit of a primary, immediate behavioral objective.

In line with these considerations, decision making in national and international crises (see Leng, this volume) also tends to show the discussed deterioration of rationality. It has been observed that the prolonged experience of stress eventually clouds the judgment of leaders and negotiators. Perceptions of opponents' intentions become somewhat paranoid, and exaggerated assessments of danger are the result. Characteristically, such judgmental bias then restricts the search for alternatives to hostile solutions to conflict, and it fosters the adherence to strategies and policies that are more belligerent than the circumstances warrant.

## Cognition in Anger

The various processing-resources models suggest that individuals in acute anger are cognitively preoccupied with immediate actions aimed at the cessation of the endangerment that generated anger, and that other cognitive functions suffer as a result. Unfortunately, the models leave unclear which particular functions should suffer the expected impairment. Domains of anger-impaired cognition may be constructed, however, on the basis of common observation and the available research evidence.

During acute emotional states, attention and information processing concentrate on events there and then. In anger, aversion is anticipated, and efforts are planned or executed to avert the threatening aversive experiences. If anger in all its physical manifestations were not to materialize, individuals would be free to contemplate numerous behavioral options, contemplate immediate and future consequences, and the like, as indicated in Table 3.1. As acute anger develops, however, and individuals become preoccupied with immediacy, consideration of the implications of their actions and of future events is temporarily relegated to insignificance. Anticipations concentrate on the immediate impact of actions. They are, presumably, less likely to be executed and applied to the situation, the more remote, in time, a consequence appears to be. It is common knowledge that persons seething with anger "don't give a damn" about what happens to them tomorrow and thereafter as a result of actions taken in anger. Their anticipatory skills concerning future coercive contingencies and future contingencies of social approval and reproach seem greatly diminished. Time (i.e., immediacy vs. remoteness) thus emerges as a dimension along which the anger impairment of cognition can be mapped.

Another dimension of interest derives from stress research, specifically from the examination of worries and anxieties (e.g., Hamilton, 1980; Hartley, Morrison, & Arnold, 1989). Eysenck (1984), for instance, proposed that worries could lead to exaggerated self-concern. Such self-concern also typifies acute anger. Analogous to anxiety, it may foster a preoccupation with anticipations of aversion to be suffered by self. Anticipations of others' suffering should diminish as anger grows intense. This is another way of saying that, in acute anger, empathic sensitivities deteriorate and become defunct (cf. Zillmann, 1991). The proposal of enhanced and exaggerated self-concern hints at a cognitive explanation for such change in empathy.

The deterioration of empathic sensitivity seems of paramount importance in the consideration of anger escalation. In the initial stages of conflict, a particular provocation may have little impact because the person reacting to it is still capable of taking the opponent's perspective. At advanced stages, after this ability faded, the same provocation should be deemed contemptuous behavior, if not an intolerable assault. In general, the later in a provocation sequence a specific provocation occurs, the greater its emotional impact is likely to be. This reasoning, it should be noticed, projects evaluative changes on the basis of altered conditions for information processing. It also indicates that the escalation of anger may be, in large measure, cognitively defined. Moreover, it suggests that, because of changed judgmental conditions, provocations late in the escalation sequence may have a disproportionally strong effect despite their reduced excitatory contribution (see the discussion of the law of initial values under Excitatory Escalation).

Finally, it has been proposed that the catecholamine rush associated with the fight-or-flight reaction fosters an illusion of power and invulnerability (Zillmann, 1979). Interoception of muscular tension may prompt exaggerated assessments of physical preparedness and strength, and such assessments may trivialize perceptions of risk and vulnerability. Anticipations of the success and failure of coping reactions (see Table 3.1) should shift away from failure and move toward success. Anticipations of costs should be similarly trivialized. More specifically, the coercive power of self should be overestimated, that of others underestimated. Stable and transitory punitive abilities of self and others should undergo the same judgmental distortions. Opposing situational forces should also come to be taken lightly. All these judgmental partialities should become manifest at exceedingly high levels of sympathetic activity. And all, it should be noticed, favor aggressive actions there and then over nonaggressive alternatives then or at later times.

The physiological mechanics of the indicated cognitive changes during escalating anger have been the subject of much speculation. It has been suggested, for example, that small amounts of the catecholamines that mediate sympathetic excitation in the peripheral structures, especially epinephrine and norepinephrine, cross the brain blood barrier and affect central processes (Rothballer, 1967) that favor immediate action against threats and dangers. It has also been suggested that particularly active areas of the cortex (i.e., groups of neurons engaged by mental efforts) attract disproportional blood flow and energizing hormones (Warburton, 1979, 1986; Warburton & Wesnes, 1985), this at the expense of support to regions less called upon to perform. However, with regard to acute anger, the operation of such specific, cognition-mediating processes has not been demonstrated as yet. (See Potegal, this volume, for a discussion of the amygdala as a potential subcortical substrate of these effects.) Technological advances in measurement (e.g., positron emission tomography or nuclear magnetic resonance scanning) may well produce the necessary validation before too long. But until such time it is prudent to accept the hypothetical status of the various proposals that were made to shed light on the relationship between heightened excitation and selective cognitive incapacitation.

Pertinent Research

Evidence for the impairment of cognition in condition assessments during acute anger and angry aggressive behavior comes from an investigation by Zillmann, Bryant, Cantor, and Day (1975). In this investigation, male subjects were or were not strongly prearoused by invigorating strenuous physical exercise. The exercise consisted of riding a bicycle ergometer. Reactions to this task had shown it to be affectively neutral. Subjects neither particularly liked nor disliked the assignment, and none of them found it irritating, tiresome, or unreasonable. The subjects were then instigated to aggression by a male experimenter's abusive behavior and eventually provided with an opportunity to retaliate. Just prior to getting their opportunity to get even, a female confederate had occasion to enter the laboratory, calling the experimenter to the phone. He left with a snide remark, giving her a chance to comment on the fact that he was under a lot of stress from exams.

At moderate levels of excitation, such mitigating information should be received, processed, applied to the circumstances, and ultimately curtail hostile, retaliatory actions. This aggression-reducing effect of mitigating information has been observed in numerous studies (e.g., Burnstein & Worchel, 1962; Pastore, 1952; Rule, Dyck, & Nesdale, 1978; Zillmann & Cantor, 1976). At very high levels of excitation, however, the effect should not materialize because of cognitive incapacitation.

The findings, summarized in Fig. 3.2, were as expected. Mitigating information strongly reduced retaliatory hostility at moderate levels of excitation. This outcome corroborates the earlier findings. The novel finding concerns the behavior at high levels of excitation. At these levels, the provision of mitigating information proved to be without appreciable effect on hostile behavior.

Unanticipated data from this investigation suggest that mitigating information is similarly received but is processed differently at different levels of excitation. The prearoused subjects apparently comprehended the information but rejected it vehemently. Upon the confederate's revelation of stress from exams, these prearoused subjects uttered assessments like "That's just too bad!" Other utterances expressed the same sentiment, but in so doing used the strongest vulgarities the English language has to offer. The expression of such vulgarities is, of course, a characteristic accompaniment of impulsive agonistic behavior.

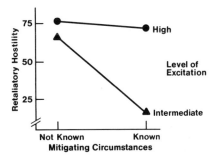

FIG. 3.2.   Impairment of cognitive response guidance in hostile behavior associated with high levels of sympathetic excitation. (From Zillmann, 1979. Reprinted with permission.)

Regardless of the intensity of the language used, however, the comments suggest that acutely angry, extremely excited persons become unforgiving and obsessed with retaliatory desire. They are determined to "get even" with their tormentors, and they appear to become oblivious to consequences such as social condemnation of their actions and likely reprisals by their opponents.

The apparent changes in cognitive functioning do not so much pertain to the perception of events as they manifest a shift in judgment. This shift is consistent with all rationales entertained earlier. For instance, processing-resources reallocation could explain the lack of appropriate judgmental integration of secondary information. Excessive concern for self and impoverished empathy for others predict the same outcome. So does the illusion-of-power model, as reprisals are not to be considered or feared. Because the effects of extreme excitedness on particular cognitive processes have not been demonstrated and may prove elusive in future exploratory efforts, these proposals have to be treated as confounded. All that can be said at present is that cognition capable of curtailing hostile behavior at moderate levels of sympathetic excitation fails to hold off aggression when anger is associated with extremely high levels of excitation.

### Drugs and Anger

Cognition that serves to inhibit and curtail violent action is, of course, not only influenced by changes in sympathetic activity. The so-called "mind-altering" drugs have a direct impact on the proficiency of cognitive operations, especially on operations involved in monitoring events in the environment and in preparing rationally sound response strategies (Hull, 1981). In the exploration of violence among intimates and acquaintances, alcohol is the drug to be considered. Ethanol intoxication is a condition under which a large portion of violent, abusive behavior occurs (e.g., Kantor & Straus, 1987; Leonard, Bromet, Parkinson, Day, & Ryan, 1985; Pagelow, 1984).

### Pertinent Research

Experimental research has shown with considerable consistency that the provocation of alcohol-intoxicated persons leads to stronger aggressive reactions than does the same provocation of sober persons (Taylor & Leonard, 1983), presumably because of a relaxation of inhibitions resulting from the impaired anticipation of consequences. An investigation by Leonard (1989) suggested that intoxicated persons are particularly insensitive to cues that under normal circumstances convey the victim's willingness to cease fighting, and that aggravated conflict often continues and escalates because of this intoxication-generated insensitivity.

Related research (Zillmann & Bryant, 1990) indicates that alcohol intoxication facilitates aggression most when the provocation predates the intoxication. Male subjects were either aggressively instigated prior to ethanol ingestion or thereafter. With time between provocation and retaliation kept constant, they eventually, but always while intoxicated, were given an opportunity to aggress against their tormentor. Ethanol intoxication was found to intensify aggressive reactions in both sequences: intoxication/provocation and provocation/intoxication. However, in the latter sequence, aggression proved to be facilitated to a markedly higher degree than in the former sequence.

These findings suggest that sober persons, in contrast to intoxicated ones, experience more fully the blow of demeaning treatments and personal attacks. The greater intensity of feelings of anger may be expected to instigate the contemplation of stronger retaliatory actions. If intoxication comes about in the wake of such retaliatory plans and commitments, it is likely to remove remaining inhibitions from the execution of these plans and thus allow violence to happen. The sociological literature (e.g., Bard & Zacker, 1971; Bowker, 1983; Pagelow, 1984) is laden with examples of violent actions that are perpetrated under these circumstances. It has been suggested, in fact, that alcohol intoxication is used, often deliberately, as an excuse for violent action. Such action, if perpetrated, may seem impulsive but obviously is not. In this connection, Gelles (1974) argued that, because drinking is a "socially approved excuse for violent behavior, . . . individuals who wish to carry out a violent act become intoxicated *in order to carry out the violent act*" (p. 117). The findings are certainly consistent with this possibility of intentionally shifting blame from self to a toxin.

## IMPULSIVE AGGRESSION

The consideration of cognitive deficit in escalating anger extends directly into models of impulsive aggressive behavior. Although most theories of impulsive aggression largely failed to account for the etiology of such deficit, all have invoked it in one form or another (e.g., Averill, 1982; Berkowitz, 1974; Gelles, 1974). Additionally, theories of this kind have emphasized that behavior guidance reverts to comparatively primitive mechanisms, such as stimulus and reinforcement control (e.g., Berkowitz, 1970, 1983).

A theory of impulsive aggression in which the selective impairment of cognitive functioning is explicitly linked to emotionality manifest in excessive sympathetic activity has been proposed by Zillmann (1979, 1988). This theory also predicts a reversion to basic and robust mechanisms of behavior guidance. However, in contrast to alternative models, it stipulates escalated anger and, especially, exceedingly high levels of excitation as a necessary condition for the reversion. Furthermore, this theory emphasizes the reversion to well-established habits, and it places the formation and evocation of these habits under stimulus and reinforcement control. Table 3.2 illustrates stages pertinent to the theory.

Analogous to the escalation of anger, the important consideration is that, as conflict grows in intensity and sympathetic activity reaches extreme levels, individuals become less proficient in devising coping responses whose conception requires complex cognitive operations. In

**TABLE 3.2**
**Principal Stages in the Provocation Sequence**

| Response | Provocation | | |
| | Stage 1 | Stage 2 | Stage 3 |
| --- | --- | --- | --- |
| Cognitive | Exhaustive appraisal of circumstances and consequences; balanced judgment; | Selective appraisal of circumstances and consequences; increased self-concern; diminished empathy; | Highly limited appraisal of circumstances and consequences; excessive self-concern; lack of empathy; illusion of power and invulnerability; |
| | irritation; | annoyance, anger; | spite, hatred; reversion to S–R guidance; |
| Excitatory | Low, moderate; increment upon recognition of endangerment; | Moderate, high; residues from earlier stage; heightened readiness for action; | High, excessive; residues from earlier stages; acute readiness for vigorous action; |
| Behavioral | Cautiously assertive, nonimpulsive, argumentative; | Strongly assertive, unyielding, hostile, aggressive; | Impulsive, explosive, irresponsible, reckless, violent; |

Note: The operation of interdependencies between cognitive and excitatory processes in the escalation of anger and angry aggression from Stage 1 to Stage 3 is detailed in the text.

this state, individuals are unimaginative and readily resort to well-rehearsed and much practiced reactions to given situations. Anxieties, for instance, are known to produce the indicated reversion, fostering increasingly rigid and reflexive reactions (Geen, 1985). Habitual reactions of this kind constitute, in fact, a fallback or default system for failing cognitive guidance.

Poor cognitive proficiency can, of course, be brought about by alternative means, such as ethanol intoxication, and eventuate a similar reliance on habits. Violent action depends, however, on a sufficient amount of sympathetic activity and coordination. It cannot be expected for intoxication to the point of physical incapacitation.

The discussed theory of impulsive aggression, then, predicts that hyperexcited persons, or excited persons whose cognitive capabilities are reduced by toxins, will resort to performing behaviors that have been practiced and reinforced in the past. Those who succeeded with aggression, who were able to resolve conflict to their advantage by brutalizing others, will be sure to take this course of action again. Others who failed with aggression—who, instead of being victorious, became victims of brutality—are likely to exhibit actions, or rather inactions, that are commonly subsumed under the heading of "learned helplessness" (Seligman, 1975). Although these actions are vastly different, both types are impulsive in the sense that the behavior is quasi-automatic and entails little rationality. Once such impulsive behavior materializes in situations of social conflict, efforts at resolving the conflict through persuasion and bargaining tend to be counterproductive. Furthermore, if the conflict involves habitual aggressors, it is bound to become physical. Resolutions will be sought, and possibly achieved, by brute force.

## REFERENCES

Appley, M. H., & Trumbull, R. (Eds.). (1986). *Dynamics of stress: Physiological, psychological, and social perspectives*. New York: Plenum.

Averill, J. R. (1982). *Anger and aggression: An essay on emotion*. New York: Springer-Verlag.

Bacon, S. J. (1974). Arousal and the range of cue utilization. *Journal of Experimental Psychology, 102*, 81–87.

Baddeley, A. D., & Hitch, G. (1974). Working memory. In G. H. Bower (Ed.), *The psychology of learning* (Vol. 8, pp. 74–98). London: Academic Press.

Bandura, A. (1973). *Aggression: A social learning analysis*. Englewood Cliffs, NJ: Prentice-Hall.

Bard, M., & Zacker, J. (1971). Assaultiveness and alcohol use in family disputes: Police perceptions. *Criminology, 12* (3), 281–292.

Baron, R. A. (1977). *Human aggression*. New York: Plenum.

Berkowitz, L. (1970). The contagion of violence: AN S-R mediational analysis of some effects of observed aggression. In W. J. Arnold & M. M. Page (Eds.), *Nebraska Symposium on Motivation* (Vol. 18, pp. 95–135). Lincoln: University of Nebraska Press.

Berkowitz, L. (1974). Some determinants of impulsive aggression: Role of mediated associations with reinforcement for aggression. *Psychological Review, 81,* 165–176.

Berkowitz, L. (1983, November). Aversively stimulated aggression: Some parallels and differences in research with animals and humans. *American Psychologist,* 1135–1144.

Bowker, L. H. (1983). *Beating wife-beating.* Lexington, MA: Lexington.

Bryant, J., & Zillmann, D. (1977). The mediating effect of the intervention potential of communications on displaced aggressiveness and retaliatory behavior. In B. D. Ruben (Ed.), *Communication Yearbook 1* (pp. 291–306). New Brunswick, NJ: ICA-Transaction Press.

Bryant, J., & Zillmann, D. (1979). Effect of intensification of annoyance through unrelated residual excitation on substantially delayed hostile behavior. *Journal of Experimental Social Psychology, 15,* 470–480.

Burnstein, E., & Worchel, P. (1962). Arbitrariness of frustration and its consequences for aggression in a social situation. *Journal of Personality, 30,* 528–540.

Cannon, W. B. (1929). *Bodily changes in pain, hunger, fear and rage: An account of researches into the function of emotional excitement* (2nd ed.). New York: Appleton-Century-Crofts.

Cantor, J. R., Zillmann, D., & Einsiedel, E. F. (1978). Female responses to provocation after exposure to aggressive and erotic films. *Communication Research, 5,* 395–411.

Clark, M. S., & Williamson, G. M. (1989). Moods and social judgements. In H. Wagner & A. Manstead (Eds.), *Handbook of social psychophysiology* (pp. 347–370). Chichester: Wiley.

Dobash, R. E., & Dobash, R. P. (1978). Wives: The appropriate victims of marital violence. *Victimology, 2* (3–4), 426–442.

Easterbrook, J. A. (1959). The effect of emotion on cue utilization and the organization of behavior. *Psychological Review, 66,* 183–201.

Eysenck, M. W. (1982). *Attention and arousal: Cognition and performance.* Berlin: Springer-Verlag.

Eysenck, M. W. (1984). *A handbook of cognitive psychology.* London: Lawrence Erlbaum Associates.

Finkelhor, D. (1986). *A sourcebook on child sexual abuse.* Beverly Hills, CA: Sage.

Frankenhaeuser, M. (1979). Psychoneuroendocrine approaches to the study of emotion as related to stress and coping. In R. A. Dienstbier (Ed.), *Nebraska Symposium on Motivation, 1978* (pp. 123–161). Lincoln: University of Nebraska Press.

Frankenhaeuser, M. (1986). A psychobiological framework for research on human stress and coping. In M. H. Appley & R. Trumbull (Eds.), *Dynamics of stress: Physiological, psychological, and social perspectives* (pp. 101–116). New York: Plenum.

Freeman, G. L. (1940). The relationship between performance level and bodily activity level. *Journal of Experimental Psychology, 26,* 602–608.

Geen, R. G. (1985). Test anxiety and visual vigilance. *Journal of Personality and Social Psychology, 49,* 963–970.

Gelles, R. J. (1974). *The violent home.* Beverly Hills, CA: Sage.

Gibson, M. (1991, March 3). Quoted in M. Ryan, "I admire people with self-control." *Parade Magazine,* pp. 8, 10.

Gil, D. G. (1973). *Violence against children: Physical child abuse in the United States.* Cambridge, MA: Harvard University Press.

Gray, J. A. (1971). *The psychology of fear and stress.* New York: McGraw-Hill.

Hamilton, V. (1980). An information processing analysis of environmental stress and life crises. In I. G. Sarason & C. D. Spielberger (Eds.), *Stress and anxiety* (Vol. 7, pp. 13–30). Washington, DC: Hemisphere.

Hartley, L. R., Morrison, D., & Arnold, P. (1989). Stress and skill. In A. M. Colley & J. R.

Beech (Eds.), *Acquisition and performance of cognitive skills* (pp. 265–300). Chichester: Wiley.

Heiligenberg, W. (1974). Processes governing behavioral states of readiness. In D. S. Lehrman, J. S. Rosenblatt, R. A. Hinde, & E. Shaw (Eds.), *Advances in the study of behavior* (Vol. 5, pp. 173–200). New York: Academic Press.

Hull, J. (1981). A self-awareness model of the causes and effects of alcohol consumption. *Journal of Abnormal Psychology, 90,* 586–600.

Isen, A. M., & Diamond, G. A. (1989). In J. S. Uleman & J. A. Bargh (Eds.), *Unintended thought* (pp. 124–152). New York: Guilford.

Johnston, W. A., & Heinz, S. P. (1978). Flexibility and capacity demands of attention. *Journal of Experimental Psychology* (General), *107,* 420–435.

Kantor, G. K., & Straus, M. A. (1987). The "drunken bum" theory of wife beating. *Social Problems, 34,* 213–230.

Kelley, H. H., Condry, J. C., Jr., Dahlke, A. E., & Hill, A. H. (1965). Collective behavior in a simulated panic situation. *Journal of Experimental Social Psychology, 1,* 20–54.

Leonard, K. E. (1989). The impact of explicit aggressive and implicit nonaggressive cues on aggression in intoxicated and sober males. *Personality and Social Psychology Bulletin, 15,* 390–400.

Leonard, K. E., Bromet, E. J., Parkinson, D. K., Day, N. L., & Ryan, C. M. (1985). Patterns of alcohol use and physically aggressive behavior. *Journal of Studies on Alcohol, 46,* 279–282.

Leshner, A. I. (1978). *An introduction to behavioral endocrinology.* New York: Oxford University Press.

Leventhal, H. (1974). Emotions: A basic problem for social psychology. In C. Nemeth (Ed.), *Social psychology: Classic and contemporary integrations* (pp. 1–51). Chicago: Rand McNally.

Levi, L. (1967). Stressors, stress tolerance, emotions and performance in relation to catecholamine excretion. In L. Levi (Ed.), *Emotional stress: Physiological and psychological reactions; medical, industrial and military implications* (pp. 192–199). New York: American Elsevier.

Malmo, R. B. (1959). Activation: A neuropsychological dimension. *Psychological Review, 66,* 367–386.

Marks, I. M. (1969). *Fears and phobias.* New York: Academic.

Mintz, A. (1951). Non-adaptive group behavior. *Journal of Abnormal Social Psychology, 46,* 150–159.

Navon, D., & Gopher, D. (1979). On the economy of the human-processing system. *Psychological Review, 86,* 214–255.

Norman, D. A., & Bobrow, D. G. (1975). On data-limited and resource-limited processes. *Cognitive Psychology, 7,* 44–64.

Pagelow, M. D. (1984). *Family violence.* New York: Praeger.

Pastore, N. (1952). The role of arbitrariness in the frustration–aggression hypothesis. *Journal of Abnormal and Social Psychology, 47,* 728–731.

Quarantelli, E. L. (1954). The nature and conditions of panic. *American Journal of Sociology, 60,* 267–275.

Ramirez, J., Bryant, J., & Zillmann, D. (1982). Effects of erotica on retaliatory behavior as a function of level of prior provocation. *Journal of Personality and Social Psychology, 43,* 971–978.

Rose, R. M. (1985). Psychoendocrinology. In J. D. Wilson & D. W. Foster (Eds.), *Williams textbook of endocrinology* (7th ed., pp. 653–681). Philadelphia: Saunders.

Rothballer, A. B. (1967). Aggression, defense and neurohumors. In C. D. Clemente & D. B. Lindsley (Eds.), *Aggression and defense: Neural mechanisms and social patterns: Vol. 5. Brain function* (pp. 135–170). Berkeley: University of California Press.

Rule, B. G., Dyck, R., & Nesdale, A. R. (1978). Arbitrariness of frustration: Inhibition or instigation effects on aggression. *European Journal of Social Psychology, 8*, 237–244.

Schachter, S. (1964). The interaction of cognitive and physiological determinants of emotional state. In L. Berkowitz (Ed.), *Advances in experimental social psychology* (Vol. 1, pp. 49–80). New York: Academic.

Schultz, D. P. (1964). *Panic behavior*. New York:Random House.

Seligman, M. E. P. (1975). *Helplessness: On depression, development, and death*. San Francisco: Freeman.

Selye, H. (1950). *The physiology and pathology of exposure to stress*. Montreal: Acta.

Shupe, A., Stacey, W. A., & Hazlewood, L. R. (1987). *Violent men, violent couples*. Lexington, MA: Lexington.

Sternbach, R. (1966). *Principles of psychophysiology*. New York: Academic.

Straus, M. A., Gelles, R. J., & Steinmetz, S. K. (1980). *Behind closed doors: Violence in the American family*. Garden City, NY: Anchor.

Taylor, S. P., & Leonard, K. E. (1983). Alcohol and human physical aggression. In R. G. Geen & E. I. Donnerstein (Eds.), *Aggression: Theoretical and empirical reviews. Vol. 2. Issues in research* (pp. 77–101). New York: Academic.

Turner, C. D., & Bagnara, J. T. (1971). *General endocrinology* (5th ed.). Philadelphia: Saunders.

Walker, L. E. (1979). *The battered woman*. New York: Harper Colophon.

Warburton, D. M. (1979). Stress, arousal and performance. In V. H. Hamilton & D. M. Warburton (Eds.), *Stress and cognition* (pp. 469–476). London: Wiley.

Warburton, D. M. (1986). A state model for mental effort. In G. R. J. Hockey, A. W. K. Gaillard, & M. G. H. Coles (Eds.), *Energetics and human information processing* (pp. 217–232). Dordrecht: Martinus Nijhoff.

Warburton, D. M., & Wesnes, K. (1985). Cholinergic mechanisms and cognitive dysfunction. In M. M. Singh, D. M. Warburton, & H. Lal (Eds.), *Central cholinergic mechanisms and adaptive dysfunction* (pp. 132–145). New York: Plenum.

Wilder, J. (1957). The law of initial values in neurology and psychiatry: Facts and problems. *Journal of Nervous and Mental Disease, 125*, 73–86.

Yerkes, R. M., & Dodson, J. D. (1908). The relation of strength of stimulus to rapidity of habit formation. *Journal of Comparative Neurology and Psychology, 18*, 459–482.

Zillmann, D. (1971). Excitation transfer in communication-mediated aggressive behavior. *Journal of Experimental Social Psychology, 7*, 419–434.

Zillmann, D. (1978). Attribution and misattribution of excitatory reactions. In J. H. Harvey, W. J. Ickes, & R. F. Kidd (Eds.), *New directions in attribution research* (Vol. 2, pp. 335–368). Hillsdale, NJ: Lawrence Erlbaum Associates.

Zillmann, D. (1979). *Hostility and aggression*. Hillsdale, NJ: Lawrence Erlbaum Associates.

Zillmann, D. (1983a). Arousal and aggression. In R. G. Geen & E. I. Donnerstein (Eds.), *Aggression: Theoretical and methodological issues* (pp. 75–101). New York: Academic.

Zillmann, D. (1983b). Transfer of excitation in emotional behavior. In J. T. Cacioppo & R. E. Petty (Eds.), *Social psychophysiology: A sourcebook* (pp. 215–240). New York: Guilford.

Zillmann, D. (1984). *Connections between sex and aggression*. Hillsdale, NJ: Lawrence Erlbaum Associates.

Zillmann, D. (1988). Cognition-excitation interdependencies in aggressive behavior. *Aggressive Behavior, 14*, 51–64.

Zillmann, D. (1991). Empathy: Affect from bearing witness to the emotions of others. In J. Bryant & D. Zillmann (Eds.), *Responding to the screen: Reception and reaction processes* (pp. 135–167). Hillsdale, NJ: Lawrence Erlbaum Associates.

Zillmann, D., & Bryant, J. (1990). *Effects of ethanol intoxication before versus after provocation on aggressive behavior*. Unpublished manuscript, University of Alabama.

Zillmann, D., Bryant, J., Cantor, J. R., & Day, K. D. (1975). Irrelevance of mitigating circumstances in retaliatory behavior at high levels of excitation. *Journal of Research in Personality, 9,* 282–293.

Zillmann, D., & Cantor, J. R. (1976). Effect of timing of information about mitigating circumstances on emotional responses to provocation and retaliatory behavior. *Journal of Experimental Social Psychology, 12,* 38–55.

Zillmann, D., Hoyt, J. L., & Day, K. D. (1974). Strength and duration of the effect of aggressive, violent, and erotic communications on subsequent aggressive behavior. *Communication Research, 1,* 286–306.

Zillmann, D., Johnson, R. C., & Day, K. D. (1974). Attribution of apparent arousal and proficiency of recovery from sympathetic activation affecting excitation transfer to aggressive behavior. *Journal of Experimental Social Psychology, 10,* 503–515.

Zillmann, D., Katcher, A. H., & Milavsky, B. (1972). Excitation transfer from physical exercise to subsequent aggressive behavior. *Journal of Experimental Social Psychology, 8,* 247–259.

# CHAPTER 4

# Aggressive Arousal: The Amygdala Connection

Michael Potegal
*Walter Reed Army Institute of Research*

*Sometimes the light's all shinin' on me,*
*other times I can barely see.*

—From "Truckin'," words by Robert Hunter,
music by Jerry Garcia, Bob Weir, and
Phil Lesh ("The Grateful Dead"), 1971,
1973, Ice Nine Publishing Co.

The major thesis of this chapter is that there exist central processes of aggressive arousal within individuals that mediate overt aggressive behavior. This aggressive arousal is distinct from general arousal (should such a thing exist) or sexual arousal. Aggressive arousal is an organizing principle for a variety of phenomena relating to aggression within, between, or among individuals. The amygdala is identified as an important component of the neural circuitry mediating aggressive arousal; its neuroanatomical connections and physiological properties are consistent with its role as a supraordinate organizer of aggression-related behaviors. Parallels between aggression in humans and in other animals are identified, on the hypothesis that these parallels may stem from similarities in the neural circuitry of emotional expression.

## SEPARATING THE PROVOCATION OF AGGRESSION FROM THE TARGET OF AGGRESSION

In an elegant quantitative study of two species of cichlids, Heiligenberg (1974) provoked an increase in the aggressive behavior of adult male fish by briefly presenting to each subject a male conspecific outside of the subject's tank. While the subjects watched the stimulus fish during this presentation, few attacks occurred; after the stimulus was withdrawn, there was a dramatic increase in the number of subject's attacks directed against the blind fingerling fish that inhabited each subject's tank. Aggression was provoked by the male conspecific but was directed against the fingerling fish. Another extensively investigated experimental example of this distinction is schedule-induced aggression in pigeons, in which a conspecific target (live bird, model, or picture) is continuously accessible but is routinely attacked during only one phase of the schedule (e.g., during extinction; Azrin, Hutchinson, & Hake, 1966). The provocation here is a schedule-related event, the target is a species-relevant stimulus.

This theoretical separation between provocation and target is akin to the ethological distinction between stimuli that motivate behavior and those that release or trigger it (e.g., Adams, 1979). In schedule-induced aggression in pigeons, for example, the more lifelike the target, the greater the likelihood of attacks; the head of the target is a particularly effective "releaser" of attack (e.g., Cohen, Yoburn, Pennington, & Ball, 1979). In the case of hamsters, whose aggressive behavior is discussed in greater detail later, if one places into the cage of a known aggressive animal an intruder drugged to the point of immobility, this intruder will be thoroughly explored but not attacked. If the intruder begins to move, it will be attacked within a few minutes. Its movement is the releasing stimulus (cf. Grant & Mackintosh, 1963, and Grant, Mackintosh, & Lerwill, 1970 for reports of flight by one hamster eliciting chase by another). On the other hand, 1 minute's exploration of an anesthetized conspecific is sufficient to significantly reduce the latency of attack upon a subsequently presented moving target. Exploration of the intruder provides motivating stimuli, most likely in the form of pheromonal cues.


## AGGRESSIVE AROUSAL AS A
## MOTIVATIONAL STATE


Aggression shows all the classical defining characteristics of a motivated behavior (e.g., the same stimulus, presented on different occassions, may or may not elicit aggression depending on the internal state of the organism). Animals presented with an invariant, attack-provoking stimulus often show a rise and then a fall in the rate and/or intensity of their attacks. Such temporal shifts have been referred to as the sensitization and habituation of aggression, emphasizing a link with learning processes (e.g., Peeke & Peeke, 1982; Bronstein, this volume) and as attack priming and satiation, emphasizing a motivational perspective (Potegal & tenBrink, 1984). Aggression is goal directed in the sense that the organism may alter its strategies during repeated attempts at attacking a given target. For example, resident rats will dig under and turn over an anesthetized intruder presented in the supine position to deliver a bite to its dorsal surface, the usual target site for offensive attacks (Blanchard, Blanchard, Takahashi, & Kelley, 1975). Evidence that the expression of aggression can be reinforcing under the appropriate conditions has been reviewed earlier (Baenninger, 1974; Potegal, 1979).

A well-replicated and particularly striking phenomenon illustrating the motivational aspect of aggression is found in experiments in which rats or pigeons were trained to use attack as an operant by having been given food or water reinforcement for attacking a restrained target animal. When two such trained and food-or water-deprived subjects are initially placed together, they attack each other and then continue to fight for some time, ignoring the presentation of food or water (Azrin & Hutchinson, 1967; Killeen, 1975; Reynolds, Catania, & Skinner, 1963; Ulrich, Johnston, Richardson, & Wolff, 1963). Aggressive motivation overrides the original motivation for food. In these experimental situations, the stimuli from the other animal act to maintain or even increase aggressive motivation. However, aggressive behavior can persist even after the provoking stimulus has been withdrawn (e.g., Heiligenberg, 1974). Such *temporal persistence* (Hinde, 1970), also called *motivational inertia* (Fentress, 1973; Lorenz, 1957) or *momentum* (Marler, 1976), is the most important motivational feature of aggression for the present purposes. In the context of aggression, Heiligenberg (1974) used the term *attack - readiness* to indicate the internal state controlling the overt behavior; I use the term *aggressive arousal*. Using the attack-priming paradigm described next, I have found that aggressive arousal in hamsters and rats persists over intervals of at least 30 minutes following provocation (Potegal, 1992a). Because there was no external stimulation during these intervals, such persistence clearly must be mediated by internal processes (cf., Cairns, this volume, who similarly invokes internal physiological, "neurobiological" states that support attack and fighting).

## STUDIES OF AGGRESSIVE AROUSAL IN
## HAMSTERS AND RATS

Female hamsters have been the main subject of my studies of intraspecific aggression because a high proportion of them are aggressive when singly housed, but, like other female rodents, their bites on conspecifics are partially inhibited so they inflict little or no tissue damage (cf. Blanchard, Kleinschmidt, Fukanaga-Stinson, & Blanchard, 1980). Aggressive arousal in these animals is studied via the attack-priming effect, a behavioral paradigm derived from the work of Lagerspetz (1969): When a female hamster is allowed a single biting attack on an intruder placed into its home cage, the latency to attack a second, "probe" intruder, is reduced and the probability increased (Potegal & tenBrink, 1984). The intruders in these experiments are treated with methotrimeprazine, a long-acting analgesic/sedative that reduces the variability in their behavior, eliminating wild flight in particular, and protects them against the stress of being attacked. Because the hamsters do not appear to discriminate one drug-treated intruder from another (Potegal, 1991), the change in latency from priming to probe trial must be internally mediated (i.e., it must involve a change in aggressive arousal).

Attack priming is specific to aggression in that primed animals show no changes in eating or in locomotion in a running wheel (Potegal & tenBrink, 1984). Mounting an attack on a conspecific involves detecting, tracking, and biting the other animal. To determine if the priming effect might depend on this particular combination of acts per se, hamsters were trained to pursue a hamster-sized block of wood moving back and forth through their cage to obtain the sunflower seeds that had been taped to it. The animals quickly learned to follow the block and remove the seeds; they also often spent some time gnawing on the block. Each hamster was then given, in ABBA or BAAB order, two priming or probe trial pairs and two woodblock or probe trial pairs (i.e., in the first trial the hamsters attacked an intruder or pursued and gnawed on a woodblock. In either case they were presented with a probe intruder on the second trial). Statistical analyses showed that latencies to attack the probe were significantly shorter following a priming attack than following interaction with a woodblock. These results indicate that the priming effect is not dependent on the sensorimotor acts of pursuit and biting.

## ATTACK-INDEPENDENT AND ATTACK-DEPENDENT AGGRESSIVE AROUSAL

At least two theoretically separable processes may account for the priming effect. One is that exposure to and exploration of the first intruder increases aggressive arousal to the point at which an attack is elicited. When the second intruder is presented, arousal is already high and an attack occurs more quickly. Note that under this interpretation the attack on the first intruder is merely a "marker" of the change of state; that is, the first attack signals that a change of state is occurring but does not itself play a causal role in reducing subsequent attack latency. The alternative possibility is that it is the occurrence of the first attack itself that somehow shortens the subject's latency to perform the second attack.

In support of the first alternative, a substantial body of evidence shows that the aggressive behavior of hamsters, like that of other rodents, is strongly controlled by olfactory/vomernasal stimuli (e.g., Murphy, 1976; Payne, 1974). These cues determine whether sexual or aggressive behavior will be directed to a conspecific. The importance of these stimuli for priming in hamsters was first suggested by the observation that the priming effect is more consistent and pronounced if time in contact with the intruder is used as the dependent measure instead of the more usual measure of elapsed time since introduction of the intruder (Potegal, 1991). During contact the subject explores the intruder's anogenital region, ear, corner of mouth, eye, and flank, all of which bear specialized glands. Experiments carried out following this discovery showed that allowing subjects to investigate an anesthetized intruder systematically reduced subsequent attack latency; the longer the durations of contact, the shorter the subsequent attack latencies. With 90 seconds of contact the latencies fall to an asymptotic level that is almost as short as that produced by attack priming.

The fact that attack latency shortens systematically with increasing exposure to an anesthetized intruder argues against the possibility that priming is basically a step change in state. However, even the maximally effective 90-second exposure to an anesthetized intruder did not completely reduce attack latencies to the level achieved by attack priming. What other stimuli might be involved? As noted previously, several studies show that movement of the opponent can release aggression in rodents (see Potegal, 1992b, for review). It has been found that enucleation does not reduce hamster aggression (Murphy, 1976), suggesting that visual movement is not necessary for attack. It may be sufficient, however. Lagerspetz and Portin (1968) found that mice would attack a moving but not a motionless bottle brush. Because a brush presumably does not provide pheromonal cues, movement may also be an attack-motivating stimulus that increases aggressive arousal. Thus, it is possible that exposure to the appropriate combination of sensory stimuli from the intruder would suffice to reproduce the priming effect in its entirety (i.e., to reduce attack latency to that which follows a priming attack). This possibility could be tested by experiments in which hamsters are exposed to anesthetized conspecifics mounted on a moving platform.

A very different possibility is that priming is partially response dependent. On this hypothesis, a change in internal state is associated with the commission of the first attack; this change contributes to the reduced latency of the second attack. In other words, the full magnitude of the priming effect can be obtained only when the subject has carried out an attack. At least three sources of information might be involved. Purely external feedback would involve cues from the intruder (e.g., their vocalization and movement upon being bitten). In a preliminary study these responses were elicited from intruders by means of a forceps pinch while the aggressive subjects were in contact with them; this maneuver completely failed to facilitate subjects' attacks. Somatic feedback (e.g., proprioceptive signals from the subject's jaws when biting) is another possible source of state-changing information. However, it is clear from the woodblock experiment cited before that pursuit and biting of an object per se are insufficient to produce a reduction in attack latency. Purely central "feedforward" signals within the central nervous system preceding and during attack and/or feedback signals following the attack comprise a third set of possibilities for triggering this hypothetical change of state. From a functional viewpoint, the operation of any of these mechanisms would imply that priming is an instance of a positive feedback process: Performing the first attack makes the second attack more likely. Positive feedback processes have been claimed to contribute to episodes of extreme violence in humans (Baenninger, 1974; Zimbardo, 1969). Experimental examination of these complex and subtle possibilities presents a formidable challenge.

## NEURAL MECHANISMS OF AGGRESSIVE AROUSAL: NEUROANATOMICAL LOCALIZATION AND BEHAVIORAL SPECIFICITY

My investigation of the brain mechanisms of aggressive arousal began with a search for the neural loci mediating the priming effect. The recently developed technique of using the expression of the proto-oncogene c-fos as a marker of neuronal activity was the key to this investigation. c-fos is one of a number of "early intermediate" genes whose protein products are expressed in neurons within 30 minutes of activation (depolarization and calcium release); the expression of c-fos protein persists for an hour or 2 thereafter (see Sheng & Greenberg,

1990, for review). In my laboratory this technique has recently shown that the corticomedial amygdala (CMA) is a potential locus mediating aggressive arousal: The number of activated neurons in and around the medial nucleus of the amygdala is higher in attack-primed hamsters then in unperturbed animals of matched baseline aggressiveness (Potegal, Ferris, & Skaredoff, 1991). This effect was neuroanatomically specific in that no such increases were found elsewhere including the lateral, basolateral, or central amygdaloid nuclei, or a number of other limbic and hypothalamic structures. The effect was also behaviorally specific in several ways: There were no significant differences in the general activity of primed and control animals in the hour that elapsed between the final observation and sacrifice. Furthermore, there was no correlation between CMA *c-fos* expression and the motor activity that followed the priming trial (note that motor activity has often been used as a measure of general arousal). *c-fos* expression was also unrelated to any specific behaviors that occurred in this period.

Further evidence for behavioral specificity comes from a yoked control group of hamsters each of which had been matched for baseline aggressiveness with an animal in the priming group. After pretraining on the woodblock pursuit task described earlier, the yoked controls were allowed to pursue, make contact with, and gnaw on the block for a period of time equal to the duration of a priming trial of the matched animal in the priming group. CMA *c-fos* expression also was greater in primed animals than in these yoked controls. Thus, the greater *c-fos* expression in attack-primed animals was not simply due to the localization, pursuit, and biting of a salient object but is specifically related to aggressive behavior.

In an additional series of *c-fos* studies, ovariectomized female hamsters were injected with estrogen and progesterone over several days to induce an hormonal state of estrous. While in this state half of these animals were also allowed to interact with a stud male until they assumed the sexually receptive lordorsis posture of arched back and raised tail. Hormonal injections by themselves lowered CMA *c-fos* counts below baseline levels. Sexual interaction raised the number of nuclei above the hormone treatment level. The number of activated CMA nuclei in animals showing lordosis was still less than the number in attack-primed animals, however, and their neuroanatomical distribution was different: Attack priming increased the number of nuclei expressing *c-fos* more or less uniformly along the rostro-caudal extent of the CMA, whereas activation was greater in the caudal aspect of the CMA in sex-primed animals (Potegal, Ferris, & Skaredoff, 1991). The dissociation between CMA *c-fos* patterns of aggressive and sexual behavior is evidence for at least a partial separation of these motivational systems. It would be of interest to compare CMA activation patterns in male hamsters that can turn rapidly from one to the other behavior and in which aggressive and sexual motor patterns are more alike.

The foregoing observations on different behaviors strongly suggest the CMA activity is specific to aggression. Further evidence comes from within the primed group: The aspect of aggressive behavior most clearly associated with the number of CMA cells expressing *c-fos* was the mean priming latency over all trials. Longer contact durations correlated with higher nuclear counts. When similar experiments were carried out with aggressive male rats in the resident/intruder situation, the same relationship between CMA *c-fos* expression and mean latency was obtained.

The CMA is the major site of olfactory and vomeronasal input to the amygdala (e.g., Scalia & Winans, 1975). That *c-fos* expression increased with longer exposure to the intruder might be expected from the nature of the input; more prolonged contact with the intruder implies a more prolonged stimulation of the cells receiving the input. In another experiment, a 1-minute exposure to an anesthetized intruder increased *c-fos* expression in the posterior part of the CMA to levels found in primed animals. This suggests that exposure to the olfactory and vomernasal cues from an intruder is sufficient to activate CMA neurons, even when an attack is not carried out. These latter findings are consistent with the importance of contact in producing the priming effect, and with the observation that contact with an anesthetized intruder is sufficient to reduce subsequent attack latency almost to the primed level. However, *c-fos* expression was more associated with the *mean* contact duration on all trials than with the particular duration of contact on the trial that just preceded sacrifice. One possible interpretation of this finding is that *c-fos* expression reflects the general level of sensory-neural CMA activation required to release attack rather than the particular acute history of CMA stimulation.

A final comment on these observations needs to be made. *c-fos* expression has attained a certain notoriety as a neuroanatomically diffuse response that can be elicited by the most trivial of stimuli. In part, this reputation stems from its association with generalized seizure activity, this being the experimental circumstance in which its expression in the CNS was discovered (Morgan, Cohen, Hempstead, & Curran, 1987). That *c-fos* expression was so selectively restricted in the current studies may well relate to the facts that animals were tested in their home cage in their home room, that having attacked intruders in their cages on a number of prior occassions they were well habituated to the test situation, and that they had experienced no counterattacks on these occassions.

## THE FUNCTIONAL SIGNIFICANCE OF THE CMA
## LOCALIZATION

The functional significance of the CMA localization was evaluated by bilateral radio frequency lesions of the area. To examine the effect of passing an electrode through the tissue lying dorsal to the CMA, electrode track puncture wounds were made in one control group. A cortical lesion was made in a second group to control for the effects of destroying a volume of brain tissue. CMA lesions significantly increased the latency and reduced the number of attacks relative to the control groups. This finding is consistent with earlier lesion studies in hamsters (e.g., Shipley & Kolb, 1977; Takahashi & Gladstone, 1988), rats (e.g., Koolhaas, Schuurman, & Wiepkema, 1980; Luiten, Koolhaas, Boer, & de Koopman, 1985), and mice (Kemble, 1981). Histological examination revealed that CMA lesions were distributed along the rostro-caudal length of the amygdala. Correlation analysis showed that the more rostral the lesion the longer the mean elapsed time to the first bite on either trial. This relationship between lesion site and behavioral effect was confounded by the fact that the more anterior lesions were larger. However, the correlation between lesion volume and attack latency was nonsignificant, and a partial correlation between lesion site and attack latency that removed the effect of lesion size remained significant.

CMA lesion and control animals were also given two consecutive 10-minute trials in a running wheel. There were no significant differences among the groups in latency to enter the wheel and no correlation within the CMA group between entry latency and lesion site or size. There were also no differences between groups in the number of revolutions they turned in the wheel. However, all animals in both control groups and 10 of the 11 CMA animals increased the number of turns in the second trial. This produced a highly significant locomotor practice effect. A lack of interaction indicated that this practice effect occurred equally strongly in all groups. These findings indicate that CMA lesions do not increase general timidity, do not produce a general locomotor impairment, and do not affect hamster's ability to increase their behavior through experience. The elimination of these alternative explanations strengthens the hypotheses that CMA *c-fos* expression marks a process coupled to aggressive arousal and that the CMA is part of the neural circuitry mediating aggressive arousal.

Clearly, the CMA exercises a relatively specific control over intraspecific aggression in rodents. The contributions of anterior and posterior parts of the CMA remain to be resolved. It may be that, although proportionately greater *c-fos* expression occurs in the posterior CMA during priming, the neurons controlling attack are located more anteriorly. Alternatively, it remains possible that the posterior CMA neurons are those that control attack, and that the anterior electrolytic lesions destroyed caudally directed afferents to and/or rostrally directed projection fibers from these neurons. These possibilities need to be investigated with axon-sparing ibotenic acid lesions placed at different sites within the CMA.


## THE TIME COURSE OF C-FOS EXPRESSION AND THE PERSISTENCE OF AGGRESSIVE AROUSAL

In both female hamsters and male rats, the priming effect is robust at 30 minutes following the initial attack but is less before and after this time point (Potegal, 1992a). This observation is of interest in view of the well-established delay of about 30 minutes between neuronal stimulation and the appearance of *c-fos* protein. Aggressive arousal may well depend on several neural processes partially overlapping in time, at least one of which involves genomic modulation of neural events.

That the amygdala is part of the circuitry responsible for the prolongation of aggressive arousal should come as no surprise. Effects that build up slowly and then persist for awhile are a motif of amygdala function: While recording from single cells in the medial amygdala of behaving animals during the presentation of olfactory and acoustic stimuli, Saphier, Mor, and Feldman (1988) and Saphier (personal communication, 1992) noted that "there were delays in the onset of responses that were on the order of several seconds. These delays were not absolute but took the form of ramped increases in activity that reached a steady-state plateau of elevated activity after some seconds." In complementary fashion, responses in some amygdala neurons persist for tens of seconds following termination of stimulus presentation (O'Keefe & Bouma, 1969). On a behavioral level, amygdala lesions reduce the duration of intraspecific fighting in dogs (Fuller, Rosvold, & Pribram, 1957) and post shock fighting in hamsters (Shipley & Kolb, 1977). Conversely, autonomic and behavioral signs of aggression in cats frequently persist for periods as much as 2 to 3 minutes following stimulation of the amygdala. These post stimulation effects occur more frequently and last longer following amygdala stimulation than following stimulation of either hypothalamus or central gray in same animals (e.g., Hilton & Zbrozyna, 1963). Kruk (1991) noted that hypothalamic stimulation in rats and cats that is subthreshold for eliciting attack can facilitate subsequent stimulation effects. The half life for this effect is on the order of 10 seconds. Because lesion and stimulation studies show that the amygdala exerts its effects on aggression by acting through the hypothalamus and central gray, the greater persistence of aggressive behavior following amygdala stimulation may be the consequence of activating this larger mass of neural tissue. Alternatively, there may be special, intrinsic characteristics of amygdaloid circuitry that tend to prolong activation; these may involve the same properties that contribute to amygdaloid kindling and seizure susceptibility.

Are these speculations relevant to the persistence of anger in humans? In 3 of 4 surveys of anger scattered over more than half a century, American and Japanese college students reported that the median duration of an episode of anger was 10 to 20 minutes (Gates, 1926; Meltzer, 1933; Ueda, 1962). Subjects in a fourth set of surveys, which included nonstudent community residents, had bimodal distributions of anger durations (Fridhandler & Averill, 1982). The shorter mode in two thirds of this most recent set of surveys was 5 to 10 minutes, in agreement in the previous observations. These retrospective estimates are consistent with experimental demonstrations of the persistence of aggressive arousal over a delay imposed between provocation and test. Kornadt (1974) and Konecni (1975) found increases in projective and overt behavioral measures of aggressiveness in subjects up to 13 minutes after they had been provoked by insult and/or frustration, whereas Doob and Climie (1972) and Buvinic and Berkowitz (1976) failed to find such effects after delays of 20 or 60 minutes. These durations are within the temporal range of the attack-priming effect.

The second mode of anger duration in Fridhandler and Averill's surveys consisted of episodes a day or more in duration. These episodes tended to be broken into discontinuous periods of experienced anger. Such intermittent effects presumably involve "rumination" (i.e., the tendency to keep recalling and rehearsing past provocations, to plan real or symbolic revenge, etc.). Caprara (this volume) found that identifying individuals as *ruminators* or nonruminators has important predictive value for their aggressive behavior, accounting for much or all of the variance in several experimental situations. Maybe the individuals reporting protracted episodes of anger in Fridhandler and Averill's study were ruminators. Because rumination is presumably based on our advanced cognitive capacities, it is difficult to imagine the animal analog. Do hamsters roam their cages after carrying out an attack saying to themselves "Just wait till that guy comes back"? Maybe not. However, aggressive arousal in attack-primed hamsters and rats does not decay smoothly but waxes and wanes reliably over the course of minutes and hours (Potegal, 1992a; Potegal & Popken, 1985). Perhaps intermittent angry rumination is the consequence of physiological processes mediating aggressive arousal.

## BEYOND RODENTS

The priming effect has been replicated in male rats (Potegal, 1992a). So has the finding of increased CMA *c-fos* expression associated with priming. These findings highlight the importance of the medial amygdala in the control of aggression in hamsters and rats, two species of rodent. Because olfactory and vomeronasal input has such a major control over aggression in rodents, the question must be raised whether this area of the brain retains a crucial role in the aggressive arousal of microsomatic species where olfactory/vomernasal stimuli are of lesser importance. The functions of the CMA in aggression should be examined across a wider range of species. It would be particularly important to examine the role of the CMA in primate species. In this context it is important to note that, not only are medial amygdala neurons in monkeys responsive to visual stimuli, they are attuned to facial expression (e.g., Brothers, Ring, & Kling, 1990), suggesting that they play a role in mediating social interactions in this species.

## PHENOMENA THAT MAY BE EXPLICABLE IN TERMS OF AGGRESSIVE AROUSAL

Up to this point, aggressive arousal has been inferred from changes in the probability of overt attack. It is unlikely that the influence of the internal processes that control attack probability would be narrowly restricted to just this aspect of aggressive behavior. There are a diversity of phenomena in the domain of aggressive behavior that may be influenced by these same processes. These are noted briefly in the next section.

### Escalation of Aggressive Sequences, "Threat/Intention" Displays, and the Prediction of Conflict Outcome

Ethological field observations have shown that agonistic encounters usually involve species-typical threat displays, sequences of postures and acts that sometimes culminate in physical attacks. The predictive value of these threat displays for overt aggression varies according to species and circumstance. Among free-living blue tits, for example, certain combinations of head, wing, and body posture predict attack with as much as a 50% probability, depending on the season of the year (Stokes, 1962). In encounters between barnyard hens, in contrast, if both birds assume a "Deep Crouch" posture, the probability of a fight is 1.0 (Foreman & Allee, 1959, Table V). In some cases it seems as if displays differ in the degree of aggressive arousal required to activate them; as arousal increases, successively higher thresholds are crossed and the corresponding displays appear in an orderly sequence. If the encounter continues, arousal will eventually reach the threshold for overt attack. Laboratory examples include the much studied agonistic behavior of the rat, in which lateral threat posture typically precedes a full aggressive posture that precedes a bite-and-kick attack (e.g., Lehman & Adams, 1977). This description also fits observations on species as diverse as fighting fish (Simpson, 1968) and shrews (Crowcroft, 1957). Differences between antagonists in the latency, rate, and/or intensity of their displays can actually predict the winner of the fight. A classic case is encounters between red stags, where the winner may be predicted by its relatively greater rate of roaring before combat is joined (Clutton-Brock & Albon, 1979). The probability of fighting and/or winning can be predicted by gill erection, body, and/or eye color in various species of fish (e.g., Evans, 1985; Martin & Hengstebeck, 1981, Bronstein, this volume; Stacey & Chizar, 1975). Initial agonistic postures predict contest winners in both chickens (Foreman & Allee, 1959) and jungle fowl (Wilson, 1974).

In other cases threat displays result from a conflict between the tendency to attack and some other tendency (e.g., most usually to flee, sometimes to mate, etc.). It is certainly true that full intensity, unambivalent attacks not preceded by any display have been reported in mice (Kahn, 1951), voles (Banks, 1962), shrews (Olsen, 1969), meercats (Ewer, 1973), and monkeys (Adams & Schoel, 1982). Some of the best evidence for the conflict hypothesis can be found in Blurton-Jones' (1968) work on the conflict between attack and flight in the great tit (for an overview of the controversy, see Hinde, 1970). In the present context, the important point is that the type and intensity of display can be determined in part or in whole by the level of aggressive arousal. Conversely, in favorable cases threat type and/or intensity may be used as indices of aggressive arousal.

In either variant the ethological view of threat is that it expresses an inner motivational state. This view can be contrasted with game theoretic analyses of animal conflicts in which display is equivalent to a move in a game, which may or may not have "emotional" significance (see Archer & Huntingford, this volume). One prediction arising from game theory is that such autonomic and behavioral signals would be more adaptive as bluff concealing actual intent than as veridical advertisement of aggressive arousal, because it is less risky to scare off a rival by looking and acting fierce than to reveal information on the true readiness to fight (e.g., Turner & Huntingford, 1986). This bluff hypothesis has been disconfirmed in some cases including those cited earlier. Although attack generally cannot be predicted with a probability of 1.0, these behavioral and autonomic stigmata do indicate an increased probability of aggression. (For a more detailed discussion of the interaction between the expressive aspect of display and its communication/negotiation function, see Hinde, 1985.)

Threat and attack can be dissociated by experimental manipulation. Reductions in threat and increases in attack occur in rats upon hypothalamic stimulation (Kruk, 1991) and in monkeys after frontal lesions (Miller, 1976), for example. Breeding mice for high levels of aggression produces the same effect (Cairns, this volume). Such observations can be accommodated within the versions of the aggression arousal hypothesis. In the successive threshold version, arousal could rise to the attack threshold so quickly that displays would not have time to be released. Alternatively, these experimental manipulations might uncouple display from arousal (e.g., by eliminating input to the neural substrate for a particular display). In the conflict interpretation, the manipulations might eliminate threat by reducing fear.

Fight Duration Distributions

When it comes to actual fighting, the distribution of agonistic-encounter durations in many species tends to be bimodal or J-shaped with many brief encounters and a smaller number of prolonged fights (e.g., Tooker & Miller, 1980). The occurrence of the longer fights, especially in the bimodal case, could be accounted for by the simultaneous increase in the aggressive arousal of both combatants. Most animal conflicts are terminated by the retreat of the subordinate animal. If neither retreats in the early stages, retaliatory exhanges can lock them into a positive feedback loop (e.g., Rushen & Pajor, 1987). Increased levels of aggressive arousal may also produce an internal "commitment" to aggression (Bronstein, 1981a), possibly because this arousal renders the combatants less sensitive to painful and/or other distracting stimuli as noted previously.

Alterations of Sensorimotor Function and the
Narrowing of Attention during Combat

Several lines of evidence suggest that there are alterations in sensorimotor function during combat. Regulation of these functions could be
part of that change with aggressive arousal level.

*(1) Pain.* It is well established that being subject to intense attack
induces a pronounced analgesia. This presumably subserves the maintenance of defense in the face of painful injury. Analgesia has also been
reported in some studies of mice that are initiating attack (e.g., Seigfried
& Frischknecht, 1988). This effect has not been found in rats (Rodgers &
Hendrie, 1982).

*(2) Touch.* In a classic study, MacDonnell and Flynn (1966) found that
the same electrical stimulation of the hypothalamus that induced
predatory attack by a cat on a rat would also activate a biting reflex: A
touch on the cat's lips that would ordinarily induce a withdrawal would
elicit a bite when the cat was being stimulated. Similar stimulation-
dependent effects have been reported in the cutaneous sensory fields
that trigger paw strikes (for review, see Kruk, 1991). Although such
sensorimotor effects have not yet been reported in animals aggressively
aroused by natural stimuli, it is reasonable to suppose that hypothalamically induced reflex mechanisms may mediate attack under normal
conditions. If so, the report that stimulation of various amygdaloid
nuclei modulates these hypothalamic effects (Block, Siegel, & Edinger,
1980) in turn implies that these effects could be regulated as part of an
aggressive arousal level set by the amygdala.

*(3) The Distance Senses.* Hypothalamic activation has also been
shown to facilitate eye movements for tracking prey in cats (for review,
see Kruk, 1991). Some perceptual consequences of such oculomotor
effects may be revealed in field reports indicating that significant,
maladaptive reductions in antipredator vigilance occur during intraspecific conflicts. Human observers find that they can move closer than
usual to the animals without eliciting flight during such events (e.g.,
Rand, 1942). Observers in field studies of voles (Colvin, 1973) and
laboratory studies of marmosets (Lipp, 1978) even report instances in
which they were easily able to capture animals engaged in an agonistic
encounter, presumably because the animals' attention was focused on
their antagonist and not on the human "predator." At least one instance
of real, lethal predation upon an animal engaged in high-intensity
conspecific threat has been reported in blackbirds (Dabelsteen & Peder-

sen, 1990). These anecdotal accounts of the narrowing of attention during combat need to be verified by systematic studies. Analogous situations arise among humans in which intense anger is accompanied by a narrowing of attention and a disregard of danger (Potegal, 1979; Zillmann, this volume).

Redirection and Displacement

A relatively common situation in which aggression is systematically directed against targets other than the provoker can be found in field observations of the *redirection* of attack, so named by Bastock, Morris, and Moynihan (1953), in which an animal involved in an aggressive interaction subsequently seeks out and attacks another individual that was uninvolved in the original encounter. The victims of these attacks are often animals with which the aggressor has had amicable relations. Redirection has most often been reported in colonies of monkeys where a subordinate attacked by a dominant will seek out a still lower ranking animal (e.g., Kawamura, 1967). Among mice, females are ordinarily not subjected to aggression by males but may become the target of redirected attack (e.g., Eisenberg, 1962; Simmel & Walker, 1970). The phenomenon of redirection, too, has been recreated in the laboratory: Alberts and Galef (1973) noted that presenting an anesthetized intruder to one of a pair of peacefully cohabiting resident feral rats elicited aggression that was redirected to the companion animal. Obviously, for attack to be redirected, an aggressive arousal is required that persists throughout the delay between the original provocation and the search for a suitable target. From the perspective of a theoretical distinction between provoker and target, redirected aggression is not a special case; in most cases aggression just happens to be directed at the object that provoked it.

Anecdotal instances of human aggression redirected to inanimate objects are offered by Eibl-Eibesfeldt (1971). Averill's (1979) retrospective survey of 80 episodes of anger caused by "everyday" provocations included two instances of redirected anger. Clinicians have claimed that aggression resulting from sexual frustration, usually on the part of the male partner, can be directed against the couple's children (Zillmann, 1984, p. 8). Attempting to make a connection with the "displacement" of emotions in psychoanalytic theory, Miller's (1948) reformulation of the frustration–aggression hypothesis drew theoretical attention to this aspect of human aggression by incorporating rules for the redirection of hostility from the provoker to substitute targets. A brief review of experimental demonstrations of redirected human aggression can be found in Fitz (1976); a review of studies of redirection in the context of the frustration–aggression hypothesis can be found in Zillmann (1979, pp. 139–144). At the social psychological level, the frustration–aggression theorists argued that the redirection of aggression in the form of "scapegoating" is at the root of social prejudice and intolerance (Berkowitz, 1962; Miller & Bugelski, 1948; but see Tedeschi, Smith, & Brown, 1974). Strictly speaking, the latter phenomena probably do not involve aggressive arousal in the sense of a transient emotional state but as a more enduring attitude; discussion of relationships between aggressive states and traits are beyond the scope of this chapter. Anthropologists' field reports suggest that redirection can play an important role in instigating warfare among hunter-gatherer peoples when short-term emotional conflicts arising within the group fuel the planning of raids on neighboring groups (Vayda, 1968; Whiting, 1944).

Ethologists have applied the term *displacement behavior* to seemingly inappropriate acts, usually digging in the substrate or grooming, which appear in the course of aggressive conflicts in birds and fish (Hinde, 1970). In wild rats, Alberts and Galef (1973) found that presentation of an anesthetized intruder elicited displacement digging as well as attack on a cohabiting conspecific. This suggests that stimuli from the anesthetized animal increased aggressive arousal that was expressed in alternative ways in the presence of a less than adequate releasing stimulus. In a complementary observation, Potegal, Gimino, Marotta, and Glusman (1979) noted that, when muricidal rats are deprived of the opportunity to dig, the number of their attacks on mice increases. Aggressive arousal can increase the probability of a narrow range of behaviors other than those directly related to attack.

Reinforcing Effects: Attack Priming as
Incentive Motivation for Aggression

An earlier paper described the evidence suggesting that some forms of aggression can be reinforcing under the appropriate conditions (e.g., if the animal has had a history of prior victories, Potegal, 1979). Few papers on this issue in animals have been published since (e.g., Melvin, 1985). For humans, the odd reporter's story of recreational fighting among young men on land or sea can be added to the evidence (e.g., Buford, 1992; Gusterson, 1986, Rawls, 1980). Historical examples and anecdotal reports about human aggression also suggest that assault and homicide become more pleasurable with both arousal and practice; for at least some individuals, aggression may be reinforcing only or particularly when aggressive arousal is high (Potegal, 1979). In other animals, attack priming can function as incentive motivation for committing further attacks. Thus, mice that have just had a fight will cross a grid with higher shock levels or make more T maze choices in order to attack another mouse (e.g., Lagerspetz, 1969; Tellegen & Horn, 1972). Hogan and Bols (1980) demonstrated the existence of a priming effect in fighting fish using a T maze; they suggested that attack-primed fish more often chose the arm in which another fish was visible, rather than the arm containing food, because the priming manipulation had made attack more reinforcing. Bronstein (1981b) challenged this interpretation, proposing instead that the "choice" of the arm containing the fish was due to a priming-induced increase in a reflex-like tendency to lunge toward a close, visible target. An important counterargument to this challenge is that even when attack primed the fish did not attack on all trials, suggesting that their behavior had not simply fallen under the control of a low-level, reflex-like response. Furthermore, the subjects erected their gill covers at the sight of the target fish even on trials when they failed to approach it. This indicates that (a) they actually saw the target and (b) that the decision to attack was reached at a higher level of processing. The subjects were making a choice, in some sense, and that choice was influenced by their state of aggressive arousal. Bronstein's point about the ambiguity of the reinforcement interpretation is well taken, however, and additional evidence would be necessary to demonstrate that the effect of priming was due to an increase in the reinforcing value of attack. Such evidence could involve instrumental learning for the opportunity to attack and/or further demonstrations that the preference for attack (versus other consummatory behaviors) was systematically altered by priming. Insofar as reinforcement requires the activation of the median forebrain bundle/lateral hypothalamic pathways, the CMA projections to the preoptic area and parts of the hypothalamus are in a position to facilitate such activation.

## Contagion of Aggression

A common laboratory example of the contagion of aggression occurs when grouped mice begin bouncing around the cage, the ensuing violent contacts provoking indiscriminate attack and fighting among cage mates. Bohstedt, in this volume, refers to contagion in rioting, a process presumed to involve imitation. Contagion can be seen at work in the formation of a crowd of peers around two arguing boys, the crowd then urging the boys to escalate their argument into a fight. Fistfights between hockey fans in the stands that inspire fights in the rink and vice versa are common instances of contagion that have been documented (Russell, 1983; Smith, 1983, pp. 168–170). These phenomena involve more than mechanical imitation of the "Simon says" variety. They must be based upon empathic (but not prosocial) processes in which seeing someone behave in a state of aggressive arousal induces a similar state in other group members. Those in the center of the action may come to blows whereas others on the sidelines will stop at verbal expression. The essential point in the present context is that it is the affect as least as much as the overt behavior that is contagious.

## ANGER AND VIOLENCE IN HUMANS; AGGRESSIVE AROUSAL AND OFFENSE IN OTHER ANIMALS

How might aggressive arousal manifest itself in humans? As implied in several of the preceding sections, one possibility is that we subjectively experience aggressive arousal as anger, according to Berkowitz (1965) a distinct, transient emotional state associated with "a readiness for aggressive acts" (p. 308). It is a long way from an intraspecific biting attack by rodents to our subjective feelings. Nonetheless, the connection has been made quite explicitly by Caroline and Robert Blanchard, who have distinguished between offensive and defensive aggression in rodents and other animals and argued that offense in animals is analagous with angry attack in people (e.g., Blanchard, 1984). In their view, which has been a major heuristic influence on animal aggression research for the last 10 or 15 years, offense is provoked by a conspecific "challenge" (e.g., for territory ownership) whereas defense is provoked by direct, painful attack. These behavior complexes also differ in their topography and targets of attack. In offense nonlethal body areas like the shoulder or rump are selected for attack; the choice of target area being a species-typical function. In defense the nearest offending body part, often the opponent's snout, is bitten. However, these distinctions are somewhat problematic even with regard to the animal data. Resident montane voles use the classic offense pattern of lateral approach when attacking conspecific intruders, for example, but resident prairie voles use jump attacks (Pierce, Pellis, Dewsbury, & Pellis, 1991), a response that has been classified as defensive. Locations of wounds inflicted by presumptively offensive male rats vary as a function of test chamber size (Mos, Olivier, van Oorschot, & Dijkstra, 1984). The latter results imply that targets of attack are not determined by the presumptive type of aggression but by the space available for the opponent's countermoves. Arguing from the results of extensive studies of attack elicited in rats by hypothalamic stimulation, Kruk (1991) suggested that presumptive offense–defense differences may be more a matter of "intensity" of activation because raising current levels shifts the form of attack from a less violent, offense-like pattern to a more violent, defense-like pattern. These caveats notwithstanding, there are often clear cases in which one animal is the attacker and the other the defender (e.g., within established social dominance hierachies), whereas in other, equally clear, cases, both may be on the offensive (e.g., in territorial disputes).

Blanchard (1984) argued that basic motivations underlying these behavior patterns differ: Offense and defense reflect tendencies to attack ("hit or hurt") and to escape from danger, respectively. In the case of humans, these motivations are identified with the affects of anger and fear, respectively. A most effective provoker of anger across cultures around the world is an insult, whereas a deadly assault will evoke fear. Blanchard (1984) described one questionnaire study in which people were asked to describe their imagined actions, emotions, and goals in response to one of these two prototypical situations. The subjects responding to insult/challenge reported an (inhibited) desire to kick or hit; Blanchard argued that this inhibited desire to strike was analagous to the attack on a nonvulnerable body part in offensive animals. Subjects responding to stranger assault imagined escaping, or, failing to escape, to hitting back. Rather than being categorical differences in the mode of aggressive response, these differences could be more parsimoniously viewed as due to differences in the "intensity" of the response. This is reminiscent of the point about offense versus defense made by Kruk (1991). In general, it is difficult to see the presence of a conspecific as a "challenge" in the usual sense. Rats do not fight over food, access to females, or territory in any direct way. Offense in this species is triggered by certain stimuli from same-sex conspecifics, and the resulting attack happens to produce the favorable result of removing these stimuli. Distal evolutionary ends (the preservation of resources necessary to maintain inclusive fitness) are subserved by proximal neurobehavioral mechanisms that are independant of the end being served (see Archer & Huntingford, this volume). In general, the Blanchards' analogies require a willing suspension of disbelief. If we do suspend our disbelief, however, the fact that the hamster attacks reported previously are unmistakably offensive aggression implies that the *c-fos* data reported here could represent the first steps toward identifying the neural substrate of felt anger.

## AUTONOMIC ACTIVATION, ANGER, AND AGGRESSIVE AROUSAL

From Seneca's first-century treatise on anger, *De Irae*, through the 19th-century writings of Charles Darwin and William James, all based on casual observation and common knowledge, much was made of the autonomic concomitants of anger. The frequent occurrence of such reactions has been subsequently demonstrated empirically. In two surveys spanning more than three quarters of a century, 63% to 87% of American adults reported experiencing facial flushing in conjunction with anger (Averill 1982; see also Blanchard, 1984; Hall, 1899). Facial pallor occurred in fewer of those surveyed whereas some individuals reported alternations between flushing and pallor. Eighty nine percent of laboratory studies published since 1961 found an increase in systolic blood pressure following provocations meant to elicit anger, 63% reported increases in diastolic pressure, and 56% found heart rate increases (Potegal, review in preparation).

In 1962, Schachter and Singer moved autonomic arousal back to the central position in the theory of emotion espoused by James by their finding that subjects injected with epinephrine, a drug that produces autonomic activation, experience either euphoria or anger as they are cued to do so by a manic or angry individual in their environment. They advanced the general proposition that autonomic arousal is an essential but nonspecific energizer of emotion; the particular emotion experienced is a function of the cognitive "labeling" of the emotion as that is guided by environmental cues and by the subject's past experience and understanding of his or her current situation (Schacter, 1964). Anger is the result of an autonomic arousal associated with a provocation that the individual understands as one to which anger is an appropriate response (e.g., an insult); if the same autonomic arousal were to occur in the presence of flight-producing cues, it would be experienced as fear. This proposition and its variants with regard to anger and aggression are discussed in detail by Zillmann and by Caprara in this volume. In brief, the sets of data supporting this claim are: (a) Activation induced by a variety of stimuli including exercise, drugs, and noise enhances aggressive responding as long as the activation can be attributed to the apparent provocation, (b) attribution of activation to sources other than the provoker reduces aggressive responding; (c) reduction or elimination of autonomic activation by pharmacological blockade of peripheral $\beta$-adrenergic receptors reduces self-reports of felt anger (Erdmann & van Lindern, 1980). A single clinical case report suggests that it may also reduce aggressive behavior (Polakoff, Sorgi, & Ratey, 1986). In Hohmann's (1966) widely cited study, patients whose sympathetic outflow was cut off by spinal cord injury reported that they experienced anger less strongly since being injured. The higher the injury in the spinal cord (i.e., the more extensive the sensory loss), the greater was the reduction in emotional intensity.

There are caveats, of course. At least as important as the high incidence of autonomic concomitants in the surveys just noted is the observation that they are not completely ubiquitous (i.e., some individuals become angry without experiencing autonomic activation). The findings with spine-injured patients are striking, but it may be such patients shut off their feelings as a way of coping with the otherwise unbearable psychological burden of such severe and life-altering injury (Reisenzein, 1983). Furthermore, a recent extensive replication of Hohmann's work by Bermond, Nieuwenhuyse, Fasotti, and Schverman (1991) completely failed to substantiate his conclusions. Of particular interest in the present context was their question about changes in the duration of anger; 64% of the respondents reported no change, whereas the number reporting decreases was slightly outweighed by the number reporting increases. Bermond et al. (1991) also reviewed a number of other studies that disconfirm Hohmann's (1966) report. Nonetheless, the consistency of the other types of evidence for Schacter's counterintuitive hypothesis is still impressive. Where the hypothesis fails is in regard to the role of autonomic arousal in the aggressive behavior of animals. Cannon's classical experimental study found that surgical interruption of outflow through the sympathetic ganglia did not alter affective defense in cats (Cannon, Newton, Bright, Menken, & More, 1929). More recently, Kaplan and Manuch (1989) failed to find any effects of $\beta$-adrenergic blockade on aggression in monkeys using propanolol doses that clearly suppressed peripheral autonomic responsivity. In the hamster studies cited earlier, there was essentially no c-fos expression in the central nucleus of the amygdala. Because of the strong reciprocal connections of the central nucleus with the dorsal motor nucleus of the vagus and other brainstem sites regulating autonomic activity, this lack of c-fos expression suggests that autonomic activation, or its feedback to the CNS, was not a major contributor to the hamsters' aggressive arousal. Note that these hamsters were well-practiced aggressors. In both mice (Kahn, 1951) and monkeys (Kaplan, personal communication, 1992) autonomic activation is reduced or absent in experienced, successful aggressors. (It is, of course, also possible that the central nucleus was indeed activated but that this activation was not coupled to c-fos expression.) In trying to accommodate such results, Schachter (1964) suggested that the autonomic arousal might be essential to anger but not to aggressive behavior. This would seem to be an odd arrangement given the evidence for hemodynamic changes during fighting (Bacelli, Mancia, Adams, & Zanchetti, 1968; Rader, Stevens, Meechan, & Henry, 1974; Viken, Johnson, & Knutson, 1991; Zanchetti, Baccelli, Mancia, & Elison, 1972) and the general presumption that the autonomic nervous system exists to support emergency behaviors.

The evidence that autonomic arousal plays an important, if not obligatory, role in felt anger but is not necessary for aggressive behavior presents a problem for the notion that anger is simply the subjective experience of aggressive arousal as the term has been used here. Note, however, that the data suggest that nonspecific autonomic activation enhances anger; they do not preclude the simultaneous existence of an aggression-specific brain state. Perhaps the human equivalent of aggressive arousal is the impulse to hit or hurt (Berkowitz, 1965); the activation of the CMA in us produces a specific preparedness for hostile action. A possible laboratory model of such a specific, aggression-facilitating state may be found in studies in which people are exposed to an experimental manipulation like frustration in such a way that they deliver more "punishment" to another individual although they do not report being angry (e.g., Berkowitz, 1978; cf. Reisenzein's 1983 review concluding that this is a typical outcome in laboratory studies).

It is difficult to imagine or name the subjective feeling that might be associated with the pure impulse to aggression in real life. Perhaps it is whatever affect accompanies displays of status and dominance by school-yard bullies, belligerent campus jocks, English football thugs (Buford, 1992), street gang members looking for a fight, or skinheads spoiling for "a bit of bovver." Consider also the affect communicated to the fans at boxing and wrestling matches and hockey games, ball players who run out of the dugout to join a fight on the field, the contagion of aggression in riots, or the "battle joy" of warriors and soldiers (Potegal, 1979), what Lorenz (1966, Chapter 13) described as feelings of *militant enthusiasm*. This affect, when coupled with autonomic activation, is experienced as conscious anger.

In contrast to the Schacterian hypothesis, I propose that "labeling" a stimulus as anger appropriate results in a specific impulse to hit/hurt that is reified in particular amygdala circuitry. The processing of such provocations is different from other cognitive activity in that it results in a localized brain state with a short but definite life-span, a clear implication for action and, when combined with autonomic activation, a strongly felt emotion. One basis for this proposal is that the *c-fos* expression in the amygdala that is characteristic for attack priming is different from that for sexual arousal and probably also different from that for fear. In the context of this book, a possible path to escalation occurs when a provocation produces an impulse to action, acting on this impulse increases autonomic arousal, and the combination intensifies felt anger justifying further action.

TEMPORAL LOBE EPILEPSY, THE AMYGDALA, AND
ANGER IN HUMANS: WHAT'S A NASTY STRUCTURE
LIKE THIS DOING IN A NICE SPECIES LIKE YOU?

Ounsted, Lindsay, and Richards (1987) proposed that rage is one of a large class of "paroxysmal" behaviors that includes grand mal epileptic seizures. A more commonly held opinion, that there is a higher than normal incidence of hostility and violence in temporal lobe epileptics, derives from reports that began appearing about 40 years ago (Gibbs, 1956; Rey, Pond, & Evans, 1949). Consider the following clinical impressions by Gloor (1975): "episodic violent behavior in temporal lobe epileptics is characterized by a low rage threshold. Such patients even in response to the most trifling provocation may fly into a violent rage which is totally out of proportion to the triviality of the triggering event" (p. 30). Walker and Blumer (1975) noted (cf. Geschwind, 1975, p. 278):

> The aggressivity in patients with temporal lobe epilepsy is of a peculiar type. It has been termed impulsive-irritable behavior characterized by relatively unmotivated paroxysmal outbursts of anger, abusiveness, or assaultiveness, quite in contrast with the person's usual behavior. Between the outbursts the individual is usually very good natured, so that the abrupt change is striking. (p. 394–395)

A few of these individuals have been implanted with chronic, indwelling depth electrodes to determine if subcortical seizure foci might be the cause of their problem. Some neurologists and neurosurgeons who have dealt with these patients have been impressed by the association between the attacks and seizure activity recorded from the amygdala (e.g., Ferguson, Rayport, & Corrie, 1986; Heath, 1981; Mark & Ervin, 1970; Saint- Hilaire, Gilbert, Bouvier, & Barbeau, 1980; Smith, 1980).

The significance of these rage attacks has been downplayed by investigators who argue that, although they appear very forceful and may result in damage to household objects, they generally do not result in serious injury to other people. But is not this true of most ordinary episodes of anger? A more serious criticism has been raised by psychologists whose large-scale surveys have failed to show increased aggressive behavior in temporal lobe epileptics (TLE) or greater evidence for violence in convicted criminals with TLE than in those without (e.g., Brandt, Seidman, & Kohl, 1985; for review see Whitman, King, & Cohen, 1986). Gloor (1975) is often cited in this context: "In our observations, which cover hundreds of patients explored for temporal lobe epilepsy . . . we never saw a patient in whom positive evidence was uncovered that violence or even rage was ictal in origin" (p. 29). This school of thought holds that, at best, the clinicians have been deluded by the purely coincidental co-occurrence of TLE with a dramatic, if not lurid, behavioral pathology. At worst, the argument goes, blaming aggression on epilepsy is a sociobiological fallacy; politically incorrect thinking that stigmatizes a neurological minority and draws attention away from the true sources of aggression: poverty, racism, sexism, and the other ills of society. Note, however, that most of the aggressive epileptic patients reported in the literature are White males who are not from the poorest stratum of society.

One possible explanation for the discrepancies between the case studies and the surveys is that rage is particularly associated with seizures in the amygdala which lies in the depths of the temporal lobe. In a few instances where both surface and depth recordings were made simultaneously, the depth electrodes sometimes picked up pathological activity that the surface ones did not (Heath, 1981; Smith, 1980). If it is seizures of the amygdala that are critical, the routine diagnosis of temporal lobe epilepsy with scalp electroencephalograms (EEGs) will provide false negatives (i.e., patients whose scalp EEGs fail to reveal the seizures in the depths) and may also generate false positives (i.e., patients with cortical but not subcortical seizure foci). Furthermore, as Monroe (1975) noted, tense and agitated patients are unlikely to cooperate in EEG recording procedures, reducing the chances of observing abnormalities at the time when they are most likely to be occurring.

A second kind of explanation is that fear is the emotion that is most typically experienced in spontaneous TL seizures and is evoked by electrical stimulation in the clinic (Gloor, 1975). This observation may be rooted in the fact that basolateral nuclei of the amygdala mediate fear-related processes (e.g., Sananes & Davis, 1992), and that these nuclei, being relatively much larger than the CMA in primates, are more likely to be host to any localized pathological process. By the same token, in the event of more global amygdaloid pathology, the output of the basolateral nuclei may dominate and suppress the sensations of anger associated with CMA activation. Position emmission tomography (PET) scan studies of cerebral blood flow have recently shown that "panic attacks," a form of acute, severe anxiety accompanied by tachycardia, sweating, and flushing, are associated with activitation of the temporal pole (Reiman, Fusselman, Fox, & Raichle, 1989, but see Drevets, Videen, MacLeod, Haller, & Raichle, 1992, for a methodological critique). This connection between anxiety and temporal pole activation is in keeping with the finding that fear is the most common emotion associated with TLE. A recent report of interest in this context is of "anger attacks," sudden outbursts of anger with little or no provocation, which resemble the more typical panic attacks in the co-occurrence of autonomic signs, the subjective experience of being out of control, and a good clinical response to tricyclic antidepressants (Fava, Anderson, & Roenbaum, 1990). Perhaps rage and anxiety attacks represent pathological events arising in corticomedial and basolateral amygdala, respectively, both of which engage amygdalofugal brainstem autonomic mechanisms. Because such events are not triggered by the usual cortically mediated perceptions of the external environment (e.g., the appearance of a threat), the emotions are experienced as inappropriate, giving rise to feelings of a loss of control. These "events" may be epileptoid: Mattes' (1986) review of the literature on the pharmacological treatment of adult "temper tantrums" in individuals with no signs of TLE suggests that the efficacy of carbamazapine in controlling such outbursts may be related to its anticonvulsant properties. Propanolol and lithium have also been reported to be effective; all three of these drugs reduce CNS GABA ($\gamma$-aminobutyric acid) turnover (Mattes, 1986).

## INAPPROPRIATE AGGRESSIVE AROUSAL AND PATHOLOGICAL ACTIVITY IN THE MEDIAL AMYGDALA

Consider a less often cited addendum to Gloor's (1975) famous quote: "It is important to emphasize, however, that in spite of rarity of documented ictal rage in temporal lobe epileptics, the association of aggressive behavior and temporal lobe epilesy is a real one" (p. 30). Geschwind and Bear and others have also claimed that increased irritability is part of an interictal TLE syndrome (e.g., Bear, Levin, Blumer, Chetham, & Reider, 1982; Walker & Blumer, 1975, Table II). Clinical reports that TLE seizures may be preceded by long-lasting mood shifts of increased irritability (e.g., Ervin, 1976; Smith, 1980; Walker & Blumer, 1975) has been confirmed by more systematic cataloguing of TLE prodromae (Adamec, 1990). How might this come about? Imagine that the level of aggressive arousal is determined by the ongoing activity in certain amygdalo–hypothalamic circuits. When activity is low, a major provocation is required to increase it to the threshold necessary to trigger felt anger and/or an overt attack. As baseline activity rises, less and less stimuli are required to trigger these responses. When baseline activity hovers near threshold, an extended "bad mood" of irritability results; small random fluctuations will produce "spontaneous" outbursts of temper. In the absence of intrinsic pathology, high baseline levels may result from continuing environmental stress or conditions like nicotine withdrawal in habitual smokers. High baseline activity and occasional spontaneous outbursts may also result from abnormal, epileptoid activity in the putative amygdalo–hypothalamic circuits. There are probably differences in quality as well as quantity of amygdaloid activity in TLE. Heath (1981) reported 0.5- to 1.0 second spindle bursts of 12- to 18

Hz waves in the amygdalae of nonepileptic, psychotic patients experiencing anger during the recall of painful early memories. In epileptics experiencing the prodroma of irritability, spindles did not appear; instead, spiking was superimposed on slow wave activity. In view of the evidence implicating the amygdala in the persistence of aggression in animals, it is of interest that the irritability preceding outbursts of anger in TLE may persist for hours or even days (e.g., Ervin, 1976; Walker & Blumer, 1975). Lewis, Pincus, Shanok, and Glaser (1982), noted also that the "inability to stop fighting once having started" (p. 884) was one index of aggressiveness that correlated significantly with other signs of psychomotor epilepsy in aggressive, incarcerated adolescents.

Adamec (1990) reviewed his work and that of others showing that kindling of amygdala seizures in animals by repeated stimulation increases the likelihood of "spontaneous" manifestations of defense and/or enhances such responses to below-threshold stimulation (e.g., startle to touch in rats and attack to low levels of hypothalamic stimulation in cats). The studies in cats are in general agreement with the rodent CMA data described earlier in that it is the medial nuclei of the amygdala that produces the aggression-enhancing effects (e.g., Brutus, Shaikh, Edinger, & Siegel, 1986). Adamec suggested that kindling may be an experimental model of interictal pathology in human TLE. It is thus particularly noteworthy that, in TLE patients with rage attacks, the rage was associated with spontaneous seizures and electrical stimulation of the more medial aspect of the amygdala (Heath, 1981; Mark & Ervin, 1970; Smith, 1980).

## A MODEST PROPOSAL

Whether or not kindling is a good experimental model for the pathology underlying TLE, there remains the question of how to reconcile the striking clinical case reports of TLE symptoms associated with anger in selected individuals and the failure to find such association in large sample surveys of TLE patients. The statistical connection between anger and TLE may not be unlike the relationship between criminality and various physical and physiological stigmata: Within populations of violent individuals, the frequency of these signs is often higher than that of control populations (see Brennan, Mednick, & Kandel, 1991, for minor physical anomalies, Virkkunen, 1982, and Benton, Kumari, & Brain, 1982, for hypoglycemia, Hinton, 1981, and Buikhuisen & Mednick, 1988, for psychophysiological and EEG indices, and Ervin, 1976, for neurological signs). However, as in the case of TLE, populations selected for any one of these signs may not show significantly increased rates of hostility and violence. Such observations may be reconciled by an interactional, multiplicative, or threshold model in which several factors must coincide before there is any increase in risk. To take an oversimplified example, suppose there are factors X, Y, and Z, each with an incidence of 10% in a population, and that these factors are distributed at random (i.e., they are uncorrelated, as in Hinton's 1981 study). Further imagine that each factor alone has no effect but, when they all co-occur within an individual, they increase his or her risk of being aggressive 50 fold (e.g., from a baseline of 0.01 to a level of 0.5). A survey of the aggressive individuals in this population would show that 14% of them exhibit factor X (or Y or Z). However, a survey of individuals bearing X (or Y or Z) would show that just 1.5% of them are aggressive, which is not appreciably different from the 1.0% incidence of aggression for this population at large. In this model the co-occurrence of XYZ factors would account for only 5% of the subpopulation that is aggressive. Note, however, that if one of these factors is TLE it is just that 5% that would eventually show up in neurologists' offices. Ervin (1976) found that 7 out of 130 individuals self-referred to a clinic for excessive violence had classic, undiagnosed TLE. This rate is 2- to 17-fold greater than 2.4% to 0.3% incidence of TLE estimated in poor and middle-class communities, respectively (cf. Whitman et al. 1986). This speculation about interactive risk factors is not without precedent; a model of naturalistic sexual aggression involving interactions among several factors has been shown to be a better predictor of behavior than an additive model (Malamuth, 1986). Furthermore, Ervin (1976) remarked that when one of these indicators is a medically treatable condition, treatment often leads to a reduction in violence.

## CATHARSIS REVISITED

Catharsis has a multitude of historical interpretations but, as applied to anger and aggression by social psychologists during the middle decades of this century, it was an hypothesis about the conservation of emotional energy: Anger once provoked must be expressed in one form or the other. The expression of the anger reduces it, leading to feelings of relief and satisfaction. The analogy to sexual arousal and satisfaction is obvious; the appropriateness of the analogy is less obvious. Nonetheless, the TLE literature provides some extraordinary anecdotes concerning what seem to be catharsis-like effects. For example, Mark and Ervin (1970) described a TLE patient named Thomas who would brood for hours over an imagined insult, working himself up to rage that would last 5 or 6 minutes during which he would assault his wife or children, "after which he would be overcome by remorse or grief and sob as uncontrollably as he had raged. He would then go to sleep and wake up feeling refreshed and eager to work" (pp. 93–94). Remarkably, these patients may feel relaxed, at peace, or even sometimes euphoric following a rage seizure. Ounsted et al. (1987) believed that an "afterglow" is universal after paroxsymal events including rage. The details of sequence and time course of such events in different patients are strikingly similar (cf. Smith, 1980).

The feelings of relief that follow these fits of rage are reminiscent, on a shorter time scale, of the *catathymic crisis* first described by Wertham in 1937. This term denotes the situation of an individual who ruminates obsessively about a violent act he or she has decided to commit, experiencing increasing thought disorder and emotional tension that builds over the course of weeks or months until he or she tries to or successfully manages to commit the act. Following the assault, these individuals experience a relief of tension and a return to apparent normality (Wertham, 1978). Superficially, these descriptions of the buildup of emotional tension followed by release resemble the popular picture of catharsis.

As reviewed by Quanty (1976), various aspects of the catharsis hypothesis have been amply disconfirmed by a majority of studies that show that being exposed to aggressive stimuli and/or acting aggressively generally leads to an intensification of aggressive and hostile feelings and actions (see also Heelas, 1983, for fascinating but ultimately unconvincing anthropological accounts of cathartic dog beating by Utku eskimos and anticathartic cock fighting by Balinese). On the other hand, it is true that people sometimes feel badly if they fail to respond to a hostile challenge and they feel better when they do. Physical or verbal counteraggression may not be necessary to achieve this effect, however. What is required is some coping response that allows the challenged individual to restore his or her self-esteem. Coping responses other than retaliation that lead to relaxation of tension and restoration of self-esteem have been described anecdotally (Blanchard, 1984) and demonstrated experimentally (Hokanson, Willers, & Koropsak, 1968).

In the case of TLE, having a rage may not be necessary to resolve dysphoric feelings. Relief of prodromal irritability can be provided by a generalized seizure terminating the episode. Monroe (1975) noted: "depth electrode studies suggest that seizural discharges in subcortical areas associated with subjective dysphoria are terminated if seizural activity spreads to cortex with its accompanying classical epileptic attack" (p. 339). Blumer (1976) similarly observed: "A need for occasional seizures in the interest of emotional well being is apparent in patients who display a protracted prodromal phase marked by increasing angry explosiveness terminated by a seizure" (p. 218). Conversely, it is neurological folklore, if not clinical experience, that reducing or eliminating seizures with dilantin or other antiepileptics (forcing "normalization" of the EEG) can lead to a worsening of behavior, particularly in children (Livingston, 1972). Seizures often end fairly abruptly; electrophysiological studies showing pronounced postictal neuronal hyperpolarization indicate that active inhibitory processes rather than metabolic "fatigue" accounts for this rapid termination. Although the responsible endogenous antiepileptic agents have yet to be identified (Dragunow, 1986), it is reasonable to suppose that the activity of such agents in the amygdala of affected individuals would be experienced as relief. Termination of nonepileptic rage may involve some of the same mechanisms.

Having crawled out to the tip of the thinest branch of speculation, I now saw the branch off. As noted at the beginning of this section, there appears to be a common sequence of events in adults in which an intense outburst of anger is followed by feelings of remorse, guilt, or shame, and then by a resolution of dysphoric feeling. Mark and Ervin (1970) said of TLE patient Julia: "Her behavior between seizures was marked by severe temper tantrums followed by extreme remorse" (p. 97). Could it be that activation of the aggressive arousal circuitry primes other circuits that then produce the next emotions in the sequence? Electrical stimulation of the lateral amygdala turns off rage and produces relaxation and calming (Mark & Ervin, 1970; Smith, 1980). This sequence of emotions is overdetermined: Adults certainly know when they have been inappropriately aggressive and have gone beyond socially approved limits. Remorse is an emotionally appropriate response to a rupturing of valued social bonds, whereas a display of remorse is also the conventional, socially approved way to apologize and restore the bonds. However, this same sequence is seen in the temper tantrums of small children who have not yet learned all the contingencies (see Einon & Potegal, this volume). In children, as in adults, resolution of anger can include behaviors aimed at reconciliation and restoration of social bonds. Of course, there are other possible sequelae of rage including sullenness, guilt, and so on. In monkeys and apes, an aggressive encounter can be followed by a redirection of aggression or by attempts at affiliation with the former opponent (e.g., Cords, 1988, York & Rowell, 1988). It is conceivable that sequences of postaggressive behaviors are channeled by the intrinsic excitatory and inhibitory connections between the circuits underlying these behaviors.

## FIGURE/GROUND REVERSAL IN THE
## UNDERSTANDING OF AGGRESSION

Hans-Lukas Teuber used the perceptual metaphor of a figure/ground reversal to describe the change in focus produced by some major scientific discoveries. Physiological discoveries have so altered the focus in several lines of psychological research. Where dreams were once regarded as a primary phenomenon of sleep, the observation of distinctly different brain states associated with REM (rapid eye movement) and nonREM sleep has relegated dreaming to being one aspect of REM sleep. The research described in the first part of this chapter was designed to identify the neural circuitry dedicated to aggressive arousal. Thus, attack priming is based upon a naturalistic stimulus situation uncontaminated by the drugs, footshocks, brain lesions, or brain stimulation that are often used to elicit aggression in the laboratory. It has, in fact, led to the identification of a locus of neural activity specifically associated with aggression. Now suppose that subsequent research shows that the magnitude of CMA activation in any particular situation predicts attack probability in that situation. Imagine that threat is associated with low levels of CMA activation and overt fighting with high levels. Further suppose that when the CMA is activated and there is no opportunity to attack, displacement behaviors occurred. We might then want to refocus our efforts from defining the behavioral characteristics of attack priming to defining the behavioral characteristics of CMA activation. This might foster the development of a nonarbitrary, physiologically based typology of aggression lacking the problems of the current offense–defense distinction. It would not be a surprise to discover that much of what is now called offense corresponds to CMA-type aggression, however, whereas much of what is now called defense is a function of basolateral amygdala activation.

Consider the potential virtues of this figure/ground reversal. Suppose we find subtle or not so subtle changes in feeding or sexual behavior in CMA-activated animals. Instead of having found worrisome evidence for behavioral nonspecificity, we will have simply defined additional characteristics of the brain state whose primary effect is massive changes in attack probability. When the behavioral consequences of CMA activation in the rat and the cat, the monkey and the human are compared, species differences in neurobehavioral function may become more comprehensible. Finally, theoretical claims have been made for the existence of subthreshold, inhibited, or suppressed aggression in animals (e.g., in conflict situations), repressed or unconscious anger in people, and so forth, which are inferred from certain behavioral cues or their lack. Now these claims can be evaluated directly; open the black box and look at the CMA.

## ACKNOWLEDGMENTS

I would like to thank Jim Meyerhoff and Craig Ferris for their contributions, implicit and explicit, to this work. Thanks are due John Knutson for his suggestions, heeded and unheeded, for improving this chapter. And thanks to you, dear reader, for indulging me in this opportunity for unbridled speculation.

## REFERENCES

Adamec, R. E. (1990). Does kindling model anything clinically relevant. *Biological Psychiatry, 27,* 249–279.

Adams, D. B. (1979). Brain mechanisms for offense, defense, and submission. *Behavioral and Brain Sciences, 2,* 201–241.

Adams, D. B., & Schoel, W. M. (1982). A statistical analysis of the social behavior of the male stumptail macaque (*Macaca arctoides*). *American Journal of Primatology, 2,* 249–273.

Alberts, J. R., & Galef, B. G. Jr. (1973). Olfactory cues and movement: Stimuli mediating intraspecific aggression in the wild Norway rat. *Journal of Comparative and Physiological Psychology, 85,* 233–242.

Averill, J. R. (1979). Anger. In H. Howe & R. Dienstbier (Eds.), *Nebraska Symposium on Motivation 1978* (Vol. 26, pp. 1–80). Lincoln: University of Nebraska Press.

Averill, J. R., (1982) *Anger and aggression* New York: Springer-Verlag.

Azrin, N., & Hutchinson, R. R. (1967). Conditioning of the aggressive behavior of pigeons by a fixed interval of reinforcement. *Journal of the Experimental Analysis of Behavior, 10,* 395–402.

Azrin, N., Hutchinson, R. R., & Hake, D. F. (1966). Extinction induced aggression. *Journal of the Experimental Analysis of Behavior, 9,* 191–204.

Baccelli, G., Mancia, G., Adams, D. B., & Zanchetti, A. (1968). Hemodynamic patterns during fighting behavior in the cat. *Experientia, 24,* 1221–1223.

Baenninger, R. (1974). Some consequences of aggressive behavior: A selective review of the literature on other animals. *Aggressive Behavior, 1,* 17–38.

Banks, E. M. A. (1962). A time and motion study of prefighting behavior in mice. *Journal of Genetic Psychology, 101,* 165–183.

Bastock, M., Morris, D., & Moynihan, M. (1953). Some comments on conflict and thwarting in animals. *Behaviour, 6,* 66–84.

Bear, D., Levin, K., Blumer, D., Chetham, D., & Reider, J. (1982). Interictal behavior in hospitalized temporal lobe epileptics: Relationship to idiopathic psychiatric syndromes. *Journal of Neurology, Neurosurgery, and Psychiatry, 45,* 481–488.

Benton, D., Kumari, N., & Brain, P. F. (1982). Mild hypoglycaemia and questionnaire measures of aggression. *Biological Psychology, 14,* 129–135.

Berkowitz, L. A. (1962). *Aggression: A social psychological analysis*. New York: McGraw-Hill.

Berkowitz, L. (1965). The concept of aggressive drive: Some additional considerations. In L. Berkowitz (Ed.), *Advances in experimental social psychology* (Vol. 2, pp. 301–330. New York: Academic.

Berkowitz, L. (1978). Do we have to believe we are angry with someone in order to display "angry" aggression toward that person? In L. Berkowitz (Ed.), *Cognitive theories in social psychology* (pp. 455–463). New York: Academic.

Bermond, B., Nieuwenhuyse, B., Fasotti, L., & Schuerman, J. (1991). Spinal cord lesions, peripheral feedback, and intensities of emotional feelings. *Cognition and Emotion, 5,* 201–220.

Blanchard, D. C. (1984). Applicability of animal models to human aggression In K. J. Flannelly, R. J. Blanchard, & D. C. Blanchard (Eds.), *Biological perspectives on aggression* (pp. 49–74). New York: Alan Liss.

Blanchard, R. J., Blanchard, D. C., Takahashi, T., & Kelley, M. J. (1975). Attack and defensive behavior in the albino rat. *Animal Behaviour, 25,* 622.

Blanchard, R. J., Kleinschmidt, C. F., Fukanaga-Stinson, C., & Blanchard, D. C. (1980). Defensive attack behavior in male and female rats. *Animal Learning and Behavior, 8,* 177–183.

Block, C. H., Siegel, A., & Edinger, H. (1980). Effects of amygdaloid stimulation upon the trigeminal sensory fields of the lip that are established during hypothalamically-elicited quiet biting attack. *Brain Research, 197,* 39–55.

Blumer, D. (1976). Epilepsy and violence. In D. J. Madden & J. R. Lion (Eds.), *Rage, hate, assault and other forms of violence* (pp. 207–222). New York: Spectrum, Halsted, Wiley.

Blurton-Jones, N. G. (1968) Observations and experiments on causation of threat displays of the great tit (*Parus major*). *Animal Behaviour Monographs, 1,* 2.

Brandt, J., Seidman, L. J., & Kohl, D. (1985). Personality characteristics of epileptic patients: A controlled study of generalized and temporal lobe cases. *Journal of Clinical and Experimental Neuropsychology, 7,* 25–38.

Brennan, P., Mednick, S., & Kandel, E. (1991). Congenital determinants of violent and property offending. In D. J. Pepler & K. H. Rubin (Eds.), *The development and treatment of childhood aggression* (pp. 81–92). Hillsdale, NJ: Lawrence Erlbaum Associates.

Bronstein, P. (1981a). Commitments to aggression and nest sites in male *Betta splendens. Journal of Comparative and Physiological Psychology, 95,* 436–449.

Bronstein, P. (1981b). Social reinforcement in *Betta splendens*: A reconsideration. *Journal of Comparative and Physiological Psychology, 95,* 943–950.

Brothers, L., Ring, B., & Kling, A. (1990). Response of neurons in the macaque amygdala to complex social stimuli. *Behavioral Brain Research, 41,* 199–213.

Brutus, M., Saikh, M. B., Edinger, H., & Siegel, A. (1986). Effects of experimental temporal lobe seizures upon hypothalamically elicited aggressive behavior in the cat. *Brain Research, 366,* 53–63.

Buford, B. (1992). *Among the thugs*. New York: Norton.

Buikhuisen, W., & Mednick S. A. (Eds.), (1988). *Explaining criminal behavior*. Leiden, The Netherlands: E. J. Brill.

Buvinic, M. L., & Berkowitz, L. (1976). Delayed effects of practiced vs. unpracticed responses after observation of movie violence. *Journal of Experimental and Social Psychology, 12,* 283–293.

Cannon, W. B., Newton, H. F., Bright, E. M., Menken, M. & More, R. M. (1929). Some aspects of the physiology of animals surviving complete exclusion of sympathetic nerve impulses. *American Journal of Physiology, 89,* 84–107.

Clutton-Brock, T. H., & Albon, S. D. (1979). The roaring of red deer and the evolution of honest advertisement. *Behaviour, 68,* 145–170.

Cohen, P. S., Yoburn, B. C., Pennington, R. V., & Ball, R. (1979). Visual target control of schedule-induced aggression in white king pigeons (*Columbia livia*). *Aggressive Behavior, 5,* 291–307.

Colvin, D. V. (1973). Agonistic behavior in males of five species of voles *Microtus. Animal Behaviour, 21,* 471–480.

Cords, M. (1988). Resolution of aggressive conflicts by immature long-tailed macaques *Macaca fascicularis. Animal Behaviour, 36,* 1124–1135.

Crowcroft, P. (1957). *The life of a shrew.* London: Max Reinhardt.

Dabelsteen, T., & Pedersen, S. B. (1990). Song and information about aggressive responses of blackbirds, *Turdus merula,* evidence from interactive playback experiments with territory owners. *Animal Behaviour, 40,* 1158–1168.

Doob, A. N., & Climie, R. J. (1972). Delay of measurement and effects of film violence. *Journal of Experimental and Social Psychology, 8,* 136–142.

Dragunow, M. (1986). Endogenous anticonvulsant substances. *Neuroscience and Biobehavioral Review, 10,* 229–242.

Drevets, W. C., Videen, T. O., MacLeod, A. K., Haller, J. W., & Raichle, M. E. (1992). PET images of blood flow changes during anxiety: *Correction. Science, 256,* 1696.

Eibl-Eibesfeldt, I. (1971). Love and hate. (G. Strachan, Trans.) New York: Holt, Rinehart & Winston.

Eisenberg, J. F. (1962) Studies on the behavior of *Peromsycus maniculatus gambelli* and *Peromyscus californicus parasiticus. Behaviour, 19,* 177–207.

Erdmann, G., & van Lindern, B. (1980). The effects of beta-adrenergic stimulation and beta-adrenergic blockade on emotional reactions. *Psychophysiology, 17,* 332–338.

Ervin, F. (1976). Evaluation of organic factors in patients with impulse disorders and episodic violence. In W. L. Smith & A. Kling (Eds.), Issues in brain/behavior control (pp. 23–32). New York: Spectrum, Halsted, Wiley.

Evans, C. S. (1985). Display vigor and subsequent fight performance in the Siamese fighting fish, *Betta splendens. Behavioural processes, 11,* 113–121.

Ewer, R. F. (1973). *The ethology of mammals.* London: Elek Science.

Fava, M., Anderson, K., & Rosenbaum, J. F. (1990). "Anger attacks": Possible variant of panic and major depressive disorders. *American Journal of Psychiatry, 147,* 867–870.

Fentress, J. C. (1973). Specific and non specific factors in the causation of behaviour. In P. P. G. Bateson & P. H. Klopfer (Eds.), *Perspectives in ethology* (pp. 155–224) New York: Plenum.

Ferguson, S. M., Rayport, M., & Corrie, W. S. (1986). Brain correlates of aggressive behavior in temporal lobe epilepsy In B. K. Doane & K. E. Livingston (Eds.), *The limbic system: Functional organization and clinical disorders* (pp. 183–193). New York: Raven.

Fitz, D. (1976). A renewed look at Miller's conflict theory of aggression displacement. *Journal of Personality and Social Psychology, 33,* 725–732.

Foreman, D., & Allee, W. C. (1959). A correlation between posture stance and outcome in paired contests of domestic hens. *Animal Behaviour, 7,* 180–188.

Fridhandler, B. M., & Averill, J. R. (1982). Temporal dimensions of anger: An exploration of time and emotion. In J. R. Averill (Ed.), *Anger and aggression* (pp. 253–280). New York: Springer-Verlag.

Fuller, J. L., Rosvold, H. E., & Pribram, K. H. (1957). The effect on affective and cognitive behavior in lesions of the dog pyriform-amygdala-hippocampal complex. *Journal of Comparative and Physiological Psychology. 50,* 89–96.

Gates, G. S. (1926). An observational study of anger. *Journal of Experimental Psychology., 9,* 325–336.

Geschwind, N. (1975). The clinical setting of aggression in temporal lobe epilepsy. In W. S. Fields & W. H. Sweet (Eds.), *Neural bases of violence and aggression* (pp. 273–284). St. Louis, MO: Warren H. Green.

Gibbs, F. A. (1956). Abnormal electrical activity in the temporal lobe and its relationship to abnormalities of aggressive behavior. *Research Publications, Association for Research in Nervous and Mental Disease, 36,* 278–284.

Gloor, P. (1975) Electrophysiological studies of the amygdala (stimulation and recording): Their possible contribution to the understanding of neural mechanisms of aggression. In W. S. Fields & W. H. Sweet (Eds.), *Neural bases of violence and aggression* (pp. 5–40). St. Louis, MO: Warren H. Green.

Grant, E. C., & Mackintosh, J. H. (1963). A comparison of the social postures of some common laboratory rodents. *Behaviour, 21,* 246–259.

Grant, E. C., MacKintosh, J. H., & Lerwill, C. J. (1970). The effect of a visual stimulus on the agonistic behaviour of the golden hamster. *Zeitschrift für Tierpsychologie, 27,* 73–77.

Gusterson, H. (1986, August 18). A young man's exercise in ritual on the high seas. *The Guardian,* p. 18.

Hall, G. S. (1899). A study of anger. *American Journal of Psychology, 10,* 516–591.

Heath, R. G. (1981). The neural basis for violent behavior: Physiology and anatomy. In L. Valzelli & L. Morgese (Eds.), *Aggression and violence: A psycho/biological and clinical approach. Proceedings of the first Saint Vincent Special Conference* (pp. 176–194). Edizioni Saint Vincent, Italy.

Heelas, P. (1983). Anthropological perspectives on violence: Universals and particulars. *Zygon, 18,* 375–404.

Heiligenberg, W. (1974). Processes governing behavioral states of readiness. In D. S. Lehrman, J. S. Rosenblatt, R. A. Hinde, & F. Shaw (Eds.), *Advances in the study of behavior* (Vol. 5, pp. 173–200). New York: Academic.

Hilton, S. M., & Zbrozyna, A. W. (1963). Amygdaloid region for defense reactions and its efferent pathway to the brainstem. *Journal of Physiology, 165,* 160–173.

Hinde, R. A. (1970). *Animal behaviour: A synthesis of ethology and comparative psychology* (2nd. ed.). New York: McGraw-Hill.

Hinde, R. A. (1985) Was "The expression of the emotions" a misleading phrase? *Animal Behaviour, 33,* 985–992.

Hinton, J. W. (1981). Adrenal cortical and medullary hormones and their psychophysiological correlates in violent and in psychopathic offenders. In P. Brain & D. Benton (Eds.), *The biology of aggression* (pp. 291–300). Alphen aan den Rijn, The Netherlands: Sijthoff & Noordhoff.

Hogan, J. A., & Bols, R. J. (1980). Priming of aggressive motivation in *Betta Splendens. Animal. Behaviour, 28,* 135–142.

Hohmann, G. W. (1966). Some effects of spinal cord lesions on experienced emotional feelings. *Psychophysiology, 3,* 143–156.

Hokanson, J. E., Willers, K. R., & Koropsak, E. (1968). The modification of autonomic response during aggressive interchange. *Journal of Personality, 36,* 386–404.

Kahn, M. W. (1951). The effect of severe defeat at various age levels on the aggressive behavior of mice. *Journal of Genetic Psychology., 79,* 117–130.

Kaplan, J. B., & Manuch, S. B. (1989). The effect of propanolol on behavioral interactions among adult male cynomolgous monkeys (*Macaca fascicularis*) housed in disrupted social groupings. *Psychosomatic Medicine, 51,* 449–462.

Kawamura, S. (1967). Aggression as studied in troops of Japanese monkeys. In C. Clemente & D. Lindsley (Eds.), *Aggression and defense, brain function* (pp. 195–224). Berkely: University of California Press.

Kemble, E. (1981). Some behavioral effects of amygdaloid lesions in Northern grasshopper mice. In Y. Ben-ari (Ed.), *The Amygdaloid Complex, IRSERM Symposium No 20.* (pp. 305–315). Amsterdam: Elsevier.

Killeen, P. (1975). On the temporal control of behavior. *Psychological Review, 82,* 89–100.

Konecni, V. J. (1975). Annoyance, type and duration of post annoyance activity and aggression: The "cathartic effect." *Journal of Experimental Psychology, 104,* 76–102.

Koolhaas, J. M., Schuurman, T., & Wiepkema, P. R. (1980). The organisation of intraspecific agonistic behaviour in the rat. *Progress in Neurobiology, 15*, 247–268.

Kornadt, H.-J. (1974). Toward a motivational theory of aggression and aggression inhibition: Some considerations about an aggression motive and their application to TAT and catharsis. In J. de Wit & W. W. Hartup (Eds.), *Determinants and origins of aggressive behavior* (pp. 567–578). The Hague: Mouton.

Kruk, M. R. (1991). Ethology and pharmacology of hypothalmic aggression in the rat. *Neuroscience and Biobehavioral Reviews, 15*, 527–538

Lagerspetz, K. (1969). Aggression and aggressiveness in laboratory mice. In S. Garattini & E. B. Sigg (Eds.), *Aggressive behavior* (pp. 77–85). New York: Wiley.

Lagerspetz, K., & Portin, R. (1968). Simulation of cues eliciting aggressive responses in mice at two age levels. *Journal of Genetic Psychology, 113*, 53–63.

Lehman, M., & Adams, D. B. (1977). A statistical and motivational analysis of the social behaviors of the male laboratory rat. *Behaviour, 61*, 238–275.

Lewis, D. O., Pincus, J. H., Shanok, S. S., & Glaser, G. H. (1982). Psychomotor epilepsy and violence in a group of incarcerated adolescent boys. *American Journal of Psychiatry, 139*, 882–887.

Lipp, H. P. (1978). Aggression and flight behavior of the marmoset monkey *Callithrix jacchus*: An ethogram for brain stimulation studies. *Brain, Evolution and Behavior, 15*, 241–259.

Livingston, S. (1972). *Comprehensive management of epilepsy in infancy, childhood and adolescence.* Springfield, IL: Thomas.

Lorenz, K. (1957). The past twelve years in the comparative study of behavior. In C. H. Schiller (Ed.), *Instinctive Behavior* (pp. 288–310). New York: International Universities Press.

Lorenz, K. (1966). *On aggression* (English translation). New York: Harcourt, Brace, & World.

Luiten, P. G. M., Koolhaas, J. M., Boer, S., & de Koopmans, S. J. (1985). The cortical-medial amygdala in the central nervous system organization of agonistic behavior. *Brain Research, 332*, 283–297.

MacDonnell, M. F., & Flynn, J. P. (1966). Sensory control of hypothalamic attack. *Animal Behaviour, 14*, 399–405.

Malamuth, N. M. (1986). Predictors of naturalistic sexual aggression. *Journal of Personality and Social Psychology, 50*, 953–962.

Mark, V. H., & Ervin, F. R. (1970). *Violence and the brain.* New York: Harper & Row.

Marler, P. (1976). On animal aggression: The roles of strangeness and familiarity. *American Psychologist, 31*, 239–246.

Martin, F. D., & Hengstebeck, M. F. (1981). Eye colour and aggression in juvenile guppies, *Poecilia reticulata* Peters. *Animal Behaviour, 29*, 325–331.

Mattes, J. A. (1986). Psychopharmacology of temper outbursts. *Journal of Nervous and Mental Disease, 174*, 464–470.

Meltzer, H. (1933). Student adjustments to anger. *Journal of Social Psychology, 4*, 285–308.

Melvin, K. B. (1985). Attack/display as a reinforcer in *Betta splendens*. *Bulletin of the Psychonomic Society, 23*, 350–352.

Miller, M. (1976). Dorsolateral frontal lobe lesions and behavior in the macaque: Dissociation of threat and aggression. *Physiology and Behavior, 17*, 209–213.

Miller, N. E. (1948). Theory and experiment relating psychoanalytic displacement to stimulus–response generalization. *Journal of Abnormal and Social Psychology, 43*, 155–178.

Miller, N. E., & Bugelski, B. R. (1948). Minor studies of aggression: II. The influence of frustrations by the in-group on attitudes expressed toward out-groups. *Journal of Psychology, 24*, 437–442.

Monroe, R. (1975). Drugs in the management of episodic behavioral disorders. In W. S. Fields & W. H. Sweet (Eds.), *Neural bases of violence and aggression* (pp. 328–348). St. Louis, MO: Warren H. Green.

Morgan, J. I., Cohen, D. R., Hempstead, J. L., & Curran, T. (1987). Mapping patterns of *c-fos* expression in the central nervous system after seizure. *Science, 237,* 192–197.

Mos, J., Olivier, B., van Oorschot, R., & Dijkstra, H. (1984). Different test situations for measuring offensive aggression in male rats do not result in the same wound pattern. *Physiology and Behavior, 32,* 453–456.

Murphy, M. (1976) Olfactory stimulation and olfactory bulb removal: Effects on territorial aggression in male Syrian golden hamsters. *Brain Research, 113,* 95–110.

O'Keefe, J., & Bouma, H. (1969). Complex sensory properties of certain amygdala units in the freely moving cat. *Experimental Neurology, 23,* 384–398.

Olsen, R. W. (1969). Agonistic behavior of the short-tailed shrew (*Blarina brevicauda*). *Journal of Mammalogy, 50,* 494–500.

Ounsted, C., Lindsay, J., & Richards, P. (1987). *Temporal lobe epilepsy 1948–1986: A biographical study.* Blackwell. Mac Keith, Oxford:

Payne, A. P. (1974). The effects of urine on aggressive responses by male golden hamsters. *Aggressive Behavior, 1,* 71–80.

Peeke, H. V. S., & Peeke, S. C. (1982). Parental factors in the sensitization and habituation of territorial aggression in the convict cichlid (*Cichlasoma nigrofasciatum*). *Journal of Comparative and Physiological Psychology, 96,* 955–966.

Pierce, J. D. Jr., Pellis, V. C., Dewsbury, D. A., & Pellis, S. M. (1991). Targets and tactics of agonistic and precopulatory behavior in montane and prairie voles: Their relationship to juvenile play-fighting. *Aggressive Behavior, 17,* 337–350.

Polakoff, S. A., Sorgi, P. J., & Ratey, J. J. (1986). The treatment of impulsive and aggressive behavior with nadolol. *Journal of Clinical Psychopharmacology, 6,* 125–126.

Potegal, M. (1979). The reinforcing value of several types of aggressive behavior: A review. *Aggressive Behavior, 5,* 353–373.

Potegal, M. (1991). Attack priming and satiation in female golden hamsters: Tests of some alternatives to the aggression arousal interpretation. *Aggressive Behavior, 17,* 327–335.

Potegal, M. (1992a). Time course of aggressive arousal in female golden hamsters and male rats. *Behavioral and Neural Biology, 58,* 120–124.

Potegal, M. (1992b). Aggression and aggressiveness in female golden hamsters. In K. Bjorkqvist & P. Niemela (Eds.), *Of mice and women: Aspects of female aggression.* (pp. 330–350). San Diego: Academic.

Potegal, M., Ferris, C., & Skaredoff, L. (1991). The corticomedial amygdala and hamster agonistic behavior. *Society for Neuroscience Abstracts, 17,* 877.

Potegal, M., Gimino, F., Marotta, R., & Glusman, M. (1979). Factors in the waning of muricide in the rat. II. Digging behavior. *Aggressive Behavior, 5,* 283–290.

Potegal, M., & Popken, J. (1985). The time course of attack priming effects in female golden hamsters. *Behavioral Processes, 11,* 199–208.

Potegal, M., & tenBrink, L. (1984). Behavior of attack-primed and attack-satiated female golden hamster (*Mesocricetus auratus*). *Journal of Comparative Psychology, 98,* 66–75.

Quanty, M. B. (1976) Aggression catharsis: Experimental investigation and implication. In R. G. Green & E. C. O'Neal (Eds.), *Perspectives on aggression* (pp. 99–132). New York: Academic.

Rader, R. D., Stevens, C. M., Meehan, J. P., & Henry, J. P. (1974). Telemetered renal responses to avoidance and aggression in dogs. *Biotelemetry, 1,* 3–11.

Rand, A. L. (1942). Results of the Archbold expeditions. *Bulletin of the American Museum of Natural History, 44. U,* 517–524.

Rawls, W. (1980, July 5). Good ol' mountain boys of Tennessee brawl to be meanest of 'em all. *New York Times,* p. 6.

Reiman, E. M., Fusselman, M. J., Fox, P. T., & Raichle, M. E. (1989). Neuroanatomical correlates of anticipatory anxiety. *Science, 243,* 1071–1074.

Reisenzein, R. (1983). The Schachter theory of emotion: Two decades later. *Psychological Bulletin, 94,* 239–264.

Rey, J. H., Pond, D. A., & Evans, C. C. (1949). Clinical and electroencephalographic studies of temporal lobe function. *Proceedings of the Royal Society of Medicine, 42,* 891–904.

Reynolds, G. S., Catania, A. C., & Skinner, B. F. (1963). Conditioned and unconditioned aggression in pigeons. *Journal of the Experimental Analysis of Behavior, 6,* 73–74.

Rodgers, R. J., & Hendrie, C. A. (1982). Agonistic behaviour in rats: Evidence for non-involvement of opioid mechanisms. *Physiology and Behaviour, 29,* 85–90.

Rushen, J., & Pajor, E. (1987). Offence and defence in fights between young pigs (*Sus scofa*). *Aggressive Behavior, 13,* 329–346.

Russell, G. (1983). Psychological issues in sports aggression. In J. H. Goldstein (Ed.), *Sports violence* (pp. 157–181). New York: Springer-Verlag.

Saint-Hilaire, J. M., Gilbert, M., Bouvier, G., & Barbeau, A. (1980). Epilepsy and aggression: Two cases with depth electrode studies. In P. Robb (Ed.), *Epilepsy updated: Causes and treatment.* pp. 145–176 Miami: Symposia specialists.

Sananes, C. B., & Davis, M. (1992). N-methyl-D-aspartate lesions of the lateral and basolateral nuclei of the amygdala block fear-potentiated startle and shock sensitization of startle. *Behavioral Neuroscience, 106,* 72–80.

Saphier, D., Mor, G., & Feldman, S. (1988). Neurogenic stimuli alter preoptic area and amygdala unit activity: Central effects of olfactory projections on paraventricular nucleus units. *Experimental Neurology, 100,* 71–82.

Scalia, F., & Winans, S. (1975). The differential projections of the olfactory bulb and accessory olfactory bulb in mammals. *Journal of Comparative Neurology, 161,* 31–56.

Schacter, S. (1964). The interaction of cognitive and physiological determinants of emotional state. In L. Berkowitz (Ed.), *Advances in experimental social psychology* (Vol. 1, pp. 401–432). New York: Academic.

Seigfried, B., & Frischknecht, H-R. (1988). Naltrexone-reversible pain suppression in the isolated attacking mouse. *Behavioral and Neural Biology, 50,* 354–360.

Sheng, M., & Greenberg, M. E. (1990). The regulation and function of *c-fos* and other intermediate early genes in the nervous system. *Neuron, 4,* 477–485.

Shipley, J. E., & Kolb, B. (1977). Neural correlates of species-typical behavior in the Syrian golden hamster. *Journal of Comparative and Physiological Psychology, 91,* 1056–1073.

Simmel, E. C., & Walker, D. A. (1970). Social priming for agonistic behavior in a "docile" mouse strain. *American Zoologist, 10,* 486–487.

Simpson, M. J. A. (1968). The display of the Siamese fighting fish. *Animal Behaviour Monographs, 1,* 1–73.

Smith, J. S. (1980). Episodic rage. In M. Girgis & L. G. Kiloh (Eds.), *Limbic epilepsy and the dyscontrol syndrome* (pp. 255–266). Amsterdam: Elsevier.

Smith, M. D. (1983). *Violence and sport.* Toronto: Butterworth.

Stacey, P. B., & Chizar, D. (1975). Changes in the darkness of four body features of bluegill sunfish (*Lepromis macrochirus Rafinesque*) during aggressive encounters. *Behavioral Biology, 14,* 41–49.

Stokes, A. W. (1962). Agonistic behaviour among blue tits at a winter feeding station. *Behaviour, 19,* 118–137.

Takahashi, L. K., & Gladstone, C. D. (1988). Medial amygdaloid lesions and the regulation of sociosexual behavioral patterns across the estrous cycle in female golden hamsters. *Behavioral Neuroscience, 102,* 268–275.

Tedeschi, J. T., Smith, R. B., & Brown, R. C. (1974). A reinterpretation of research on aggression. *Psychological Bulletin, 84,* 540–562.

Tellegen, A., & Horn, J. M. (1972). Primary aggression motivation in three inbred strains of mice. *Journal of Comparative and Physiological Psychology, 78*, 279–304.

Tooker, C. P., & Miller, R. J. (1980). The ontogeny of agonistic behaviour in the blue gourami, Tricogaster trichopterus (*Pisces, Anabantoidei*). *Animal Behaviour, 28*, 973–988.

Turner, G. F., & Huntingford, F. A. (1986). A problem for game theory analysis: Assessment and intention in male mouthbrooder contests. *Animal Behaviour, 34*, 961–970.

Ueda, T. (1962). A study of anger in Japanese college students through the controlled diary method (2). *Journal of Nara Gakugei University, 10*, 342–348.

Ulrich, R., Johnston, M., Richardson, J., & Wolff, P. (1963). The operant conditioning of fighting behavior in rats. *Psychological Record, 13*, 465–470.

Vayda, A. (1968). Hypothesis about functions of war. In M. Freid, M. Harris, & R. Murphy (Eds.), *War* (pp. 85–91). New York: The Natural History Press.

Viken R. J., Johnson, A. K., & Knutson, J. F. (1991). Blood pressure, heart rate, and regional resistance in behavioral defense. *Physiology and Behavior, 50*, 1097–1101.

Virkkunen, M. (1982) Reactive hypoglycemic tendency among habitually violent offenders. *Neuropsychobiology, 8*, 35–40.

Walker, E. A., & Blumer, D. (1975). Long term effects of temporal lobe lesions on sexual behavior and aggressivity. In W. S. Fields & W. H. Sweet (Eds.), *Neural bases of violence and aggression* (pp. 392–400). Warren H. Green. St. Louis, MO:

Wertham, F. (1978). The Catathymic Crisis. In I. L. Kutash, S. B. Kutash, & L. B. Schlesinger (Eds.), *Violence: Perspectives on murder and aggression.* (pp. 165–170). San Francisco: Jossey-Bass.

Whiting, J. (1944). The frustration complex in Kwoma society. *Man, 44*, 140–144.

Whitman, S., King, L. N., & Cohen, R. L. (1986). Epilepsy and violence: A scientific and social analysis (pp. 285–302). In S. Whitman & B. P. Hermann (Eds.), *Psychopathology in epilepsy.* New York: Oxford University Press.

Wilson, R. (1974). Agonistic postures and latency to the first interaction during initial pair encounters in the red jungle fowl *Gallus gallus. Animal Behaviour, 22*, 75–82.

York, A. D., & Rowell, T. E. (1988). Reconciliation following aggression in patas monkeys. *Erythrocebus patas. Animal Behaviour, 36*, 502–509.

Zanchetti, A., Baccelli, G., Mancia, G., & Ellison, G. D. (1972). Emotion and the cardiovascular system in the cat. In D. Hill (Ed.), *Physiology, emotion and psychosomatic illness* (pp. 213–218). Amsterdam: Elsevier.

Zillmann, D. (1979). *Hostility and aggression.* Hillsdale, NJ: Lawrence Erlbaum Associates.

Zillmann, D. (1984). *Connections between sex and aggression.* Hillsdale NJ: Lawrence Erlbaum Associates.

Zimbardo, P. G. (1969). The human choice: Individuation, reason, and order vs deindividuation, impulse and chaos. In W. J. Arnold & D. Levine (Eds.), *Nebraska Symposium on Motivation* (pp. 237–309). Lincoln: University of Nebraska Press.

# CHAPTER 5

# Aggression Waxing (Sometimes Waning): Siamese Fighting Fish

Paul M. Bronstein
*University of Michigan-Flint*

Although not a subject of intense concern to the North American variety of animal rights activists (not yet, at least), domesticated Siamese fighting fish (*Betta splendens*) might be considered the "white rat" of the aquatic world. They are highly domesticated animals, relatively easily cared for and inexpensive. Also, they readily exhibit a great deal of social behavior, and these activities have been a subject favored for study among psychologists—especially those interested in social behavior and learning.

Some investigators (e.g., Peeke, 1984) have considered these animals so artificially selected as to cast doubt on whether their behavior bears much of a relationship to the life histories of "wilder" species, including even undomesticated *Betta splendens*. However, following the lead of psychologists who consistently have shown a concern for understanding animals' life histories (e.g., Bolles, 1970), in the middle 1970s I began to suspect that, beneath their colorful, ferocious, and inbred exteriors, *Betta* might be revealed to possess many behavioral tactics similar to those of less domesticated and territorial teleosts.

My studies of aggression in *Betta splendens* also emerged from some theoretical notions of animal conflict that had begun to be developed in the domain of game theory. Highly escalated fighting, it has been argued, should be observed mostly when and where animals might improve their inclusive fitness, either directly or indirectly (Maynard-Smith, 1976). In addition, observations of many other species often

**113**

characterized animals as quite tentative and selective in escalating their intraspecific fights (see Huntingford & Turner, 1987; also Archer & Huntingford, this volume). In contrast, the literature on male *Betta* then available appeared not to describe much selectivity in the fighting decisions exhibited by these animals; rather, they were depicted as "fighting fish" (i.e., hawks that would escalate fights wantonly whenever challenged by a conspecific; see Bronstein, 1981a; Hogan & Roper, 1978). Noting that *Betta splendens* may be unusual subjects—due to either artificial selection for aggressiveness or because of experimenters choosing mainly highly aggressive subjects for inclusion in particular studies—it was likely, nonetheless, that these animals might be capable of a greater degree of agonistic selectivity than had been documented previously.

In response to the apparent discrepancy between the empirical literature on *Betta* then available on the one hand, and, on the other, observations of other species, as well as the predictions of game-theoretic models of fighting, studies of agonistic and reproductive behavior in domesticated *Betta* were undertaken. Individuals and small groups of fish were observed in tanks of various sizes and shapes, with these results, turning out to represent a description of animals that can be quite selective in escalating their fighting—competing for and defending isolated breeding areas with their agonistic activities.

## AGONISTIC TACTICS OF *BETTA SPLENDENS*

Male Siamese fighting fish in reproductive condition build nests (clumps of bubbles at the water surface); they use these nests as breeding sites and for accumulating eggs toward which the males also direct caretaking activities. The paternal behavior (mostly mouthing eggs and fry and also adding to the size of bubble nests) prevents the growth of fungi lethal to their offspring (Bronstein, 1982). Crevices that are visually isolated from other males are preferred nest areas and are defended against conspecifics with aggressive behavior (Bronstein, 1980, 1981a, 1982); intruder males typically respond to attack by taking flight, although not before many hours of mutual biting and chasing have occurred.

When a male is confronted for several hours either by its own mirror image or by another male displaying in a stationary container, a three-phase ethogram is revealed (Bronstein, 1981a, 1983a, 1983a, 1985a). As shown in Fig. 5.1, fish initially approach the site of stimulation, issue gill-cover and fin-extension displays when they are within

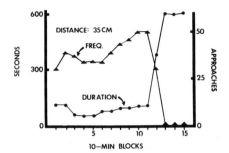

FIG. 5.1. The onset of combat: Behavior of a single male *Betta splendens* reacting to a highly aggressive male conspecific enclosed in a clear plastic container 35 cm from the subject's nest. For the first 110 minutes (Phase 1), this fish remained primarily at its nest, approaching the opponent 3 to 5 times per minute, and spending 2 to 4 seconds near the opponent (within two body lengths) upon each approach. During the final 30 minutes of testing (Phase 2), escapes from the opponent ceased, and the subject attacked its opponent for almost all the final 1800 seconds.

about two body lengths (8 cm) of the stimulus, and then flee. Escapes (during which males can swim more than a meter per second), with further approaches and displays, often continue for more than 30 minutes. These activities define Phase 1, a "mixed phase," with both attack and escape occurring. The second phase of social interaction, attack, occurs when escape movements cease and males remain continually within one-to-two body lengths of the stimulus, displaying and biting all the while. Finally, typically after hours of combat, fish retreat from the stimulation area and fail to reinitiate display for some hours (Phase 3).

The transitions in agonistic behavior—from the mixed phase, to attack, to retreat—are determined by the duration of visual stimulation, as well as by subjects' individual differences in aggressiveness. Intermittent stimulation (e.g., an opponent that only rarely emerges from hiding behind a visually opaque barrier) results in a prolonged mixed phase from virtually all males. However, when environments are arranged so that the image of a proximate displaying male cannot be escaped (i.e., few barriers to mutual visual stimulation), a bimodal distribution of animals is revealed (with some intermediate cases) as a consequence of persistent visual stimulation: Some fish are stimulated to attack, retaliating in direct proportion to the duration of social stimulation provided; others persist in escaping (Bronstein, 1983a). Furthermore, agonistic behavior noted early in an encounter is a reliable predictor of subsequent aggression. Fish that escalate their behavior from the mixed phase to pure attack (Phase 2) soon after being stimulated are the most tenacious fighters (Bronstein, 1983a, 1985a,

1985b; Bronstein in press). Furthermore, males reliably maintain their individual attack dispositions for as long as 1 month (i.e., they have reliable "personalities"; (Bronstein, in press).

Some escalation of aggression can be accomplished by as little as 10 minutes of continual visual stimulation by a conspecific male; such stimulation results in a significant increase in the volume of personal space defended (Bronstein, 1983b). Males cease fighting when visual contact between combatants is interrupted, even briefly (Bronstein, 1981a, 1983a). However, 15 minutes of stimulation by a male restrained behind glass results in a heightened readiness for attack that is retained for at least 1 minute after that stimulation ceases (Bronstein, 1989a). Fifteen minutes of exposure to the image of a male conspecific is adequate also to cause another male to remain near the site of that stimulation for at least another 30 minutes (Bronstein, 1986, 1988). As in other species *Betta* appear to learn the location of prior agonistic encounters (Bronstein, Parmigiani, Torricelli, & Brain, 1988; Peeke & Veno, 1973), due perhaps to classical conditioning (see Domjan & Hollis, 1988; Hollis, Cadieux, & Colbert, 1989).

Minor variations in this three-part ethogram are noted when a free-swimming opponent, rather than a spatially restricted image, is employed as the social stimulus. First, mobile and live opponents are attacked more intensely than are images of males visible at one fixed locale (Bronstein, 1981a). Second, the agonistic repertoire interacts with nest-building activity (Bronstein, 1980, 1981a, 1984a). When a resident male and live intruder first encounter each other, they approach, display, and escape (Phase 1). The resident departs to its nest at which time further nest building occurs. The intruder also flees but, if the animals continue to have visual contact, continuation of the mixed phase by one or both fish is observed; display and attack occur throughout the tank, with the nest area apparently not becoming the primary focus of intense fighting.

Fights typically escalate from Phase 1 to Phase 2 after some tens of minutes of approach–escape activity, escape movements being eliminated as opponents then fight continually for hours within one body length of each other. Aggressive contests between males nearly always result in stable dominance/subordinancy relations after 12 to 24 hours of fighting, with the subordinate fish persistently escaping from the victorious male. This prolonged combat, occurring prior to the resolution of contests, also is seen in tanks of many sizes (Bronstein, 1984a). Fights often terminate quickly when one or both fish escape the scene of combat, thus reducing mutual stimulation (Bronstein, 1981a, 1983a, 1983b). Studying thousands of fights and partial fights has resulted in the conclusion that dominant males (a) are relatively large, (b) build relatively large nests, (c) have become familiar with the visual and/or tactile characteristics of their combat environments, and (d) escalate the intensity of their fighting from Phase 1 to Phase 2 (i.e., cease escaping) relatively quickly when first encountering an opponent. *Betta* seem unusual because of their long fight durations, and in general, it is relatively persistent aggression that results in a male *Betta* attaining dominance, with characteristics (c) and (d) known to correlate positively with fight persistence (Bronstein, 1981a, 1984a, 1985a, 1985b).

Furthermore, there are marked consequences of an animal attaining social dominance: Dominant males control both breeding sites and females near those areas (Bronstein, 1984a). When a female is added to a male's tank, copulation usually is noted within 30 hours (Bronstein, 1982). Males initially respond to females as they do to male intruders—approaching, displaying, and then quickly retreating to elaborate their nests. However, females react to males with behaviors that lower the probability of injurious attack. First, females develop dark vertical bars; these reduce males' biting (Robertson & Sale, 1975). Second, females escape into crevices or clumps of vegetation where the bars can act as cryptic coloration (Bronstein, 1982). Females also remain relatively immobile unless closely pursued by a male, at which time they escape rapidly. For the first day of cohabitation, males alternate between nest building and directing approach–display–escape sequences at females. Females then follow males to their nests and copulations occur intermittently for several hours. Males next chase females from their nests and continue nest-building behavior, which now includes the mouthing of eggs and fry. Offspring are protected by males' attacks that drive off predatory adult conspecifics. However, this reproductive relationship between a male and a female is disrupted severely by the presence of a second male even when he is confined behind clear glass. Such an intruder stimulates male–male aggression and consequently reduces the time spent in reproduction. This stimulation leads to at least a 50% drop in the offspring produced by resident males (Bronstein, 1982).

Motivationally, *Betta* are not the ubiquitously aggressive animals as suggested by either their common English name or by the literature available in the 1970s. They have a social system where males are motivated to defend their privacy with, if successful, a consequent elevation in breeding potential: First, nests are built to be visually isolated from other males (Bronstein, 1980, 1981a). Second, the biting, gill-cover erection and fin-expansion behaviors of aggressive males repel intruders and also cause males to return to their own isolated nest sites (Bronstein, 1981a, 1982). Third, a period of residency in social isolation causes a male to become both increasingly aggressive and attached to its nest; thus, some period of privacy increases the likelihood subsequently of an isolated resident maintaining its privacy by expelling intruders (Bronstein, 1984a, 1985a; cf. Potegal, this volume). Fourth, a resident male fights against a conspecific with an intensity that is inversely proportional both to the distance between the two fish and to the distance from the resident's nest to the challenger (Bronstein, 1981a, 1983a, 1983b). Heightened commitment to fighting occurs when the isolation of the resident and its nest is threatened by a nearby male, with line-of-sight communication used to assess the intensity of the threat (Bronstein, 1983a). Fifth, if privacy is experimentally denied to resident males by exposing them inescapably to the visual image of a second male, the courtship and breeding of those residents is greatly reduced (Bronstein, 1982). Clearly, what one has here are not ferocious "fighting fish" but selectively aggressive, potentially territorial, animals.


## CONCLUSIONS


In retrospect, the game-theoretic and zoological view of animal conflict served as a useful heuristic for further understanding fighting in domesticated male *Betta*. Rather than rigidly escalating whenever challenged by another male (i.e., playing the hawk), they fight most intensely in situations where the potential for successful reproductive behavior is threatened most by the presence of a same-sex conspecific. As noted in several previous papers (e.g., Bronstein, 1981b, 1985c, 1986, 1989b), earlier overestimations of *Betta* aggression stemmed mostly from attempts to use these fish as exemplars of operant conditioning. Replacement of Skinnerian procedures and concepts by those of ethology and comparative psychology resulted in a fuller appreciation of how fighting is but one tactic in the integrated social life of this species.

Also, with the addition of new information several problems have emerged that now becloud earlier attempts to understand male *Betta* by using Skinnerian techniques (i.e., presenting a conspecific image contingent upon the occurrence of a particular behavior; see Hogan & Roper, 1978, for a review of that literature). First, the conclusion emerging from those data, that these animals are ubiquitous fighters, was revealed to be something of an overgeneralization. As noted earlier, *Betta* are selective as to when and where they escalate their combat. Second, none of the animal movements used in the operant-conditioning studies to define learning in *Betta* are unambiguously learned; and each can be interpreted as variations of the *un*learned species-typical approach–escape (Phase 1) sequences elicited by the conspecific image (the alleged reinforcer; see Bronstein, 1981b, 1984b,

1985c, 1989b). Third, regardless of uncertainty over whether certain actions of the fish are learned or unlearned, it turned out (Bronstein, 1985a) that the swimming movements most commonly assumed to be indicative of high levels of aggression in those social-reinforcement studies do not predict performance in actual combat. The construct validity of perhaps the most fundamental operational definition of aggression in operant attempts to condition male *Betta* has been overwhelmed by recent data.

Male *Betta* do employ social learning in defending specific areas around their nests against male conspecifics (Bronstein, 1986, 1988). Following the experience of fighting near distinctive visual and/or spatial cues, fish approach those stimuli and at times initiate gill-cover displays when near the cues that had been paired with aggression. There is no reason to either suggest or exclude the possibility of a Skinnerian explanation for those data.

Social-reinforcement procedures have been successful in changing the behavior of other teleost species (Davis, Harris, & Shelby, 1974; Rasa, 1971). It remains uncertain in my view whether a naturally occurring social-reinforcement process (as distinct from effective experimental social-reinforcement procedures) provides any explanation for social behavior in *Betta splendens* (cf. Gardner & Gardner, 1988).

Finally, one important aspect of game theory has not been confirmed in studies of *Betta* aggression. As stated clearly by Archer and Huntingford (see their chapter, this volume), when intense, injurious fighting is one behavioral option, one would expect aggression to be preceded by a preliminary stage of communication during which each opponent's fighting potential is assessed by its adversary, with animals, in effect, "deciding" whether to risk the injury of continued escalation. It has been shown repeatedly that male *Betta* reliably reveal their agonistic potential (resource-holding potential) during their first 30 minutes of exposure to a same-sex conspecific (Bronstein, 1981a, 1985a, 1985b). However, it is apparent also that, whereas human experimenters can predict accurately and quickly which member of a dyad will eventually be victorious, the fish themselves seem not to use this potential information to retreat from asymmetrical contests prior to the most intense combat, thus escaping subsequent injury in the jaws of a decidedly superior opponent. Rather, *Betta* seem oblivious to their relative status until something like a war of attrition has been fought. It may be that in *Betta* artificial selection has resulted in many males that use the display of other fish more as a releaser for continued fighting than as information about their own potential dominance or defeat. A major exception to this conclusion occurs when one fish is considerably larger than its opponent. Under such circumstances, not only does the smaller animal almost always become subordinate, but a relatively small fish often gives up after some display, but prior to escalation and the occurrence of injurious biting (Bronstein, 1984a). These data suggest that male *Betta* can assess an opponent's size prior to extensive fighting; however, the capacity for the rapid assessment of opponents' fighting ability appears to be either limited or not to exist in size-matched pairs (cf. Turner & Huntingford, 1986). Thus, whereas domesticated *Betta* are not ubiquitous fighters, they, nonetheless, are "fighting fish" in that their bouts of combat are extremely prolonged. Convict cichlids (*C. nigrofasciatum*), for instance, regularly settle their disputes after but a single, brief bite delivered by the victor (Bronstein & Brain, 1991; Figler & Peeke, 1978), whereas pairs of male *Betta* struggle on and on for dozens of hours (for comparison with other species, see Potegal, this volume). One cause for the failure of male *Betta* to quickly cease fighting has recently been discovered (Bronstein, in press): Fighting with a male conspecific for 1 day (or the presence of a male across a clear glass barrier for 5 days) greatly elevates aggressiveness.

Figure 5.2 shows the results of 30-minute aggression tests given twice to male *Betta*. These tests permit an isolated male to approach and display to an aggressive conspecific enclosed in a clear plastic container for up to 1,800 seconds, and animals' scores are positively correlated with their becoming dominant in actual fights (Bronstein, 1985a, in press). Pretests occurred several days prior to fighting; posttests occurred several days after combat; and control fish were given the same two tests, but without any intervening social experience. Fighting

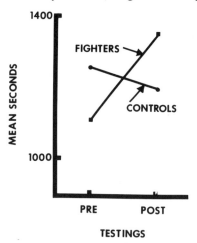

FIG. 5.2. Mean seconds of approach to a male conspecific (behind clear glass) by groups of *Betta* in each of two 30-minute tests. Interposing daylong fights between testings results in a robust elevation of approach in the postfight test.

greatly elevates scores on the second test. Furthermore, this heightened potential for fighting occurred equally among both winners and losers of the intervening fights.

Whether one male *Betta* can evaluate the agonistic potential of an equal-size conspecific is uncertain. However, it seems clear why males fail to retreat when confronted by a fish that human beings would predict to be a superior fighter: Fighting sensitizes subsequent fighting in these animals.

## ACKNOWLEDGMENTS

This chapter and most of the research on which it is based was supported by grants from the Research Advisory and Faculty Development and Awards Committees at the University of Michigan-Flint. It is dedicated to Professor George H. Collier, one of my teachers, on the occasion of his retirement from Rutgers University. (Retirement, in this case pseudoretirement, will mean little more than a change in title. Research will continue as George hobnobs with his fellow emeriti.)

## REFERENCES

Bolles, R. C. (1970). Species-specific defense reactions and avoidance learning. *Psychological Review, 77*, 32–48.

Bronstein, P. M. (1980). *Betta splendens*: A territorial note. *Bulletin of the Psychonomic Society, 16*, 484–485.

Bronstein, P. M. (1981a). Commitments to aggression and to nest sites in male *Betta splendens. Journal of Comparative and Physiological Psychology, 95*, 436–449.

Bronstein, P. M. (1981b). Social reinforcement in *Betta splendens*: A reconsideration. *Journal of Comparative and Physiological Psychology, 95*, 943–950.

Bronstein, P. M. (1982). Breeding, paternal behavior, and their interruption in *Betta splendens. Animal Learning and Behavior, 10*, 145–151.

Bronstein, P. M. (1983a). Agonistic sequences and the assessment of opponents in male *Betta splendens. American Journal of Psychology, 96*, 163–177.

Bronstein, P. M. (1983b). Onset of combat in male *Betta splendens. Journal of Comparative Psychology, 97*, 135–139.

Bronstein, P. M. (1984a). Agonistic and reproductive interactions in *Betta splendens. Journal of Comparative Psychology, 98*, 421–431.

Bronstein, P. M. (1984b). A confound in the application of fixed-ratio schedules to the social behavior of male Siamese fighting fish (*Betta splendens*). *Bulletin of the Psychonomic Society, 22*, 484–487.

Bronstein, P. M. (1985a). Predictors of dominance in male *Betta splendens. Journal of Comparative Psychology, 99*, 47–55.

Bronstein, P. M. (1985b). The prior residence effect in *Betta splendens*. *Journal of Comparative Psychology*, *99*, 56–59.

Bronstein, P. M. (1985c). Toxiphobia, "social reinforcement," comparative psychology, and Pat Capretta. In N. Braveman & P. M. Bronstein, (Eds.), Experimental assessments and clinical applications of conditioned food aversions. *Annals of the New York Academy of Sciences*, *443*, 158–170.

Bronstein, P. M. (1986). Socially mediated learning in male *Betta splendens*. *Journal of Comparative Psychology*, *100*, 279–284.

Bronstein, P. M. (1988). Socially mediated learning in male *Betta splendens* III: Rapid acquisitions. *Aggressive Behavior*, *14*, 415–424.

Bronstein, P. M. (1989a). A short-term memory for aggression in *Betta splendens*. *Animal Behavior*, *37*, 165–166.

Bronstein, P. M. (1989b). Some operant misengineering of behavior. In R. J. Blanchard, P. F. Brain, D. C. Blanchard, & S. Parmigiani (Eds.), *Ethoexperimental analysis of behavior* (pp. 674–690). Dordrecht: Kluwer.

Bronstein, P. M. (in press). On the predictability, sensitization and habituation of aggression in male Bettas (*Betta splendens*). *Journal of Comparative Psychology*.

Bronstein, P. M., & Brain, P. F. (1991). Successful prediction of dominance in convict cichlids, *Cichlasoma nigrofasciatum*. *Bulletin of the Psychonomic Society*, *29*, 455–456.

Bronstein, P. M., Parmigiani, S., Torricelli, P., & Brain, P. F. (1988). Preference for the sites of fighting in two teleost species. *Aggressive Behavior*, *14*, 363–370.

Davis, R. E., Harris, C., & Shelby, J. (1974). Sex differences in aggressivity and the effects of social isolation in the Anabantoid Fish, *Macropodus opercularis*. *Behavioral Biology*, *11*, 497–509.

Domjan, M., & Hollis, K. L. (1988). Reproductive behavior: A potential model system for adaptive specializations in learning. In R. C. Bolles & M. D. Beecher (Eds.), *Evolution and learning* (pp. 213–237). New York: Lawrence Erlbaum Associates.

Figler, M. H., & Peeke, H. V. S. (1978). Alcohol and the prior residence effect in male convict cichlids (*Cichlasoma nigrofasciatum*). *Aggressive Behavior*, *4*, 125–132.

Gardner, R. A., & Gardner, B. T. (1988). Feedforward versus feedbackward: An ethological alternative to the law of effect. *Behavioral & Brain Sciences*, *11*, 429–493.

Hogan, J. A., & Roper, T. J. (1978). A comparison of the properties of different reinforcers. In J. S. Rosenblatt, R. A. Hinde, C. Beer, & M. C. Busnel (Eds.), *Advances in the study of behavior* (Vol. 8). New York: Academic. Press.

Hollis, K. L., Cadieux, E. L., & Colbert, M. M. (1989). The biological function of Pavlovian conditioning: A mechanism for mating success in the Blue Gourami (*Trichogaster trichopterus*). *Journal of Comparative Psychology*, *103*, 115–121.

Huntingford, F. A., & Turner, A. (1987). *Animal conflict*. London: Chapman & Hall.

Maynard-Smith, J. (1976). Evolution and the theory of games. *American Scientist*, *64*, 41–45.

Peeke, H. V. S. (1984). Habituation and the maintenance of territorial boundaries. In H. V. S. Peeke & L. Petrinovich (Eds.), *Habituation, sensitization, and behavior* (pp. 393–421). New York: Academic.

Peeke, H. V. S., & Veno, A. (1973). Stimulus specificity of habituated aggression in the stickleback (*Gasterosteus aculeatus*). *Behavioral Biology*, *8*, 427–432.

Rasa, O. A. E. (1971). Appetence for aggression in juvenile damsel fish. *Zeitschrift für Tierpsychologie, Supplement*, *7*, 1–67.

Robertson, C. M., & Sale, P. F. (1975). Sexual discrimination in the Siamese fighting fish (*Betta splendens* Regan). *Behavior*, *54*, 1–26.

Turner, G. F., & Huntingford, F. A. (1986). A problem for game theory analysis: Assessment and intention in male mouthbrooder contests. *Animal Behaviour*, *34*, 961–970.

# CHAPTER 6
# Studies of Individual Differences in Aggression

Gian Vittorio Caprara, Marco Perugini,
Claudio Barbaranelli
*University of Rome*

This chapter is intended to provide a review of the most salient results of more than a decade of research devoted to the examination of individual differences in relation to the expression of aggression. When this research program began and the vast amount of previous experimental work on aggression was reviewed, what impressed us more than the variety of approaches taken by various investigators was the apparently contradictory results obtained from studies that were substantially based on the same theories and utilized similar procedures. Given the similarity of operational definitions, paradigms, and methods used among these studies, it seemed unlikely that the contradictions among studies were due to conceptual problems; these may become a factor when different theoretical positions or different disciplines are compared.

In the majority of studies we reviewed, aggression was defined as a behavior aimed at delivering noxious stimulation to another person or a person substitute, and most of the research focused on the situations that may elicit or facilitate such behavior in an interpersonal context. In attempting to understand the apparent differences in outcome among studies, we hypothesized that personality variables may play a role; that is, we wondered whether an understanding of relatively stable individual tendencies might facilitate the elucidation of theories of aggression that were primarily focused on the nature of stimuli and responses. It seemed plausible that, by considering the general emotional and cognitive processes of individuals that could mediate the relations between environmental events and aggression (cf. Bandura, 1973; Berkowitz, 1962; Zillmann, 1979), it would be possible to gain an understanding of inconsistencies among studies. Of course, this interest in the role of personality and individual differences in aggression did not develop in isolation. In recent years, many authors (Dengerink, O'Leary, & Kasner, 1975; Fraczek, 1984; Malamuth, 1984; Olweus, 1978, 1980, 1984; Pitkanen-Pulkkinen, 1981) have paid greater attention to the role specific personality characteristics can play in mediating the expression of aggressive behavior.

We hoped that by taking dispositions into account, we would gain better access to the mechanisms and processes that sustain and regulate various forms of aggression. In this respect, we were confident that by combining the study of personality and individual differences with experimental laboratory work we would go beyond the mere noting of differences and correlations to a formulation of better general laws of aggression. Such an approach is consistent with comments by Lewin (1951), who noted that general laws and individual differences are merely two aspects of one problem; they are mutually dependent on each other, and the study of one cannot proceed without the study of the other. Ideally, personality constructs that are anchored to more general theoretical formulations would have enhanced explanatory power by being derived from demonstrated relations among dispositions, situations, and behaviors that can be systematically observed and manipulated under controlled conditions. Thus, we had as a goal a better understanding of the basic processes that sustain and mediate the interaction of the individual with the environment to yield aggression. Basically, we were hoping to follow Allport's (1937) recommendation for developing laws, or at least hypotheses, that explain how uniqueness comes about.

## IRRITABILITY AND EMOTIONAL SUSCEPTIBILITY

In an attempt to validate the Italian version of the Buss and Durkee (1957) Hostility Inventory, a series of item analyses were conducted to identify constructs that would be more precisely defined, although more limited, than aggression. Two relatively new constructs, *Irritability and Emotional Susceptibility*, and the scales to assess them, were identified as being appropriate for research on dispositions that could influence aggression (Caprara, 1983). Both constructs were assumed to reflect a tendency to overreact emotionally to events that are perceived as frustrating, as well as tendency to perceive events as frustrating.

Irritability was defined as the tendency to react impulsively, controversially, or rudely at the slightest provocation or disagreement. The Irritability scale consisted of 30 items (20 effective and 10 control), including such items as "I think I am rather touchy" and "Sometimes I shout, hit, kick, and let off steam." Emotional Susceptibility was defined as the tendency of the individual to experience feelings of discomfort, helplessness, inadequacy, and vulnerability. The Emotional Susceptibility measurement scale consisted of 40 items (30 effective and 10 control), including such items as "Fear of failure worries me more than necessary" and "Sometimes I feel on edge."

A series of studies then established the psychometric properties of the scales. With regard to their internal consistency, results of principal components analyses performed on the Italian, English, and French versions of the scales with different groups of subjects were favorable (Caprara, Cinanni, Passerini, Renzi, & Zelli, 1983). Subsequent studies with Japanese (Hata, 1989), Polish (Drwal, 1986), and Spanish versions (Sanchez-Elvira, Bermudez, & Perez Garcia, 1988) consistently confirmed the high degree of stability of the factorial structure of the two scales. Thus, based on samples of subjects representing different languages, nationalities, and cultural contexts, the Irritability and Emotional Susceptibility scales resulted in comparable data. Moreover, test–retest reliability and split-half reliability assessments were satisfactory for both scales on all populations tested.

With regard to construct validity, Irritability showed a high positive correlation with reports of assault, as well as indirect and verbal aggression. The Emotional Susceptibility scale was found to correlate positively with self-aggression and with various indices of anxiety and difficulties in emotional adjustment (Caprara, Cinanni, Passerini, Renzi, & Zelli 1983; Drwal, 1986).

Consistent with the basis for their development, both scales proved particularly suitable for exploring the role of dispositions in the frustration-aggression (F-A) hypothesis (Dollard, Doob, Miller, Mowrer, & Sears, 1939) and corollaries of the frustration-aggression hypothesis concerning forms of impulsive and reactive aggression in which excitatory and involuntary processes are likely to play a major role. With the intention of assessing the contribution of irritability and emotional susceptibility in frustrative aggression, irritability and emotional susceptibility were systematically included as factors in experimental studies using a slightly modified version of the Buss (1961) aggression machine paradigm. Subjects were first assigned a memory task and then they were exposed to a frustration manipulation in the form of either a positive or a negative evaluation of their performance by the experimenter. Following these manipulations, they were offered the opportunity to deliver shocks of varying intensities to an innocent confederate who had failed an "extrasensory perception" task.

In a number of studies following this basic methodology aimed at investigating the F-A hypothesis, highly irritable subjects and highly emotionally susceptible subjects selected higher shocks than subjects who were either low on Irritability or low on Emotional Susceptibility, respectively. The pattern was especially strong when subjects had previously been provoked (Caprara, 1982; Caprara & Renzi, 1981; Caprara, Renzi, Alcini, D'Imperio, & Travaglia, 1983). These findings regarding irritability and emotional susceptibility were replicated in studies exploring the influence on subsequent aggression of interpolating events between the instigation and the opportunity to aggress. Interpolated events included exposure to aggression-eliciting cues such as slides portraying weapons (Caprara, Renzi, Alcini, D'Imperio, & Travaglia, 1984; Caprara, Renzi, Amolini, D'Imperio, & Travaglia, 1984), or strenuous physical exercise (i.e., continuous pedaling for 2 minutes on a bicycle ergometer adjusted so that the S's external energy expenditure was 150 W, regardless of the rate of pedaling), which increases sympathetic excitation (Caprara, Renzi, D'Augello, D'Imperio, Rielli, & Travaglia, 1986). The former interpolated activities were selected to explore the weapon effect hypothesis described by Berkowitz (1974) and Berkowitz and La Page (1967), and the latter was intended to test Zillmann's (1979) transfer of excitation hypothesis (see also Zillmann, this volume).

Confirming expectations, these studies of the influence of interpolated events showed that the inclusion of measures of individual differences embedded in studies of other hypotheses expanded the opportunities to critically test, generalize, and refine these hypotheses. In the case of the F-A hypothesis, it was not surprising that highly irritable and highly emotionally susceptible subjects, after having been exposed to minor frustrations like failure on a memory task, selected higher levels of shocks than less irritable and less emotionally susceptible subjects in experiments where other alternative behaviors were precluded. However, the findings that less irritable subjects and less emotionally susceptible subjects also selected higher levels of shocks after failure provided strong evidence in favor of the F-A hypothesis. Also, it was not surprising to find that more irritable and more emotionally susceptible subjects selected higher levels of shocks than less irritable and less emotionally susceptible subjects when exposure to aggressive slides was interpolated between the instigation and the opportunity to aggress. Strong evidence in support of the "weapon effect" hypothesis (Berkowitz, 1974) came from the finding that less irritable and less emotionally susceptible subjects selected higher levels of shocks after being exposed to "aggressive slides" than after being exposed to "neutral slides."

In the case of the transfer of excitation hypothesis, the findings of the experiments in which physical exercise and the associated sympathetic excitation were interpolated between the instigation and the opportunity to aggress suggested the possibility of integrating two different theoretical formulations: (a) the neo-Hullian position (Berkowitz, 1983), which asserts that physical exercise by itself could facilitate subsequent aggression; (b) the transfer of excitation position (Zillmann, 1983), which says that physical exercise would facilitate subsequent aggression when associated with previous instigation. Although the results of the experiment were congruent with the former theory when irritability was a factor (i.e., high-and low-irritable subjects selected higher levels of shocks after physical exercise and independent from previous frustration), the latter theory is more consistent with the data from the experiment in which emotional susceptibility was considered (i.e., highly emotionally susceptible male subjects selected higher levels of shocks, especially when physical exercise followed a previous frustration).

In all these experiments derived from the frustration-aggression hypothesis, both the Irritability and Emotional Susceptibility scales were found to account for a substantial proportion of the variance in aggressive responses. It must be noted, however, that across experiments, irritability accounted for a consistently higher percentage of variance than emotional susceptibility. It may be that, whereas emotional susceptibility is a step removed from specific behavioral manifestations of aggression and closer to a more general emotional lability response, irritability is probably more directly connected with the emergence of aggression.

## RUMINATION AND DISSIPATION

The importance of temporal factors in the expression of aggression has been recognized by many investigators. The importance of temporal factors can be seen in connection with variations in aggressive conduct over the entire time span of an aggressive encounter as well as within the passage of time between an instigation to aggress and the opportunity to aggress (e.g., Bandura, 1973; Caprara, 1986; Goldstein, Davis, & Herman, 1975; Konecni, 1975, 1984). Based on investigations of variability in aggression due to the passage of time between instigation and opportunity to aggress, Konecni (1975) described the phenomena of dissipation and rumination. The former refers to a decrease in aggressive conduct as a function of the time elapsed between the instigation to aggress and the moment when it becomes possible to react aggressively, whereas the latter refers to an increase in the probability of aggression as a function of time between the instigation and the opportunity to aggress.

From a personality perspective, it seemed reasonable to hypothesize that dissipation and rumination could be considered as opposite ends of a single dimension of behavior and, therefore, as opposite poles along a parallel continuum of a personality construct. This personality construct would be characterized at one extreme by an inclination toward rapid dissipation and minimal rumination and at the other extreme by an inclination toward slow dissipation and prolonged rumination. Thus, with the passage of time "dissipators" were expected to resolve ill feelings or desires to retaliate quickly, whereas "ruminators" were expected to maintain or even increase their feelings of ill will and desire for vengeance over time.

To test hypotheses derived from assumptions regarding a personality construct of rumination and dissipation, a new scale was developed. The Rumination-Dissipation scale consisted of 20 items (15 effective and 5 control) and contains items such as "It takes many years for me to get rid of a grudge" and "I do not forgive easily once I am offended." Assessments of psychometric characteristics indicated that the internal consistency and stability of the scale were very satisfactory in both the Italian and English versions (Caprara, Cinanni, D'Imperio, Passerini, Renzi, & Travaglia, 1985; Caprara, 1986). Results of principal components analyses performed on the Italian and English versions confirmed the high stability of the factorial structure of this scale with respect to samples drawn from populations of different languages, nationalities, and cultural backgrounds.

Paralleling the earlier studies of irritability and emotional susceptibility, experimental studies were conducted to clarify the nature of the personality construct in relation to reactive aggressive behavior. First, the role of dissipation-rumination was examined in replications of the previously described experiments aimed at investigating the frustration-aggression hypothesis and its corollaries. In contrast with what was found when irritability and emotional susceptibility were considered, the interaction between the personality trait of rumination-dissipation and experimental manipulation was only marginally significant and the main effect of rumination was significant. In the experiments where frustration and rumination and dissipation were examined, only the main effects due to the personality trait and frustration emerged. In studies of the weapon effect, the influence of the interpolated aggressive slides was mitigated by the fact that, whereas dissipators tended to show the expected effects, ruminators tended to give higher shocks when exposed to the interpolated neutral slides than when exposed to interpolated aggressive slides. In an experiment where physical exercise was interpolated between frustration and opportunity to aggress and where dissipators and ruminators were contrasted, the only significant effect was due to the personality trait.

Because of the outcome of these studies, another set of experiments was developed to further explore the frustration-aggression hypothesis using different procedures. Instead of manipulating frustration through failure in a learning task as in the previous experiments, in this new procedure, threats to self-esteem were used. Subjects were first either threatened or not threatened in their self-esteem by a confederate's negative or positive evaluation, respectively, and then given the opportunity to reciprocate by selecting the level of shock to deliver to the same confederate to communicate to him his mistakes in an extrasensory perception task and by evaluating him for a position on the experimental staff. In the first experiment where irritability, emotional vulnerability (a very similar construct to emotional susceptibility), and rumination were considered, only rumination was significantly associated with higher manifestations of aggression and hostility (Caprara et al., 1987). In another experiment designed to examine the role of rumination-dissipation in association with different time intervals between instigation and the opportunity to retaliate, ruminators were more inclined to aggression or hostility than dissipaters (Caprara, 1986). However, contrary to expectations, there was no significant interaction between time and the trait of rumination-dissipation. Taken together, this series of experiments caused a reconsideration of the original focus on time as a factor in rumination to a focus on the cognitive processes of rumination; that is, the storing and elaboration of resentment that seem to characterize rumination took on greater importance than the temporal aspects of rumination.

## TOWARD A DISTINCTION BETWEEN IMPULSIVE AND COGNITIVE COMPONENTS OF AGGRESSION

An important question arising from data accumulated across studies concerns whether hypothesized relationships and hypothesized distinctions among constructs and the different processes to which they refer are actually supported. With regard to correlations among scales, in several studies Emotional Susceptibility and Irritability showed a correlation of approximately.60. The Dissipation-Rumination scale correlated approximately.30 and approximately.65 with Emotional Susceptibility and Irritability, respectively. Thus, it seems plausible from these results that irritability and emotional susceptibility share a common dimensional link to emotional lability. This hypothesis was confirmed by multivariate analyses, including canonical correlation and conjoint factor analysis, originally conducted on the two scales (Caprara, Cinanni, D'Imperio, Passerini, Renzi, & Travaglia, 1985). In contrast, Dissipation-Rumination seems to manifest a stronger link to the "offensive" aspects of emotional lability than to the "defensive" ones, as suggested by its relatively low correlation with Emotional Susceptibility.

With regard to experimental studies, comparisons between experiments with different operational definitions of frustration (i.e., failure on a memory task vs. a self-esteem threat), as well as the comparisons between the relevant role of dissipation-rumination and the marginal role of emotional susceptibility and irritability in those studies using threat to self-esteem as a frustrative event, led to an evaluation of the dissimilarities of experiments and of the dissimilarities between personality characteristics to gain greater insight into the underlying psychological processes determining the emergence of aggression.

The role of both irritability and emotional susceptibility emerged as decisive in those experiments where impulsive or reactive aggression was the primary outcome measure when subjects were required to respond immediately after the frustrative event. In contrast, the role of dissipation-rumination emerged as decisive in the experiment where cognitive processing was a prominent factor and the opportunity to respond aggressively was delayed. It was not surprising that both highly irritable subjects and highly emotionally susceptible subjects selected higher shocks immediately after frustration than less irritable subjects and less emotionally susceptible subjects, given that other behavioral choices were precluded. The fact that the recipient of shocks was an innocent confederate appears to be a further indicator that the procedure used is appropriate for examining a kind of aggression whose release is primarily an indicator of the emotional control of the respondent. Furthermore, it was not surprising that, in spite of obvious differences, highly irritable and highly emotionally susceptible subjects behaved in similar ways in situations that demonstrated their common inadequacy to resist excitation and to maintain full emotional self-control in the presence of frustration. In those experiments where failure was manipulated, it is likely that there was a quasi-automatic association between the experience of failure and the increasing level of shocks delivered to an innocent confederate.

On the other hand, in the experiment in which the self-esteem threat was manipulated, it is likely that the subjects were aware of the possibility of retaliation they were offered in the form of delivering shocks or denigrating their own provoking agent. It is likely that the nature of the instigation and the opportunity to retaliate against the provoking agent significantly reduced the role of impulsiveness by altering the resistance of the subjects to aggress from the beginning. It is also likely that greater awareness of the situation as a provocation entailed a variety of cognitive processes in perceiving, attributing, and evaluating the inequity of the insult, as well as reaching a decision on the appropriate response. In fact, it should be obvious that cognitive processes are implied in rumination where a subject stores feelings regarding the suffered offense and waits for an opportunity to retaliate. In contrast, these cognitive processes, by definition, play only a minor role in irritability and in emotional susceptibility.

## INVESTIGATING ATTITUDES TOWARD VIOLENCE

Concern over the multiple manifestations of violence in the differing experimental and natural settings has led to an examination of the possible mechanisms and processes that can lead to the justification of violent conduct. To develop an objective indicator of proneness toward violence, an examination of the role of various attitudes toward violence was made. The *Tolerance Toward Violence* scale was developed as part of a larger study financed by the Italian Government to investigate young people's attitudes toward violence (LABOS, 1989). The scale contains 29 items (26 effective and 3 control) formulated on the basis of their relationship to three criteria: (a) violence with ideological and political connotations, (b) violence against people and their property, and (c) apparently gratuitous violence for its own sake.

Sample items from the scale are: "Because society is basically violent it does not make any sense to punish the single individual who resorts to violence" and "Today there are many more reasons to resort to violence than in the past."

With regard to validity, results of principal components' analysis performed on both Italian and English versions with different groups of subjects supported the presence of a general factor underlying the various statements (Caprara, Cinanni, & Mazzotti, 1989; Caprara,

Mazzotti, & Prezza, 1990. Internal consistency and stability appear satisfactory for both versions of the scale. However, the monofactorial structure of the present scale was less clear than for scales developed previously, such as Irritability, Emotional Susceptibility, and Dissipation-Rumination. It is likely that this could be due to the lower specificity of the construct as well as to the greater variability of item choices that concern either general patterns of behavior or evaluations of one's own behavior. With regard to construct validity, Tolerance Toward Violence (LABOS, 1989) was found to correlate with the probability of being involved as victims or as agents in violent acts seen as being under an external locus of control and the tendency to justify recourse to violent acts to defend one's own image and reputation. In various studies, Tolerance Toward Violence showed correlations of approximately .45 with Irritability, .40 with Rumination, and .15 with Emotional Susceptibility. All these correlations seem to suggest a more complex network of attitudes, dispositions, and mental representations in which recourse to violence appears to be a prevalent and self-perpetuating strategy.

## THE ROLE OF GUILT: AS AN INHIBITOR OR FACILITATOR OF AGGRESSION?

More recently the research focus was turned toward studying possible mechanisms mitigating aggressive conduct. In this regard, it seemed important to examine the role of guilt and guilt feelings in the emergence of aggressive behavior. Historically, psychologists working from many different theoretical perspectives have examined the guilt–aggression phenomenon without coming to any agreement. Although most of the experimental literature (i.e., Fincham & Jaspars, 1979; McGraw, 1987) has focused on the antecedents of guilt and has emphasized its inhibitory role in aggressive conduct, in the psychoanalytic tradition different authors (i.e., Freud, 1915; Klein, 1948) have underlined the role that guilt might play in determining aggression and in transforming feelings of hatred, envy, and fear into gratitude, depression, or more subtle forms of hostility.

More recently, Zahn-Waxler and Kochanska (1989) proposed a multidimensional construct of guilt; its main phenomenological aspects are feelings of responsibility for others and feelings of self-blame and concern over the harmful consequences of one's own actions. In their sociocognitive developmental approach, guilt has a functional or dysfunctional outcome for individual adjustment primarily depending on whether it is ultimately "empathy guided" or "fear driven." Therefore, in contrast with much of the experimental literature but in accord with the psychoanalytic tradition and the contemporary sociocognitive developmental approach, there seem to be two different dimensions for considering the phenomenology of guilt rather than one.

Based on this premise, a series of studies was conducted to clarify the controversial role that individual differences in proneness to guilt could play in relation to aggression. First, a study by Caprara, Perugini, Pastorelli, and Barbaranelli (1990) was completed in which the dual nature of guilt was confirmed. In this study, a pool of items was developed according to an empirical definition of "what is prototypical of guilt." This item pool was then factor analyzed, with two main factors emerging. The first factor was called *Fear of Punishment* and the second termed *Need for Reparation*.

Based on various analyses, two new scales were constructed. The Fear of Punishment scale consisted of 30 items (23 effective and 7 control) and included such items as: "I sometimes feel I am about to be punished" and "I sometimes experience feelings of guilt." This scale measured a proneness to experience feelings of persecution, oppression, and tension linked to the anticipation and fear of impending punishment. The Need for Reparation scale, which consisted of 20 items (15 effective and 5 control), contained such items as: "When faced with my mistakes, I want to make up for them as soon as possible" and "Sooner or later the bad things that one has done come to light." This scale measured a tendency to experience feelings of remorse, embarrassment, disturbance, tension, and desire for justice linked to the need for reparation of the negative results of guilt-eliciting actions.

Statistical analysis confirmed the internal consistency and reliability of the two scales. More recently, a study conducted on a sample of American students (Caprara, Manzy, & Perugini, 1992) confirmed the results obtained using the Italian version of the scales. The English version of the guilt scales also measured the two distinctive dimensions of guilt and met the required psychometric characteristics regarding internal consistency, reliability, and discriminative validity. In both the Italian and the U.S. studies, the correlation between the two scales was approximately .25. In relation to our other scales, the Fear of Punishment scale showed correlations of approximately .70 with Emotional Susceptibility, .55 with Irritability, .40 with Rumination, and .25 with Tolerance Toward Violence. Need for Reparation correlated of approximately .40 with Emotional Susceptibility, .15 with Irritability, .05 with Rumination, and -15 with Tolerance Toward Violence. In summary, our studies showed a differentiated pattern of relations between the dimensions of guilt and the "amplification" constructs of aggressive conduct. What may make the two forms of guilt different may be the "locus of control" over the consequences of one's own perception of wrongdoing.

In the case of fear of punishment, one worries about the consequences of his or her wrongdoing as if he or she had no control over them. In the case of need for reparation, one takes responsibility of his or her wrongdoing and is actively engaged in mastering the consequences. In the first case, one is at the mercy of "forces" he or she does not control; in the second case, there is the belief that he or she can do something to repair the act or to reestablish equity and fairness. Different feelings, beliefs, and expectations may, therefore, be associated with the experience of guilt. Thus, fear of punishment would correspond to "fear driven" guilt, and need for reparation would correspond to "empathy guided" guilt.

## THE STRUCTURAL LEVEL: RELATIONS AMONG INDICATORS OF AGGRESSIVE BEHAVIOR

The empirical data that has been collected repeatedly forces a reconsideration of the essential nature of the personality dimensions underlying aggression and their relations. First of all, the high correlation between the Emotional Susceptibility and Irritability scales has led to the hypothesis of a common second-order factor. This hypothesis was only partially confirmed by the multivariate analyses originally completed on the two scales (Caprara, Cinanni, D'Imperio, Passerini, Renzi, & Travaglia, 1985).

A second line of inquiry concerned the link between irritability and emotional susceptibility, on the one hand, and dissipation-rumination, on the other. It was hypothesized that it might be worth distinguishing between those personality variables, such as irritability and emotional susceptibility, which prove decisive in situations in which impulsive-reactive aggression is under examination, and those personality variables, such as dissipation-rumination, which are operative when less impulsive aggression is considered. In the latter case, it is clearly implied that a wider variety of cognitive processes related to intentionality and voluntary control of aggression, as well as attribution of causality and responsibility, might be operative. It is important to note, however, that it is unlikely that these dimensions belong to completely separate systems. An examination of the various correlations led to the assignment of crucial importance to irritability for it correlates positively and significantly with emotional susceptibility and with dissipation-rumination, whereas, emotional susceptibility is not highly correlated with dissipation-rumination.

It is also plausible that the construct referred to as emotional susceptibility largely reflects internal components and dynamics of a primarily temperamental nature; and what has been termed *Dissipation-Rumination* may correspond to traits and attitudes that reflect adaptation styles or strategies that are anchored to specific social experiences and training. The pattern of correlations among the dimensions of personality studied has become more complex and intriguing with the inclusion of the variables of Tolerance Toward Violence, Need for Reparation, and Fear of Punishment scales. To clarify the links between these various factors in aggressive behavior, two preliminary studies were conducted on small groups of Italian and American subjects (Caprara & Pastorelli, 1989; Caprara, Perugini, Pastorelli, & Barbaranelli, 1990). In these studies, subjects were administered all the scales with the exception of Need for Reparation. A more recent study (Caprara et al., 1992) was conducted on a larger group of American subjects; in this case, subjects were administered all of our scales, including Need for Reparation. In all of these studies, following the correlational analyses between the scales, second-order factor analyses (Loehlin, 1987) and latent variable model analysis (Bentler, 1980; Joreskog, 1978; Loehlin, 1987) were completed. Based on the two preliminary studies, the second-order factor analyses identified two main factors: The Emotional Susceptibility and Fear of Punishment scales loaded primarily on the first factor, whereas Rumination and Tolerance Toward Violence loaded primarily on the second factor. The Irritability scale loaded in an intermediate position.

The theoretical model relating these constructs that emerged from the latent variable analyses was very similar in both studies. In these two studies, emotional susceptibility was identified as a basic antecedent of irritability and also of fear of punishment. Irritability had a direct impact on both rumination and tolerance toward violence, and rumination had an impact on fear of punishment. There was also an additional influence of rumination on tolerance toward violence in the American study. Guilt as measured by fear of punishment was positively associated with rumination.

In a more recent study (Caprara et al., 1992), which also included the Need for Reparation scale, we expected to find support for the bidimensional hypothesis of guilt and, in particular, elements supporting an antagonistic role of need for reparation with respect to the emergence of aggression. Results of this study substantially confirmed those obtained in the preliminary studies; that is, a second-order factor analysis (Loehlin, 1987) was completed using the varimax rotation and the two-factor solution proved to be optimal, with the two factors jointly explaining 70% of the variance. As represented graphically in Fig. 6.1, tolerance toward violence (.816), irritability (.779), rumination (.751), and fear of punishment (.501) primarily loaded on the first factor. The first factor seemed to reflect a general dimension of justification and expression of aggressive behavior; thus, it was labeled *proneness to aggression*. Emotional susceptibility (.792), need for reparation (.763), fear of punishment (.663), and irritability (.440) loaded primarily on the second factor. This factor seemed to reflect a general dimension of lack of emotional control and of pronounced emotional responsivity in the presence of frustrating and aversive situations; thus, it was labeled *emotional responsivity*.

It is important to note the different placement of the sense of guilt dimensions with respect to the two extracted factors. Fear of Punishment and Need for Reparation mainly differed from each other with regard to their loading on the first factor. The former loaded positively on the *Proneness to Aggression* factor; the latter loaded negatively on the same factor. Both scales loaded highly positively on the second factor as well.

A structural equation model approach was then used to test the hypothetical of relations between latent variables. The hypothetical model was evaluated using the normal theory, maximum likelihood

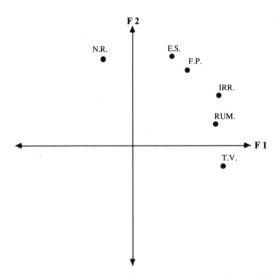

FIG. 6.1. Graphical representation of second-order factor analysis. (*Note.* Solution with Varimax rotation.) F1 = Proneness to Aggression; F2 = Emotional Responsivity; E.S. = Emotional Susceptibility; F.P. = Fear of Punishment; IRR = Irritability; N.R. = Need for Reparation; RUM = Rumination; T.V. = Tolerance toward Violence.

strategy, as implemented in the EQS program (Bentler, 1989). This statistical technique analyzes the relations between variables as represented in a covariance matrix. It should be stressed, however, that such correlational and cross-sectional data do not allow for causal interpretations (see Cliff, 1983). Therefore, the interpretation of results is mostly conjecture and needs further empirical work for clarification and verification. With that caveat in mind, the model depicted in Fig. 6.2 fits the data very well (chi-square-3.47, $df = 7$, $p = .84$, Normed Fit Index $= .98$), with all path coefficients being significant. This model adds new and significant information to earlier models based on this research. In particular, the insertion of a nonrecursive path between Fear of Punishment and Rumination must be noted, whereas the previously identified path directed to fear of punishment from rumination suggests that the more people ruminate the more they fear punishment. The new path aimed at rumination from fear of punishment implies that, in turn, once fear of punishment increases, the inclination to ruminate is reduced. However, these two paths can also be considered by looking first at fear of punishment: The more one is afraid of punishment, the less rumination there is, and the less rumination there is, the less one is afraid of

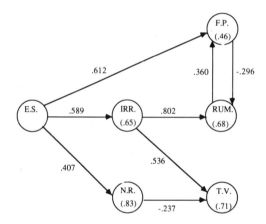

Chi-square= 3.47   d.f.= 7   p= .84
Normed Fit Index (NFI) = .98
Goodness of Fit Index (GFI) = .988
Adjusted Goodness of Fit Index (AGFI) = . 964
Root Mean Square residuals (RMS) = .032

FIG. 6.2. Model of relations between latent variables. (*Note.* Numbers in parentheses mean unique portions of variance of the constructs.) E.S. = Emotional Susceptibility; F.P. = Fear of Punishment; IRR = Irritability; N.R. = Need for Reparation; RUM = Rumination; T.V. = Tolerance Toward Violence.

punishment. Thus, the more guilt becomes associated with a fear of potential sanctions, the less likely a subject will maintain hostile feelings over time. However, the more hostile feelings are maintained over time, the more a subject may fear potential punishment. In sum, fear of punishment seemed to be a moderating mechanism for rumination, and rumination an amplifier for fear of punishment.

In addition to the previously discussed nonrecursive path, the important role of irritability should also be noted. Irritability seems to play a critical role in the transformation of emotional susceptibility into rumination and tolerance toward violence, which are both strictly associated with the deliberate expression and moral justification of hostile behavior. The Need for Reparation scale was linked to Emotional Susceptibility as well as to Tolerance Toward Violence, suggesting that emotional susceptibility is an antecedent of need for reparation, whereas need for reparation serves as a mitigator of tolerance toward violence.

## THE SEMANTIC SPACE OF AGGRESSIVE
## PHENOMENOLOGY AT A DESCRIPTIVE LEVEL

The second-order factor analysis completed on the scales (see Fig. 6.1) described in the previous section suggested that there may be a circumplex order among the various forms of aggressive conduct. A circumplex model is indicative of a particular pattern of relations among variables such that they are better represented in a bidimensional space rather than on a line, with all the variables represented as points of a circumplex with the axes of opposing variables being represented by the two factors (Wiggins, 1979; Wiggins, Steiger, & Gaelick, 1981). The primary advantages of a circumplex model over a linear one are its representativeness and its potential for predictive precision. The greater representatives of the circumplex model is achieved by capturing the complexity of the phenomenon under investigation. At the same time, the capacity for predictive precision of a circumplex model in comparison to a linear one is increased notably because various aggregation points of the variables are identifiable as a function of differentiated associations with respect to external criteria. With that in mind, the plausibility of a circumplex structure of aggressive phenomenology was investigated (Perugini, 1993a, 1993b).

### Theoretical Rationale

The rationale behind the approach taken had as a basic assumption that a distinction between two different forms of aggression had been effectively made in the field of aggression research. Although the two forms of aggression have been given different labels by different investigators (e.g., reactive and proactive by Dodge & Coie, 1987; hostile and instrumental by Berkowitz, 1989, and by Feshbach, 1964), and although distinctions have been made with respect to various research criteria (e.g., stimuli, targets, functional relations), there is sufficient agreement on the basic characteristics of the two forms of aggression. One type of aggression (hostile or reactive) is characterized by a strong affective-emotional component; the other (instrumental or proactive) is less affective and much more planned and methodical. Moreover, the studies outlined earlier led to the identification, by means of psychometric scales, of various forms of aggressive dispositions that were congruent with the notion of two general forms of aggressiveness. The almost general convergence of research investigating these two dimensions of aggression, coupled with the studies described earlier, suggested the possibility of researching a general reference structure to encompass the entire phenomenon of aggressiveness. The advantages of such a structure are evident both as a point of reference for studies examining particular aspects of aggressiveness and for a theoretical synthesis of different laboratory paradigms. The central theoretical hypothesis to be assessed was that aggressive conduct is largely describable through its relative composition with respect to two general and basic factors.

The first of these general factors is Negative Affect. This factor corresponds to the capacity to handle negative feelings and is associated to the level of responsivity to various stimuli, that are potentially noxious and frustrating. Whereas high Negative Affect is characterized by nervousness, anguish, and sadness, low Negative Affect is characterized by stability, optimism, and cheerfulness. In mutating the same notion used by Watson and Tellegen (1985) we intended to take into account our previous findings on "Emotional Responsivity" posing greater emphasis on the "negative" connotations of emotional involvement. Also, we intended to incorporate in this notion what in the five-factor model of personality traits has been indicated as Neuroticism (McCrae & Costa, 1987; Peabody & Goldberg, 1989).

The second hypothesized basic and general factor is Self-Centered versus Other-Centered Interpersonal Orientation. This factor corresponds to positive versus negative attitudes in interpersonal behavior. Whereas Self-Centered Interpersonal Orientation is characterized by despotism, indifference, and arrogance, Other-Centered Interpersonal Orientation is characterized by altruism, sensitivity, and charity. This factor is similar to what we previously indicated as "Proneness to Aggression," but is broadened to include what in the five-factor model of personality traits has been indicated as Agreeableness (McCrae &

Costa, 1987), and in the Wiggins (1979) circumplex model of interpersonal traits has been indicated as Love.

From an empirical perspective, it was assumed that, at least in an initial phase, it would be possible to operationalize the theoretical hypotheses of two general factors by using a pool of adjectives representative of aggressive phenomenology. To develop the pool of adjectives, a strategy consistent with Cattell's (1945) sedimentation hypothesis was adopted. This has been the approach that has provided the basis for much of the contemporary research on personality, and, in particular, research on the so-called "Big Five" dimensions of personality (see Digman, 1989; Goldberg, 1981; John, 1990; McCrae & Costa, 1985). The sedimentation hypothesis assumes that the most salient and socially relevant individual differences in a person's life will be codified in their language. The more important a personal difference, the more probable it will be expressed with a single word. Thus, in light of this hypothesis, natural language can be considered as containing an exhaustive grouping of attributes of individual differences in personality with respect to the most relevant social manifestations of personality. It follows, then, that because aggressive phenomenology is socially salient it should be possible to find all its principal characteristics described by adjectives in a language dictionary. Once this pool of terms has been identified, a first test of the hypotheses regarding the two general factors of aggressiveness could be conducted based on the self-evaluative responses of an adequate number of subjects. It is apparent that this work is primarily research on the semantic space of aggressiveness. Nevertheless, in light of the number of studies that indicate the convergence between the underlying structure of semantic space and behavioral space (see Gifford & O'Connor, 1987) and between the structures underlying self-evaluative space and other-evaluative space (see Peabody & Goldberg, 1989; Hampson, 1990), it was hypothesized that any conclusions reached from this work may represent a first broad theoretical conceptualization of aggressive conduct.

An empirical representation of this consideration benefits from the use of a circumplex model as the reference structure; that is, it can be hypothesized that the various forms of aggressive conduct can be placed along the circumference of the circle that encompasses the two axes representing the two general factors in question, namely, Negative Affect and Interpersonal Orientation. Moreover, it should be possible to place all the different forms of aggressive conduct in the space generated by these two factors. The following is a description of the first phases of the construction of a new empirical instrument, the Adjective Checklist of Aggressive Phenomenology (ACAP), developed to operationalize theoretical hypotheses regarding a two-factor circumplex model of aggression.

Development of Adjective Checklist of Aggressive
Phenomenology (ACAP)

The initial pool of adjectives used for developing the scale was comprised of 492 adjectives chosen on the basis of their usefulness in describing personality for research focused on verifying the factorial structure of the Big Five dimensions of personality and identifying the pool of adjectives most useful in describing personality (see Caprara & Perugini, 1990). Thus the original aims of this work was not focused in the same area as that of the present research. This pool of 492 useful adjectives was formed in a series of phases. In the first phase, all adjectives in an Italian abridged dictionary (8,534) were evaluated by four expert judges on the basis of several criteria. In particular, the criterion of the "usefulness" of an adjective for describing personality was employed to reduce the initial pool of adjectives to 1,337. In the second phase, these 1,337 adjectives were judged by 22 lay judges. On the basis of a 5-step Likert Scale, they were asked for quantitative judgments with respect to four different criteria: (a) Clarity of Meaning, (b) Utility for Describing Personality, (c) Social Desirability, and (d) Frequency of Use. However, only the rating of Utility for Describing Personality was used as a rationale for selecting the adjectives at this second phase. Based on these ratings the 492 adjectives were retained, and an average interjudge correlation of .25 and a composite score reliability (Cronbach's Alpha) of .88 was obtained on those ratings.

In a third phase, these retained adjectives were presented to 220 subjects with instructions to evaluate their own personality using a 7-step Likert scale ranging from "Not at all (0)" to "Completely (6)." These data were then used in the original research on the Big Five personality dimensions (see Caprara & Perugini, 1990) and later provided the basis for the present research on aggression.

First, on the basis of theoretical considerations and empirical considerations, four initial pools of adjectives to define each pole of the two dimensions were selected. Theoretical selection involved choosing those that were believed to potentially define the pole. Empirical selection involved choosing adjectives to maximize correlations between items defining opposite poles and minimizing correlations between adjectives defining the independent or orthogonal poles. On the basis of this strategy, eight adjectives were chosen as marker variables for each of the four poles (see Perugini, 1993a, 1993b). The adjectives were then aggregated for each of the poles and the correlations among the four aggregated scores were examined. Analysis of the principal components of the four groupings clearly confirmed the existence of the two independent bipolar dimensions. The remaining 460 adjectives were then correlated with the four poles formed by the selected marker adjective variables. From this, 142 of the 492 adjectives were chosen as being sufficiently in line with the two-factor solution. On the basis of theoretical considerations and similarity of meaning with adjectives selected empirically, another 40 adjectives were added to the 142. These additional 40 adjectives were not present on the original list of 492 adjectives selected on the basis of "Utility." The entire pool of 182 adjectives was then administered to a sample of 212 university students (73 males and 139 females) with an average age of 20.88 (s.d. = 5.33). As shown in Table 6.1, the four poles were identified relative to the two general hypothesized factors. Moreover, both the pattern of correlations between the four poles and the result of a principal components analysis (see Table 6.2) established the adequacy of a bidimensional space for representing the data.

Additionally, four intermediate groupings were identified between two-pole couples at a distance of 45 degrees from the two referenced poles. To verify the level of circumplexity of the structure, the analysis strategy proposed by Wiggins et al. (1981) was conducted. Results of this analysis substantially confirm the plausibility of a circumplex model. The percentage of variance explained by the circumplex compo-

**TABLE 6.1**
**Marker Adjectives for the Four Poles**

| Negative Affect | |
| --- | --- |
| High | Low |
| Hesitating (Titubante) | Constant (Costante) |
| Pessimist (Pessimista) | Stable (Stabile) |
| Tormented (Tormentato) | Cheerful (Allegro) |
| Nervous (Nervoso) | Strong (Forte) |
| Unsatisfied (Insoddisfatto) | Optimist (Ottimista) |
| Anguished (Angosciato) | Happy (Felice) |
| Sad (Triste) | Pleased (Contento) |
| Tense (Teso) | Sure (Sicuro) |

| Interpersonal Orientation | |
| --- | --- |
| Self-centered | Other-centered |
| Supercilious (Strafottente) | Tenderhearted (Sensibile) |
| Arrogant (Arrogante) | Nonviolent (Nonviolento) |
| Proud (Superbo) | Humble (Umile) |
| Rude (Rude) | Condescending (Condiscendente) |
| Despotic (Dispotico) | Docile (Docile) |
| Indifferent (Menegreghista) | Merciful (Clemente) |
| Pitiless (Spietato) | Charitable (Caritatevole) |
| Tyrannical (Tirannico) | Humane (Umano) |

TABLE 6.2
Correlations and Principal Component Analysis
for the Four Poles

| | Correlations | | | |
|---|---|---|---|---|
| | N.A(h) | N.A.(1) | I.O.(s) | I.O.(o) |
| N.A.(h) | 1 | | | |
| N.A.(1) | −.81 | 1 | | |
| I.O.(s) | −.17 | .10 | 1 | |
| I.O.(o) | −.05 | .02 | −.64 | 1 |

| Principal Component Analysis | | | |
|---|---|---|---|
| Factors | Eigenvalues | % of variance | |
| F1 | 1.870 | 46.8 | |
| F2 | 1.600 | 40.0 | |
| F3 | .348 | 8.7 | |
| F4 | .181 | 4.5 | |
| Loadings | F1 | F2 | |
| N.A.(h) | −.951 | .041 | |
| N.A.(1) | .946 | −.013 | |
| I.O.(s) | .082 | .911 | |
| I.O.(o) | .138 | −.902 | |

Note.   N.A.(h) = Negative Affect high. N.A.(l) = Negative Affect low. I.O.(s) = Interpersonal Orientation self-centered. I.O.(o) = Interpersonal Orientation other-centered.

nent (70.1%) clearly prevailed over the other components (general: 2.4 %; polar: 11.5%; orthogonal: 11.0%; specific: 5.1%) and confirmed the basic circumplex positioning of the variables.

Once the level of circumplexity of the structure was determined, a technique similar to that used by Wiggins, Trapnell, and Phillips (1988) was developed, which allowed for the plotting of adjectives on a well-defined theoretical structure. Two factors defined by the four theoretical poles were extracted and correlated with all adjectives. Then, using the formula for the transformation of Cartesian coordinates into polar coordinates, three values for each adjective were obtained. These values indicated, respectively, their position in degrees on the circumplex sphere, the ray-vector that defines the sphere including their position, and their communality within the circumplex model. On the basis of the length of the ray-vector, adjectives were assigned to three different bands of prototypes (most prototypical, above .45; intermediate, from .36 to .45, least prototypical, below .35) relative to the phenomenon under investigation (aggression). Adjectives with ray-vectors greater than .25 (165 out of 182) were then retained. Figure 6.3 shows several examples of the placement of these adjectives.

Because this research is still in progress, any definitive conclusions

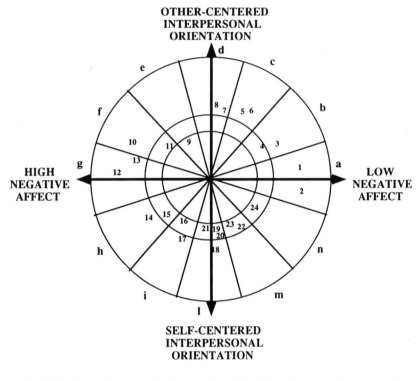

FIG. 6.3. Circumplex model of ACAP (Adjectives Checklist of Aggressive Phenomenology: Examples of positioning of some adjectives. (Note: Letters from "a" to "n" mean belonging of adjectives to slices.)

would be premature. Nevertheless, some results are worthy of note. Above all, the theoretical hypothesis regarding the adequacy of two general dimensions for encompassing aggressive phenomenology seems to be substantially corroborated by our second-order factorial studies. In fact, the primary characteristics of aggressive conduct can be represented in the semantic space defined by the two factors.

Before considering additional attempts to further examine the nature of these two factors, it is important first to comment on their fundamental differences. The *Negative Affect* factor can be usefully considered as a measure of the quality of emotional involvement in terms of negative feelings (see Watson & Tellegen, 1985) and of the capacity for emotional control. In contrast, the *Interpersonal Orientation* factor can be usefully considered as a measure of the direction of the prevalent attitude in interpersonal relations in terms of attitude toward others and of attitude against others.

Thus, considering aggressive conduct to be decomposable into two fundamental elements (Negative Affect and Interpersonal Orientation) seems justified. In this way, a characterization of all aggressive conduct at a descriptive-semantic level and in terms of the relative degree of involvement with respect to the two fundamental dimensions seems possible. Although data are not yet available to relate the factorial solution of the ACAP to those of the other scales from this laboratory, the remarkable resemblance between the two factors extracted in the two different research strategies is notable. A study to thoroughly examine these relations is planned; and it is expected that there will be a high degree of congruence between the two factorial solutions. Finally, it is important to emphasize that the proposed two-dimensional basic structure does not imply that other theoretical differentiations are erroneous, but, on the contrary, the current formulation may allow for a very high hierarchical level of conceptualization to bring the different formulations together within a common framework.

## THE DYNAMIC LEVEL:
## ROLE OF TEMPORAL PATTERNS

As noted by many authors (e.g., Goldstein et al., 1975; Potegal, 1979), temporal patterns deserve greater attention as far as the dynamics of aggression are concerned. There are a number of reasons for this. Daily events reported in the popular media and clinical experience cry out for research that revises the relatively "static" concept of aggressive conduct proposed by traditional laboratory research. Indeed, all aggressive conduct from the triggering event to the ultimate completion may be said to take place in a temporal context. Aggressive conduct clearly has a variable duration. Moreover, it may vary in intensity and quality during the time span between initial provocation and ultimate conclusion. Thus, whereas psychological research has generally treated aggression as a static concept, primarily examining its magnitude or initial probability following certain antecedents or instigators, it is clear that aggression is a dynamic process that develops and varies over time. Unfortunately, there are very few empirical or experimental studies that have attempted to shed light on the processes and mechanisms that contribute to the regulation of aggressive conduct over a span of time.

In the laboratory situation, one finding frequently obtained with the Buss aggression machine paradigm is an upward drift of the shock intensity selected by subjects across trials. Assuming that such an effect is not an artifact, Goldstein et al. (1975) referred to it as a case of escalation of aggression in humans. However, it remains controversial whether such an escalation reflects an increase in the drive to behave aggressively or a decrease in the inner restraints that most people have internalized against aggression; that is, a reduction in moral and social inhibition to aggress. Because it is very likely that different mechanisms may be operative in different situations as well as in different subjects, it is doubtful that the term escalation of aggression is fully adequate to cover all the mechanisms and processes that may be implied, especially in humans.

In attempting to account for escalation of aggression in humans, Goldstein et al. (1975) proposed a number of possible mechanisms referring to different theoretical frameworks, such as the frustration-aggression theory, the adaptation level theory, the cognitive conflict theory, and the disinhibition and deindividuation theory. Given the Buss aggression paradigm in which the subject is led to shock an experimental confederate over successive trials where there has been, or has not been, a prior instigation to aggress, all the preceding explanations could account for the upward drift of shock intensities selected by subjects over trials. Thus, for example, the successive mistakes of the confederate may represent new sources of frustration that intensify subsequent aggression. Similarly, subsequent shocks used by subjects may become more intense if the unsuccessful consequences of initial shocks results in a perception of a decrease in their effectiveness in influencing the performance of the confederate. Selection of shocks of increasing intensity may be justified by minimizing their painful consequences or by devaluating the target. Subjects may also become progressively habituated or less inhibited with respect to delivering shocks to another person. Thus, these various interpretations of the increase in intensity of selected shocks across trials do not appear mutually exclusive, nor do they exclude the various reinforcement explanations that have been proposed, mainly in animal studies (e.g., Knutson, Fordyce, & Anderson, 1980; Potegal, 1979).

In some of the studies in this laboratory, the escalation hypothesis has been investigated with the aim of examining the role of dispositions and situations in determining whether any upward drift of shock intensity used by subjects over trials would occur in the presence and absence of previous instigation to aggress from a failure experience. From a dispositional hypothesis, individual differences in irritability and in emotional susceptibility (Caprara, Renzi, Alcini, D'Imperio, & Travaglia, 1984), and in rumination–dissipation were taken into account in an assessment of post-instigation situational variables; that is, the effect of previous instigation on escalation of aggression was examined in a paradigm where four different conditions were interpolated between the instigation to aggress and the opportunity to aggress: these four different conditions included (a) an interval of 10 minutes, (b) the projection of 10 aggressive slides, (c) the projection of 10 neutral slides, and (d) physical exercise. Following instigation, it was found that, with few exceptions, all groups increased the level of shocks used across trials independent of the interpolating condition. However, under conditions of no instigation, most groups did not increase the level of shocks selected to present to the confederate across trials. Moreover, individual differences in irritability, emotional susceptibility, and in rumination–dissipation did not influence the escalation of shock intensity across trials.

Although the results of this research did not suggest a role for personality factors in the emergence of escalation, it may be argued that subjects who have been exposed to failure experiences in a previous task may be more inclined to increase the intensity of electric shocks they administer to an experimental confederate over trials as a means of avoiding another experience of failure. Thus, as instrumentally motivated aggression, administering electric shocks to the other person is a form of aggression that increases in intensity over trials as a result of the previous instigation. Such an analysis suggests that the escalation effect is not a mere artifact induced by the Buss machine per se.

Without a doubt, the escalation phenomena underscore the role played by temporal factors in the dynamics of aggressive behavior. However, whereas most research on aggression has studied short-term episodes in which instigators precede aggressive consequences by 10 to 15 minutes, it is likely that the probability and the intensity of aggression would vary significantly depending on the time interval that separates the instigation to aggress from the actual opportunity to aggress. In addition, various factors may interact with the duration of the time interval with regard to the initiation of aggressive conduct. For example, the type of processes (excitation and/or cognitive) primarily involved in the task, the type of instigating stimuli, the forms of aggressive acts available, the sociocultural context in which the aggressor finds her or himself, and various personality dispositions could all interact with the interval between the instigation and the opportunity to aggress. Based on research from this laboratory, it is important to consider the modulating role played by personality dispositions. In the case of aggressive conduct that develops in a very short period of time, the personality dimensions that seem to be most important in modulating aggressive conduct are those in which the role of arousal control processes are greatest—namely *Irritability* and *Emotional Susceptibility*. Probably in these rapid reaction situations the role played by arousal processes is much greater than that played by cognitive processes, although any rigid distinction would be questionable.

In contrast, as the time interval between instigation and aggressive behavior increases, a greater role seems to be played by processes of storage, recall, and elaboration. Thus, in those situations in which there is a very long interval between provocation and opportunity to aggress, the role played by personality dimensions that relate to specific regulatory processes and cognitive mediation, such as Rumination–Dissipation, should be greater. Clearly, the possibility of ruminating over wrongs experienced implies a fundamental role played by cognitive processes both at the level of recall and elaboration and at the level of legitimizing with respect to personal normative standards, as well as intentions to vindicate, and the desire to re-establish equity and justice.

Although speculative, the time lapse between instigation and action may be equally important for the elaboration of personal conduct and "reprovable" acts. In this sense the temporal dimension undoubtedly constitutes a fundamental aspect of the assignment of blame. The assignment of blame seems to involve processes, more or less conscious, linked to the elaboration of one's own wrongdoing, which, on one hand, leads to feelings of persecution (as in the case of fear of punishment) and, on the other, to the will to put into action atonement-type behaviors (as in the case of need for reparation). From the point of view of the temporal dimension, guilt seems to be, at least in part, a phenomenon of rumination. In this case, "rumination" refers to an injury (real or imagined) caused to others and not necessarily an injury experienced by others.

It is important to understand the various outcomes of the different processes implied by the personality dimensions identified in the present research. In this regard, it is useful to refer to empirical results deriving from the structural equation model tested previously and presented in Fig. 6.2. In particular, the importance of the nonrecursive path between Dissipation–Rumination and Fear of Punishment is emphasized. It is reasonable to suppose that the temporal dimension of aggressive conduct plays a decisive role in the dynamics of the relationship between these two constructs; that is, the process by which an increase in rumination is transformed into an increase in fear of punishment, which, in turn, can lead to a decrease in rumination and a decrease in fear of punishment, which then may result in an increase in rumination, which, when it reaches a certain level can again results in an increase in fear of punishment, is comprehensible only within a temporal dimension. By necessity, such a pattern must transcend a single episode in which the subject has caused an injury and, thus, is fearful of the consequences deriving from his or her act (fear of punishment) or has experienced an injury and is meditating vengeance (rumination). This recursive process must imply a network of episodes and behavioral outcomes dependent on the dynamic equilibrium between emotional and behavioral states connected to the various situations in which the subject finds himself.

## CONCLUSIONS

This program of research began with the intention of measuring aggressiveness. A series of factorial studies led to the identification of two dimensions of individual differences that related to aggressivity: Irritability and Emotional Susceptibility. Subsequent investigations led to a recognition of the need to shift the research focus to more specific, though more limited, constructs than aggressiveness. This conviction was further reinforced by a series of studies in which the combining of experimental and correlational design worked toward clarifying the frustration-aggression hypothesis. Interest in the temporal dimension of aggressive phenomenology directed our attention toward a new personality dimension (i.e., rumination-dissipation), corresponding with the inclination toward prolonged rumination, increasing or at least maintaining the desire to retaliate following an instigation. The examination of the rumination-dissipation dimension in experiments analogous to those previously conducted, whereas controlling for irritability and emotional susceptibility, led to a re-examination of the traditional distinctions between the various forms of aggression. We propose an alternate definition of aggressive manifestations based on the amount of variability accounted for by the impulsive and cognitive components of aggression. Then, the study of the possible antagonists of aggressive conduct suggested the importance of distinguishing two different manifestations of guilt, Fear of Punishment and Need for Reparation, which can be differentiated also on the basis of their association with other constructs linked to aggressive conduct.

The examination of the relations among all these constructs led to the development of a structural model able to take into account the various links between the different constructs and their association with two basic dimensions of aggressivity, labeled Emotional Responsivity and Proneness to Aggression. From this model, a conceptual framework was developed in which the various aggressive manifestations take form as part of a circumplex system capable of structuring examinations of the semantic space of aggression. Although we still have far to go before arriving (if we ever do arrive) at a complete understanding of the phenomenon of aggressiveness and its escalation, we hope that the research contribution summarized in this chapter is stimulating to other investigators, and that it can lead to a better understanding of the phenomenon.

## ACKNOWLEDGMENTS

This study was partially supported by two grants from C.N.R. n. 87.01886.08 and n. 88.00990.08

## REFERENCES

Allport, G. W. (1937). The functional autonomy of motives. *American Journal of Psychology, 50,* 141–156.
Bandura, A. (1973). *Aggression: A social learning analysis.* Englewood Cliffs, NJ: Prentice-Hall.
Bentler, P. M. (1980). Multivariate analysis with latent variables: Causal modeling. *Annual Review of Psychology, 31,* 419–456.
Bentler, P. M. (1989). *EQS structural equations program manual.* Los Angeles: BMDP Statistical Software.
Berkowitz, L. (1962). *Aggression: A social psychological analysis.* New York: McGraw-Hill.
Berkowitz, L. (1974). Some determinants of impulsive aggression: The role of mediated association with reinforcement for aggression. *Psychological Review, 81,* 165–176.
Berkowitz, L. (1983). The experience of anger as a parallel process in the display of "angry" aggression. In R. G. Geen & E. I. Donnerstein (Eds.), *Aggression: Theoretical and empirical reviews* (Vol. 1, pp. 103–133). New York: Academic.
Berkowitz, L. (1989). Frustration-aggression hypothesis: Examination and reformulation. *Psychological Bulletin, 106* (1), 59–73.
Berkowitz, L., & La Page, A. (1967). Weapons as aggression-eliciting stimuli. *Journal of Personality and Social Psychology, 7,* 202–207.
Buss, A. (1961). *The psychology of aggression.* New York: Wiley.
Buss, A., & Durkee, A. (1957). An inventory for assessing different kinds of hostility. *Journal of Consulting Psychology, 21,* 343–348.
Caprara, G. V. (1982). A comparison of the frustration-aggression and emotional susceptibility hypotheses. *Aggressive Behavior, 8,* 234–236.
Caprara, G. V. (1983). La misura dell' aggressivita': Contributo di ricerca per la costruzione e la validazione di due scale per la misura dell' irritabilita' e della suscettibilita' emotiva

[A research contribution via the construction and the validation of two scales for the measurement of irritability and emotional susceptibility]. *Giornale Italiano di Psicologia,* 9, 91–111.

Caprara, G. V. (1986). Indicators of aggression: the dissipation-rumination scale. *Personality and Individual Differences,* 7, 23–31.

Caprara, G. V., Borgogni, L., Cinanni, V., Di Giandomenico, F., & Passerini, S. (1985). Indicatori della condotta aggressiva. [Indicators of aggressive behavior]. *Giornale Italiano di Psicologia,* 12, 515–539.

Caprara, G. V., Cinanni, V., D'Imperio, G., Passerini, S., Renzi, P., & Travaglia, G. (1985). Indicators of impulsive aggression: Present status of research on irritability and emotional susceptibility. *Personality and Individual Differences,* 6, 665–674.

Caprara, G. V., Cinanni, V., & Mazzotti, E. (1989). Measuring attitude toward violence. *Personality and Individual Differences,* 10, 479–481.

Caprara, G. V., Cinanni, V., Passerini, S., Renzi, P., & Zelli, A. (1983). Caratteristiche e sviluppi di due scale per la misura dell' irritabilita' e della suscettibilita' emotiva: Indicazioni di ricerca in ambito clinico [Characteristics and development of two scales for the measurement of irritability and emotional susceptibility: Research findings in a clinical setting]. *Psicologia Clinica,* 3, 323–346.

Caprara, G. V., Gargaro, T., Pastorelli, C., Prezza, M., Renzi, P., & Zelli, A. (1987). Individual differences and measures of aggression in laboratory studies. *Personality and Individual Differences,* 8, 885–893.

Caprara, G. V., Manzy, J., & Perugini, M. (1992). Investigating guilt in relation to emotionality and aggression. *Personality and Individual Differences,* 13, 519–532.

Caprara, G. V., Mazzotti, E., & Prezza, M. (1990). Una scala per la misura dell'atteggiamento verso la violenza [A scale for the measurement of attitude toward violence]. *Giornale Italiano di Psicologia,* 17, 107–120.

Caprara, G. V., & Pastorelli, C. (1989). Toward a reorientation of research on aggression. *European Journal of Personality,* 3, 121–138.

Caprara, G. V., & Perugini, M. (1990 June). *Personality described by adjectives: Could the "Big Five" be extended to the Italian context?* Paper presented at the fifth European Conference on Personality, Rome.

Caprara, G. V., Perugini, M., Pastorelli, C., & Barbaranelli, C. (1990). Esplorazione delle dimensioni comuni della colpa e dell' aggressivita' [Exploration of the common dimension of aggression and guilt]. *Giornale Italiano di Psicologia,* 17, 665–681.

Caprara, G. V., & Renzi, P. (1981). The frustration-aggression hypothesis versus irritability. *Recherche de Psychologie Sociale,* 3, 75–80.

Caprara, G. V., Renzi, P., Alcini, P., D'Imperio, G., & Travaglia, G. (1983). Instigation to aggress and escalation of aggression examined form a personological perspective: The role of irritability and emotional susceptibility. *Aggressive Behavior,* 9, 354–358.

Caprara, G. V., Renzi, P., Alcini, P., D'Imperio, G., & Travaglia, G. (1984). Istigatori e mediatori della condotta aggressiva [Instigators and mediators of aggressive conduct]. *Giornale Italiano di Psicologia,* 10, 113–128.

Caprara, G. V., Renzi, P., Amolini, P., D'Imperio, G., & Travaglia, G. (1984). The eliciting cue value of aggressive slides reconsidered in a personological perspective: The weapons effect and irritability. *European Journal of Social Psychology,* 14, 312–322.

Caprara, G. V., Renzi, P., D'Augello, D., D'Imperio, G., Rielli, I., & Travaglia, G. (1986). Interpolating physical exercise between instigation and aggression: The role of irritability and emotional susceptibility. *Aggressive Behavior,* 12, 83–91.

Cattell, R. (1945). The description of personality: Principles and findings in a factor analysis. *American Journal of Psychology,* 58, 69–90.

Cliff, N. (1983). Some cautions concerning the application of causal modeling methods. *Multivariate Behavioral Research,* 18, 115–126.

Dengerink, H. O., O'Leary, R., & Kasner, K. (1975). Individual differences in aggressive responses to attack: Internal–external locus of control and field dependence–independence. *Journal of Research in Personality, 9*, 191–199.

Digman, J. (1989). Five robust trait dimensions: Development, stability, and utility. *Journal of Personality, 57*, 195–214.

Dodge, K. A., & Coie, J. D. (1987). Social information processing factors in reactive and proactive aggression in children and peer groups. *Journal of Personality and Social Psychology, 53*, 1146–1158.

Dollard, J., Doob, L. W., Miller, N. E., Mowrer, O. H., & Sears, R. R. (1939). *Frustration and aggression.* New Haven: Yale University Press.

Drwal, R. (1986). Reliability and validity of the irritability and emotional susceptibility scales in Poland. *Rassegna di Psicologia, 2*, 3–20.

Feshbach, S. (1964). The function of aggression and the regulation of aggressive drive. *Psychological Review, 71*, 257–272.

Fincham, F. D., & Jaspars, J. M. (1979). Attribution of responsibility to self and other in children and adults. *Journal of Personality and Social Psychology, 37*, 1589–1602.

Fraczek, A. (1984). *Aggressive personality.* Paper presented at the sixth biennal International Society for Research on Aggression meeting.

Freud, S. (1915). *Character-types in psychoanalytic work: 3. Criminality from a Sense of Guilt. Standard Edition, Vol. 14.* London: Hogarth.

Gifford, R., & O'Connor, B. (1987). The interpersonal circumplex as a behavior map. *Journal of Personality and Social Psychology, 52*, 1019–1026.

Goldberg, L. (1981). Language and individual differences: The search for universals in personality lexicons. In L. Wheeler (Ed.), *Review of personality and social psychology* (Vol. 2, pp. 141–165). Englewood Cliffs, NJ: Sage Publications.

Goldstein, J. H., Davis, R. W., & Herman, D. (1975). Escalation of aggression: Experimental studies. *Journal of Personality and Social Psychology, 31*, 162–170.

Hampson, S. (1990). Reconciling Inconsistent information: Impressions of personality from combinations of traits. *European Journal of Personality, 4*, 157–172.

Hata, K. (1989). Findings on the Japanese versions of the irritability and emotional susceptibility scales. *Japanese Journal of Psychology, 60*, 49–58.

John, O. P. (1990). The "big five" factor taxonomy: Dimensions of personality in the natural language and in questionnaires. In L. A. Pervin (Ed.), *Handbook of personality: Theory and research* (pp. 66–100). New York: Guilford.

Joreskog, K. G. (1978). Structural analysis of covariance and correlation matrices. *Psychometrika, 43*, 443–477.

Klein, M. (1948). On the theory of anxiety and guilt. *International Journal of Psycho-Analysis, 29*,

Knutson, J. F., Fordyce, D. J., & Anderson, D. J. (1980). Escalation of irritable aggression: Control by consequences and antecedents. *Aggressive Behavior, 6*, 347–359.

Konecni, V. (1975). Annoyance type and duration of postannoyance activity and aggression: The cathartic effect. *Journal of Experimental psychology, 104*, 76–102.

Konecni, V. (1984). Methodological issues in human aggression research. In R. M. Kaplan, V. J. Konecni, & R. W. Novaco (Eds.), *Aggression in children and youth* (pp. 1–43). The Hague: Martinus Nijhoff.

LABOS (1989). *Giovani e violenza [Youth and violence].* Rome: Edizioni T.E.R.

Lewin, K. (1951). Field theory in social science: Selected theoretical papers. In D. Cartwright (Ed.), New York: Harper & Row.

Loehlin, J. C. (1987). *Latent variable models: An introduction to factor, path, and structural analysis.* Hillsdale, NJ: Lawrence Erlbaum Associates.

Malamuth, N. (1984). The mass media, individual characteristics and aggression against women. In R. M. Kaplan, V. J. Konecni, & R. W. Novaco (Eds.), *Aggression in children and youth* (pp. 264–281). The Hague: Martinus Nijhoff.

McCrae, R., & Costa, P. (1985). Updating Norman's adequate taxonomy: Intelligence and personality dimensions in natural language and in questionnaires. *Journal of Personality and Social Psychology, 49,* 710–721.

McCrae, R. R., & Costa, P. T. (1987). Validation of the five-factor model of personality across instruments and observers. *Journal of Personality and Social Psychology, 52,* 81–90.

McGraw, K. M. (1987). Guilt following transgression: An attribution of responsibility approach. *Journal of Personality and Social Psychology, 53,* 247–256.

Olweus, D. (1978). *Aggression in the schools: Bullies and whipping boys.* Washington, DC: Hemisphere.

Olweus, D. (1980). The consistency issue in personality psychology revisited with special reference to aggression. *British Journal of Social and Clinical Psychology, 19,* 337–380.

Olweus, D. (1984). Stability in aggressive and withdrawn inhibited behaviors pattern. In R. M. Kaplan, V. J. Konecni, & R. W. Novaco, (Eds.), *Aggression in children and youth* (pp. 89–104). The Hague: Martinus Nijhoff.

Peabody, D., & Goldberg, L. (1989). Some determinants of factor structures from personality-trait descriptors. *Journal of Personality and Social Psychology, 57,* 552–567.

Perugini, M. (1993a). *Un approccio cireomplesso gerarchico alla individuazione di una Tassonomia delle caratteristiche di personalitá [A circumplex hierarchical approach to the individuation of a Taxonomy of personality characteristics].* Doctoral Thesis, Faculty of Psychology, University "La Sapienza" of Rome.

Perugini, M. (1993b). *Lo spazio semantico dell'aggressione: Sviluppo di un modello circomplesso delle caratteristiche di personalitá legate alla Fenomenologia Aggressiva [The semantic space of aggression: Development of a circumplex model of personality characteristics linked to aggressive phenomenology].* Manuscript submitted for publication.

Pitkanen-Pulkkinen, L. (1981). Long-term studies on the characteristics of aggressive and nonaggressive juveniles. In P. F. Brain & D. Benton (Eds.), *Multidisciplinary approach to aggression research* (pp. 215–243). Amsterdam: Elsevier North Holland.

Potegal, M. (1979). The reinforcing value of several types of aggressive behavior: A review. *Aggressive Behavior, 5,* 353–373.

Sanchez-Elvira, M., Bermudez, J., & Perez Garcia, A. (1988, June). *Irritability and emotional susceptibility scales: Preliminary results in Spanish samples.* Paper presented at the 4th European conference on personality, Stockholm, Sweden.

Watson, D., & Tellegen, A. (1985). Toward a consensual structure of mood. *Psychological Bullettin, 98,* 219–235.

Wiggins, J. (1979). A psychological taxonomy of trait-descriptive terms: The interpersonal domain. *Journal of Personality and Social Psychology, 37,* 395–412.

Wiggins, J., Steiger, J., & Gaelick, L. (1981). Evaluating circumplexity in personality data. *Multivariate Behavioral Research, 16,* 263–289.

Wiggins, J., Trapnell, P., & Phillips, N. (1988). Psychometric and geometric characteristics of the revised interpersonal adjective scale (IAS-R). *Multivariate Behavioral Research, 23,* 517–530.

Zahn-Waxler, C., & Kochanska, G. (1989). The origins of guilt. In R. A. Thompson (Ed.), *1988 Nebraska symposium on motivation* (pp. 183–258). Lincoln: University of Nebraska Press.

Zillmann, D. (1979). *Hostility and aggression.* Hillsdale, NJ: Lawrence Erlbaum Associates.

Zillmann, D. (1983). Arousal and aggression. In R. G. Geen, & E. I. Donnerstein, (Eds), *Aggression: Theoretical and empirical reviews* (Vol. 1, pp. 75–101). New York: Academic.

# PART III

## Aggression Dynamics in Development: Interactions Within and Outside the Family

# CHAPTER 7

# Temper Tantrums in Young Children

Dorothy Einon
*University College London*

Michael Potegal
*Walter Reed Army Institute of Research*

*She goes red in the face, cries, and throws herself onto the floor where she kicks and screams, crying, screaming and shouting at me. She then stops, wriggles to the nearest object and throws it—screaming at the same time. It then continues with her screaming, hitting, and kicking the floor and anything in her way.*
—A mother's description of her 3-year-old girl's tantrum.

By the time a child is 7 months old and capable of intentional communication (Greenspan & Greenspan, 1985), most parents recognize that he or she is sometimes angry (Sroufe, 1979). By 18 months, when the child is better able to understand what others want and feel, he or she may also know how to make his or her parents and siblings angry (Greenspan & Greenspan, 1985). No one who has lived through their child's "Terrible twos" doubts that children of this age engage in, and induce, conflict. Parents have told us that around this age their children seek to augment conflict and anger; they become deliberately contrary and insist on doing things they know are forbidden. They invite frustration, demanding "Me do it" when they know from experience that the task is too difficult. And when their wishes are denied by parents or they fail at the task, they have a tantrum. From the parents' perspective, tantrums present a challenge with which they must cope (Chamberlin, 1974).

Tantrums also raise questions from a theoretical perspective: Are there biological roots of tantrum behavior? What functions do they serve in the family situation? Challenges in the course of development are faced by all children; some react with tantrums, some do not. Even among those who have tantrums, there is a broad distribution of tantrum frequency. Surely some of this variance must reflect individual differences. What do tantrums imply about a given child's emotional development and personality? Are these differences transient developmental events or do they persist over time? Studies of development have used tantrums as an identifying characteristic of the "difficult" child; tantrums have also been used as an index of hostility, anger, and aggression, although it is not known if anger is a necessary or even a frequent component of tantrums. The clearest thing about tantrums is what they are not, and what they are not is well understood.


## DEFINITION OF TANTRUMS


Whereas it may be argued that everyone knows what a tantrum is, an adequate formal definition has not been found. Needlman, Howard, and Zuckerman (1989) described a range of behaviors that include angry crying through physical thrashing. The problem of definition is highlighted when we try to distinguish crying from tantrums at a later age. As we note later, crying is one of the two most common behaviors in tantrums. Shouting, screaming, sobbing, flushing, arm flailing and leg kicking, arched back, rigid legs, tears, whimpering, heavy breathing, and pulling away are others. In listing the most common elements of tantrums, one is inevitably listing the components of certain bouts of inconsolable crying in young babies. The behaviors that are "exclusive" to tantrums such as running away, stamping, throwing oneself on the floor, and hitting objects and people are more a function of the child's age and motor maturity than a distinct profile of behaviors. One thing that differentiates tantrums from inconsolable crying in babies is the social context. Babies cry by themselves in their cribs; we suspect that children do not have many tantrums while sitting alone in their rooms.


## THE SURVEY AND ITS ANALYSES


*Anger in Young Children*, published 60 years ago by Florence Goodenough, remains one of the few thorough studies of temper tantrums. Goodenough (1931) collected parents' reports of 1, 878 tantrums had by a sample of 45 normal children whose ages ranged from birth to 7 years.

To update the data base, we recently carried out a survey among the readers of *Parents* magazine in the United Kingdom examining the ontogeny, structure, and context of tantrums. Parents were asked to observe the next tantrum shown by one of their children and fill in a questionnaire describing it. The questionnaire included some more general questions about the frequency and severity of their child's tantrums and details of their own feelings and actions. Gender, age, number of siblings, birth order in the family, early sleep and crying patterns, weaning, toilet training, speech development, and other social interactions were also covered.

Just over 1,000 people returned the main questionnaire. In keeping with the large number of responses, most questions asked of the data were answered by $\chi^2$ analyses of frequency. Only significant results are reported here. These analyses were supplemented by two other statistical techniques. An SPSS–X factor analysis of the physical aspects of the tantrums identified 5 factors. A cluster analysis carried out with the SPSS–X "Quick cluster" algorithm yielded an interpretable pattern of organization when just nine clusters had been formed. Three of the five factors were clearly identical with the picture provided by the cluster analysis. Crying, for example, was identified both as an independent factor and also as the distinguishing feature of a cluster of 119 cases.

In addition to the questionnaire, we invited parents to enclose a letter giving the details of the sequence of behaviors composing the tantrum. We received 120 letters. We added an examination of the behavior sequences derived from narrative descriptions of 74 tantrums. This chapter reviews some interesting findings that appeared interpretable from the various analyses and places them in appropriate developmental, personality, and sociobiological contexts.

## THE ORGANIZATION OF TANTRUMS: PHYSICAL CHARACTERISTICS AND EMOTIONAL CONTENT

### Duration of Tantrums and Relative Rates of Tantrum Development and Subsidence

The temporal changes in affect that occur during a tantrum provide an interesting window onto the internal regulation of anger and associated emotions because tantrums are, as a rule, less controlled by the moment-to-moment behavior of others than is the course of events in other aggressive interactions between individuals. In our survey, as in

Goodenough's (1931), the most common duration of tantrum recorded for every age was 1 to 4 minutes. Similarly, Miller and Sperry (1987) remarked on the brevity of most of the incidents of anger observed during their extensive longitudinal in-home observations of three 2-year-old girls. These episodes are shorter than the mean duration of episodes of anger, generally 10 to 20 minutes, reported in surveys of adults over the past 50 years (see Potegal, this volume). Also like Goodenough (1931), we found no noticeable shifts in the distribution of durations with age, suggesting that the change to longer durations of anger occurs after age 7.

We asked parents to rate the relative speeds (quick or slow) with which the tantrum developed and then subsided. More than half of tantrums begin quickly. Cairns (this volume) reported that interpersonal confrontations between older children also escalate rapidly. The single most common up-and-down pattern for tantrums was "quick, quick," which accounted for 40% of tantrums, reflecting that fact that most of them are brief. The next most common pattern was "slow, slow." Together these two patterns account for 69% of all tantrums, suggesting that the speed of subsidence tends to mirror the speed of arousal. The distribution of temporal patterns was the same for boys and girls and for tantrums in which the child was angry or was crying.

Temporal Structure of Tantrums

Parens, Scattergood, Singletary, and Duff (1987) have noted that longer tantrums have a temporal structure. They described ascending and descending phases of emotional intensity upon which are superimposed secondary fluctuations. They did not identify the behaviors upon which their estimates of emotional intensity are based, however. Our survey included a list of 4 facial expressions, 6 kinds of vocalizations, and 17 actions that respondents could use to describe their child's tantrum. The items that were included on the questionnaire are *italicized* for identification the first time they appear in the discussion that follows.

Seventy-four of the letters that were returned with the survey contained enough information to determine a sequence of two or more events. A table consisting of the order of events or sets of events in each tantrum was constructed. For example, the events in a letter saying: "The child shouted No! (1), then he hit and kicked. (2) Later, he cried and sobbed." (3) would be ordered as indicated by the numbers in parentheses. The relative frequency of ordered behaviors in tantrums in which two to five sets of sequential events could be discriminated is shown in Fig. 7.1. (There were a few tantrums in which six to eight sets of events were discerned, but these were collapsed into five to increase

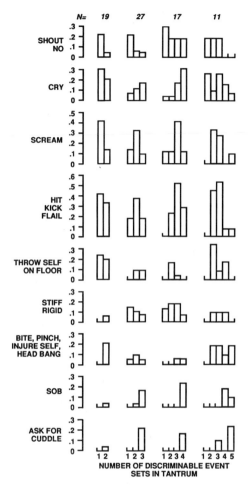

FIG. 7.1.  Ordering and relative frequency of different behaviors in tantrums in which there were two to five sets of sequential events. Tantrums were grouped by the number of event sets discriminable in the description in the letter (see bottom label). The number of tantrums in each of these groups is indicated in the top row ($N =$). The ordinate for each behavior indicates the decimal fraction of the tantrums in which that behavior occurred. This fraction was calculated separately for each group. In the group of 27 tantrums in which three event sets could be discriminated (i.e., the second column), for example, "shout/no" occurred six times among the first set of events, twice in the second, and once in the third.

sample size by putting the most similar behaviors into one set of events, e.g., "cry" with "sob" or "scratch" with "pinch".) We discovered that, in general, the sequence of events described could be resolved into four action/emotion stages with a systematic order of transition between stages. These stages were as follows:

***Stage 1: Prodroma.*** Some tantrums appear "out of the blue," surprising the parents, or are triggered by a minor frustration that would not ordinarily upset the child. These instances speak to the operation of internal factors. Other tantrums have a clear prodroma such as whining, bad moods, or irritability, and defiant looks. Parents remarked that they could sometimes see it coming for hours. Some children exhibit unusual signs that a tantrum is brewing; their parents wrote of "strange moods," speaking in a "queer voice," or having a "hang dog look." More typical comments are "She was stubborn beforehand" or "He'd been moody and contrary all morning." One parent wrote: "He says he wants something, and when you offer it to him he says he doesn't and then cries when you say OK, don't have it then."

Making the same request persistently, and having it repeatedly refused, precedes and precipitates a number of tantrums. Some children appear to deliberately goad parents by disobedience or naughtiness. These behaviors invite punishment that, in turn, triggers a tantrum. In this sense the prodroma of tantrums are akin to those occasions in which one child will deliberately do something that gains him or her no desired end but which he or she knows will anger a sibling. As Lewis Carroll (1965) wrote, "He only does it to annoy because he knows it teases" (p. 68).

***Stage 2: Confrontation.*** The tantrum proper generally begins with a confrontation, then can escalate to a point where the child appears to be overcome by emotion, maintaining a distance from loved ones by violent and seemingly disorganized behavior. The flavor of what happens is given in the following quotes:

> He cries or shouts, then he finds me (or at least makes sure he has an audience), he then throws himself on his back, often hurting himself intentionally, he kicks and cries.

> He starts with short angry screams. Then he screams continuously shaking his arms and legs and hitting out at me. He then runs away. If I give him his dummy (pacifier) it will be taken from me and thrown as will anything else he can get hold of. If I go near him he hits me, pinches and pulls my hair.

*Shouting* appeared in 47% of tantrums. In these tantrums it was likely to be the first event (see Fig. 7.1). *Saying "No"* and shouting comprised one factor in the factor analysis (loadings of 0.66 and 0.68) indicating defiance. Indeed, several parents commented on defiant looks as a salient tantrum feature. One of the two most common events was *screaming,* which occurred in 61% of tantrums. Shouting, which most often occurs at the beginning, is a more coherent and articulate form of expression involving speech. Screaming, which tends to occur in the middle of the tantrum when emotion is more intense, does not involve speech and is, in this sense, more primitive. A negative loading of screaming on the *"No"/shouting* factor indicates that shouting and screaming do not often occur in the same tantrum. This implies that there is no "general vocalization" element.

Screaming and *hitting* load on a second factor (0.6 and 0.74, respectively); they also tend to occur together at the middle stages of the tantrum (see Fig. 7.1). Also occurring during these stages are *flailing arms* and *kicking,* which each have loadings of 0.65 on a third factor. Screaming, hitting, and kicking together are wilder, more unorganized behaviors that develop as the tantrum progresses. The most common variant on hitting reported in the letters is throwing things followed by pushing food off the high chair (in younger children), and door slamming (in older children). The common physical factor in these acts is the abrupt and forceful activation of major muscle groups. The verbal equivalent of this is "I hate you, Mummy," "You're stupid," and so on. The pinching, biting, scratching, and hair pulling that were described in the letters are more deliberately hostile aggression. They are relatively rare and tend to happen only after the tantrum has started. Hitting, kicking, and screaming probably reflect anger that is not specifically directed, whereas pinching, biting, scratching, and hair pulling are aggressive acts intended to produce pain. The latter may be differentiated from simple expressions of anger by being more directed and coordinated muscular activity.

Not only do children lash out at people and objects, but they hurt themselves as well. Our attention was drawn to this self-directed aggression by the letters. Head banging is the most common behavior of this type. In our sample, head banging appeared most likely at a year and a half: six of the eight head bangers in the letters were 18 months old (the other two were 16 and 24 months). This age range is consistent with French and American surveys showing that head banging in populations of normal children appears at about 8 months and disappears by about 36 months. The peak incidence, which occurs from 9 to 18 months, has been estimated as 4% to 17% in different surveys (for review see Baumeister & Rollings, 1976). Head banging is several times more common in boys than girls. A host of explanations for head banging have been offered, ranging from organic factors to possibilities that the behavior is shaped by social reinforcement, but none of these is fully satisfactory (for review see Baumeister & Rollings, 1976; de Catanzaro, 1978). Head banging is most likely to appear during teething episodes (Kravitz & Boehm, 1971). At least one child in our survey had struck his head severely enough to chip a tooth, cut his lip, and bloody his nose. When children bite and pinch themselves or pull out their own hair, it is very worrisome to parents. The prevalence data suggest that such self-directed aggression continuing after age 3 is a sign of serious pathology, and parental worry would be justified.

From a comparative perspective, frustration-induced self-scratching and hair pulling have been observed in normal chimpanzees (Finch, 1942) as are other forms of aggression directed toward the self in rhesus monkeys (Gluck & Sackett, 1974). Self-directed aggression is, in fact, relatively common in rhesus and stumptailed macaques after several years of living in laboratories and zoos, especially if they have been socially isolated during rearing (Anderson & Chamove, 1980). It is not seen in feral, free-living monkeys. These observations make it unlikely that self-directed aggression in primates is closely related to tantrums in children. However, grooming another monkey substantially reduces self-directed aggression but receiving such grooming does not (Goosen & Ribbens, 1980). This may parallel observations on the child's willingness to cuddle after a tantrum, as described next.

Escape, avoidance, and rejection also occur in tantrums. Relatively early in the tantrum a child may push away food, clothes, toys, or other objects. *Turning away* from the parent was relatively rare and associated with "milder" tantrums. A small number of children run away and hide. One mother wrote: "She cries, then sulks and hides behind the sofa till she has calmed down." When these children are approached, they may back up against a wall or door. They resent and resist being touched or held and may re-escalate the tantrum if parents attempt to do so. There is a sense from the letters that the children create and prolong their own emotional hurting. The rejection of parental overtures is part of this as is the self-directed aggression noted previously. That parents' attempts to touch or cuddle can intensify the tantrum demonstrates that the child has not simply become insensitive to such stimulation, contrary to the suggestion of Parens et al. (1987). There is, instead, a passive or active avoidance of what was (and will be again) pleasant tactile stimulation. It is as if the sign of the hedonic value had been temporarily reversed and the most loved one (and tantrums almost always involve the child's most loved one) is now the most hated. Curiously, a similar reversal appears to occur with mother's odor as well as her touch. Welch (1988) stated: "At least half the children I have seen . . . comment about disliking their mother's scent (during a tantrum), only to tell her later that they love it" (p. 215). Olfaction is a phylogenetically older sense and is very important in the control of social behaviors in lower vertebrates (see chapter 4, this volume). This observation underscores the phylogenetic continuity of social motivational processes.

Sudden and dramatic postural changes are another tantrum characteristic. *Lying on the floor* was found in 40% of tantrums. Sitting down or falling to the knees, reported in several letters, may be variants on this behavior. This behavior has been reported in the first tantrums of very young children, before they ever had the opportunity to see another child do it. It is, in this sense, unlearned. It may be a reversion to babyhood when the child, lying on his back, could only kick and thrash.

Becoming *stiff* and making *legs rigid* was reported in 27% to 21% of tantrums, respectively. It is often followed by *going floppy*. In a few children, as in grand mal patients, rigidity can happen so quickly and strongly that the child topples over involuntarily. Parents of these children naturally worry about catching them before they fall and hurt themselves. Biomechanically, this posture results from the strong simultaneous activation of agonist and antagonist muscles. The head is often thrown back, facilitating extensor tone. This effect is exploited by weight lifters when lifting and by runners in the final sprint. "Stiff/rigid legs" together defined a single factor that appeared in a subset of tantrums with crying; it did not appear in tantrums with anger alone. We have not yet found an association between this response and going floppy or any other characteristic of the tantrum or the child. We suspect that this behavior has both learned and unlearned aspects. In some children it may appear as a spontaneous, expressive, even involuntary reaction. Subsequently, the child learns that going rigid makes it more difficult to pick him up from the floor, dress him, spoon feed him, or put him in a stroller. In other children it may be part of a strategy of resistance from the outset.

In spite of the fact that most tantrums in our survey began with a conflict, not all involved obvious angry expressions. Overall, *"angry face"* was seen in 50% of tantrums, *"cry face"* in 44%. The percentage of angry face expressions increases slightly with age, from 44% in children up to age 3 to 53% in older children. Within every age group, angry face was roughly 30% more common in boys than girls. At these ages, angry expressions correlate with aggressive behavior (see Table 7.1); hitting was significantly more likely to occur when the child had an angry face than when he or she had a cry face [$\chi^2(1) = 5.3$, $p < .02$]. Boys were more likely to hit than girls, particularly over the age of 4 (see Table 7.1). This is consistent with many earlier reports that by the time boys reach school age they are more aggressive than girls (Maccoby & Jacklin, 1980) and are more likely to be referred to mental health agencies for aggressiveness (Cullinan & Epstein, 1982).

TABLE 7.1
Percentage of Children Hitting During Tantrum as a Function
of Facial Expression and Gender

| Age | Expression | | Gender | |
|---|---|---|---|---|
| | Angry | Crying | Boys | Girls |
| ≤1 | 26 | 21 | 27 | 20 |
| 2 | 29 | 18 | 28 | 23 |
| 3 | 27 | 18 | 24 | 22 |
| ≥4 | 48 | 18 | 41 | 20 |

*Crying* is the other most common element in our data, found in 61% of tantrums in the sample and likely to be found at every stage (see Fig. 7.1). The cluster analysis revealed that 14% of the tantrums formed a cluster defined by the presence of cry face plus crying. In other surveys of children's tantrums, crying is the most common behavior reported. Insofar as crying is a sign of distress or sadness, the high preponderance of crying simply confirms that tantrums are unpleasant experiences for the child.

**Stage 3: Sobbing.** The third stage includes intensified crying and *sobbing* (sobbing was an event in 44% of tantrums; see Fig. 7.1). This is presumably the descending phase of the tantrum as described by Parens et al. (1987). Quotes from three letters describe this stage: "The wild actions eventually calm into crying and soon after into sobs." "He went stiff again, but he was only sobbing and looked very unhappy." "Near the end tears come."

The third stage is quieter and more subdued. Parents talk of sobs rather than shouts, of stillness rather than thrashing, of being floppy rather than stiff. Protests are less full blooded and the most obvious emotion is sadness. Feelings of grief, guilt, or remorse may be present, perhaps relating to the felt loss of emotional bonding and/or a sense of vulnerability at being out of control (cf. Caprara et al.'s Need for Reparation scale, this volume). Some children stay close to, but separate from, the caregiver; others actively seek contact. Some children apologize. The impression is of sorrowful children starting to regain self-control and re-establishing communication. However, a number of parents reported that their child could easily be provoked into further tantrums at this stage. The third stage is usually shorter than the preceding one; it may be a transition between the earlier angry emotions and the eventual resolution, as the following comment indicates: "Eventually he will come and stand next to me. I am not allowed to pick him up until he puts his arms up, otherwise he will start again."

***Stage 4: Reconciliation (Contact, Reassurance, and Social Communication).*** Eventually tantrums are resolved: Occasionally the *parent gave in* (5.5%), more often the *child gave in* (29%), sometimes it was a *compromise* (18%). Thirty-five percent of tantrums ended in a *cuddle* (see Fig. 7.1). Many times this was initiated by parents. But some children do not wait for a cuddle, they ask for one: "She will suddenly stop and come to me for a cuddle and a tissue to wipe her eyes." "He tries to seek comfort for the pain he caused himself" (this boy had bitten his own arm).

Asking for a cuddle signals the end of the tantrum and is a request for contact, reassurance, and reconciliation. Variants in asking for and getting a cuddle include hugging mother (Miller & Sperry, 1987), leaning against the mother (Parens et al., 1987), clutching her legs, cuddling a favorite teddy bear, and sucking on a pacifier. Proximity and physical contact are the recurrent themes in these behaviors. One 3-year-old girl apologizes for her tantrums. By saying "I'm sorry, Daddy" she verbally accomplishes what other children do by touching. After his mother had carried him screaming from a shop, a 3-year-old boy demanded "Mummy, say sorry," trying to lay off blame while at the same time reestablishing contact. Of this brilliant stroke of emotional economy his mother writes "Ha! The cheek of it." Such apologies strengthen the hypothesis that the sobbing phase involves feelings of guilt or embarrassment. Making amends by complying with the previously resisted demand is another solution. "After awhile he came out with the box in his hand to show me he had picked the puzzle up." Roiphe (1991) suggested that the basic pleasure in defiance and submission is the reestablishment of emotional closeness.

### Aftereffects

For 55% of the tantrums the response to the question "What happened afterwards?" was "It was as if nothing happened." Similarly, Miller and Sperry (1987) noted that "Most arguments simply faded out as the parties lost interest" (p. 25). However, 12.5% of all tantrums were followed by what Goodenough called an *aftereffect* (i.e., a persistence of *anger, upset,* or *sulkiness*). We found, as did Goodenough (1931), that the prevalence of aftereffects increased strongly with age. Table 7.2 shows the close similarity between our observations and Goodenough's. That our figures for the two younger ages are slightly lower than Goodenough's may be due to the fact that only 10% of her sample were cuddled afterward. In the subsample matched for age and tantrum length that is shown in Table 7.3, we found that children who were

**TABLE 7.2**
**Percentage of Children Having Aftereffects as a Function**
**of Age**

| | Age | | | | |
|---|---|---|---|---|---|
| | <1 | 1 | 2 | 3 | 4 |
| Einon and Potegal | 4 | 6 | 8 | 12 | 32 |
| Goodenough (1931) | | [a]10 | | 12 | 31 |

[a]Goodenough grouped data from children up to 3 years old.

**TABLE 7.3**
**Percentage of Children Having Aftereffects as a Function of**
**Cuddling at the End of the Tantrum**

| | Child's State after the Tantrum | | |
|---|---|---|---|
| | Back to Normal | Sulky/Upset | Angry |
| Child cuddled | 46 | 25 | 18 |
| Child not cuddled | 54 | 75 | 82 |

Note: Parents endorsed one or more statements about their child's state after the tantrum. Three of these states, "Back to normal", "sulky/upset", and "angry", form the columns of this table. The numbers are the percentages of all the children reported in a given state who had or had not been cuddled.

cuddled were significantly less likely to show aftereffects than those who were not [$x^2(1) = 17.8$, $p < .01$]. The increase in aftereffects with age may presage the brooding and rumination that are responsible for the prolongation and recurrence of episodes of anger in adults (see Caprara, this volume). This, in turn, may relate to increases in cognitive and memory capacity with age.

## COMMENTS AND CAVEATS

Individual tantrums described in the letters consisted of one or more of these stages. But if stages can occur or fail to occur, in what sense can a sequence be said to exist? It is that, if more than one stage appears, they will do so in the order described. Note also that it is not the case that one stage clearly ends before another begins, but they overlap. For example, some parents noted that, even at the inception of the resolution phase, their children could be easily provoked into further tantrums.

As a methodological caveat, we note that differences in the number, progression, or emotional content of stages identified in the tantrums of individual children are confounded by possible differences in the attentiveness of parents in identifying, and thoroughness in reporting, different behaviors. These hypotheses remain to be confirmed by sequence analysis of a more systematically collected set of data.

## PARALLELS TO THE ANGER–SORROW–RECONCILIATION SEQUENCE OF TEMPER TANTRUMS

***Holding Therapy for Children.*** Welch (1988) presented a three-phase "tight holding" technique for forestalling or terminating tantrums. The first, *confrontation*, phase is initiated by the mother holding the child tightly, making direct eye contact, and talking to him or her. This quickly precipitates the "rejection" phase in which the child avoids gaze by eye closure and tries to escape from being held by physical struggles and verbal protests (e.g., older, more articulate children will explain why this is a bad time to engage in this interaction). If the child is in the beginning or middle of a tantrum when tight holding is initiated, it immediately exacerbates the anger, provoking screams, writhing, spitting, kicking, butting, biting, pinching, or hair pulling. Even if the child is calm and willing at the onset of tight holding, defiance and anger appear relatively quickly as it continues. If the parent continues to hold, a final "resolution" phase appears, signaled by a relaxation of tension, smiling, and active cuddling on the part of the child (not just passive acceptance of it). Five of our letter writers said or implied that they used this technique (e.g., "I cuddle her very tightly so she can't struggle and the tantrum gives way to tears and cuddles from her"). The resolution phase is characterized by intense feelings of physical and emotional closeness between child and parent. One telling sign of this change in emotional tone is the child's willingness to make eye contact, but the really critical indicator is that continued tight holding no longer elicits resistance. This change into the third phase is so sudden and dramatic that Welch labels it catharsis. Furthermore, according to Welch, this procedure affects the child's (and mother's) affect and behavior for a considerable period of time thereafter. In this sense, it appears to resemble the sense of well-being, even euphoria, that can occur after temporal lobe seizures (Potegal, this volume).

This process can take an hour or more, especially the first time the mother does it; with practice the cycle duration can be reduced to a few minutes. It takes longer if the "resolution" is incomplete; child and mother can go through several rejection/resolution cycles before resolution is achieved. This feature of tight holding resembles ordinary tantrums in some children who can be provoked into resuming the tantrum at the transition from sorrow to reconciliation.

What tight holding can do is to initiate a tantrum ab initio. This effect was noted over 70 years ago by Watson and Watson (1921), who pointed out that physical restraint is a very powerful provoker of tantrums. If Welch is to be believed, the unusual aspect of tight holding is that, when prolonged, it brings about a reconciliation phase intensified well beyond that which occurs spontaneously. She reported that occasionally the predominant emotion of the rejection phase is not anger but "hurt, sadness, jealousy or fear." It appears that the experience of some negative emotion is an integral first step because it occurs even when children are used to tight holding, like it, and ask for it. The long-term bonding that is claimed to result from repeated cycles of tight holding may reflect the effects of alternating sequences of punishment and reinforcement that have been demonstrated to strengthen infantile bonding in humans and a number of other species (Rajecki, Lamb, & Obmasche, 1978) and are conjectured to play a role in trapping women into abusive relationships (Dutton, 1988). No wonder the children in Welch's narratives are often ambivalent about tight holding.

***Spouse Abuse Among Adults.***   For a comparison of tantrum structure with the more brutal interactions that occur within couples, we draw on two sources: (a) Walker's (1979) summary of her conversations with abused American and English women who sought her out for psychotherapeutic help and (b) Dobash and Dobash's (1984) account of their more systematic and standardized interviews with Scottish women living in shelters. Each study involved over 100 women; the Dobashes' interviews were supplemented by analyses of police reports in which men had used violence against their female partners. Walker (1979) described a three-phase cycle of behavior in the batterers. The first phase is a period of rising tension and anger that, as it intensifies, includes "possessive smothering and brutality," "psychological humiliation," and "minor" physical assault (p. 59). The second phase is a frenzied eruption of physical attack that is most often set off by events external to the relationship (e.g., some external setback or internal state that affects the husband). Walker (1979) noted that "It is not uncommon for the batterer to wake the woman out of a deep sleep to begin his assault" (p. 61), from which it may be inferred that a period of rumination precedes the attack. The assault phase usually continues for 2 to 24 hours; the cause of its termination remains unclear but may be due to his "exhaustion and emotional depletion." The third phase is marked by calmness, extreme contrition, and exaggerated, loving attention to the woman, which is designed to win her back. He begs forgiveness; he is all sweetness and light. The women often liken the man's behavior to that of a little boy who has been caught doing something wrong. Potegal (chapter 4, this volume) cites other instances in which an intense outburst of anger in adults is followed by feelings of remorse, guilt, or shame and then by a resolution of dysphoric feeling.

The Dobashes' study confirms some of Walker's observations and offers a number of parallels between spouse abuse and tantrums. In their study, 84% of the assaults occurred within the home (for tantrums in our survey the figure is 75%). Two thirds of them arose from an argument; the other third began without warning. In 54% of the former cases, the argument had lasted less than 5 minutes before the assault began (recall that 63% of tantrums begin quickly). Unlike the women interviewed by Walker, those questioned by the Dobashes (1984) said that the man's assault usually began when he perceived her to be "questioning his authority or challenging the legitimacy of his behavior" (p. 274). The Dobashes, like Walker, reported that, once the attack began, blows were struck repeatedly. Walker (1979) stated: "The violence has an element of overkill to it, and the man cannot stop even if the woman is severely injured." (p. 62). Although the men's violent acts are physically well coordinated to inflict pain and injury, the loss of emotional control is reminiscent of a child's tantrum.

In a parallel to tantrum aftereffects, the Dobashes noted that intimidation and coercion, slaps and shoves may continue for some time after the beating. Recall that the post-tantrum persistence of irritability in children increases as they get older. In contrast to Walker's finding that the final stage of apology and loving attention is quite common and very pronounced, the Dobashes reported that only 35% of Scottish men were contrite and apologized or tried to make amends in other ways after their first assault. This number declined to 22% following subsequent assaults. Most typically, the men acted as if nothing had happened. Discussion of the methodological, cultural, or other factors that might account for the differences in the Scottish and American studies is beyond the scope of this chapter, but we note that the Need for Reparation scale described by Caprara and colleagues in this volume loads heavily on a (negative) emotionality factor that is orthogonal to their Interpersonal Attitude, hostility-related factor. This is consistent with the idea that these can be independent emotional traits. We note also the Dobashes' (1984) observation that "It was not uncommon for a man to indicate that it was all over . . . by beginning to make requests for domestic service . . . albeit in a somewhat conciliatory rather than demanding fashion" (p. 280). This alteration in tone might reflect a very mild form of reestablishing contact.

*Aggression and Reconciliation in Other Animals.* The existence of a biological basis for these aggression/reconciliation transitions is suggested by anecdotal reports and formal studies of postaggression social bonding in a number of mammalian species, particularly primates (e.g., de Waal, 1989; Cords, 1988; York & Rowell, 1988). After aggressive interactions, the number of affiliative behaviors between the combatants increases relative to baseline levels and relative to affiliation with animals not involved in the encounter. Van-Lawick Goodall (1988) wrote: "Once I watched (an adult male) chimpanzee pound and drag an old female during one of his displays while her screaming infant clung beneath her; then, almost before he had stopped attacking her, he turned around to embrace, pat, and kiss her" (p. 153). Adult male chimps will touch, embrace, and kiss each other on the mouth just after an agonistic exchange, behaviors that occur only rarely in other contexts (de Waal & van Roosmalen, 1979). A particularly striking ape–human parallel is that chimps will hold out their hand after a fight, a species-typical signal for soliciting contact. In rhesus macaques reconciliation takes the form of a rapid postaggression switch to grooming other animals and a particular tendency to embrace the just former opponent (de Waal & Yoshihara, 1983). In both rhesus and long-tailed macaque, the initiator of friendly contact is routinely the former aggressor who is also the more dominant animal (Cords, 1988; de Waal & Yoshihara, 1983).

The rapidity of the mood shifts may suggest a strong need to maintain bonds in groups of socially living animals. de Waal and Yoshihara's (1983) observations were made over a 20-minute postaggression period suggesting that a state of aggressive arousal has been replaced by a different state. It is conceivable that there are brain mechanisms that support this need by increasing the probability of such transitions from one mode of social functioning to the next. Note that this is in accord with the standard advice to parents to comfort their children after a tantrum. Children's tantrums differ from these examples of primate aggression in many respects, including the understanding by both parent and child that the individual initiating the outburst is not the dominant one. However, the reconciliation process is similar in that it is the child who has the tantrum and it is the child who initiates the contact.

## ONTOGENY OF TANTRUMS

Age Related Changes in Incidence and Frequency

Jenkins, Owen, Bax, and Hart (1984) reported that 50% of the population of 2-year-olds they surveyed had tantrums, Macfarlane, Allen, and Honzik (1954) reported a 60% to 70% incidence, whereas Chamberline (1974) put the figure as high as 83%. The frequency distribution of the ages at which tantrums were reported to have begun in our sample is shown in Table 7.4. The modal age of tantrum onset, between 1 and 2 years, was reported by 62% of our respondents. This corresponds well with the age distribution of children in our sample very few of whom were under 1. One in 15 of the children in our sample who began to have tantrums before they were 2 persist until 4. They comprise 53% of the children having tantrums at this age. Of the remaining 47%, almost half (22%) began at 2 and 24% at 3 or later. In our survey there are relatively few 4-year olds and still fewer 5-year olds, together accounting for 10% of our sample. Jenkins et al. (1984) similarly reported that the number of children having tantrums diminished to 11% by age 4 ½. It appears that most children in the United Kingdom have stopped tantruming by age 4. The drop out rates with age in American children reported by Goodenough (1931) and Macfarlane et al. (1954) appear much lower than those found by Jenkins or ourselves.

The frequency of tantrums as a function of age is shown in Fig. 7.2. Note that there are a variety of factors that might bias the observed distribution. Parents' likelihood of filling out our questionnaire might vary as they become less sensitive to their children's tantrums over a year or two, the tantrums themselves may become more (or less) irritating, and so on. However, our weighted mean hourly frequencies

**TABLE 7.4**
**Percentage of Children Starting Tantrums at Different Ages**
**as a Function of Age at Time of Survey**

| Age Tantrums Began (Months) | Percentage of Whole Sample Beginning at This Age | Age (Months) at Time of Survey | | | | | |
|---|---|---|---|---|---|---|---|
| | | 0–12 | 12–24 | 24–36 | 36–48 | 48–60 | >60 |
| 0–12 | 19 | 3 | 10 | 3 | 3 | 0 | 0 |
| 12–24 | 62 | | 19 | 29 | 9 | 4 | 1 |
| 24–36 | 14 | | | 4 | 7 | 2 | 1 |
| 36–48 | 4 | | | | 2 | 2 | 0 |
| Percentage of total sample at this age | | 3 | 29 | 36 | 21 | 8 | 2 |

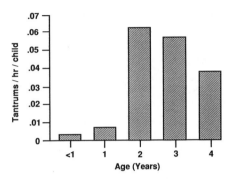

FIG. 7.2. Histogram of the mean frequency of tantrums as a function of age. Frequencies are displayed as hourly rates to make our data directly comparable to Goodenough's (1931).

of tantrums at each age are comparable with Goodenough's that were collected under different circumstances. Both data sets reach a peak at age 2. The agreement between our data and Goodenough's suggests that reporting biases are probably small.

## Life Events and Perceptual, Cognitive, and Emotional Development at Age 2

What is happening in the lives of 2-year-olds that increases the risk of tantrums? By this age the average child is mobile, vocal, and curious. The opportunities for conflict have thus multiplied. By this age children have also had the opportunity to learn that tantrums are a dramatic and effective means of getting what they want. The child can become a practitioner of behavior modification, manipulating his or her parents by the classical technique of negative reinforcement (reinforcement by withdrawal of an aversive stimulus; cf., "demand-related" tantrums; Carr & Newsom, 1985). A few of our letter writers intimated that their children had mastered this art; their tantrums stopped immediately when they had gotten what they wanted. Another kind of evidence along this line comes from the association between parental acquiesence to the child's demands and tantrum frequency. This evidence is discussed in the section on parental influences forthcoming.

The potential for the manipulation of others by tantrums is facilitated by the development of the awareness of the self and others that can be seen as the basic core of social development (Kagan, 1971). A child who can monitor his or her own behavior becomes aware that things do not always go as planned, and one might argue that a self-aware child is more capable of using conflict to get his or her way. Temper tantrums also coincide with the beginning of social awareness (Kagen, 1984). They continue for a period of 1 to 2 years, by which time the child is 3 or 4 and has a theory of mind—that is to say that the child recognizes that every individual has unique experiences, thoughts, perceptions, and feelings, and that, whereas these are private and distinct from the child's, they are nonetheless similar to the ones that the child would experience in a similar situation. Between these two mileposts a great deal of social knowledge is acquired.

Social referencing also begins to develop at much the same time. By 12 months most babies will glance at their mothers when placed in a strange situation, and their behavior is influenced by the facial expressions of the parent. Inevitably, children who continually make reference to parents rapidly become aware of any inattention or disapproval. Our data suggests that most tantrums occur when the child wishes to do one thing and the parents another. However, the mere fact that other animals have tantrums suggests that, although the maturity of the child's social skills might augment the opportunities for tantrums (and learning through tantrums), it is hardly a prerequisite for them to occur.

Some children are artful tantrumers but for most it is not a very successful strategy. Overall, only 5.5% of tantrums are ended by the parents giving in to the children, whereas 29% of tantrums ended with children giving in to their parents. On simple reinforcement principles one would expect the behavior to extinguish fairly rapidly. It does not. The average child probably continues to have tantrums on an almost daily basis for at least a year. The majority of parents are not upset, embarrassed, or angered by their child's tantrums. Even when they are, it is unlikely that the emotional upset experienced by the parent is as intense as that experienced by the child. In the extreme cases, the child's anger even results in self-directed aggression. The person most hurt by the tantrum appears to be the child. What do children gain by such behavior? In Dunn's (1988) long-term study of children in 52 families through their second and third years, she found that "it was those issues which children at 18 months were most distressed or angry about that at 36 months they were most likely to justify . . . the children produced their most mature behavior when dealing with those issues they cared most about" (p. 10). Yet this cannot be the only answer. Children induce conflict about silly things as well as about important issues. They quarrel with a younger sibling for standing too close to their chair, touching something they have forbidden him or her to touch, or for looking through "their" car window. They are well aware of the impact of these behaviors on others. Dunn (1988) and Goodenough (1931) found that by 18 months children deliberately perform acts that have been expressly forbidden, either to gain attention or in retaliation for something done by the person in authority. Parens (1979) and Roiphe (1991) related similar observations made in research nurseries. Our letter writers tell us of children deliberately seeking an audience before beginning a tantrum. Children over 4 may laugh raucously, knowing that it is irritating to others. The picture of the "innocent" young child overcome by uncontrollable emotion when faced with an important matter of principle is clearly not the whole story.

Some of the major issues that children, like adults, are concerned with in social contexts are the avoidance of helplessness and the maintenance of some power and control within their familial relationships. Young children's lack of control in family situations is likely to make them angry. In other contexts, a child who has less control over a situation may become more angry (Bandura & Walters, 1959). Goodenough (1931) noted that as age advances an increasing percentage of outbursts show at least one stage during which energy is directed in more appropriate channels. Even at 14 months (before most children have full-blown tantrums), children recognize the effect of their angry outbursts on their parents; they even sometimes smile during such outbursts (Dunn & Munn, 1986). Tantrums may be about learning to use anger (or just the tantrum behaviors themselves) to manipulate their parents and assert control. As we report later, aggressive children have more tantrums. This observation is consistent with the suggestion that these children lack the social skills to control situations in other ways (e.g., Rubin, Bream, & Rose-Krasnor, 1991).

*A Sociobiological Perspective.* The preceding arguments presume that tantrums occur at age 2 because the child's developing perceptual, cognitive, and social abilities at that age make it more capable of social manipulation. However, many tantrums express confusion and disorientation at least as much as manipulation. Tantrums can continue even after the desired object is offered; it seems as if the child has "forgotten" what it wanted (see the quote in the Prodroma section earlier). If tantrums are a tool, they are not an easily controllable tool.

A different hypothesis that fits tantrums into the developmental timetable starts with a few reports from parents of children who appear to have had their first (and sometimes their only) tantrum without example or practice. Consider also that animals of other species behave in ways that strike observers as remarkably reminiscent of human temper tantrums. Such tantrums, which include intense screaming, crouching, hurling the self on ground, running, and occasionally attacking the mother, are relatively common in infant and juvenile chimpanzees (Hamburg & van Lawick Goodall, 1974). On-back tantrums have been witnessed in laboratory-reared baby chimps that are known never to have seen or practiced tantruming (e.g., Hebb, 1945). For both humans and apes, it is not necessary to learn how to tantrum.

From an evolutionary, game-theoretic perspective, there is a basic conflict between parent and offspring about how much time should be spent in parental care (Trivers, 1985). In most species the risk of mortality in the first year of life is very high. Correspondingly, most birds and mammals spend a very large proportion of their time and energy caring for their young in the initial phase of development. It is in the interest of the young to hold on to their parents protection and take the food they provide for as long as possible. From the parents' point of view, however, there comes a point at which their inclusive fitness would be better served by spending less time with this offspring and more time going about the business of producing the next set of offspring. So as the young grow and are capable of greater autonomy, the parents spend greater amounts of time off the nest or offering the nipple less readily and more briefly. In many species the mother retrieves or feeds her young, then quickly withdraws to a place where she may watch them without being in direct physical contact. The young, being "crazy like a fox" as Trivers (1985) put it, have counterstrategies. de Waal (1989) noted that female chimps prevent their young from nursing by threatening them and pushing them away. The youngster often responds by pouting and whimpering and by an occassional temper tantrum. The mother's response to this is to cuddle the youngster on the condition that it keeps its head turned away from the nipple. A compromise has been reached. By the age of 2, children in Western culture are long past weaning. Historically, however, 2 was the age of weaning in Western culture as it remains in other cultures to this day. The timing of tantrums may not be coincidental. A disposition to tantrum that develops at an age when weaning occurred over most of human history might well reflect a strategy to reassert command of parental attention. The fact that tantrums often end in cuddles may not be accidental.

*Learning Emotional Control and Conflict Management.* Independent of whether and how much operant learning, self- and social awareness, or sociobiological factors contribute to tantrum causation, children's eventual mastery of their tantrums may teach them valuable lessons in the use and control of emotions and the management of conflicts that arise between themselves and others. Judy Dunn (1988) wrote: "It is the child's egoism in the context of family relationships which motivates him to understand others" (p. 10). Anger is present in the young baby who cries with rage when hungry, hurt, or left alone.

Overt anger disappears in the child who is abandoned for long periods and protest is replaced by depression (Bowlby, 1969). Both responses are largely controlled in adults who may feel angry and upset but do not fly into rages or sink into depression. Anger is a necessary part of our makeup, enabling us to hold or compete for resources. Consider the behaviors of groups of strangers (of one or another age) competing for a boxful of toys or the bargains at a winter sale. Most of us do not behave like this at other times because we have regard for others within our social group and have learned to deal with compromise, win and lose conflicts, without resorting to battle. The gains made from aggressively fighting for resources must be balanced against the benefits of group living that demand that most of us keep anger in check in nearly all circumstances. Given the complexities of the human social environment, this probably requires some direct experience of conflict. Children must learn when to fight and when to step aside, when to express anger and when to supress it, and how to assert their will without losing control. Hay and Ross (1982), observing children in experimental settings, noted that they are adept at moving in and out of conflict, quickly abandoning arguments, yielding, and joining forces as necessary. Although on the surface the concerns of children in the nursery classroom and the home may be similar (e.g., the possession of toys, the friendship and esteem of others), conflict within the family is likely to be more intense because of the pre-existing emotions of love, jealousy, envy, and possessiveness embedded in the family context and because the struggle with older siblings and parents is less equal.


## IMMEDIATE CAUSE OF TANTRUMS


Parents attribute the majority (52%) of tantrums in children less than a year old to frustration or attention seeking. Frustration was equally divided between frustration with objects, people, and the child's own inabilities (cf. Miller & Sperry, 1987). For children older than a year, the single major cause of tantrums changes dramatically to conflicts with parents, whereas the number of tantrums attributed to attention seeking drops to less than 5%. These changes in attributed cause across age were statistically significant [$\chi^2$ (3) = 36.2, $p <$. 001]; Goodenough (1931) noted similar developmental trends. The conflicts followed requests as reasonable as the child asking to watch a video while the parent was watching TV or as outrageous as the child's insistence that he drive the family car. The most common issue of confrontation was eating (16.7%), closely followed by confining the child in a stroller, chair, or shopping cart (11.6%). The latter issue is consistent with Watson and Watson's (1921) classic observation that holding and restraining a child is a very effective stimulus to tantrum. Dressing accounted for 10.8% of tantrums. There were no noticeable gender differences in these figures. The temporal pattern varied with the situation provoking the tantrum, however. When parents refused children's wishes, the tantrum was perceived as beginning more quickly [$\chi^2(2) = 10.2, p < .01$] and persisting longer [$\chi^2(2) = 6.9, p < .05$] than when the child refused the parents' demand or frustration was the trigger.

A number of other conditions are known to increase tantrum probability. Goodenough (1931) noted a daily rhythm of tantrums with peaks in the late morning (i.e., before lunch, when children are hungry) and early evening. Parents in our survey similarly reported that tantrums were associated with fatigue; 35% occurred within an hour of bedtime (cf. Miller & Sperry, 1987). Goodenough (1931) also found that children who are in the process of becoming dry by night have almost twice as many tantrums on days following nights in which they wet their beds. There were also more tantrums on days following nights of restless sleep.

## INFLUENCES OF PARENTAL BEHAVIOR

That interactions with the mother are important in learning to control aggression is suggested by the increased aggressiveness of children deprived of maternal care (Ainsworth, 1973; Rutter, 1979). Even among children with continuous parental care, the nature of that care affects subsequent aggressiveness. Dunn (1988) suggested that the way in which parents deal with their own conflicts forms a model for the child's own behavior when engaged in conflict with others. A parent who hits provides one model, a parent who reasons another. In support of this position it should be recalled that induction (i.e., discipline based on reasoned discussion) and parental power assertion are two prominent forms of discipline that have been consistently linked to different ways that children think and behave in peer groups (e.g., Hart, De Wolf, Wozniak, & Burts, 1992). Parental rejection and inconsistency, punitive discipline, family discord, and maternal lack of self-esteem all increase children's aggressiveness (e.g., Patterson, Capaldi, & Bank, 1991).

*Cuddling.* There is within this survey some evidence that parental acceptance of the child's anger and its resolution (given in the form of a cuddle with or without discussion) can influence tantrum duration and frequency. Children who were cuddled at the end of the sample tantrum had tantrums that were significantly shorter [$\chi^2(4) = 12.2$, $p < .02$] and less frequent [$\chi^2(3) = 10.9$, $p < .02$] than children who were not. Although cuddling is one remedy for tantrums advocated by our respondents, it may not be the major influence. In our letter sample, almost all parents who wrote sympathetically about the need to understand their child's conflicts, or sat with the child and discussed the reasons and resolutions of the tantrum, cuddled the child. So did those whose forgiveness was reinforced by reading stories or by playing with the child. It is also possible that the causality goes in the opposite direction (i.e., that parents are more likely to cuddle children whose tantrums are shorter or less frequent). It is worth noting, nonetheless, that discipline based on induction rather than parental power assertion (Parke & Slaby, 1983) has been linked with greater self-discipline, lower hostility, and fewer aggressive interactions with peers (Baumrind, 1971; Bearison & Cassel, 1975).

*To Give In, or Not to Give In, or Both.* An immediate solution to stopping a tantrum is to give in. Parents are normally advised not to do so. Does the short-term solution have a long-term price? In our sample 5.5% of parents gave in to the child having the tantrum, at least on the occasion recorded. If tantrums are operants, it follows that children should be reinforced for having them and that tantrum frequency should increase. For children having more than five tantrums a day, the rate of acquiesence was a significantly higher 23%. A further test of this hypothesis was carried out by forming pairs of children matched for age and gender, the parents of one of whom gave in and the parents of the other did not (*n* = 57 pairs). As Table 7.5 shows, children who "got their own way" following a tantrum had longer [$\chi^2(3) = 27.5$, $p < .001$] and more frequent tantrums [$\chi^2(3) = 14.4$, $p < .005$]. This is quite consistent

TABLE 7.5
Distribution of Tantrum Frequency as a Function of
Parental Acquiescence

|  | Child's Tantrum Frequency | | |
|---|---|---|---|
|  | < 1/week | 1–7/week | ≥ 2/day |
| Parent acquiesces | 6 | 56 | 38 |
| Parent does not acquiesce | 4 | 80 | 16 |

Note: The top row contains the percentage distribution of tantrum frequencies for children whose parents said they gave in to the sample tantrum. For example, 6% of these children tantrumed less than once a week. The bottom row is the percentage distribution of children whose parents did not give in.

with Goodenough's (1931) original findings and with the report of Patterson et al. (1991), that roughly 14% of the coercive behaviors used by normal children within the family obtain the desired ends, whereas 22% of such maneuvers are successful when tried by aggressive children who use them more frequently.

In the survey as a whole, 45% of tantrums occurred when parents refused their child's wishes; a similar rate occurred in the subsample of 57 children whose parents did not give in. If we consider only those parents who subsequently give in, 77% of tantrums arose because the parents refused their child's wishes. Assuming that the overall rate at which children refuse to comply with parents is not affected by parent acquiesence, it appears that children who win also may make more demands on their parents.

The last question in the survey concerned the parents' policy of discipline; one of the four choices that could be endorsed for that question was "No policy—it depends on mood." Twenty percent of parents overall selected this answer. Among those who reported giving in, this figure rose to 38%, a significantly higher proportion than in the main sample [$\chi^2(1) = 26.2$, $p < .005$]. Thus, the higher tantrum rates in children whose parents acquiesced may in part be due to their parents' lack of consistency.

*Emotions and Behaviors of Parents of Children with Extreme Tantrums.* As the data on *giving in* suggest, it is instructive to examine parents' responses to the extremes of tantrum behavior. These data are shown in Table 7.6. Unsurprisingly, the mothers of children with the highest frequency and the longest duration of tantrums were more likely to report that they were angry and/or upset at the tantrum (more than twice as likely in the case of frequent tantrumers). If what is reported as a response to a particular tantrum actually reflects chronic mood states, it is possible that the higher incidence of anger in these mothers is a cause rather than an effect. This indeed seems to be the perception of the mothers of children with the highest frequency of tantrums, 40% of whom reported that their own mood and/or family upset was influencing their child compared to 28% of the mothers in the sample as a whole. The situation appears quite different for mothers of children with the longest duration of tantrums, only 3% of whom felt that their mood influenced their child. This difference among the groups was among the most striking and significant in our survey [$\chi^2(2) = 27.1$, $p < .001$].

Parental inattention may be another tantrum-facilitating factor. The mothers of children having five or more tantrums a day were less than half as likely to be caring for their child at the time of the tantrum. They were also less likely to be engaged in housework, which arguably can

TABLE 7.6
Behavior of Mothers of Children at the Extremes of Tantrum
Frequency and Duration

| | Characteristics of Child's Tantrum | | |
| --- | --- | --- | --- |
| | Frequency > 5/Day | Whole Sample | Duration ≥ 20 Minutes |
| Mother's reaction to tantrum | | | |
| Feels angry | 50 | 21 | 39 |
| Acts angry | 35 | 16 | 21 |
| Feels upset | 50 | 20 | 29 |
| Believes her mood is a causal factor in child's tantrum | 40 | 28 | 3 |
| Mother's activity during tantrum | | | |
| Attend to tantruming child | 15 | 37 | 25 |
| Attend to other child[a] | 34 | 10 | 0 |
| Attend to other things | | | |
| Housework/shopping | 15 | 40 | 43 |
| Other activities[b] | 40 | 15 | 32 |

Note: In the upper section of this table, the respondent could endorse one or more of these reactions to the tantrum; the figures shown are the percentage of respondents in the respective (sub)samples who endorsed each choice. The lower section of the table shows percentages of only those respondents who endorsed a single activity. [a]This subsample includes only families with more than one child. [b]Other activities include: Talking/being with friends and Washing/dressing/reading/doing things for myself.

be carried out while interacting with the child, and more likely to be with friends, watching TV, or reading. Children probably perceive these latter activities as excluding them and respond accordingly. This impression is strengthened by examination of subsamples of children with high or low frequency of tantrums who have been matched for numbers of siblings. This analysis showed that when a tantrum was thrown by a child with a lower frequency of tantrums, the mother was almost four times as likely to be attending to the tantrumer as another sibling (Table 7.5). Quite the opposite was the case for mothers of high-tantruming children who were more than twice as likely to be attending to another child. Blurton Jones et al. (1979) reported that mothers of aggressive 1- and 3-year-olds are less attentive to their child's crying than are mothers of less aggressive children. Their report is consistent with our observations because, as described next, frequently tantruming children are more hostile than other children.

Mothers of children at the extremes of tantrum behavior were also more likely to shout at, threaten, and strike their children. Overall, only 4% of our respondents indicated that they struck their child because he or she had a tantrum. In sharp contrast, striking was reported by 15% of parents of longest tantrumers and 17% of parents of the most frequent tantrumers. Children who were struck after the sample tantrum had significantly higher frequencies of tantruming [$\chi^2(3) = 21.4$, $p < .001$] but not longer tantrums [$\chi^2(4) = 5.0$, NS]. Are children's tantrums frequent or prolonged because their mother is inattentive and uses physical punishment, or are the mothers' inattention and their negative emotions and behavior a function of their children's excessive tantrums? This survey cannot resolve cause and effect. However, preliminary results from a subsequent survey indicate that high rates of tantruming are associated with high rates of punishment unrelated to the particular tantrum surveyed, suggesting that it is parental behavior that is shaping tantrum rate.

## THE CONSISTENCY OF TANTRUMS
## AND THEIR IMPORTANCE AS AN EARLY INDICATOR
## OF TEMPERAMENT

There is increasing evidence that traits like shyness and hostility emerge early in development and are informative predictors of adult personality and behavior (see, e.g., Malatesta, Culver, Tesman, & Shepard, 1989, for review). Because tantrums are such a common feature of early childhood, engaged in by at least half of all 2-year-olds, the fact that a given 2-year old has a tantrum may not convey much information about that child. Having a high frequency of tantrums might be more informative, particularly if such behavior were consistent and persistent. In a longitudinal study that repeatedly evaluated various problems of 252 "normal" children between 21 months and 14 years, MacFarlane et al. (1954) found that tantruming was a consistent trait in 58% of boys and 35% of girls. Within-subject, interage correlations were consistently high after age 8. In younger children, Jenkins et al. (1984) found that children with a high frequency of tantrums tend also to be those who persist in tantrums. About a third of their sample who had more than one tantrum a day at age 2 were still tantruming at 4½. A similar trend appeared among the 4-year-olds in our survey: The earlier they had begun, the higher their rate. Children who began to tantrum at age 3 have a mean rate of 5.1 per week at age 4, those beginning at 2 have 5.9 tantrums per week at 4, and those who started tantruming before the age of 2 have tantrums at a mean rate of 7.7 per week. The later rate is actually higher than the contemporaneous mean rate for 1- and 2-year-olds, 6.5 and 6.8 per week, respectively. This suggests that tantrum rates increase for the persistent subgroup, or, more likely, the persistent children are those with the higher rates to begin with. Thus, there are some children who can be characterized as early, frequent, and persistent tantrumers. What does this characteristic portend about other aspects of their personality?

*"Difficulty" and Illness.* Thomas and Chess (1977) defined difficult children by a set of characteristics including low adaptability, withdrawal from new stimuli, and low levels of rhythmicity. These children also had high rates of tantruming. Manning and Sluckin (1983) noted two types of "difficult" children, those who were quarrelsome, bossy, and prone to anger, and those who were pestering and dependent. Factor-analytic studies by Bates and colleagues suggested that the label of *difficulty* is assigned to children displaying frequent and intense episodes of negative emotion; a classification of difficult at 6 and 24 months was predictive of anxiety, hostility, and hyperactivity at age 3 (Bates, Bayles, Bennett, Ridge, & Brown, 1991). Jenkins et al. (1984) found that 2- and 3-year-old children having more than four tantrums a day are likely to be rated by their mothers as demanding of attention and difficult to manage. Macfarlane et al. (1954) found that temper tantrums were related to overdependence and negativism in both boys and girls at several ages. The latter authors further noted that "For a number of children, tantrums tapered into *over-sensitiveness, mood swings, or excessive reserve*" (p. 137, italics theirs).

To determine if there were any such relationships in our sample, we compared children at the high end of the distribution of tantrum frequency with age- and gender-matched children from the low end of the range. We first looked for a history of "colic" (i.e., "excessive" and inconsolable crying in early infancy; Brazelton, 1962; St. James Roberts, 1989). Although we found no significant associations with 6-week colic, children who had two or more tantrums a day were significantly more likely to have had a history of frequent crying in the first year of life compared to those whose tantrum frequency was less than one a week [$\chi^2(1) = 16.8$, $p < .005$]. They were also more likely to have started tantrums before the age of 1 [$\chi^2(1) = 6.8$, $p < .01$]. Macfarlane et al. (1954) reported that temper tantrums in boys correlated positively with food finickiness and speech problems at 21 months and sleep disturbances up to age 12. Our survey revealed no evidence for a relationship between tantrum frequency and any other problem such as poor sleep pattern, difficult weaning, or delayed speech.

Eleven percent of tantrums in our survey were associated with illness such as a mild cold or infectious disease (cf. Miller & Sperry, 1987). There is reason to suppose that inconsolable crying and tantrum frequency could be related to a history of ill health. Sick babies cry; Goodenough (1931) presented evidence for a direct relationship between the number of illnesses a child had experienced and the frequency of tantrums, even if the child were well at the time of the survey. Macfarlane et al. (1954) found a correlation of 0.41 between illness and tantrums in girls but not in boys at 21 months. It is possible that sick children develop a demanding style of interaction, and that this increases the level of confrontation between parent and child. In the preceding section we presented evidence that parental anger may increase the frequency of tantrums in children. Equally, it is possible that parents of sick children may be less patient with, and more physically abusive of, their children, as parents of handicapped children and children whose emotional reactions are intense and demanding sometimes are.

*Hostility.* Anger and aggression are clearly major emotional components of tantrums. The pioneering studies of Olweus in Sweden, Farrington in England, and Eron and Huesmann and others in America have demonstrated the consistency of antisocial behavior and aggressiveness as a recognizable personality trait from around age 6 to 8 through to early adulthood (see Farrington, 1991, for review). In identifying an "early starter" route from childhood antisocial behavior to later criminal violence, Patterson and colleagues (e.g., 1991) suggested that this trait can be recognized even earlier, starting at age 4, when it is being strengthened by the parents' inadvertent reinforcement of the child's coercive behaviors. These behaviors include temper tantrums. Consistent with this suggestion, tantrums persisting at age 5 and later are associated with antisocial personality. Macfarlane et al. (1954) found that persistent tantruming in boys and girls is associated with irritability at age 12. Factor-analytic studies of normal and clinical samples of children between 4 and 16 have found that temper tantrums load highly on a factor clearly identifiable as aggression or hostility (Achenbach, 1978; Elithorn, 1974): In both studies the factor included disobedience and fighting and, in the Achenbach study, it also included such items as argues, is cruel to others, and threatens and attacks people. These findings indicate that temper tantrums in middle and later childhood are one of several manifestations of an underlying trait of aggressiveness.

Are consistently high levels of tantrum behavior in preschool children an even earlier indicator of an enduring personality trait? We addressed the question of tantrums as indicators of personality in several ways. The first approach was to select children who were at the extremes of tantrum frequency or duration and determine if they were more likely to behave aggressively. As Table 7.7 shows, children who were reported as having five or more tantrums a day had higher incidences of aggressive

TABLE 7.7
Characteristics of Children at the Extremes of Tantrum
Frequency and Duration

| | Characteristics of Child's Tantrum | | |
|---|---|---|---|
| | Frequency > 5/Day | Whole Sample | Duration ≥ 20 Minutes |
| Behaviors within tantrum | | | |
| Angry expression | 55 | 55 | 65 |
| Hits objects | 41 | 26 | 13 |
| Hits people | 41 | 33 | 26 |
| Bites people | 31 | 10 | 1 |
| Behaviors outside tantrum | | | |
| Aggression toward others | | | |
| Bullies other children | 28 | 10 | 4 |
| Retaliates if attacked | 58 | 33 | 26 |
| Aggression from others | | | |
| Picked on by other children | 7 | 7 | 13 |
| Shouted at by parents | 26 | 21 | 15 |
| Smacked by parents | 17 | 4 | 15 |

Note: The figures are the percentage of respondents in the respective (sub)samples endorsing each choice.

behaviors both within the tantrum (hits objects, hits people, bites) and more generally in peer relations (retaliates, bullies others). This was not true of children whose reported tantrum lasted 20 minutes or more. The latter children responded rapidly and looked angry but were less likely than the average child to act aggressively within the tantrum or toward other children outside the tantrum. They were almost twice as likely to be picked on by other children. It may be that long tantrums are characteristic of the second kind of "difficult" children described by Manning and Sluckin (1983; i.e., those who are pestering and dependent). As noted in the preceding section, mothers may also treat children who have long tantrums differently than those with frequent tantrums, paying more attention to the former than the latter.

To pursue the relationship between tantrum frequency and aggressiveness, we took an approach complementary to the preceding one by identifying children rated as particularly aggressive in peer relations and then evaluating their tantrum frequency. Sixty-seven children were selected based upon their parents' choice of "often" in response to one or both of the following two statements: "This child teases or insults other children" and "This child hits or bullies other children." These children were matched by age and gender with 67 other children for whom the parents' response to both questions had been "never." The aggressive children had significantly more frequent tantrums [$\chi^2(4) = 29.4$, $p < .001$]. Considering the extremes of tantrum frequency, 54% of the aggressive children had more than two tantrums a day compared to 14% of the comparison group. We also evaluated the cross-situational consistency of aggressiveness in tantrums and in peer relations. Tantrums were rated for aggressiveness by assigning 1 point each for "angry face" and "makes a fist" (symbolic expressions of anger) and 2 points for each gross physical activity like screaming, kicking, and flailing. As mentioned earlier, spitting, pinching, biting, scratching, and hair pulling are less frequent and more deliberately harmful acts. Each of these was awarded a score of 3. The maximum obtainable score was 24. As Fig. 7.3 shows, the distribution of tantrum aggressiveness scores in the aggressive children was strongly and significantly skewed toward the high end [$\chi^2(5) = 16.1$, $p < .01$].

Our results suggest that hostility appears as a consistent cross-situational trait even earlier than previously shown, and that tantrum frequency is one aspect of that trait. Longitudinal studies will be required to determine the stability of this trait, and if those who are highly hostile as young children are the ones who continue to tantrum past the age of 5. Dodge's (1991) studies of boys 5 through 12 years old distinguish between proactive and reactive forms of overt aggressive

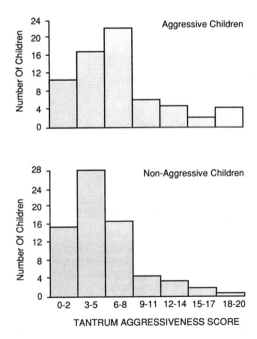

FIG. 7.3.  Distribution of tantrum aggressiveness score for children classified as aggressive ($N = 67$) or non aggressive ($N = 67$). Criteria for classification and scoring of tantrum behaviors are described in the text.

behavior. The former consists of object acquisition, bullying, and dominance over peers; the latter is displayed as anger or temper tantrums. The most significant characteristic distinguishing between forms is the absence or presence of anger. The question of whether hostile 2- to 4-year-olds with a high frequency of tantrums go on to become the reactive aggressors described by Dodge could also be resolved by longitudinal studies.

## TANTRUMS AS THE CONSEQUENCE OF EMOTIONAL INTENSITY AND LABILITY; BEING "OUT OF CONTROL"

Children look angry during tantrums and the behaviors performed such as foot stamping, kicking, flailing, screaming, and deliberate injury to themselves and others certainly suggest anger that has escalated. We know in other social contexts children's emotions are "fierce" and often extreme. One has only to watch a group of young children running in and out of a garden sprinkler to recognize the intensity of their shared pleasure. The open joy, anger, possessiveness, jealousy, or love displayed toward his or her family by a 2-year-old would be considered pathological in an adult. If the lability of a child's moods persisted to adulthood, it would give cause for concern. In principle, there is no reason for a child to feel such intense emotions nor for that intensity to be largely confined to the family relationships. Teachers and child minders confirm that tantrums are rare in day care and nursery schools, even when children spend much of their waking hours in such places. Studies in nursery schools indicate that conflict between the children lessens as they get to know one another. Why does not familiarity, surely greater within families than outside the family, also reduce the excesses of sibling rivalry? Perhaps children, like adults, expose themselves to intense emotion only when it is safe to do so. It is within our own homes and cars that most of us tend to lose our tempers. If we throw things or hit, it is usually a loved one at the receiving end.

Malatesta et al. (1989) argued that certain facial expressions such as pursed lips are associated with the suppression or "neutralization" of unpleasant emotions; the increasing frequency of such expressions during the first 2 years of life indicates the learning of emotional control, a control that helps the child avoid the experience of "toxic" emotions. Tantrums may occur when this learning fails: Needlman et al. (1989) commented that "tantrums occur when emotions exceed the child's ability to control them" (p. 12). Goodenough (1931) remarked that "in younger children . . . the behavior has the appearance of an explosive form of emotional outlet" (p. 66).

In apparent contrast to the foregoing observations, some parents noted that their child's tantrums appear to be performed for the benefit of an audience. Children will move directly in front of the parent and perform any manner of other maneuvers to ensure attention to their tantrum. Furthermore, their aggressive acts are sometimes well directed; they will hit or throw things with some accuracy and will wriggle into position to kick a particular object. Tantrums can also sometimes be defused: One mother reported that when *she* lay on the floor and screamed, her child stopped. Another wrote that when she laughed, it allowed her child to stop. In contrast, several respondents noted that their laughter would intensify the child's tantrum. In either case, the children were responding to events in their environment; they were not cut off. The degree to which a child is out of control may well depend on the particular child; it may also depend on the particular stage of the tantrum. Parens et al. (1987), and our letter writers, too, talked about a point of no return before which an adroit intervention can forestall a tantrum and after which any intervention, no matter how adroit, will only make it worse. It is in the second and third stages that the child may seem "out of control." Because they first maneuver to be seen does not mean that they then do not really lose control. Temporal lobe epileptics about to have a seizure have been known to warn people to leave the room, but it is a real, uncontrollable seizure that they then have.

What elements might be involved in the loss of control? One element is a paradoxical intentionality, a deliberate abandonment of self-control. Children in the midst of a tantrum protect their own emotional state. They reject parents' advances and prolong the tantrum by re-escalating if parents try to stop or comfort them. A second element is a narrowing of attentional focus. This is a common phenomenon in adults; angered individuals ignore stimuli that would ordinarily capture their attention and proceed without caution to say and do things they would ordinarily not (Potegal, 1979; Zillmann, this volume). As noted previously, there is also a change in responsiveness to stimuli such as being held. On a more physiological level, the somatosensory and proprioceptive signals generated during a tantrum could act to intensify and prolong it. The act of frowning has been reported to intensify felt anger, for example (Laird, 1974; see Collier, 1985, for review). The vigorous behaviors and autonomic concomitants of a tantrum may act in similar positive feedback fashion (Zillmann, this volume). It is also possible that mechanisms intrinsic to the central nervous system act to intensify and prolong anger; Potegal (this volume) reviews the evidence for such mechanisms.

## ARE SOME TANTRUMS MILD, TRANSIENT,
## LOCALIZED SEIZURES OF THE TEMPORAL LOBE?

When a particular 2½-year-old in our survey was forbidden to do something she wanted, she would scream and then induce a fit by holding her breath. Eventually she would pass out. She is not the first or the only child to act in this way. Five lines of argument can be adduced to support the proposition that some temper tantrums may involve an extreme instance of "out of control," a localized seizure of the temporal lobe:

1. Tantrums are found to be common in children with temporal lobe foci although most of the children in these studies were well past normal tantrum age (Elithorn, 1974; Keating, 1961; Nuffield, 1961). The correlation is higher with temporal lobe foci than with foci elsewhere (Elithorn, 1974; Nuffield, 1961).

2. The abrupt onset of many tantrums, with or without a prodroma, the apparent obliviousness to the environment at the peak of the tantrum (if not before), and the relatively quick return to a normal state are reminiscent of the sequence and time course of some seizures (Smith, 1980).

3. The classic temporal lobe seizure, like many tantrums, involves autonomic signs including pallor followed by flushing, salivation, lacrimation, and sweating. Autonomic signs also accompany adult temper tantrums (see Potegal, this volume).

4. Making the body stiff and rigid occurred in roughly 25% of tantrums in our survey. This arching of the back and rigid extension of the limbs resembles the tonic stage of extensor muscle activation occurring in grand mal and some other seizure disorders. In a few children, as in grand mal patients, stiffening can happen so quickly and strongly that the child topples over involuntarily. An age-related susceptibility to seizures is suggested by the existence of febrile seizures and by the Lennox-Gastaut syndrome whose major period of onset is between 1 and 3 years. This syndrome includes purely tonic seizures with extension of the extremities and rigid stretching of the body. Unlike tantrums, however, these seizures occur during sleep. The syndrome also includes drop attacks during waking and mental retardation. The parents of three young children (12 to 22 months) in our survey mentioned that their child's arms go up into the air at the beginning of the tantrum; head turning and arm raising are characteristic of seizures involving the supplementary motor area. Of course, these cortical regions may become activated during tantrums without frank seizures occurring.

5. The extremes of emotion in the reconciliation mode described by Welch (1988) for holding therapy and Walker (1979) for spouse abuse are reminiscent of the intense states of well-being and even euphoria occurring after some temporal lobe seizures (Smith, 1980).

There are, in addition, a great many differences between temporal lobe seizures and tantrums. Temporal lobe epilepsy is rare and pathological, for example, whereas temper tantrums are common and normal. Furthermore, the claim that having a temporal lobe focus predisposes the affected individual to anger and aggression is still controversial (see Potegal, this volume, for review). We conjecture that during the terrible twos and threes the limbic–temporal lobe circuitry whose activation causes anger undergoes a developmental hypersensitivity that in most cases is mild and transient. With extreme hypersensitivity, angry tantrums can be triggered by slight provocation or even erupt without warning (cf. chapter 4, this volume). When activity in these circuits is high, as indicated by intense emotional arousal, additional circuitry is engaged, resulting in rigidity as in other types of seizure. Tantrums occur mainly when the child is at home with loved ones, and they are strongly influenced by mother's mood and behavior. Thus, this circuitry, even when hypersensitive, remains under environmental control and is activated only under specific conditions.

## CONCLUSIONS

Tantrums turn out to be largely about conflicts between the child and his or her parents and the child's resulting anger. Tantrums have a structure that usually consists of several identifiable emotional stages that precede and follow the angry confrontation phase. These stages resemble the emotional sequencing in other conflict situations where a social bond exists between the participants. Tantrums do not occur at random; they occur when there is something to fight about and when it is safe to experiment. In the safety of their homes children sometimes appear to induce tantrums by contrariness or other means, but most tantrums arise because of direct conflict between mother and child. Parents who give in to children increase the frequency of their child's tantrums, and those who react to tantrums with aggression have more aggressive children. Such children also have more frequent tantrums. Parents who offer cuddles and comfort after the tantrum is over are rewarded with fewer and less persistent tantrums.

Dunn (1988) found that, even at 14 months, children have some sense of their family's interpretation of the rules of justice. She suggested that children develop this knowledge by engaging in family conflicts. Perhaps children's tantrums are sometimes deliberately provoked as part of this learning process, as an experiment in lack of control when it is safe to be so. However, it seems more likely that children have tantrums when they have cause to do so and when they might gain by so doing.

## REFERENCES

Achenbach, T. M. (1978). The child behavior profile: 1. Boys aged 6–11. *Journal of Consulting and Clinical Psychology, 46,* 478–488.

Ainsworth, M. D. (1973). The development of infant–mother attachment. In B. Caldwell & H. Ricciuti (Eds.), *Review of child development research,* (Vol. 3, pp. 1–94). Chicago: University of Chicago Press.

Anderson, J. R., & Chamove, A. S. (1980). Self-aggression and social aggression in laboratory reared macaques. *Journal of Abnormal Psychology, 89,* 539–550.

Bandura, A., & Walters, R. H. (1963). *Social learning and personality development.* New York: Holt, Rinehart and Winston.

Bates, J. E., Bayles, K., Bennett, D. S., Ridge, B., & Brown, M. M. (1991). Origins of externalizing behavior problems at eight years of age. In D. J. Pepler & K. H. Rubin (Eds.), *The development and treatment of childhood aggression* (pp. 93–120). Hillsdale NJ: Lawrence Erlbaum Associates.

Baumeister, A. A., & Rollings, J. P. (1976). Self-injurious behavior. In N. R. Ellis (Ed.), *International review of research in mental retardation* (Vol. 8, pp. 1–34). New York: Academic.

Baumrind, D. (1971). Current patterns of parental authority. *Developmental Psychology Monographs, 4* (Part 1&2), 1–103.

Bearison, D. J., & Cassel, T. Z. (1975). Cognitive decentration and social codes: Communicative effectiveness in young children from different family contexts. *Developmental Psychology, 11,* 29–36.

Blurton-Jones, N., Ferreira, M. C. R., Farquhar Brown, M., & Macdonald, L. (1979). Aggression, crying and physical contact in one- to three-year-old children. *Aggression Behavior, 5,* 121–133.

Bowlby, J. (1969). *Attachment and loss.* New York: Basic Books.

Brazelton, T. B. (1962). Crying in infancy. *Pediatrics, 29,* 579–588.

Carr, E. G., & Newsom, C. (1985) Demand-related tantrums. *Behavior Modification, 9,* 403–426.

Carroll, L. (1965). *Alice's adventures in Wonderland.* (Centiennial Ed.) New York: Random House.

Chamberlin, R. W. (1974). Management of preschool behavior problems. *Pediatric Clinics of North America, 21,* Issue No. 1.

Collier, G. (1985). *Emotional expression.* Hillsdale, NJ: Lawrence Erlbaum Associates.

Cords, M. (1988). Resolution of aggressive conflicts by immature long-tailed macaques *Macaca fascicularis. Animal Behavior, 36,* 1124–1135.

Cullinan, D., & Epstein, M. H. (1982). Behavior disorders. In N. G. Haring (Ed.), *Exceptional children and youth* (3rd ed., pp. 207–242). Columbus, OH: Cambridge University Press.

de Catanzaro, D. A. (1978). Self-injurious behavior: A behavior analysis. *Motivation and Emotion, 2,* 45–65.

de Waal, F. B. M. (1989). *Peacemaking among primates.* Cambridge, MA: Harvard University Press.

de Waal, F. B. M., & van Roosmalen, A. (1979). Reconciliation and redirected affection among chimpanzees. *Behavior Ecology and Sociobiology, 5,* 55–66.

de Waal, F. B. M., & Yoshihara, D. (1983). Reconciliation and redirected affection in rhesus monkeys. *Behaviour, 85,* 224–241.

Dobash, R. E., & Dobash, R. P. (1984). The nature and antecedents of violent events. *British Journal of Criminology, 24,* 269–288.

Dodge, K. A. (1991). The structure and function of reactive and proactive aggression. In D. J. Pepler & K. H. Rubin (Eds.), *The development and treatment of childhood aggression* (pp. 201–218). Hillsdale, NJ: Lawrence Erlbaum Associates.

Dunn, J. (1988). *The beginnings of social understanding.* Oxford: Basil Blackwell.

Dunn, J., & Munn, P. (1986). Becoming a family member: Family conflict and the development of social understanding. *Child Development, 56,* 480–492.

Dutton, D. G. (1988). *Domestic assault on women.* Boston: Allyn & Bacon.

Elithorn, A. (1974). Sources of aggressivity in epileptic children. In J. de Wit & W. W. Hartup (Eds.), *Determinants and origins of aggressive behavior* (pp. 325–336). The Hague, Netherlands: Mouton.

Farrington, D. P. (1991). Childhood aggression and adult violence: Early precursors and later life outcomes. In D. J. Pepler & K. H. Rubin (Eds.), *The development and treatment of childhood aggression* (pp. 5–30). Hillsdale, NJ: Lawrence Erlbaum Associates.

Finch, G. (1942). Chimpanzee frustration responses. *Psychosomatic Medicine, 4,* 233–251.

Gluck, J. P. & Sackett, G. P. (1974). Frustration and self-aggression in social isolate rhesus monkeys. *Journal of Abnormal Psychology, 83,* 331–334.

Goodall, J. van-Lawick (1988). *In the shadow of man.* (rev. ed.) New York: Houghton Mifflin.

Goodenough, F. (1931). *Anger in young children.* Minneapolis: University of Minnesota Press.

Goosen, C., & Ribbens, L. G. (1980). Autoaggression and tactile communication in pairs of adult stumptailed macaques. *Behaviour, 73,* 155–174.

Greenspan, S. I., & Greenspan, N. T. (1985). *First feelings: Milestones in the emotional development of your baby and child.* New York: Viking.

Hamburg, D., & van Lawick-Goodall, J. (1974). Factors facilitating development of aggressive behavior in chimpanzees and humans. In J. de Wit & W. W. Hartup (Eds.), *Determinants and origins of aggressive behavior* (pp. 59–86). The Hague, Netherlands: Mouton.

Hart, C. H., De Wolf, D., Wozniak, P., & Burts, D. C. (1992). Maternal and paternal disciplinary styles: Relations with preschool's playground behavioral orientations and peer status. *Child Development, 63,* 879–892.

Hay, D. F., & Ross, M. S. (1982). The social nature of early conflict. *Child Development, 53,* 105–113.

Hebb, D. O. (1945). The forms and conditions of chimpanzee anger. *Bulletin of the Canadian Psychological Association, 5,* 32–35.

Jenkins, S., Owen, C., Bax, M., & Hart, H. (1984) Continuities of common behavior problems in preschool children. *Journal of Child Psychology and Psychiatry, 25,* 75–89.

Kagan, J. (1971). *Change and continuity in infancy.* New York: Wiley.

Kagan, J. (1984). *The nature of the child.* New York: Basic.

Keating, L. E., (1961). Epilepsy and behavior disorder in school children. *Journal of Mental Science, 107,* 161–180.

Kravitz, H., & Boehm, S. (1971). Rhythmic habit patterns in infancy: Their sequence, age of onset, and frequency. *Child Development, 42,* 399–413.

Laird, J. D. (1974). Self-attribution of emotion: The effects of expressive behavior on the quality of emotional experience. *Journal of Personality and Social Psychology, 29,* 475–486.

Maccoby, E. E., & Jacklin, C. N. (1980). Sex differences in aggression: A rejoinder and reprise. *Child Development, 51,* 964–980.

Macfarlane, J. W., Allen, L., & Honzik, M. P. (1954). *A development study of the behavior problems of normal children between twenty one months and fourteen years.* Berkeley: University of California Press.

Malatesta, C. Z., Culver, C., Tesman, J. R., & Shepard, B. (1989). The development of emotion expression during the first two years of life. *Monographs of the Society for Research in Child Development, 54,* (1–2), 1–140.

Manning, M., & Sluckin, E. (1983). The function of aggression in the preschool years. In N. Freude & H. Cault (Eds.), *Children's aggression at school.* London: Wiley.

Miller, P., & Sperry, L. L. (1987). The socialization of anger and aggression. *Merrill–Palmer Quarterly, 33,* 1–31.

Needlman, R., Howard, B., & Zuckerman, B. (1989). Temper tantrums: When to worry. *Contemporary Pediatrics, 6,* 12–34.

Nuffield, E. J. A. (1961). Neurophysiology and behaviour disorders in epileptic children. *Journal of Mental Science 107,* 438–458.

Parens, H. (1979). *The development of aggression in early childhood.* New York: Aronson.

Parens, H., Scattergood, E., Singletary, W., & Duff, A. (1987). *Aggression in our children.* Northvale, NJ: Aronson.

Parke, R. D., & Slaby, R. G. (1983). The development of aggression. In E. M. Hetherington (Ed.), *Handbook of child psychology: Socialization, personality, and social development* (4th ed. Vol. 4, pp. 547–643). New York: Wiley.

Patterson, G., Capaldi, D., & Bank, L. (1991). An early starter model for predicting delinquency. In D. J. Pepler & K. H. Rubin (Eds.), *The development and treatment of childhood aggression* (pp. 139–168). Hillsdale, NJ: Lawrence Erlbaum Associates.

Potegal, M. (1979). The reinforcing value of several types of aggressive behavior: A review. *Aggressive Behavior, 5,* 353–373.

Rajecki, D. W., Lamb, M. E., & Obmasche, P. (1978). Toward a general theory of infantile attachment: Comparative review of aspects of the social bond. *Behavioral and Brain Sciences, 1,* 417–436.

Roiphe, H. (1991). The tormentor and the victim in the nursery. *Psychoanalytic Quarterly, 40,* 450–464.

Rubin, K. H., Bream, L. A., & Rose-Krasnor, L. (1991). Social problem solving and aggression in childhood. In D. J. Pepler & K. H. Rubin (Eds.), *The development and treatment of childhood aggression* (pp. 219–248). Hillsdale NJ: Lawrence Erlbaum Associates.

Rutter, M. (1979). Maternal deprivation 1972–1978. *Child Development,* 283–305,

Smith, J. S. (1980). Episodic rage. In M. Girgis & L. G. Kiloh (Eds.), *Limbic epilepsy and the dyscontrol syndrome.* Amsterdam: Elsevier/North Holland Press.

Sroufe, L. A. (1979). Socioemotional development. In J. D. Osofsky (Ed.), *Handbook of infant development* (pp. 462–516). New York: Wiley.

St. James Roberts, I. (1989). Persistent crying in infancy. *Journal of Child Psychology and Psychiatry, 30,* 189–195.

Thomas, A., & Chess, S. (1977). *Temperament and development.* New York: Brunner/Mazel

Trivers, R. (1985). *Social evolution.* Cummings, CA: Benjamin.

Walker, L. (1979). *The battered woman.* New York: Harper & Row.

Watson, J. B., & Watson, R. R. (1921). Studies in infant psychology. *Scientific Monthly, 7,* 493–515.

Welch, M. (1988). *Holding time.* London: Century.

York, A. D., & Rowell, T. E. (1988). Reconciliation following aggression in patas monkeys *Erythrocebus patas. Animal Behaviour, 36,* 502–509.

# CHAPTER 8

# Physically Abusive Parenting as an Escalated Aggressive Response

John F. Knutson
Mary E. Bower
*University of Iowa*

## THE CONCEPT OF ESCALATION IN PHYSICAL ABUSE OF CHILDREN

Although it is possible to identify articles relevant to the maltreatment of children in the late 19th and early 20th centuries, the recognition of physical abuse of children by parents as a major public health problem dates largely from the influential paper describing the "Battered Child Syndrome" (Kempe, Silverman, Steele, Droegemueller, & Silver, 1962). Within the United States, this influential paper stimulated public and professional awareness, public policy, and legislative initiatives (cf. Nelson, 1984), as well as a dramatic growth in research. Knutson and Schartz (in press) recently reported a consideration of over 1, 200 articles pertaining to physical abuse and neglect of children since 1973. Although there has been a burgeoning of research on abuse of children, epidemiological data (e.g., Knutson & Selner, 1994; Office of Human Development Services, 1988; Straus & Gelles, 1986) do not suggest that the research and public policy initiatives have had a significant influence on the prevalence of physical abuse. Moreover, although there are some optimistic reports based on interventions with "at-risk families" (e.g., Hardy & Streett, 1989; Hornick & Clarke, 1986; Wolfe, Edwards, Manion, & Koverola, 1988), the intervention efforts that have been empirically tested with severely maltreating families are not necessarily encouraging (e.g., Cohn & Daro, 1987). Thus, physical abuse of children by parents is not a problem that has been fully understood or resolved.

When the physical abuse of children was first seriously addressed, investigators focused their efforts on the identification of serious parental psychopathology as the determinant of abuse. The early research efforts to link physical abuse and psychopathology were largely unsuccessful (see reviews by Berger, 1985; Parke & Collmer, 1975). More recent work using cluster analyses of Minnesota Multiphasic Personality Inventory (MMPI) profiles identified 13 different profile clusters in a sample ($N$ = 178) of physically abusive, emotionally abusive, or neglecting parents (James & Boake, 1988). Thus, the existing research has not identified a single, or even a few, personality types associated with abuse or neglect. Other recent work has attempted to determine whether parental affective disorders or symptoms of depression could be contributing factors in the emergence of abuse. Knutson and Schartz (in press) reviewed 11 studies attempting to link depression with abuse or neglect. Although six of these studies were able to establish an association between depression and abuse, five of the studies did not. The many methodological differences that existed among the studies compromised any possibility of reaching an unequivocal conclusion regarding affective disorders and child maltreatment; however, present data appear insufficient to establish a link between maltreatment and parental depression. Thus, efforts to understand abuse as a reflection of parental psychopathology continue to fail to pay significant dividends.

With the failure to identify parental variables that account for large amounts of the variance in physical abuse, alternative theoretical formulations have been offered that conceptualize abuse as a consequence of a combination of parent attributes, child attributes, and setting events that occasion the occurrence of maltreatment (e.g., Cicchetti, Taraldson, & Egeland, 1978; Cicchetti & Toth, 1987; Kempe & Helfer, 1972). Such an approach recognizes physical abuse as a parent–child *relational* difficulty rather than a problem residing solely in the parent (see Knutson & Schartz, in press). Within this conceptual framework, the occurrence of physical abuse by parents can be considered an example of discipline and parenting that has shifted from a normative level of interaction to one that is potentially or actually injurious. A shift in discipline from noninjurious acts to those that are injurious can be viewed as an example of an escalated coercive exchange. Using such a framework, it may be possible to account for variance in the occurrence of abuse by focusing on adult and child factors that contribute to escalation in disciplinary contexts. To that end, this chapter describes a series of analog-parenting studies designed to assess subject attributes and child behaviors that might serve to escalate disciplinary acts.

Although episodes of great cruelty and willful assault attract considerable attention in mass media outlets, the vast majority of physically abusive events occur in the context of disciplinary activity by a child caretaker; that is, identified abusive events are typically characterized by efforts of child caretakers to influence the behavior of the child under their supervision. Such abusive acts may be single discrete episodes, but most often they are described as part of more extended exchanges between the child and the caregiver. When single child behaviors are identified as proximal antecedents of the physically abusive act, they are typically seen as aversive behaviors displayed by the child (e.g., Weston, 1974), and the abuse perpetrator can be described as reacting to these negative child behaviors. It is important to note, however, that the aversive child behaviors that are antecedents to abuse are usually well within the range of naturally occurring child behaviors; that is, although the child behaviors may be aversive and irritating, they are not necessarily pathological or deviant. Thus, the abuse perpetrator is probably confronted with the same irritating child behaviors that nonabusive parents experience. As a result, considerations of abuse as an escalated series of interactions between a child caretaker and a child seem to require some attention to sources of individual differences among parents in their reaction to irritating child activities.

One possibility that has been offered by investigators in the area of abuse is the notion that abusive parents are hyper-reactive to child behaviors (see Knutson, 1978; Vasta, 1982). This approach derives in part from psychophysiological research (e.g., Frodi & Lamb, 1980) in which abusive parents were less responsive than control parents to subtle changes in infants behavior and were more likely to react negatively to the crying of an infant. Although individual differences in reactivity have been pursued in psychophysiological work, recent research has focused on parental reactivity to child behaviors in the context of expectations and perceptions of child behavior. For example, several investigators have focused on internal representational models (cf. Crittenden, 1988), or parental perceptions and expectations of children (e.g., Rosenberg & Reppucci, 1983; Twentyman & Plotkin, 1982), as attributes that may contribute to the emergence of abusive parent–child interactions. Such work seems to have some relevance to the hyper-reactivity notion, because the abusive parental reactions are seen as a consequence of distorted perceptions of child behavior.

Two research strategies have been used to support the hypothesis that abusive or neglectful parents have distorted perceptions or unrealistic expectations of their children or children in general. The first strategy has been to infer perceptions or expectations from deviant parenting behavior. For example, Gladston (1965) reported that abusive parents describe their children as if they were capable of the organized and intentional behavior of adults. Excessively high expectations for the child are then thought to mediate abuse when the child fails to meet the parent's expectation. When young children are left unattended, are required to be responsible for siblings at an inappropriately early age, or are asked to provide emotional support for parents (e.g., Dubanoski, Evans, & Higuchi, 1978; Elmer, 1977; Morris & Gould, 1963; Steele, 1976), investigators have suggested that the expectations of the parents are the mediating factors in the abuse or neglect. Unfortunately, these unrealistic expectations have generally been inferred from the abusive acts or from comments in retrospective clinical interviews. Thus, the evidence of distorted perceptions by abusive or neglectful parents has not always been based on independent assessments.

The second strategy has been to directly assess perceptions or expectations using data that are obtained independently of the abusive incidents. In one of the first attempts to directly assess parental expectations of abusive, neglecting, and comparison parents, Twenty-man and Plotkin (1982) used a questionnaire to assess expectations regarding the attainment of developmental milestones by their own children and "average" children. By basing the questionnaire on the *Vineland Social Maturity Scale*, these parental expectations could be contrasted with existing normative data. In general, the obtained group differences were modest. With respect to absolute scores, the abusive group expected its own child to attain developmental milestones at a later age than the "average" child, and the abusive and neglecting groups estimated that the average child would attain developmental milestones later than normative data would suggest. Additionally, the abusing and neglecting parents showed a pattern of both overestimating and underestimating the abilities of their youngsters relative to the control group parents. Thus, when overall differences did not obtain, there was the suggestion that it was due to the canceling effects of both over- and underestimating within maltreating groups. Abusive and neglecting parents were as likely to set low expectations for their children as they were to set high ones. In a follow-up study, Azar and Rohrbeck (1986) contrasted physically abusive mothers with mothers whose partner engaged in physical abuse of a child. The abusive mothers had significantly higher and more unrealistic expectations than the mothers who had an abusive partner. Such data suggest that more unrealistic expectations are specific to perpetrators rather than just a family characteristic.

When Perry, Wells, and Doran (1983) contrasted parents from abusing families with parents from matched nonabusing families, both fathers and mothers from the abusive families expected slower development from their children. Williamson, Borduin, and Howe (1991) reported that, when questioned regarding their expectations for an "average child," physically abusive mothers of adolescents were likely to overestimate when developmental milestones would be met, and physically neglecting and control mothers were likely to underestimate when the milestones would be met. Because different instruments were used by the Williamson et al. (1991) and the Twentyman and Plotkin (1982) studies, the apparent inconsistencies cannot be easily reconciled.

Because mere knowledge of developmental milestones might have been an inadequate test of the unrealistic expectations hypothesis, Azar, Robinson, Hekimian, and Twentyman (1984) completed a study in which neglecting and abusive parents were assessed regarding expectations for developmental milestones and expectations regarding more complex family interaction and behavioral events involving children. Parents were also asked to provide solutions to a behavioral problem. Both the neglecting and abusing mothers evidenced more unrealistic expectations in the complex family interaction context and poorer behavioral problem-solving skills than a group of matched control mothers. The data suggested that it was not just unrealistic expectations in the context of developmental milestones that distinguished maltreating from nonmaltreating mothers, but that it was unrealistic expectations in the context of dealing with normal, but potentially distressing, child behaviors. Such data are not inconsistent with the hyper-reactivity hypothesis advanced by Knutson (1978) and Vasta (1982). Related to the hyper-reactivity hypothesis, abusive parents appear to be less able to inhibit behavior than matched control group parents (Rohrbeck & Twentyman, 1986); hence, maltreatment could reflect a combination of unrealistic expectations with respect to the occurrence of distressing child behavior and a lack of inhibitory control.

In addition to reactions based on unrealistic expectations, excessively negative perceptions of the abused child by the parents has been considered a contributor to abusive interactions (cf. Gladston, 1971; Gregg & Elmer, 1969). Herrenkohl and Herrenkohl (1979) contrasted parental perceptions of abused and nonabused children from the same families. Their data suggest that the abusive mothers had more negative perceptions of the abuse victim and felt less able to influence that child's behavior relative to the sibling. Within naturally occurring disciplinary settings, the Herrenkohl and Herrenkohl (1979) data suggest that negative perceptions could contribute to parental reactions to a child that facilitate an escalated pattern of discipline.

A failure to identify more negative perceptions by abusing mothers was described by Rosenberg and Reppucci (1983). In that research, however, the control group consisted of mothers who were referred because of "parenting difficulties." Thus, the failure to obtain group differences might reflect a tendency for both the abusing parents and those having difficulty with their children to perceive their youngsters negatively. Larrance and Twentyman (1983) contrasted abusive, neglecting, and control group mothers' perceptions of their own child and another child engaging in deviant and nondeviant acts. In this study, the abusing mothers had the most negative expectations for their children and the control group mothers had the most positive expectations. Perhaps more importantly, the mothers made different attributions regarding the variables determining the depicted child acts. When negative child acts or negative consequences to the child were depicted, abusive mothers attributed the depicted event to child-specific influences, whereas when positive acts or consequences were depicted, external and capricious attributions were made. The attributions of the mothers in the control group were virtually opposite that of the abusive mothers, and the neglecting mothers were in an intermediate position. In a related analog study of parental perceptions, reactions to stressful audiotapes of parent–child interactions with either annoying child cries or irritating alarms were compared (Bauer & Twentyman, 1985). Abusive mothers were more likely to perceive the children heard on the tapes as purposely acting to annoy adults.

In general, then, there is a growing body of evidence that abusive parents may have both overly negative perceptions of their children and somewhat unrealistic expectations. It is important to note, however, that these attributes may be shared by other deviant parents, or nonabusive parents seeking services for child behavior problems. Although parental attributes of hyper-reactivity, distorted perceptions of their children, or unrealistic developmental expectations by themselves are not sufficient to account for abusive parenting, data suggest that, in a disciplinary context, such attributes may interact with other variables to occasion abuse.

Although the Weston (1974) work described what were apparently single-episode abusive events, clinical experience and research suggests that physical abuse is more likely to be embedded in extended interactions. Of course, parent–child interactions are not discrete events but are part of long-term concantenated sequences of behavior. When episodes of parent–child interaction are characterized by aversives and are extended over time, these patterns of interaction tend to result in an escalation in the level or intensity of the exchanges between parent and child (e.g., Patterson, 1976, 1982; Snyder, 1977). This process of escalation during parent–child dyadic interactions has been studied in several contexts (e.g., Patterson & Cobb, 1971; Wahler, Williams, & Cerezo, 1990), with the resulting data suggesting that a pattern of reciprocated aversive exchanges will increase in intensity as the exchange increases in duration or number of interactions. Hence, long duration exchanges between a parent who perceives the child negatively or unrealistically and a child who engages in irritating, but perhaps nondeviant, responding provide a likely context for an escalatory parental shift from normative to abusive disciplinary strategies. In such a case, abuse could be viewed as the result of escalation of normal disciplinary acts beyond acceptable boundaries.

Consistent with the notion that abuse often results from normal discipline carried to an extreme, Herrenkohl, Herrenkohl, and Egolf (1983) found that physical abuse typically occurred within a disciplinary context and was often attributed to negative child behaviors including aggression, noncompliance, fighting or arguing, and engaging in dangerous or immoral activities. Similarly, interview reports of abusive parents suggest that aggression, lying, stealing, and defiance were among the child behaviors that occasioned abusive episodes (Kadushin & Martin, 1981). In summarizing research and clinical experience, Gil (1971) argued:

> In most instances of child abuse the caretakers involved are 'normal' individuals exercising their prerogative of discipling a child whose behavior they find in need of correction. While some of these adults may often go farther than they intended . . . their behavior does, nevertheless, not exceed the normative range of disciplining children as defined by existing culture. (p. 644)

In fact, Gil (1970) concluded that uncontrolled disciplinary responses of the caretaker accounted for a large number of the 1, 380 abuse cases in his nationwide survey. Specifically, abuse was noted to have resulted from "immediate or delayed response to a specific act of the child" in 63% of the cases, and "inadequately controlled anger of the perpetrator" was a factor in nearly 73% of the cases (p. 126). Thus, abuse can be viewed as a shift of parental responses from more or less acceptable disciplinary measures to disciplinary measures that, whereas often culturally acceptable, are carried too far.

The widespread usage of physical discipline to deal with child behavior suggests that such discipline continues to represent a generally acceptable practice in the United States. For example, responses to a 1985 national survey (Straus & Gelles, 1990, p. 97) indicate that nearly 100% of the respondents had used physical discipline with children under the age of 3, and 55% of the couples reported that they had slapped or spanked a 3- to 17-year-old child. A review of the results of a large survey of opinions regarding abuse (Sapp & Carter, 1978) revealed interesting patterns in lay person definitions of abuse. Some parental acts were viewed as clearly deviant and inappropriate: Placing or holding a child in very hot water and striking a child with a fist were labeled abusive by 99% and 98% of respondents, respectively. Other physical disciplinary strategies were viewed as much more acceptable: striking with a paddle or a belt were rated acceptable by 64% and 68% of the sample, respectively. However, numerous respondents reportedly noted that even the latter, largely "acceptable," forms of physical discipline could be abusive if they were carried to extremes or were of a severity that resulted in bruises or marks on the child. Consistent with these lay attitudes, a survey of professionals found that 69% classified a scenario in which a child is injured as the result of being struck too hard by parents in the course of punishment as abusive (Gelles, 1982). Thus, even nominally acceptable forms of physical discipline are considered abusive when the delivery is characterized by sufficient force such that an injury results.

It appears that whereas some acts (e.g., biting a child) are defined as abusive by the relative deviancy of the parental behavior itself, a more common class of abusive acts consists of acts that are topographically isomorphic with generally accepted physical disciplinary responses. For example, although most people do not consider spanking a child to be abusive, many more would consider spanking abusive in a situation where physical injury resulted. Although it might be assumed that there are subcultural differences in rating events as physically abusive, when such studies have been conducted, the differences have not been apparent (e.g., Polansky, Ammons, & Weathersby, 1983). Moreover, in those studies, when disciplinary injuries occur, there is general agreement that the event is abusive (e.g., Wolock, 1982).

Kadushin and Martin's (1981) interviews of abusive parents lend credance to the notion that the escalation of acceptable forms of discipline can result in abusive episodes. Here, in 91% of the abuse cases, the first response to the child's behavior by the parents was nonpunitive (usually verbal reasoning or a warning). However, when the initial attempt was not successful in terminating the child's behavior, the parents escalated their response to physically punitive and abusive attempts to deal with the child. Nominally acceptable forms of physical discipline (e.g., striking with the hand or an instrument as opposed to punching or burning) constituted the abuse methods in 81% of the cases, and the injuries most commonly consisted of minor bruises or welts (79%). The descriptive aspects of these data are not inconsistent with the observational analyses of escalation provided by Wahler et al.

(1990), where exchanges are extended and the parenting efforts are not able to effect a favorable outcome with the child.

Patterson (1986) hypothesized that when poor parental management techniques are combined with irritating child behaviors, the stage is set for aversive interactional sequences. Once aversive interactional sequences begin, the sequences continue until one member of the dyad escalates to a level that exceeds the level tolerated by the other. In a series of studies conducted at the Oregon Social Learning Center, Patterson (1982, 1986) and Snyder (1977) obtained data to support the hypothesis that a process of negative reinforcement maintains this pattern across successive interactions between members of a dyad. As these negative and escalating exchanges are repeated across time, the risk for an episode of physical abuse increases (Reid, 1985).

Although studies from the Oregon group have established the possible role of reinforcement in the development of escalation, other research has suggested that the reinforcement may not be necessary for escalation to occur in extended coercive exchanges. Using a variation on the aggression-machine paradigm, Goldstein, Davis, and Herman (1975) investigated escalation patterns between strangers within the laboratory. In the standard teacher–learner paradigm, learners, who were confederates of the experimenter, gave the same set responses to each teacher; that is, the learners randomly made errors throughout the course of the task. Instructed to elicit particular learner responses via the use of verbal conditioning, teachers consistently escalated in their delivery of verbal punishment over the course of the task. Relative to the present work, it is interesting to note that the teachers persisted in their pattern of escalation even when learners improved their performance continuously over trials. Thus, the escalation pattern could not be attributed to the learner's apparent resistance to learning. The authors interpreted their data as consistent with a disinhibitory process in which personal inhibitions against the use of intense painful stimulation decline over time in the interaction. It is possible, however, that the learner's failure to master the task could be seen as a source of irritation to the teacher. Extrapolating to a parenting context, these data suggest that efforts to discipline could escalate if the interaction were sufficiently lengthy and, perhaps, somewhat irritating.

Additionally, there are some data to suggest that the aggression-evoking capacity of mildly aversive events can be augmented by repeated presentations of those aversive events over a relatively brief period of time. In an analog study of the escalation of aversively motivated aggression using nonhuman subjects, Knutson, Fordyce, and Anderson (1980) attempted to determine whether a series of aversive stimuli presented with great rapidity would combine to occasion greater attack than those same stimuli presented at a lower rate; that is, subjects were exposed to a train of shock stimuli under conditions that were insufficient to evoke attack when the stimuli were presented alone or infrequently. When those stimuli were presented at a high rate, the subjects displayed a greater probability of attacking a target. Such data suggest that subjects are more likely to react aggressively to repeated aversive stimulation over a short period of time than to the same stimuli presented over a relatively long period of time. Again, the data support the notion that the risk for an escalated parental disciplinary response may rise as a function of the length of an exchange and the number of aversive episodes included in the exchange.

However, an understanding of escalation requires more than just consideration of the length of interaction and the aversiveness of the antecedents, because not all parents who are confronted with lengthy and irritating interactions with a child escalate to a level that is potentially or actually injurious. The widespread differences among subjects in the speed with which they escalate suggest that there may be important individual differences in the amount of aversive stimulation and length of exchange that may be required before an escalation occurs. Among the factors that could contribute to the individual differences in disciplinary escalation is a history of severe physical discipline or physical abuse during childhood.

## TRANSGENERATIONAL PERSISTENCE OF ABUSE

The notion that abused children become the next generation of abusive parents has had considerable attention in the abuse literature for over two decades. During the 1970s and early 1980s, a relatively large literature served to perpetuate the notion that today's victims of abuse will become tomorrow's abusers (e.g., Baldwin & Oliver, 1975; Blumberg, 1974; Gelles, 1973; Gil, 1970; Kempe & Helfer, 1972; Parens, 1987; Smith, 1976; Spinetta & Rigler, 1972; Steele & Pollack, 1974). Although this literature was largely nonempirical, or based on limited data sets, the hypothesis that child abuse leads to abusive parenting had been essentially granted axiomatic status. Recently, however, the significant methodological inadequacies of early transgenerational studies led some researchers to question the validity of the transgenerational hypothesis (e.g., Berger, 1980; Herzberger, 1983; Jayaratne, 1977; Kaufman & Zigler, 1987; Widom, 1989). Although abusive parents often report abusive childhoods (e.g., Curtis, 1963; Fontana & Besharov, 1977; Gil, 1969; Spinetta & Rigler, 1972; Steele & Pollack, 1974), it has become apparent that many abusers report no history of abuse (Conger, Burgess & Barrett, 1979), and many parents who were abused during childhood are not shown to be abusive with their own children (e.g., Dietrich, Berkowitz, Kadushin, & McGloin, 1990; Hunter & Kilstrom, 1979). For example, in contrast to transgenerational predictions, one 10-year follow-up assessment of at-risk and comparison families revealed no evidence of abusive parenting for 53% of parents who were abused as children (Herrenkohl, Herrenkohl, & Toedter, 1983). Whereas such data have caused some to argue that the transgenerational hypothesis lacks any validity, even a critical appraisal of the literature suggests that transgenerational patterns cannot be discounted entirely. For example, Kaufman and Zigler's (1987) critical evaluation of three often-cited studies (Egeland & Jacobvitz, 1984; Herrenkohl, Herrenkohl, & Toedter, 1983; Hunter & Kilstrom, 1979) led them to estimate a 30% rate of intergenerational transmission of abuse.

Egeland and Jacobvitz's (1984) unpublished report of a prospective longitudinal study of mothers and their children has been described by Widom (1989) and Kaufman and Zigler (1987). Mothers participating in the study were selected on the basis of their high risk for abuse because of adolescent pregnancy, poverty, or limited parental knowledge. Disciplinary histories and present parenting practices of the mothers were assessed using a semistructured interview. Among mothers with a history of abuse, 34% reportedly described the use of abusive parenting practices with their own children. A 6-year follow-up of these mothers (Pianta, Egeland, & Erickson, 1989) indicated a 60% maltreatment rate among the 47 physically abused mothers and a 17% maltreatment rate among the comparison mothers.

Hunter and Kilstrom (1979) provided one of the few available prospective intergenerational studies, based on a 12-month follow-up of 300 infants and their families. Of the 49 parents with a history of abuse, 9 were reported for maltreatment of their child, whereas only 1 of the nonabused parents was reported. Although these data suggest that a history of abuse increases the risk for abusive parenting, the follow-up period was too short to provide an accurate estimate of the prevalence of transgenerational patterns of abuse.

Some long-term follow-up data on abused children are available, however. A study by Herrenkohl, Herrenkohl, and Toedter (1983) provided follow-up assessments of a sample of more than 500 families cited for abuse over a 10-year period. Controlling for social desirability, economic status, and number of children in the home, the relation between parental history and present parenting practices was examined. Based on a 56% prevalence of abuse history in abusive parents and a 38% prevalence in matched (nonabusive) comparison families, Herrenkohl, Herrenkohl, and Toedter (1983) concluded that childhood abuse increased the risk for abusive parenting as a adult.

Data collected from a tertiary care child psychiatry clinic also provide support for a relation between abusive childhood experiences and risk for abusive parenting (Zaidi, Knutson, & Mehm, 1989). Parents of 169 consecutively admitted children completed a standardized questionnaire to assess their childhood disciplinary experiences, whereas abuse status of the referred child was determined from social history and medical records. Although the overall abuse rate of the sample was 24%, there was documentation of abuse in the records of 32% of children who had one parent reporting an abusive childhood history. The abuse rate was 50% among the children whose parents both reported abusive childhood experiences. These data suggest that a history of physical abuse during childhood represents a risk factor of considerable importance for understanding abusive parenting.

Whereas a transgenerational persistence of 30% for such a significant health problem cannot be considered trivial, the fact that an estimated two thirds of the victims of physical abuse do not become perpetrators (cf. Kaufman & Zigler, 1987) suggests that the mechanisms of transmission may be more complex than was originally assumed. Rather than discounting the transgenerational hypothesis entirely, continued efforts to increase our understanding through tests of newer and more limited transgenerational hypotheses seem warranted. One possibility that merits consideration is that abusive histories may influence the probability that escalation will occur in disciplinary contexts. The focus of the present research is to attempt to understand the contribution of abusive histories to escalation in an analog-parenting task.

## ANALOG STUDIES OF DISCIPLINE AND ABUSE

In many areas of clinical research, it is impossible to conduct experimental studies in a clinical context. As a result, investigations of clinical phenomena are conducted in analog studies. In analog studies, an approximation of the clinical phenomenon is achieved using either nonclinical samples or independent variables that are approximations of the clinical variables. For example, animal analog studies have been conducted on the clinical problems of depression (e.g., Seligman, 1975; Suomi & Harlow, 1977), anxiety disorders (Levis, 1979), and the role of early social experience in adult aggressivity (Knutson & Viken, 1984). A substantial amount of the research on psychotherapy has also consisted of analog research (cf. Kazdin, 1978). In spite of a long tradition of conducting analog research on clinical phenomena, the use of analogs has occasioned some concerns about the utility of analog studies. In general, these criticisms have derived from the argument that analog designs suffer from their artificial nature. In response to such criticism, Kazdin (1978) noted that virtually all experimental research is essentially analog research. Moreover, Kazdin asserted that an analog test of a clinical hypothesis is not necessarily less stringent than a clinical test. Rather, by exercising control over subject selection, experimental variables, and other factors that could influence generalizability, analog studies can provide critical tests of hypotheses derived from the clinical domain. The inherent difficulties of conducting research on abusive parenting have given rise to successful analog studies of parenting and physical abuse; these studies confirm the merit of studying abuse using analog designs (e.g., Passman & Mulhern, 1977; Vasta & Copitch, 1981).

This research is part of a broader context of analog research on abuse conducted at The University of Iowa over the last several years (e.g., Berger, 1981; Knutson, Schartz, & Zaidi, 1991; Zaidi et al., 1989). In this research, abuse potential was operationalized as the willingness of young adults to select potentially injurious disciplinary strategies in response to circumstances that could confront a parent. These studies have typically involved having participants indicate their responses to a variety of child behaviors that could induce a disciplinary response from a child caretaker, with stimuli consisting either of verbal descriptions taken from case descriptions of child behaviors that were antecedents to physical abuse (Berger, 1981) or slides depicting various common but irritating child behaviors and frankly deviant child behaviors (Zaidi et al., 1989). Subjects participating in the tasks are instructed to imagine that they are the child's caretaker and to select their most likely response to the depicted child's behavior. These task are very engaging and they have yielded data suggesting that they provide a useful means of assessing the potential role of a punitive disciplinary history in the emergence of abuse by some parents (e.g., Knutson et al., 1991; Zaidi et al., 1989). Although it is impossible to directly study the extended interactions and disciplinary escalations that result in physical abuse, analog research provides an excellent opportunity to test hypotheses regarding the potential for extended aversive parent–child exchanges to lead to disciplinary escalation and abuse. In addition, analog procedures permit testing of other hypotheses regarding factors that may mediate disciplinary escalation and abuse. Thus, available analog research provides the basis for the expectation that the analog-parenting task would be useful for assessing escalation in discipline.

General Methods

**Subject Selection.**  As suggested by Bogaard (1976), studies of the potential for child maltreatment do not have to focus on parents; that is, young adults of child-rearing age, such as university students, can be studied with respect to their disciplinary preferences and behavior patterns. As a result, this research and previous work in this laboratory has selected university students as subjects. Because a primary focus of the present research and past research has been on the impact of the abusive histories of young adults, research participants are selected on the basis of their descriptions of their disciplinary histories. This selection is accomplished by administering the Assessing Environments III (AEIII) questionnaire to large numbers of undergraduate students and recruiting subjects for subsequent studies as a function of their responses to the AEIII. The AEIII is a self-report instrument with scales designed to assess childhood disciplinary history and abuse-related characteristics of the home environment of the respondent. The AEIII was developed following the rational-statistical method (see Loevinger, 1957) for producing a content-valid instrument. The psychometric properties of the AEIII, including internal consistency of the scales and test–retest reliability are acceptable (Berger, Knutson, Mehm, & Perkins, 1988; Knutson & Mehm, 1988). Additionally, the Physical Punishment scale of the AEIII has been shown to discriminate between abused and nonabused adolescents (Berger et al., 1988), correlate with direct observations made in the houses of subjects 10 years earlier (Prescott, 1991), and effectively select subjects for analog tests of the transgenerational hypothesis of abuse (Zaidi et al., 1989).

To select subjects for this series of experiments, and for pervious research, the AEIII was administered to large groups of students who elected to participate in a group testing session as one of several ways of completing a research and laboratory experience requirement of the introductory psychology courses. When research participants arrived at the test session, they were given packets of questionnaires, instructional materials, and appropriate materials to secure informed consent. The AEIII was kept separate from the other questionnaire materials, and it had a machine scoreable answer sheet that was distinguishable from the others used in the test session. Because of the sensitive nature of the AEIII, to preserve the anonymity of the respondents and facilitate candid responding, participants were instructed not to place any personally identifying information on the AEIII answer sheet. Instead, each test booklet and answer sheet had an idiosyncratic identification number that subjects entered on the answer sheets in lieu of conventional identification numbers. In addition, a 5-cm by 7-cm card with the idiosyncratic identification number was attached to the AEIII materials. Research participants were instructed to retain the card, which was then used to confirm their eligibility for the actual analog studies. The use of the idiosyncratic identification number protected respondent anonymity while allowing for linkage of AEIII data with the analog-parenting data collected at later sessions. Using this group testing procedure, at least 500 subjects were screened over a 4-day period during the first few weeks of a single semester. The result was a large pool of potential subjects from which research participants with specific childhood backgrounds could be selected. Additionally, stable estimates of the prevalence of physical abuse in the population of University of Iowa undergraduates have been obtained with this procedure (Knutson & Selner, 1994).

For the purposes of this research, the primary scale of interest from the AEIII is the Physical Punishment (PP) scale, which was designed to assess the disciplinary history of respondents. The PP Scale consists of 12 true–false items assessing the occurrence of physical disciplinary events, ranging from exemplars of mild discipline (e.g., spanking) to severe and potentially injurious events (e.g., punching, kicking, choking). Also included in the PP Scale are items representing experiences identified in the literature as forms of abusive disciplinary practices (e.g., being struck by objects, being injured by parents, (see Gil, 1970; Sapp & Carter, 1978; Straus, 1980). Based on the Berger et al. (1988) demonstration that a score of 4 or more on the Physical Punishment scale effectively discriminated abused and nonabused adolescents, persons endorsing 4 or more of the PP items were classified as having a history of Severe Physical Punishment (SPP). Respondents with PP scores of 1 to 3 were classified as members of a Mild Physical Punishment group (MPP), and those with scores of 0 were considered members of a No Physical Punishment group (NPP).

Subjects representing each of these three disciplinary histories were selected to be eligible to participate in the analog-parenting studies as a function of physical punishment group membership. All subjects in the No Physical Punishment Group and the Severe Physical Punishment Group were selected to be eligible to participate. However, because large numbers of subjects were screened, and because approximately 68% of the potential subjects were from the Mild Physical Punishment condition, random selection from that group was often utilized to limit eligibility of individuals from this high base-rate group. The idiosyncratic identification numbers of individuals selected to be eligible for the analog study were prominently posted in an area where research participants elect research experiences. When research participants arrived at the laboratory for the analog-parenting studies, their eligibility was confirmed by checking their 5 × 7 card presented against a master list of the idiosyncratic identification numbers of eligible subjects. The idiosyncratic number was used to code all testing response materials during the session. Because research participation and informed consent forms required personally identifying information (i.e., names and students identification numbers), these forms were kept separate from the actual test materials. Thus, participants in the analog study remained anonymous, and experimenters were uniformed with respect to the disciplinary histories of the research participants.

Previous Analog-Parenting Results

In one of the first studies of discipline involving the use of an analog task in this laboratory (Zaidi et al., 1989), subjects were required to select disciplinary strategies in response to slides depicting irritating child behaviors. In that study, Zaidi et al. (1989) found that young adults with severely punitive childhood histories were more likely than those with less punitive histories to select physical discipline in response to child behaviors that they deemed unacceptable. These data, together with a study of transgenerational maltreatment using a sample of parents drawn from a tertiary care child psychiatric facility, caused Zaidi et al. (1989) to conclude that there was support for the notion that persons reporting more punitive disciplinary histories on the AEIII have a lower threshold for selecting physical discipline to deal with aversive child behaviors. The question that then arises is whether these persons from more physically punitive backgrounds are also more likely to evidence disciplinary escalation in responses to repeated instances of irritating child behaviors. In the Zaidi et al. (1989) study, an attempt was made to assess escalation in the analog task by asking subjects to identify the disciplinary response they would use if the child were to persist in the depicted activity on 10 more occasions. This approach was not successful in identifying any pattern of group differences in escalation; subjects from mild disciplinary backgrounds and severe physical disciplinary backgrounds were equally likely to endorse the use of physical discipline after 10 reoccurrences of the act. Additionally, however, it seemed that large numbers of subjects could not imagine that their disciplinary acts were so ineffective that the child would persist 10 more times! As a result, alternative approaches to assessing escalation in the analog task were considered.

## ANALOG STUDIES OF ESCALATION

Because the analog-parenting task described in Zaidi et al. (1989) did not yield an effective assessment of escalation, Zaidi (1988) developed a modification of the analog-parenting task. To better assess escalation, instead of eliciting disciplinary responses to 10 occurrences of an irritating response, participants were asked to indicate how many times the child would have to continue to display the sanctioned behavior before the subject would elect to use an alternative disciplinary tactic. When the respondent indicated a change in disciplinary strategy would occur, they were asked to identify the next disciplinary strategy. When subjects changed from a nonphysical disciplinary response to a physical one, or when they shifted from mild physical discipline to potentially injurious physical discipline, the responses were classified as escalation.

A second limitation of the analog-parenting task used in the Zaidi et al. (1989) study was the limited range of depicted child behaviors. As a result, when modifying the original analog-parenting task to permit a more sensitive assessment of escalation, Zaidi expanded the number of child depictions. Additionally, to permit an assessment of the role of the type of child transgression in the emergence of escalated discipline, the revised analog task included subsets of slides depicting three prototypical domains of child transgressions that had been identified as events commonly proximal to maltreatment. These three classes of child behaviors, each represented by seven slides, were: potentially dangerous or injurious acts (e.g., sitting on the edge of a roof, hanging out the window of a rapidly moving automobile), destructive acts (e.g., tearing pages out of a book, bending a TV antenna), and socially inappropriate or rule-violating behavior (e.g., drinking a beer, smoking a cigarette).

In the first study of escalation using this modified analog task, Knutson et al. (1991) selected university students, using the procedure outlined previously, and then administered the analog-parenting task in small groups. In this research, escalation was a relatively infrequent pattern of behavior, with most subjects failing to shift from a nonphysical to a physical disciplinary choice in response to questions regarding repetitions of the proscribed acts. The escalation that did occur was related to the type of child behavior depicted: The highest rates of escalation were reported in response to destructive acts, with the lowest rates of escalation occurring in response to the socially sanctioned or rule-violating behaviors. Consistent with previous analog data from this laboratory, and from predictions derived from a transgenerational hypothesis of physical abuse, there was also a linear trend for increasing use of physical discipline (with or without escalation) as a function of the severity of childhood punishment history. Escalation was most prevalent among subjects from the Severe Physical Discipline group.

Although the analog task using the slide stimuli was effective, the use of static images precludes the depiction of some types of child behavior. Additionally, the slide task elicits the escalated response by asking subjects to indicate the number of times a transgression had to be repeated to result in a changed response. To a large extent, such an approach may not be an adequate analog of the interactive events that are hypothesized to contribute to escalation. For example, in exchanges with children, the repeated occurrences of irritating behavior may be part of a concantenated sequence rather than merely repeated occurrences of exactly the same response. For these reasons, an alternative analog-parenting task was developed using video images.

The video analog task that was developed (Knutson & Zaidi, 1989) was based largely on the experiences obtained using the slide task. A series of 9 episodes were filmed depicting destructive, rule-violating, dangerous, and interpersonally provocative activities. The 9 episodes included 1 to 6 sequentially ordered scenes that were scripted to reflect continuations or terminations of the various irritating child behaviors, as well as depictions described as occurring at a later date. The scenes were all filmed using "point-of-view" camera work, so only the child is observed (no other parties are present) and the viewer has the impression that the camera represents his or her own view of the scene. At the completion of each scene, the action is interrupted and the subject is asked to respond to a series of questions regarding the depicted child behavior. In response to each of the scenes, subjects were required to indicate their reactions to the scene and to select disciplinary responses they would use if they were responsible for the child. Although typically administered to subjects individually, the video analog task can be administered to small groups of subjects by pausing the tape player long enough for all subjects to record their responses and by seating subjects in such a way that they cannot observe the responses made by other subjects.

To assess the possibility that subjects from severely punitive childhood backgrounds would be more likely to escalate in response to repeated provocation from a child, subjects were screened using the AEIII, as described earlier. Then eligible subjects who were identified as members of the severe physical punishment condition, the mild physical punishment condition, and no physical punishment were given the opportunity to participate in a research session in which the analog-parenting task was administered. Because of other ongoing studies, the actual conduct of the study, including screening and the administration of the analog-parenting task, was accomplished during 3 of 5 academic years. Prevalence of severe physical punishment did not differ among the tested samples those years, and the procedures followed were identical across the period of testing. In total, 42 subjects from the severe physical punishment group, 136 subjects from the mild physical punishment group, and 63 subjects from the no physical punishment group completed the analog-parenting task. Test sessions were conducted with 1 to 4 subjects present per session; all responses were recorded in a manner that preserved the anonymity of the subjects.

Within the structure of the video analog task, there are two ways to assess escalation. One index of escalation is the endorsement of physical discipline as a function of the number of scenes within episodes. Alternatively, escalation can be assessed as the latency, expressed as number of scenes required, to evoke a physical discipline response. Similar to the behavior of subjects in the slide analog task, most subjects did not evidence any escalation. As a result of the large number of zero scores, the two primary escalation analyses were completed on scores using the $\log_e (X + 1)$. For analyses of both escalation measures, these scores were analyzed using a one-way analysis of variance with punishment history as the between-groups factor. Although the severe physical punishment group evidenced the greatest number of escalation responses and the shortest latencies, the differences among groups only approached statistically significance. A third strategy for considering escalation is the proportion of subjects from each condition to evidence any escalated responses. Whereas only 13% of the subjects from the mild and no physical punishment groups evidenced any escalated responses, 25% of the severe physical punishment group displayed at least one escalated response to the episodes. Thus, although the rate of escalation was low overall, the rate among subjects from the severe physical punishment group was nearly twice that of the subjects from the mild or no physical punishment group.

To assess whether escalation was influenced by the type of transgression depicted in the episode, the proportion of subjects within condition escalating to different types of scenes was assessed. The large number of zero scores and the distributions of scores precluded parametric statistical analyses. Because the slide analog task suggested that destructive acts were distinguishable from other types of transgressions in terms of their physical discipline-evoking qualities, the comparison was between depictions of destructive acts and the other transgressions. For both the mild and nonpunished groups, there was no difference in the probability that escalation would be displayed in response to the two types of scenes. For the severe physical punishment group, when escalation occurred, it was 4 times as likely to occur in response to a depiction of a destructive act than it was to a nondestructive transgression.

The video analog-parenting task is quite different from the analog task using slides; however, with respect to escalation of discipline, the results using the video task were consistent with results from the slide task described by Knutson et al. (1991); that is, most subjects did not elect to escalate their discipline from nonphysical to physical or from mild physical discipline to potentially injurious physical discipline. However, escalation was more prevalent among those who come from severe physical discipline backgrounds. Additionally, the data suggested that escalation is more likely when the child transgression involves destructive activity. The question that must then be asked is what are the vectors of influence that cause some from severe physical discipline backgrounds to report a willingness to escalate whereas others choose not to escalate. Because parenting a child is inherently associated with a degree of negative and aversive parent–child exchanges, and escalation within these exchanges does not always occur, a consideration of other factors that might contribute to a tendency for escalation appears warranted.

Huesmann's (1988) information-processing theory provides a framework for considering escalation in the context of physical abuse of children by those from severely punitive backgrounds. Huesmann (1988) proposed that aggressive behavioral scripts develop and are stored in memory as a result of childhood experiences with aggression. When confronted with a conflict situation, a person first evaluates environmental cues and then engages in a cognitive search for potential behavioral responses to the conflict situations. Retrieval of an aggressive script during this search increases the likelihood of an aggressive reaction to the conflict situation; however, whether a retrieved aggressive script is behaviorally expressed depends on a decision-making process during which the script is appraised as appropriate or inappropriate in the given context. Thus, appraisal of an aggressive script as appropriate is a critical precursor to the behavioral employment of that script.

Huesmann's theory has potential implications for understanding transgenerational patterns of child abuse. Specifically, abused childrens' extensive exposure to aggressive scripts and limited exposure to nonaggressive scripts might make it more difficult for these victims to retrieve nonaggressive scripts to deal with conflict situations, including the extended disciplinary exchanges that they may later face as parents. A tendency for abused children to exhibit higher levels of aggressive behavior than control and neglected children (George & Main, 1979; Hoffman-Plotkin & Twentyman, 1984; Newburger, Reed, Daniel, Hyde, & Kotelchuck, 1977) and for aggressive children to demonstrate difficulty generating nonaggressive solutions to conflict situations (Keltikangas-Jarvinen & Kangas, 1988; Richard & Dodge, 1982; Slaby & Guerra, 1988) is consistent with this formulation.

Furthermore, based on Huesmann's theory, a tendency for victimization to be associated with appraisal of abusive parental behavior as appropriate (e.g., Straus & Kantor, 1987) suggests that victims may be expected to act upon abusive behavioral scripts that are retrieved. Children's exposure to aggression has been speculated to potentiate the development of "retaliatory norms" that provide a moral basis for later aggressive behavior (Feshbach, 1980), whereas familial aggression may lead children to conclude that violence against family members is particularly acceptable and justified (Straus & Kantor, 1987). A nationwide survey examining long-term effects of exposure to violence (Owens & Straus, 1975) and college student evaluations of abusive case histories (Herzberger, 1983) provided empirical evidence of a relation between exposure to violence and the sanctioning of violent behavior years later. In addition, Bower (1991) demonstrated that experiencing specific forms of childhood physical discipline may contribute to the development of attitudes regarding the acceptability of those *specific types* of potentially injurious discipline (e.g., striking with an object, hitting as opposed to spanking a child, and striking with a belt or paddle). Consistent with predictions derived from Huesmann's theory, individuals who had experienced a particular form of potentially injurious physical discipline were less likely to view that specific form of discipline as abusive than those who had not experienced that disciplinary tactic. It appears that abuse victims may be at increased risk for disciplinary escalation by nature of their childhood exposure to punitive disciplinary scripts and a related tendency to accept those punitive scripts as appropriate.

Within Huesmann's theory, abusive experiences alone are likely to be insufficient to account for disciplinary escalation, because appraisal of an aggressive script as appropriate represents a necessary precursor for behavioral employment of the script (Huesmann, 1988). In the context of this theory, individuals at greatest risk for transgenerational patterns of abuse should be those who are both exposed to punitive discipline and, thus, more likely to retrieve punitive scripts, *and* accepting of their own disciplinary experiences as normative and appropriate and, thus, more likely to employ the punitive scripts that are retrieved. Given a combination of punitive disciplinary experiences and a view that those experiences are normal, an individual would appear to be at increased risk for escalation to punitive disciplinary strategies during an extended and aversive disciplinary exchange. The predictions that childhood disciplinary experiences and the acceptance of personal experiences as normative would be associated with risk for escalation was examined using the Analog-Parenting Task.

Following the procedures described previously, the AEIII was used to obtain information regarding the disciplinary histories of 1, 359 potential participants who were enrolled in introductory psychology classes at the University of Iowa during the spring and fall of 1990. Subsequent procedures, including the use of idiosyncratic identification numbers, were generally consistent with past abuse research in this laboratory (Rausch & Knutson, 1991; Zaidi et al., 1989). Briefly, persons responding affirmatively to four or more items of the Physical Punishment scale of the AEIII were classified as members of the Severe Physical Punishment (SPP) group. Individuals who obtained a Physical Punishment score of one to three were placed in the Mild Physical Punishment group (MPP), and subjects who endorsed no items on the PP scale were identified as members of a No Physical Punishment group (NPP). Data were collected during two semesters. As in the past, the need to assume an adequate sample of lower base-rate childhood histories made it necessary to limit eligibility for higher base-rate groups. As a result, eligibility during the first semester included 100% of Severe PP individuals and a randomly selected 40% of the individuals with less severe histories. To accommodate another research study in the laboratory during the second semester, the second semester AEIII sample was randomly divided into two parts. As a result, each of the AEIII respondents was eligible for only one of the two studies being conducted in the laboratory. No other limitations were placed on eligibility during the second semester.

The idiosyncratic identification numbers of AEIII respondents who were eligible for the research study were posted in a designated area where students elect to participate in psychological studies. Eligible volunteers elected to participate in research sessions in groups of no more than 12. Upon arrival at the session, individuals were asked to present their idiosyncratic identification cards, which were checked against a master list of eligible identification numbers. Individuals who did not have their cards or were ineligible were dismissed. The 207 eligible volunteers participated in the analog test session in groups of no more than 10, and the experimenter was uniformed with respect to the disciplinary histories of participants. During the test session, subjects first completed the slide version of the analog-parenting task (described previously), which required subjects to select disciplinary responses to 28 depicted child behaviors. As described previously, slides portrayed three general categories of irritating child activities: dangerous, destructive, and rule violations.

To evaluate patterns of escalation, respondents were asked to indicate how many times they would continue to attempt to deal with the child's behavior in the same way before changing to another disciplinary response. If respondents indicated a willingness to change their disciplinary strategy when the child persisted in the activity, they were asked what their next disciplinary strategy would be. Consistent with Kadushin and Martin's (1981) descriptions of normal parenting shifting to abuse, change from a nonphysical to a physical form of discipline was classified as escalation.

To examine Huesmann's theory that both exposure to aggression and attitudinal sanctioning of aggression play an important role in the expression of an aggressive behavioral repertoire, an abuse risk variable (Risk) was developed by relating responses to the AEIII Physical Punishment scale obtained during preliminary screening, to responses to the Abuse Opinion Questionnaire. First, the number of times each individual indicated having a specific physical disciplinary experience on the AEIII questionnaire *and* indicated that that specific disciplinary act was not abusive in response to the parallel item on the Abuse Opinion Questionnaire was summed. This sum was divided by the total number of physical discipline events for that respondent on the AEIII, and multiplied by 100, to yield a percentage Risk. Thus, Risk served as an indicator of each individual's tendency to deny the abusive nature of his or her own potentially injurious physical disciplinary experiences, and to accept those disciplinary acts as normative.

The relation between disciplinary history (Physical Punishment score), Risk, and the tendency to escalate from nonphysical to physical discipline on the analog-parenting task was then examined using hierarchical regression analysis. Because Physical Punishment was already known to predict escalation from previous work with the analog-parenting task, and because the question was whether the ratings of the appropriateness of personal disciplinary experiences increased the likelihood of escalation, Physical Punishment was entered into the regression equation first. As shown in Table 8.1, although Physical Punishment alone significantly predicted the tendency to escalate during extended disciplinary exchanges, most importantly there was a significant increment in the prediction of escalation when Risk was entered into a linear model already containing Physical Punishment as a predictor. Thus, consistent with Huesmann's (1988) model of aggressive behavior, experiencing severe physical punishment and appraising those experiences as nonabusive increases risk for escalations in physical punishment in response to child transgressions.

TABLE 8.1
Hierarchical Multiple Regression Predicting Escalation
to All Analog Scenes from Physical Punishment History and
Risk Scores

|  | Multiple R | R Squared | F Change | df | Beta |
|---|---|---|---|---|---|
| Physical Pun. | .17 | .03 | 5.83* | 1,204 | .17 |
| Risk | .35 | .12 | 14.15** | 2,203 | .31 |

*$p < .05$. **$p < .001$.

Because type of scene determined escalation in the previous studies, the ability of Physical Punishment and Risk to predict escalation to the three types of scenes used in the analog-parenting task was assessed in four hierarchial multiple regression analyses that paralleled the analysis of escalation to the full range of behavioral scenes. As shown in Tables 8.2 through 8.5, with the exception of the dangerous and rule violation

TABLE 8.2
Hierarchical Multiple Regression Predicting Escalation
to Destructive Scenes from Physical Punishment History and
Risk Scores

|  | Multiple R | R Squared | F Change | df | Beta |
|---|---|---|---|---|---|
| Physical Pun. | .17 | .03 | 6.30* | 1,204 | .18 |
| Risk | .32 | .10 | 11.37** | 2,203 | .27 |

*$p < .05$. **$p < .001$.

TABLE 8.3
Hierarchical Multiple Regression Predicting Escalation
to Dangerous Scenes from Physical Punishment History and
Risk Scores

|  | Multiple R | R Squared | F Change | df | Beta |
|---|---|---|---|---|---|
| Physical Pun. | .09 | .009 | n.s. | 1,204 | .10 |
| Risk | .30 | .09 | 10.35* | 2,203 | .29 |

*$p < .001$.

TABLE 8.4
Hierarchical Multiple Regression Predicting Escalation
to Rule-Violation Scenes from Physical Punishment History
and Risk Scores

|  | Multiple R | R Squared | F Change | df | Beta |
|---|---|---|---|---|---|
| Physical Pun. | .13 | .02 | n.s. | 1,204 | .14 |
| Risk | .27 | .07 | 8.19* | 2,203 | .24 |

*$p < .001$.

TABLE 8.5
Hierarchical Multiple Regression Predicting Escalation
to Control Scenes from Physical Punishment History and
Risk Scores

|  | Multiple R | R Squared | F Change | df | Beta |
|---|---|---|---|---|---|
| Physical Pun. | .14 | .02 | 4.29* | 1,204 | .15 |
| Risk | .18 | .03 | 3.52* | 2,203 | .11 |

*$p < .05$.

scenes, escalation was predicted by the linear combination of punishment history and the Risk variable. For the dangerous and rule violation scenes, only the Risk variable was predictive of escalation. Although the predictability of escalation in response to the control slides was more limited, the fact that escalation occurred at all in response to these slides and was predictable from PP and Risk variables is remarkable. These slides depict largely benign child behaviors (e.g., playing with Tinkertoys scattered on the floor) that are typically associated with very little physical discipline. These regression analyses suggest that when escalation occurs in response to these less provocative child behaviors, it too is related to punitive histories and rating those histories as appropriate.

## SUMMARY AND CONCLUSIONS

Because it is impossible to systematically observe the actual abusive interactions between parents and children, theoretical analyses of the actual dyadic interactions that yield physical abuse of children are not amenable to direct empirical tests. As a result, theoretical accounts of maltreatment are often either evaluated by patterns of data that are determined to be consistent or inconsistent with the theoretical account, or by indirect tests accomplished in analog studies. The current series of experiments conducted with analog-parenting tasks represents an indirect test of the theoretical proposition that physical abuse of children could reflect episodes of parent–child interactions that are normative patterns of discipline escalated to an injurious or potentially injurious level.

The results of the present series of experiments do provide empirical support for the notion that physical abuse of children could be a reflection of normative discipline that is carried to an extreme. First, the analog data suggest that the persistence of irritating child behaviors can increase the risk of escalated physical discipline. Second, the data from the three experiments support a modified version of the multigenerational hypothesis of abuse by demonstrating that a history of severe physical discipline can increase risk for a pattern of escalated discipline in response to child transgressions. The data, however, also suggest that the perception of those severe disciplinary events could mediate the multigenerational pattern.

The final experiment in this series provides support for an account of physical abuse derived from Huesmann's (1988) theoretical account of the development of aggressive behavior; that is, persons who experience severe discipline as children and view those specific experiences as normative are more likely to express a willingness to escalate their discipline. These results have clear implications for prophylactic and treatment efforts. A decade-long series of studies with young adults who are enrolled in higher education indicates that personal experiences that meet a conservative criterion of physical abuse are not viewed as abusive by the victims (Knutson & Selner, 1994). These data indicate that those victims who do not view the specific experiences as abusive may be at great risk for disciplinary escalation when faced with child-care responsibilities. Thus, public service announcements and treatment programs may benefit from attempts to reduce the acceptability of specific acts of discipline, rather than from the use of general terms such as *abuse* or *maltreatment*.

Another consistency in the present series of escalation experiments is the importance of the type of scene that is most evocative of escalated discipline. The depictions of destructive behavior by children was associated with the greatest risk of escalation. These data suggest that interventions with maltreating or at-risk families should direct some attention to the types of child transgressions that might be associated with greatest risk for the elicitation of escalated disciplinary exchanges.

## REFERENCES

Azar, S. T., Robinson, D. R., Hekimian, E., & Twentyman, C. T. (1984). Unrealistic expectations and problem-solving ability in maltreating and comparison mothers. *Journal of Consulting and Clinical Psychology, 52,* 687–691.

Azar, S. T., & Rohrbeck, C. A. (1986). Child abuse and unrealistic expectations: Further validation of the parent opinion questionnaire. *Journal of Consulting and Clinical Psychology, 54,* 867–868.

Baldwin, J. A., & Oliver, J.E. (1975). Epidemiology and family characteristics of severely abused children. *British Journal of Preventive and Social Medicine, 29,* 205–221.

Bauer, W. D., & Twentyman, C. T. (1985). Abusing, neglectful, and comparison mothers' responses to child related and non-child-related stressors. *Journal of Consulting and Clinical Psychology, 53* (3), 335–343.

Berger, A. M. (1980). The child abusing family: I. Methodological issues and parent-related characteristics of abusing families. *American Journal of Family Therapy, 8,* 53–66.

Berger, A. M. (1981). *An examination of the relationship between harsh discipline in childhood, later punitiveness toward children and later ratings of adjustment.* Unpublished doctoral dissertation, University of Iowa, Iowa City.

Berger, A. M. (1985). Characteristics of child abusing families. In L. L' Abate (Ed.), *Handbook of family psychology and therapy* (Vol. 2, pp. 900–936). Homewood, IL: Dorsey.

Berger, A. M., Knutson, J. F., Mehm, J.G., & Perkins, K.A. (1988). The self-report of punitive childhood experiences of young adults and adolescents. *Child Abuse and Neglect, 12,* 251–262.

Blumberg, M. L. (1974). Psychopathology of the abusing parent. *American Journal of Psychotherapy, 28,* 21–29.

Bogaard, H. (1976). *Relationships between aggressive behavior in children and parent perception of child behavior.* Unpublished doctoral dissertation, University of Oregon, Eugene, OR.

Bower, M. (1991). *Classification of disciplinary events and disciplinary choices as a function of childhood history.* Unpublished masters thesis, University of Iowa, Iowa City.

Cicchetti, D., Taraldson, B., & Egeland, B. (1978). Perspectives in the treatment and understanding of child abuse. In A. Goldstein (Ed.), *Perspectives for child mental health and education.* New York: Plenum.

Cicchetti, D., & Toth, S. L. (1987). The application of a transactional risk model to intervention with multi-risk maltreating families. *Zero to Three, 7* (5), 1–40.

Cohn, A. H., & Daro, D. (1987). Is treatment too late: What ten years of evaluative research tell us. *Child Abuse & Neglect, 11* (3), 433–442.

Conger, R. D., Burgess, R. L., & Barrett, C. C. (1979). Child abuse related to life change and perceptions of illness: Some preliminary findings. *Family Coordinator, 58,* 73–77.

Crittenden, P. M. (1988). Distorted patterns of relationship in maltreating families: The role of internal representation models. *Journal of Reproductive and Infant Psychology, 6,* 183–199.

Curtis, G. C. (1963). Violence breeds violence—perhaps? *American Journal of Psyciatry, 120,* 386–387.

Dietrich, D., Berkowitz, L., Kadushin, A., & McGloin, J. (1990). Some factors influencing abusers' justification of their child abuse. *Child Abuse & Neglect, 14,* 337–345.

Dubanoski, R. A., Evans, I. M., & Higuchi, A. A. (1978). Analysis and treatment of child abuse: A set of behavior propositions. *Child Abuse & Neglect, 2,* 153–172.

Egeland, B., & Jacobvitz, D. (1984). *Intergenerational continuity of parental abuse: Causes and consequences.* Presented at Conference on Biosocial Perspectives in Abuse and Neglect, York, ME.

Elmer, E. (1977). *Fragile families, troubled children: The aftermath of infant trauma.* Pittsburgh, PA: University of Pittsburgh Press.

Feshbach, S. (1980). Child abuse and the dynamics of human aggression and violence. In J. Gerbner, C. J. Ross, & E. Zigler (Eds.), *Child abuse: An agenda for action* (pp. 48–60). New York: Oxford University Press.

Fontana, V. J., & Besharov, D. J. (1977). The maltreated child: The maltreatment syndrome. *Children: A medical, legal and social guide.* Springfield, Il: Thomas.

Frodi, A. M., & Lamb, M. E. (1980). Child abusers' responses to infant smiles and cries. *Child Development, 51,* 238–241.

Gelles, R. J. (1973). Child abuse as psychopathology: A sociological critique and reformulation. *American Journal of Orthopsychiatry, 43,* 611–621.

Gelles, R. J. (1982). Problems in defining and labeling child abuse. In R. H. Starr (Ed.), *Child abuse prediction* (pp. 1–30). Cambridge: Ballinger.

George, C., & Main, M. (1979). Social interactions of young abused children: Approach, avoidance, and aggression. *Child Development, 50,* 306–318.

Gil, D. G. (1969). Physical abuse of children: Findings and implications of a nationwide survey, Part II. *Pediatrics, 44,* 857–864.

Gil, D. G. (1970). *Violence against children.* Cambridge, MA: Harvard University Press.

Gil, D. G. (1971). Violence against children. *Journal of marriage and the Family, 33,* 637–648.

Gladston, R. (1965). Observations on children who have been physically abused and their parents. *American Journal of Psychiatry, 122,* 440–443.

Gladston, R. (1971). Violence begins at home: The Parents' Center project for the study and prevention of child abuse. *Journal of the American Academy of Child Psychiatry, 10,* 336–350.

Goldstein, J. H. Davis, R. W., & Herman, D. (1975). Escalation of aggression: Experimental studies. *Journal of Personality and Social Psychology, 31,* 162–170.

Gregg, G. S., & Elmer, E. (1969). Infant injuries: Accident or abuse? *Pediatrics, 44,* 434–439.

Hardy, J. B., & Streett, R. (1989). Family support and parenting education in the home: An effective extension of clinic-based preventive health care services for poor children. *Journal of Pediatrics, 115* (6), 927–931.

Herrenkohl, E. C., & Herrenkohl, R. C. (1979). A comparison of abused children and their non-abused siblings. *Journal of the American Academy of Child Psychiatry, 18* (2), 260–270.

Herrenkohl, R., Herrenkohl, E., & Egolf, B. (1983). Circumstances surrounding the occurrence of child maltreatment. *Journal of Consulting and Clinical Psychology, 51* (3), 424–431.

Herrenkohl, E. C., Herrenkohl, R. C., & Toedter, L. J. (1983). Perspectives on the intergenerational transmission of abuse. In D. Finkelhor, R. J. Gelles, G. T. Hotaling, & M. A. Straus (Eds.), *The dark side of families: Current family violence research* (pp. 305–316). Beverly Hills, CA: Sage.

Herzberger, S. D. (1983). Social cognition and the transmission of abuse. In D. Finkelhor, R. J. Gelles, G. T. Hotaling, & M. A. Straus (Eds.), *The dark side of families: Current family violence research* (pp. 317–329). Beverly Hills, CA: Sage.

Hoffman-Plotkin, D., & Twentyman, C. T. (1984). A multimodal assessment of behavioral and cognitive deficits in abused and neglected preschoolers. *Child Development, 55,* 794–802.

Hornick, J. P., & Clarke, M. E. (1986). A cost/effectiveness evaluation of play therapy treatment for child abusing and high risk parents. *Child Abuse & Neglect, 10* (3), 309–318.

Huesmann, L. R. (1988). An information processing model for the development of aggression. *Aggressive Behavior, 14,* 13–24.

Hunter, R., & Kilstrom, N. (1979). Breaking the cycle in abusive families. *American Journal of Psychiatry, 136,* 1320–1322.

James, J. A., & Boake, C. (1988). MMPI profiles of child abusers and neglecters. *International Journal of Family Psychiatry, 9* (4), 351–371.

Jayaratne, S. (1977). Child abusers as parents and children: A review. *Social Work, 22,* 5–9.

Kadushin, A., & Martin, J. A. (1981). *Child abuse: An interactional event.* New York: Columbia University Press.

Kaufman, J., & Zigler, E. (1987). Do abused children become abusive parents? *American Journal of Orthopsychiatry, 57* (2), 186–192

Kazdin, A. E. (1978). Evaluating the generality of findings in analogue therapy research. *Journal of Consulting and Clinical Psychology, 46,* 673–686.

Keltikangas-Jarvinen, L., & Kangas, P. (1988). Problem-solving strategies in aggressive and nonaggressive children. *Aggressive Behavior, 14,* 255–264.

Kempe, C. H., & Helfer, R. E. (1972). *Helping the battered child and his family.* Philadelphia: Lipincott.

Kempe, C. H., Silverman, F. N., Steele, B. F., Droegemueller, W., & Silver, H. K. (1962). The battered child syndrome. *Journal of the American Medical Association, 181,* 17–24.

Knutson, J. F. (1978). Child abuse as an area of aggression research. *Journal of Pediatric Psychology, 3,* 20–27.

Knutson, J. F., Fordyce, D. J., & Anderson, D. J. (1980). Escalation of irritable aggression: Control by consequences and antecedents. *Aggressive Behavior, 6,* 347–359.

Knutson, J. F., & Mehm, J. G. (1988). Transgenerational patterns of coercion in families and intimate relationships. In Gordon W. Russell (Ed.), *Violence in intimate relationships* (pp. 67–90). New York: PMA Publishing.

Knutson, J. F., & Schartz, H. A. (in press). Evidence pertaining to physical abuse and neglect of children as parent–child relational diagnoses. In A. Frances, M. B. First, & T. Widiger (Eds.), *DSM-IV sourcebook.* Washington, DC: American Psychiatric Association.

Knutson, J. F., Schartz, H. A., & Zaidi, L. Y. (1991). Victim risk factors in the physical abuse of children. In R. Baenninger (Ed.), *Targets of violence and aggression* (pp. 103–157). Holland: Elsevier.

Knutson, J. F., & Selner, M. B. (1994) Punitive childhood experiences reported by young adults over a ten-year period. *Child Abuse and Neglect, 18,* 43–54.

Knutson, J. F., & Viken, R. J. (1984). Animal analogues of human aggression: Studies of social experience and escalation. In D. C. Blanchard, K. J. Flannelly, & R. J. Blanchard (Eds.), *Biological perspectives on aggression* (pp. 75–94). New York: Alan R. Liss.

Knutson, J. F., & Zaidi, L. Y. (1989). *The Parenting Task: A video test of parenting and discipline.* Iowa City: University of Iowa Video Center.

Larrance, D. T., & Twentyman, C. T. (1983). Maternal attributions and child abuse. *Journal of Abnormal Psychology, 92,* 449–457.

Levis, D. J. (1979). The infrahuman avoidance model of symptom maintenance and implosive therapy. In J. D. Keehn (Ed.), *Psychopathology in animals: Research and clinical implications* (pp. 257–277). New York: Academic.

Loevinger, J. (1957). Objective tests as instruments of psychological theory. *Psychological reports, Monograph Supplement, 9,* 635–694.

Morris, M. G., & Gould, R. W. (1963). Role reversal: A concept in dealing with the neglected battered child syndrome. In Child Welfare League of America (Ed.), *The neglected-battered child syndrome.* New York: Child Welfare Leagues of America.

Nelson, B. J. (1984). *Making an issue of child abuse: Political agenda setting for social problems.* Chicago: University of Chicago Press.

Newburger, E. H., Reed, R. B., Daniel, J. H., Hyde, J. N., & Kotelchuck, M. (1977). Pediatric social illness: Toward an etiologic classification. *Pediatrics, 60,* 178.

Office of Human Development Services. (1988). *Study findings: Study of national incidence and prevalence of child abuse and neglect.* Washington, DC: U.S. Department of Health and Human Services.

Owens, D. J., & Straus, M. A. (1975). The social structure of violence in childhood and approval of violence as an adult. *Aggressive Behavior, 1,* 193–211.

Parens, H. (1987). Cruelty begins at home. *Child Abuse and Neglect, 11,* 331–338.

Parke, R. D., & Collmer, C. W. (1975). Child abuse: An interdisciplinary analysis. In E. M. Hetherington (Ed.), *Review of child development research* (Vol. 5, pp. 509–590). Chicago: University of Chicago Press.

Passman, R. H., & Mulhern, R. K., Jr. (1977). Maternal punitiveness as affected by situational stress: An experimental analogue of child abuse. *Journal of Abnormal Psychology, 86* (5), 565–569.

Patterson, G. R. (1976). The aggressive child: Victim and architect of a coercive system. In E. J. Mash, L. A. Hamerlynck, & L. C. Handy (Eds.), *Behavior modification and families I. Theory and research* (pp. 131–158). New York: Bruner-Mazel.

Patterson, G. R. (1982). *Coercive family process.* Eugene, OR: Castalia.

Patterson, G. R. (1986). Performance models for antisocial boys. *American Psychologist, 41,* 432–443.

Patterson, G. R., & Cobb, J. A. (1971) A dyadic analysis of "aggressive" behaviors. In J. P. Hill (Ed.), *Minnesota symposia on child psychology* (Vol. 5, pp. 271–282). Minneapolis: University of Minnesota Press.

Perry, M. A., Wells, E. A., & Doran, L. D. (1983). Parent characteristics in abusing and nonabusing families. *Journal of Clinical Child Psychology, 12* (3), 329–336.

Pianta, R., Egeland, B., & Erickson, M. F. (1989). The antecedents of maltreatment: Results of the Mother–Child Interaction Research Project. In D. Cicchetti & V. Carlson (Eds.), *Child maltreatment: Theory and research on the causes and consequences of child abuse and neglect* (pp. 203–235). Cambridge, MA: Cambridge University Press.

Polansky, N. A., Ammons, P. W., & Weathersby, B. L. (1983). Is there an American standard of child care? *Social Work, 28* (5), 341–346.

Prescott, A. (1991). *Early aversive social interaction in the family and later retrospective reports of physical child abuse.* Unpublished doctoral dissertation, University of Oregon, Eugene.

Rausch, K., & Knutson, J. F. (1991). The self-report of personal punitive childhood experiences and those of siblings. *Child Abuse and Neglect, 15,* 29–36.

Reid, J. B. (1985). Social interactional patterns in families of abused and nonabused children. In C. Zahn-Waxler, M. Cummings, & M. Radke-Yarrow (Eds.), *Social and biological origins of altruism and aggression* (pp. 33–45). New York: Cambridge University Press.

Richard, B. A., & Dodge, K. A. (1982). Social maladjustment and problem solving in school-aged children. *Journal of Consulting and Clinical Psychology, 50,* 226–233.

Rohrbeck, C. A., & Twentyman, C. T. (1986). Multimodal assessment of impulsiveness in abusing, neglecting, and normal treating mothers and their preschool children. *Journal of Consulting and Clinical Psychology, 54* (2), 231–236.

Rosenberg, M. S., & Reppucci, N. D. (1983). Abusive mothers: Perceptions of their own and their children's behavior. *Journal of Consulting and Clinical Psychology, 51,* 674–682.

Sapp, A. D., & Carter, D. L. (1978). *Child abuse in Texas: A descriptive study of Texas residents' attitudes.* Huntsville, TX: Sam Houston State University.

Seligman, M. E. P. (1975) *Helplessness: On depression, development, and death.* San Francisco: Freeman.

Slaby, R. G., & Guerra, N. G. (1988). Cognitive mediators of aggression in adolescent offenders: 1. Assessment. *Developmental Psychology, 24,* 580–588.

Smith, S. M. (1976). *The Battered Child Syndrome.* London: Butterworths.

Snyder, J. J. (1977) A reinforcement analysis of intervention in problem and nonproblem children. *Journal of Abnormal Psychology, 86,* 528–535.

Spinetta, J. J., & Rigler, D. (1972). The child-abusing parent: A psychological review. *Psychological Bulletin, 77,* 296–304.

Steele, B. F. (1976). Violence within the family. In R. E. Helfer & C. H. Kempe (Eds.), *Child abuse and neglect: The family and the community.* Cambridge, MA: Ballinger.

Steele, B. F., & Pollack, C. B. (1974). A psychiatric study of parents who abuse infants and small children. In R. E. Helfer & C. H. Kempe (Eds.), *The battered child* (2nd ed., pp. 89–134). University of Chicago Press.

Straus, M. A. (1980). Stress and physical child abuse. *Child Abuse & Neglect, 4,* 75–88.

Straus, M. A., & Gelles, R. J. (1986). Societal change and change in family violence from 1975 to 1985 as revealed by two national surveys. *Journal of Marriage and the Family, 48* (3), 465–479.

Straus, M. A., & Gelles, R. J. (1990). How violent are American families? Estimates from the National Family Violence resurvey and other studies. In M. A. Straus, R. J. Gelles, & C. Smith (Eds.), *Physical violence in American families* (pp. 95–108). New Brunswick: Transaction.

Straus, M. A., & Kantor, G. K. (1987). Stress and child abuse. In R. E. Helfer & R. S. Kempe (Eds.), *The battered child* (pp. 42–59). University of Chicago Press.

Suomi, S. J., & Harlow, H. F. (1977). Production and alleviation of depressive behaviors in monkeys. In J. D. Maser & M. E. P. Seligman (Eds.), *Psychopathology: Experimental models* (pp. 131–173). San Francisco: Freeman.

Twentyman, C. T., & Plotkin, R. C. (1982). Unrealistic expectations of parents who maltreat their children: An educational deficit that pertains to child development. *Journal of Clinical Psychology, 38* (3), 497–503.

Vasta, R. (1982) Physical child abuse: A dual-component analysis. *Developmental Review, 2,* 125–149.

Vasta, R., & Copitch, P. (1981). Simulating conditions of child abuse in the laboratory. *Child Development, 52,* 164–170.

Wahler, R. G., Williams, A. J., & Cerezo, A. (1990). The compliance and predictability hypotheses: Sequential and correlational analyses of coercive mother–child interactions. *Behavioral Assessment 12,* 391–407.

Weston, J. T. (1974). A summary of neglect and traumatic cases. In R. E. Helfer & C. H. Kempe (Eds.), *The battered child.* (2nd. ed; pp. 61–86; 93–201). Chicago University of Chicago Press.

Widom, C. S. (1989). Does violence beget violence: A critical examination of the literature. *Psychological Bulletin, 106* (1), 3–28.

Williamson, J., Borduin, C., & Howe, B. (1991). The ecology of adolescent maltreatment: A multilevel examination of adolescent physical abuse, sexual abuse, and neglect. *Journal of Consulting and Clinical Psychology, 59,* 449–457.

Wolfe, D. A., Edwards, B., Manion, I., & Koverola, C. (1988). Early intervention for parents at risk of child abuse and neglect: A preliminary investigation. *Journal of Consulting and Clinical Psychology, 56* (1), 40–47.

Wolock, I. (1982). Community characteristics and staff judgments in child abuse and neglect cases. *Social Work Research and Abstracts, 18* (2), 9–15.

Zaidi, L. Y. (1988). *The influence of personal disciplinary experiences and childrens' behavior on disciplinary choices in an analog parenting task.* Unpublished doctoral dissertation, University of Iowa, Iowa City.

Zaidi, L. Y., Knutson, J. F., & Mehm, J. G. (1989). Transgenerational patterns of abusive parenting: Analog and clinical tests. *Aggressive Behavior, 15,* 137–152.

# CHAPTER 9

# Aggressive Escalation: Toward a Developmental Analysis

Robert B. Cairns
*University of North Carolina at Chapel Hill*

Carlos Santoyo V.
*Universidad Nacional Autónoma de México*

Keith A. Holly
*Point Loma Nazarene College*

The hypothesis that social interchanges escalate to aggression and violence is a simple and powerful idea. Cast into an interactional framework, the proposition is that hostile acts of one person toward another provide the stimuli for more hostile counteractions. All things equal, aggression begets aggression. Among peers, a positive feedback loop of negative actions–reactions may be created whereby increases in response intensity occur with each cycle. The concept of escalation has been employed to account for such diverse phenomena as the behavior of aggressive children and adolescents (Raush, 1965), violent men (Toch, 1969), coercive families (Patterson & Cobb, 1971), agonistic behavior of mammals (Cairns & Nakelski, 1970, 1971; Cairns & Scholz, 1973), "imitation" in young boys (Hall & Cairns, 1984), and violence in incarcerated adolescent girls (Perrin, 1981). Implicit in the proposal is the larger theoretical proposition that behaviors should not be divorced from the social contexts in which they occur. The escalation hypothesis has proved to be a versatile and productive proposal in several domains of social inquiry.

Yet questions remain on the hypothesis, its theoretical underpinnings, and the nature of the empirical evidence. The aim of this chapter is to comment on these issues and to outline some implications and limitations of the escalation proposal. The first part reviews the escalation proposal as it has been explored in developmental psychobiological investigations in humans. The second section examines some issues that have been raised for social development in children and adolescents and summarizes some recent empirical findings.

## ESCALATION AND DEVELOPMENTAL
## PSYCHOBIOLOGY

Forty years ago, Robert R. Sears (1951) enunciated a "new framework" for the theoretical analysis of personality and social behavior. The dyadic model that Sears described was not wholly new—in that the concepts were largely foreshadowed in the symbolic interactionism of Cottrell (1942) and the developmental concepts of J. M. Baldwin (1902)—but it was fresh for the social learning theories of mid-century psychology. The scientific problem remained to elaborate upon the testable empirical implications of the social interactional model. What was not explicitly discussed by Sears was the need to invent methods, analyses, and constructs that were compatible with this shift in attention beyond the individual to the dyad and social network. In the two decades that followed, only a handful of studies offered attempts to elaborate the interactional model. Among the more important contributions in studies of children, the work of Raush (1965), Patterson and Cobb (1971), Bell (1968), and Yarrow and Waxler (1979) deserve attention.

### Development and Interactions

Our early work attempted to define and empirically validate the major interactional concepts of Sears (1951) within a developmental framework. We felt that a failure to achieve a clear understanding of interactional concepts—including reciprocity, escalation, synchrony, bidirectionality, and interpersonal constraint—could undermine the developmental study of specific social behavior patterns, from "aggression" and "attachment" to "dependency" and "altruism." But we also believed that the study of interactions should go beyond social learning mechanisms. Implicit but not spelled out in the "new framework" was the role of biological and developmental changes, and the impact that these changes could have upon social patterns.

To this end, we proposed that comparative study—across ontogeny and across species—could help clarify the interactional syntax, developmental constraints, and social dynamics of this interchange process (Cairns, 1973, 1979). But there are pitfalls in comparative generalizations. As noted by Schneirla (1966), it is hazardous to leap from mice to monkeys to men without regard for the distinctive functions that particular behaviors serve for each species. Yet properly and carefully constructed, comparative study may be highly productive in clarifying the syntax of interchanges and how they develop within and across species, and what might go awry.

An example may clarify the last point. In an early study, we attempted to analyze the developmental sequelae of the early social interactions observed in interspecific pairs (i.e., infantile puppies and adult rabbits). What we found was that early attachments and playful interactions were paradoxically transformed over time into abusive and hurtful interchanges (Cairns & Werboff, 1967). Direct observation of the interactions from the earliest stage (when puppies were 14 to 28 days old) to later stages (64 to 78 days old) suggested that rapid physical maturation triggered changes in the quality of the interchange through escalation. As the characteristics of the puppies changed, so did the intensity of the "play," the consequences of the behavior, and the quality of the relationship. Actions that were idyllic and mutually supportive at an early developmental level subsequently became abusive when maturational changes in one partner were not synchronized with changes in the other. *Escalation* was employed to describe interchange alterations that occurred over several days and weeks. They were triggered by developmental changes in the morphology and behavior of one individual without compensatory shifts in the structures or actions of the other.

Whereas the extinction of "attachment behavior" by maturation may seem unique to this experimental setting, the interactive processes that are implicated seem to be general across species. These phenomena raise the larger issue of how inevitable developmental changes in structure and morphology necessitate parallel changes in interactional patterns. To the extent the individuals do not—or cannot—synchronize maturational and interactional changes over time, the conditions for nonreciprocity and escalation may be established (see Cairns, 1966, 1979, 1986).

## Development and Escalation in Fighting

The concept of escalation later proved useful to account for another curious and nonintuitive finding on the ontogeny of aggression (Cairns, 1973; Cairns & Nakelski, 1971). The phenomenon was that young animals (male mice) developed the ability to attack and fight in the total absence of relevant learning experiences. In this species, the traditional mechanisms of social learning—modeling, social reinforcement, shaping—proved to be unnecessary for the initial establishment of fighting. To the contrary, the ability to mount successful attacks and to fight effectively emerged in the absence of specific learning, shaping, or modeling experiences.

The irrelevance of modeling or selective reinforcement was demonstrated through a family of developmental experiments summarized in Cairns (1973). Male mice were raised in isolation from weaning and compared to other same-line same-age males with varying types of social experience. The upshot was that no specific learning experiences beyond isolation were necessary to produce animals who were highly effective in attack and defense. Contrary to social learning principles, aggressive behavior was facilitated by the *absence* of specific reinforcement for fighting. Animals that had been kept in isolation from weaning had shorter latencies to attack and showed more vigorous fighting than animals that had considerable social experience and specific training.

Our analysis of the first occurrence of fighting and attacks in ontogeny suggested an interactional alternative interpretation of the ontogeny of the phenomena. The interactional-biosocial interpretation was suggested by a detailed analysis of the dynamics of behavioral establishment. Direct observation of the first interchange by male mice that had been raised in isolation with other mice revealed some highly predictable sequences. When the experiments were conducted under controlled conditions, it could be observed that (a) isolation-reared males approached and vigorously investigated the other conspecific (i.e., same-species, same-age male), and (b) counter-responses by the other animal stimulated even higher levels of arousal and social exploration by the isolation-reared males. These interchanges typically "escalated" to attacks and counterattacks rapidly, often in the first 3 minutes of interchange.

Interchange-escalation sequence rarely occurred among animals that had had prior social experience, including those who were raised in "normal" conditions with littermates. Direct comparisons of the kinds of interchanges that occurred in animals reared in social and nonsocial conditions suggested a key difference in the propensity of the subjects to interact with and vigorously explore the conspecific partners. Isolated animals treated the "other" as if it were a novelty and showed emotional arousal with the exploratory social behaviors. The arousal was evidenced by the subject's jumpiness, piloerection (i.e., puffiness of fur), and hyper-responsiveness to touch. This heightened state was mobilized by social acts of conspecifics, not by nonsocial stimulation or by inanimate objects (Cairns, 1973). Nonisolated animals, on the other hand, were as attentive to the characteristics of the unfamiliar setting as to the other animal. Accordingly, they tended to sniff and explore the characteristics of the test compartment, including the walls, floors, and corners of the enclosure. They would check out the other animal by sniffing in passing, but it would not be the major focus of attention.

We proposed that isolation-rearing conditions heightened the likelihood of a rapid escalation in the intensity of the first social interchanges following isolation. Accordingly, the attacks that occurred represented the operation of (a) a lack of inhibition of vigorous actions and treating the conspecific as a "novel" object, (b) the states of arousal stimulated by the unfamiliar animal and its counteractions, and (c) the dyadic escalation stimulated by the feedback of the two animals acting together. The primary initiator in this sequence was the previously isolated animal. The rapid mobilization of internal physiological states (i.e., endocrine and neurobiological states) in previously isolated animals supported vigorous actions, including fighting and attacks. They were, paradoxically, better prepared biologically to initiate and execute attacks and fighting than were socialized animals. The escalation in the interchange sequence was coordinated with this biosocial advantage. Previously isolated animals typically emerged as dominant in greater than 90% of the interchanges.

An experimental series was designed to explore whether the feedback provided by the other conspecific was an essential element in stimulating attacks. The problem with seminaturalistic or controlled observations is that correlation can be confused with causation. The apparent "escalation" could have been superfluous, in that the attacks would have been determined by other events (e.g., an internal buildup of arousal that was time based, not interchange related). To explore whether the social feedback was significant in the apparent escalation, the behavioral responses of the conspecific partners were controlled systematically through drugs that decreased activity–reactivity. The findings provided clear support for the contribution of social feedback in the behavior. The more vigorous the counter-response of the partner, the more likely the attack by the subject. The probability of attacks by the previously isolated animal could be diminished from $P = 1.0$ to $P = 0.0$ by reducing the partner's activity–reactivity.

One of the interesting features of the solution was that it drew together, in the same framework, changes in the organism's morphological and neurobiological status with features of dynamic interchanges that could be provoked. "Innate" aggressive behaviors in this species are brought about by coupling (a) internal, maturational changes with (b) dynamic principles of interchange (i.e., synchrony, reciprocity, escalation) in (c) familiar contexts.

Comparative Generalizations

*A Genetic Bias Toward Escalation?* In the original experiments that
we conducted, the likelihood of escalation to attacks seemed to depend
jointly on the biosocial state of the individual and the feedback provided
by the partner. Further experiments were conducted to determine
whether systematic variations of either the internal state or the external
conditions would change the likelihood of attacks, either by shortening
or lengthening the duration of the escalation sequence. A systematic
developmental analysis demonstrated that escalation would occur
among males only after they had attained sexual maturity (approximately 42 to 45 days of age). Sexual maturity was of course associated
with the activation onset of testosterone. We reasoned further that the
internal supports for behavioral escalation could be modified by
changing the physiological makeup of the animal through genetic
selection. By genetic selection, we succeeded in producing substrains of
mice that had extraordinarily accelerated escalation sequences. In the
first assessment following isolation, the majority of the animals from
these "high aggressive" lines attacked within seconds on their first
exposure to a conspecific. Conversely, virtually no animals in the
selectively bred low aggressive lines showed escalation or attack in the
initial test. In subsequent neurobiological studies, the genetic manipulation has been associated with specific neurobiological sites (Lewis et
al., in press). More broadly, this line of work indicates that interactional
escalation depends on properties of the species as well as on the
provocative properties of the interchange.

But the genetic bias was itself relative. When the provocation is
sufficiently intense, even nonaggressive animals can be immediately
mobilized to respond actively and viciously. Beyond the immediate
conditions of dyadic responsiveness, the context in which the observations are conducted play a large role in whether or not escalation occurs,
regardless of genetic background.

*Is Learning Irrelevant for Aggressive Escalation?* Recall that the
escalation concept was initially employed to account for why social
learning appeared to play such a modest role in the initial establishment
of aggressive behaviors. Further experiments were consistent with the
original observation, in that specific learning experience is not necessary
for the observation of postpartum attacks in females or the initial
consolidation of attacks in other nonhuman mammalian species. However, learning plays a powerful role in the recurrence of attacks,
including the latency by which they occur and the contexts in which
they recur. Depending on the specific experiences of the subjects after

the first interchange, the latency is shortened or lengthened, and the probability of attacks is increased or decreased. The broader theoretical point is that the conditions that are required for the initial development and organization of attack patterns are different from the conditions that contribute to the recurrence and maintenance of attack patterns. Specific social learning experiences may play a major role in the recurrence, maintenance, and activation of the behavior pattern.

*Males and Females.* Some limitations of the animal experiments should be underscored. One is gender. The effects that were described for escalation were obtained in males. In females, the isolation-rearing research failed to show a similar pattern, due in large measure to the failure of the interchanges among females to escalate to attacks. This raises the question of why there is a gender difference, and the conditions under which attacks may be demonstrated in females.

A clue to the answer of the gender-difference question is suggested from observation of the social organization of the species under natural conditions. Mice are highly adaptable to the ecological conditions in which they must live (Brain, 1989; Crowcroft, 1966). As a species, however, they tend to develop strong dominance structures whenever possible. The strains that we studied, like most *Mus musculus,* rapidly established a dominance organization. In the present case, this meant that one animal in a group of 5 to 10 males would gain dominance by attacking and defeating all other males in the colony. Once dominance was achieved, the single male would effectively control access to capital resources in the environment, physical and social. All other males would be effectively limited to huddle together in about 5% of the available space, and the dominant animal would freely circulate in the rest of the territory where food, females, and other resources were available. These observations suggested to us that the dominant animal functionally isolated himself from other males in natural and seminatural settings (Cairns, 1973; see also Brain, 1989). From this perspective, the isolation rearing of subjects may have simply duplicated the conditions that dominant animals create for themselves in normal conditions. Moreover, the rapid interchange escalation and lower threshold for attack was similar for dominant animals and animals raised in experimental isolation.

The story for the elicitation of aggression among females in natural settings is quite different from males. Females do attack, but under different conditions. They attack intruders in the period that their offspring are immature and suckling. Under these conditions, unfamiliar males and females are both at risk for being attacked by females (Green, 1978). For postpartum females, the attacks were virtually immediate. It is as if the internal conditions overdetermined the behavior, with a sharp diminution of attack latency. Further investigation demonstrated that the likelihood of females to attack in postpartum was genetically linked to the likelihood of males to attack after being raised in isolation (Hood & Cairns, 1988). It appeared that the same genetic pathway was involved in males and females in the support of strain differences in attack behavior. The linkage has been obscured in the literature because of the failure to employ gender-relevant assessments.

These observations of gender differences suggest that escalations in the intensity of dyadic acts should be observed only under certain conditions. On the one hand, if the behavior is overdetermined, either by internal states or by contextual provocation, there should be only modest evidence for escalation. *Overdetermined* means that the aggressive actions are not regulated by a single interactional process; they may be triggered simultaneously by prior learning or interactional experiences, or they may be promoted by states of arousal and irritability. Under such conditions, escalatory provocation is unnecessary because minimal cues can elicit the actions full-blown almost immediately. On the other hand, if the behavior is inhibited, because of internal or external constraints, there may be only modest evidence for escalation despite provocation. For example, not all peers are equal. Previously established dominance–subordinance relationships can produce inhibitions whereby intense behavioral feedback would not be adequate to provoke an attack. Similarly, foreign and unfamiliar settings can inhibit social behaviors, including escalatory aggression. So can competing stimuli, as in the case of stress-producing pheromones. All this is to emphasize that there must be a balance of conditions, internal and external, to support interactional escalation.

*Across-Episode Escalation.* One other empirical finding deserves mention because it addresses an issue that has been infrequently raised in studies of escalation in humans. This is the matter of escalation that occurs across interchange episodes as opposed to the escalation that occurs within interchange episodes. Observational methodologies have, for the most part, focused upon the immediate dynamics of within-interchange control. Less attention has been given to the relationships that exist between episodes. Yet the distinction that was offered earlier between action and establishment and recurrence and maintenance suggests that it would be useful to analyze what happens after an episode has escalated.

Where across-episode escalation has been examined in nonhumans, powerful effects are observed from one interchange to the next. Specifically, once a fight has occurred and the individual emerges dominant, that individual is likely to attack more rapidly and more viciously in the next episode (Cairns & Scholz, 1973; Lagerspetz & Hautojärvi, 1967). There is a carry-over, presumably mediated by learning and a lower threshold for action, from the preceding episode. Presumably, if the time delay between the episodes is brief, psychobiological states of arousal could serve as mediators (see Potegal, this volume). This may be observed where there is a contagion of attacks in colonies, and individuals indiscriminately attack each other while bouncing from one antagonist to another.

The original aim of these investigations of developmental psychobiology was to bring contemporary functional/learning accounts of behavior more in line with the dynamics of social interchanges across development. At first blush, many of the phenomena of aggressive behavior seemed inconsistent with the expectations of the then-dominant functional model (i.e., social learning theory). The problem was that aggressive interchanges emerged in the absence of reinforcement or imitation. To the contrary, the absence of training was as effective as the presence of training. In the course of a developmental analysis of these puzzling phenomena, it became clear that inevitable changes in behavior potential should be taken into account to reach a precise analysis of the emergence of behavioral interchanges and what is learned. The escalation hypothesis was useful in organizing a considerable amount of information, including the "innate" expression of aggressive behavior in the very first encounters of previously isolated males. It was further shown, however, that escalation was not an inevitable antecedent, and that its operation was constrained by conditions within the organism, the relationship, and the context in which the interactions occurred. Learning played a major role in understanding events within episodes as well as between episodes.

## Unresolved Issues

Whereas the preceding analysis helps answer certain questions, including the reasons for robust reciprocity correlations and how two animals may be drawn into conflicts without prior experience, it leaves other questions unresolved. Some of the more important questions are summarized next, with propositions addressed to their resolution.

***Why Does Escalation not Occur More Often?*** This question presupposes that the conditions for triggering escalation occur with reasonably high frequency in everyday interchanges. Then why are blatant outbursts of aggressive escalation usually infrequent relative to episodes of quiet synchrony? The answers that have been offered to the question have focused upon events in the individual (e.g., habituation, inhibition), in the context (territorial, dominance hierarchy), and in the dynamics of interchange patterns.

Intraorganismic factors that reduce the likelihood of escalation include developmental changes as well as ones associated with learning. For escalation to occur, certain preconditions must be met in terms of age, strength, and response capabilities. For nonhumans, very young and very old individuals cannot meet the behavioral or physical preconditions for escalation and aggression. Beyond age and physical capabilities, the arousal–reactivity associated with unfamiliarity in this species can be diminished by continued exposure to conspecifics, such as the habituation involved in group rearing (Cairns & Nakelski, 1971). Habituation as a learning process seems not unrelated to active inhibition by prior injury and defeat. Escalatory counterattacks are significantly reduced in male mice that have been previously defeated in an interchange (Brain, 1989; Cairns, 1973).

The simple answer to the question on why attacks do not occur more frequently within existing groups is that safeguards exist to diminish escalatory encounters. Some of these buffers are structural and deal with the physical environment—including territories that are not violated. Other buffers are internalized, including habituation and the inhibition of such actions by subordinates that are likely to trigger escalation.

The foregoing suggests that a distinction should be drawn between the *initiation* of escalatory interchanges and the *recurrence* of escalation. Consider, for example, the initiation conditions that surround a fresh contact with a stranger. Under these conditions, it should be the case that significant weight might be given to immediate dyadic events (because there is no history of a prior interchange). But if a prior relationship had been established, the interchange that is observed will be a joint function of the history of that relationship (including a learned modification of social stimulus functions) as well as the elicitation properties of immediate cues. Full-blown attacks may emerge immediately, without prelude or apparent escalation. This short circuiting of a previous stepwise progression can occur when a pre-emptive strike is to the advantage of the subject. The bases for escalation can be hidden in the history of the interchange as much as in the immediate stimulating conditions.

Although the dyadic conditions for establishment of escalatory sequences are different from the conditions for their recurrence, behavior patterns rarely remain static and unchanged. Even in firmly established dominance relationships, there is some fluidity whereby changes can be introduced. Day-to-day observations of colonies of mice indicate probes and skirmishes that can provide the basis for reordering of the extant hierarchy. Such continual "sizing up" of each other and relationships is not limited to rhesus monkeys; it is found as well in the daily (and nightly) interactions among mice (see Brain, 1989).

*How Does Termination Occur?* With the issue of escalation infrequency, there is the question of de-escalation and termination. The escalation proposal accounts for the mutual entrapment of individuals into conflicts, but it does not indicate why and how conflicts can be terminated without destruction. If neither individual backs down, potentially all conflicts would be expected to escalate until some other system took over (e.g., physical fatigue, contextual intervention) or destruction of the other.

In most cases, other systems become activated. Even if the defeated animal has the will to continue the attack, he may not have the capabilities. Moreover, in the course of the escalation, the cues for the persistence of the attack may be eliminated for the aggressor. These cues include changes in the provocation of the victim as well as changes in the internal states of the attacker. Taken together, these processes provide reasonably broad support for the claim of classical ethology that aggression-to-death occurs rarely among nonhuman organisms (Lorenz, 1966). There are exceptions, as Kuo (1967) observed, but those instances are clearly exceptional even in mice.

*Cross-Species Generality.* The investigations described in this section were completed, for the most, with mice albeit from various strains and lines. How do these findings match with the results obtained from other mammalian species, including primates? A review completed 10 to 20 years ago found the evidence to be relatively sparse, but what was available seemed essentially supportive of the primary empirical generalizations on the isolation–aggression linkage in males (Cairns, 1973). A more recent survey is consistent with the early judgment (Cairns, Gariépy, & Hood, 1990).

Yet there are significant within-species and between-species differences. Recall that selectively breeding for nonescalation is not only possible, but it can be achieved within one-to-three generations. Whether or not escalation is adaptive for the individual and the species seems dependent on the particular social ecology in which development occurs. All this underscores another premise; namely, the study of social patterns should be relative to the social circumstances and contexts in which the patterns occur. Comparative generalizations about interactional processes may prove more robust than generalizations about interactional outcomes.

## INTERCHANGE DYNAMICS AND ESCALATION
## IN HUMANS

At this juncture, we shift attention to theoretical issues of interactional dynamics that may apply as clearly to humans as to nonhumans. This section is subdivided into two parts: one concerned with theoretical underpinnings of the escalation construct as it has been employed in analyses of human social behavior, and the other concerned with some recent empirical findings.

### Reciprocity, Synchrony, and Constraints

In natural interchanges, where Person $\alpha$ and Person $\beta$ interact, then $r_{\alpha\beta}$ (the reciprocal correlation between the two persons computed on observed features of behavior expressed in the interchange) tends to be highly significant. For example, if Person $\alpha$ expresses hostility, then Person $\beta$ will be likely to express hostility, all things equal. The same holds for rate and intensity of speaking in adults, toys played with by children, and values expressed in the conversation (see Chapter 17 in Cairns, 1979, for a review).

One presumption of social interchange analysis is that high levels of similarity are ordinarily observed among persons who are involved in an interchange. Whereas this presumption is ordinarily seen as an empirical generalization, it may also be justified on theoretical grounds. An analysis of interchanges between Person $\alpha$ and Person $\beta$ suggests that the similarities in action follow because each person provides constraints for the behavior of the other. For the behaviors to remain compatible and synchronized, the acts of each must fit into the organized stream of the other. In addition, autoconstraints exist, whereby the acts of each person are correlated with his or her own preceding acts. As long as they remain active participants in the interchange, each person's actions are in part constrained by the prior actions of the other. The ability of persons to serve two masters simultaneously—(a) the constraints provided by one's own internal organization of thoughts and actions and (b) the constraints provided by the organization of the other with whom one interacts—is truly a remarkable achievement. The fact that even small children accomplish the feat effortlessly does not diminish the magnitude of this miracle of everyday life.

The larger point is that reciprocity correlations—similarities between persons in interchanges in the expressed actions and attitudes—seem to be a by-product of this process of behavioral synchrony. As long as two or more persons remain in an interchange, they each provide mutual constraints for the behaviors of the others. But what happens when conflicts arise, as inevitably they must. When there is dysynchrony, the actions of others can be brought into line with those of the self, or the actions of the self can be brought into line with those of others, or the interchange may be redefined for both or terminated.

In this framework, escalation may be seen as an instance of behavioral synchrony, on the one hand, or an instance of an effort to forcibly bring the other into line, on the other. In both cases, the feedback provided by each person tends to constrain the degrees of freedom for the self. But escalation is a special kind of reciprocity whereby the stakes are increased in the feedback sequence. The two or more persons thus become constrained by the acts of the other to increase the intensity of their response. It then becomes increasingly difficult to diminish the intensity of the feedback or to withdraw from the interchange because of forces from within as well as from without.

In most human investigations, attention has been given to persons who are likely to escalate or to those who are likely to be victimized. Such selection suggests that some persons are more vulnerable to become engaged in escalatory series than others, for good or for ill. This raises the question what are the characteristics of persons who are more vulnerable to become involved in escalatory interchanges. Are they more likely to provoke a negative response from peers than others? Or are they more likely to interpret an ambiguous action as an insult and respond provocatively? Or do they have a lower threshold for the expression of seriously hurtful aggressive acts or have in their repertoire a greater variety of damaging actions? Or are they less likely to terminate an aggressive interchange? These four possibilities refer to individual differences in (a) initiation, (b) reciprocity and escalation, (c) intensity, and (d) termination. Potentially individual differences may reflect one, some, or all of the preceding interchange differences.

A related matter concerns the question of whether the escalation process is general and ubiquitous, or whether the process is observed in only especially vulnerable children and adults. The hypothesis that we offer on this matter is directly linked to the aforementioned consideration of social constraints. Specifically, we propose that *escalation processes are general, even though individual and contextual parameters influence escalation frequency*. But if the frequency of escalation is controlled, there should be reasonable similarity in process, regardless of whether individuals are viewed as highly aggressive or normal.

Developmental changes may figure importantly in whether the escalation processes are age bound. It is not obvious, for example, for persons who are vulnerable to become entrapped in a negative exchange, as children and adolescents are necessarily as vulnerable as young adults. Recent data suggest, however, that the occurrence of temper outbursts are reasonably predictable in males from childhood to adulthood (Caspi, Elder, & Bem, 1987). These early behaviors are linked to an unstable employment history and other problems in social adaptation at maturity.

The fact that these effects occur over time has ordinarily been explained in terms of the durability of internal individual-difference factors. Whereas that explanation is plausible—given the configuration of emotional, behavioral, cognitive, and learning factors that are involved—it is also the case that contextual and social-organizational factors may play a significant role. The social contexts that provoke and permit the continuation of escalatory patterns may themselves contribute to the continuity of individual differences. Overt patterns of aggressive expression are permitted or supported in certain contexts, and those settings may themselves become relatively stable over time for individuals. What appears to be individual-difference stability may, in fact, reflect the continuity of persons-in-contexts. More broadly, persons and social contexts should be considered together in any account of the stability of escalatory patterns.

Several issues raised in the study of escalation in nonhuman species apply to humans as well. These include the problem of how internal states can constrain or otherwise contribute to interchange escalation. Such states might reflect the enduring dispositions of either person, or they may be acute conditions associated with fatigue, irritation, mood, or substance abuse. The problem of gender differences in escalation and whether gender differences exist has not been vigorously pursued, either theoretically or empirically. There is, as well, the problem of relationships that may exist between interepisode escalation and intraepisode escalation. It may be the case, for example, that the most powerful dimensions of escalation transcend the limitations of focus on single episodes. It may be important to view the escalatory sequences on a broader time scale to understand their impact.

## THE CLS LONGITUDINAL PROJECT

In this final section, we turn to some recent findings from the longitudinal study of interchanges in children and adolescents, and how development may be a necessary consideration to unravel the secrets of human social behavior. The preceding section implied that simultaneous attention should be given to events in two time domains: the microanalyses of social interchanges, on the one hand, and the longitudinal assessments of social adaptation, on the other. A primary concern of both theory and application is to link these two time domains together, and to specify how the direct observation of interchanges relates to long-term social adjustment. To this end, the CLS longitudinal investigation was designed to assess the social development of persons from childhood through maturity. Early in the research design, it was deemed important to make a large investment in the microanalysis of behavior interchanges in the natural setting of the school.

The CLS research design and multilevel measures have recently been described elsewhere (Cairns, Cairns, Neckerman, Ferguson, & Gariépy, 1989; Cairns, Cairns, Neckerman, Gest, & Gariépy, 1988). However, a summary of the behavior data collection procedures and analysis is not readily available. Because of the need to investigate within- as well as between-episode escalation, it was necessary to track individuals for a significant amount of time each day and successively, over a 4-day period. The observation procedure called for two observers, working simultaneously at two levels of analysis to obtain one record of observation. One researcher observer focused on the subject, and the other observer focused on the classroom context.

The 80 individuals who were observed differed in terms of whether they had been nominated for being highly aggressive by at least two persons in the school, including the child's teacher, the principal, and/or the school counselor or school psychologist. Once the highly aggressive subject was identified, a matched control subject was assigned. The matching variables included the classroom enrolled, gender, race, physical size, and socioeconomic status. A total of 40 risk and 40 individually matched control subjects were identified, equal with respect to gender and grade.

A major investment was made in the behavioral observation, in that the research design called for each child and matched control to be observed over 4 consecutive days by two observers in at least two different school contexts each day. The observation followed a protocol where one person kept a running narrative account of the child's behavior over a 5-minute period, with entries made each 5 seconds. Simultaneously, the second observer observed the context of the classroom, noting the dominant activity as well as the directions and activity of the teacher and salient behaviors in the classroom. These macrosocial, contextual observation entries were made each 60 seconds.

At the end of each 5-minute interval, the two observers switched roles. The focal observer then observed the context, and the contextual observer focused on the target child and his or her social interactions. This procedure continued for the next 5 minutes, and the roles were again reversed. The switching rarely required more than 30 seconds, and typically less. At the end of three 5-minute blocks, the observers changed to the matched-control subject. The same observational procedure was continued for the three 5-minute blocks with the second subject, then switched back to the original. Adjustments were made when the persons switched classes, or when new settings were created.

Certain assumptions on the observational method we adopted should be made explicit.

***Interactions and Episodes.***   We assumed that social interchanges could be organized in units beyond the level of the dyadic action–interaction. Although formidable problems exist in identifying episodes or clusters of interchanges, we felt that these broader units of analysis could be analyzed in terms of their particular structure and interrelations. The delineation between episodes involved a joint criterion of time between interactions and identity of the other person. To detect relationships within and between episodes, it was necessary to have extended periods of observation of a given focal individual and his or her interchanges. This theoretical assumption led to the adoption of extended periods of observation each day over a 4-day period.

***Context and Interchanges.***   It was deemed important that both contextual and focal information be available for analysis and interpretation. Of the various methods that were investigated, the procedure adopted was to simultaneously involve two observers in the same context who synchronized their observations. These focal and contextual observations, independently recorded, could then be integrated subsequently in the analysis of social interchanges.

***Public Interpretation.***   We wished to make the basis for interpretation of behavior sequences open to subsequent analysis and reinterpretation. One of the problems in developmental analysis has been that the constructs available for study often require age and developmental adjustments when they are applied to persons of different ages and genders, or in diverse circumstances. Such constructs may obscure true age and gender differences in the concrete behaviors from which the judgments are inferred (Cairns, 1986). When observers are required to make on-the-spot judgments of constructs, including the intentions of the persons who are observed, the bases for interpretation are inevitably concealed. In addition, much of the responsibility for basic interpretations is assigned by default to the least sophisticated participants in the research investigation. Such observers tend, for the most part, to employ social conventions in arriving at judgments about which button to press or which category to select. Reliability assessments may only confirm the level of social conventions and the robustness of these social judgments.

The alternative we adopted in this investigation was to use concrete data language, and verbatim transcriptions of what is said and done, and by whom. Our aim was to permit subsequent public judgments and reassessments. The data collection procedure also facilitated the identification of distinct interchange episodes in the stream of naturalistic interactions.

*Social Versus Nonsocial Observations.* Because the observer has inevitable limits in terms of attention and ability to record, priority was given in all observations to social interchanges as opposed to nonsocial behavior sequences. In this regard, the actions of the focal subject with any actions–counteractions of others with respect to the subject were recorded. In the absence of social interchanges, information was recorded with respect to the ongoing behavior of subjects.

*Behavior Aggregation and Behavior Sequences.* Following the arguments offered in an earlier publication (Cairns & Green, 1979), we anticipated that different goals would be served by (a) the sequential analysis of behavioral events and episodes, and (b) the aggregation of observations over settings, relationships, and contexts. It was expected that the former strategy would be required to detect the mechanisms of interchange control, with particular reference to the processes of escalation and their expression. The latter strategy—aggregating data over persons, contexts, and time—would be useful in identifying individual differences over development and in describing group differences. Accordingly, the data were collected and stored by procedures that would permit both types of analysis.

*Reliability and Validity.* The data collection was especially suited for the assessment of the standard psychometric properties of measurement. The availability of parallel yet independent raw research protocols permitted the assessment of interobserver agreement in both conventional and distinctive ways. Perhaps the most powerful demonstration of reliability occurs when each record is analyzed independently of the other, and the conclusions with respect to particular issues compared. The multilevel assessment permitted comparisons with other methods, including ratings of teachers, school performance, official community records, peer evaluations, and self-reports. The developmental assessments provided year-to-year evaluations of individual differences associated with the behavior observations.

Findings Relevant for Escalation

A preliminary analysis of the CLS observations indicated that the children and adolescents who had been nominated for being highly aggressive did, in fact, differ markedly from the matched control group in behavior patterns. Highly reliable differences were obtained among the two groups in the rate of negative episodes observed (e.g., Cairns & Cairns, 1984). The aggregated observations of negative episodes were positively correlated with teacher ratings of aggression and peer nominations of persons who started conflicts. The effects were observed in both males and females, and in both the fourth- and seventh-grade comparisons. Further analysis indicated that the major differences between the aggressive risk and matched-control groups appeared in the hostile and blatantly aggressive episodes. This effect appeared in both genders.

***Within-Episode Analysis.*** We attempted to determine whether the groups differed in rate of initiation of hostile acts, in likelihood of reciprocity and escalation, in absolute asymptotic level of intensity, or in the failure to terminate the negative interchanges. On the basis of a simple dyadic analysis of aggressive escalation, one might expect to find that the negative episodes would present a picture of the kind shown in Fig. 9.1(a).

This theoretical figure shows the actions of the subject (whose responses are designated by the odd subscripts, $R_1$, $R_3$, $R_5$, $R_7$ . . .) and the actions of the dyadic partner (whose responses are designated by even subscripts, $R_0$, $R_2$, $R_4$, $R_6$). The subscript number also refers to the sequence of the actions, with time progressing from the left to the right. Intensity of action is shown on the vertical axis. The diagram assumes that (a) the subject over-responds to some act of the other person; (b) there is escalatory reciprocity, in that both individuals tend to reciprocate the intensity of the action of the other in an increasing stepwise sequence; (c) the subject overmatches or escalates the immediately preceding act of the other person; (d) the intensity of the subject's actions eventually leads the other to abruptly withdraw from the reciprocal matching, thereby leading to a termination of the escalation sequence. Whereas this figure is a simplification of the escalation proposal—in that it omits the role of internal constraints and external

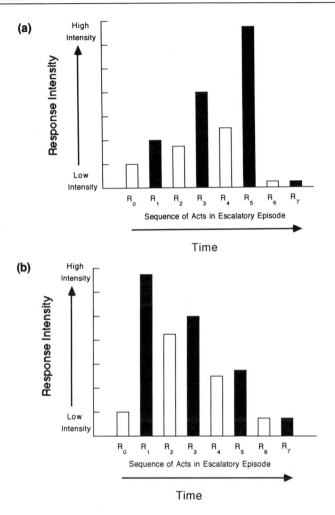

FIG. 9.1. (a) Theoretical schema showing a prototypic escalation of an interpersonal conflict. The expected response intensity of the "aggressive" subject is shown in the odd interactional steps (black columns), and the expected response intensity of the dyadic partner is shown in the even interactional steps (open columns). (b) Summary of observed "conflict" episodes from the CLS investigation of children and adolescents, with the response intensity of the "aggressive" subjects shown in the odd columns (black bars) and the response intensity of the dyadic partners in the even columns (open bars). (See text for further explanation.)

contextual inhibitions—it does not violate the essence of the basic dyadic proposal.

There was surprisingly little evidence for the preceding stepwise escalation of aggressive behavior. In the analysis of all negative episodes that occurred during the course of the CLS observation, the assumption of a stepwise escalation in the aggressive episode gained little support. The composite picture that was obtained seemed to fit, in contrast, the sequential schema shown in Fig. 9.1(b). In brief, the aggregate data indicated that the aggressive subjects differed from the matched-control subjects in the likelihood of hostile initiation in the first stage of the episode. There was a reciprocal increase in the negativity of the other's response (i.e., step $R_3$). But the tendency was to decrease—not increase—the intensity of the acts in the dyadic exchange. This decrease was observed in both the responses of the subject and those of the partner. The upshot was that the hostile interactions tended to decrease rather than increase in intensity, even when persons who had been identified as highly aggressive were involved.

This does not mean, however, that reciprocal entrapment did not occur or that aggression failed to beget aggression. To the contrary, examination of the $R_2$ and $R_4$ steps indicates that the other persons were, in fact, drawn into exchanges, and that they increased the frequency and intensity of their hostile and aggressive actions. It was also shown by the positive correlation between the aggressive acts of the two persons in interchanges. Despite this tendency to reciprocate, the overall picture indicated that most negative episodes in these observations diminished rather than increased in intensity.

The general pattern shown in Fig. 9.1(b) seemed to hold for the negative interchanges of aggressive and matched-control subjects. This set of outcomes suggests that other factors should probably be considered in the analysis of aggressive episodes, beyond the feedback provided by the partner and the provocation of the subject. Such additional factors might include the context in which the interchange occurs, and the risk that each person encounters for sanctions beyond those that might be delivered by the partner. Beyond events in the external context, there are as well self-produced events that may either support or inhibit the escalation. Such events might include the elicitation of internal controls on intensity, and the rapid recruitment of internal inhibitory processes after the impulsive action. In any case, the empirical data in this school context raise questions about the automatic engagement of individuals into patterns of exchange that are potentially mutually destructive. These data also suggest that most provocations *do not* escalate in intensity.

Further research might well be addressed to the common processes that serve to inhibit escalation or inhibit direct reciprocity. Systematic analysis is required to determine precisely how contextual and internal constraints are balanced. Evidence from this research program has shown, for example, that the occurrence of aggressive episodes is directly linked to context (i.e., the classrooms in which the observations were made differed markedly in the aggressive episode probability). But demonstrations of the importance of contextual factors does not preclude the operation of internal controls whereby the external constraints become internalized. On this score, the within-episode decrease in intensity suggests the operation of internal constraints, possibly triggered as a consequence of an impulsive outburst. Such integrative analyses seem called for if we are to understand how interactions are embedded in social contexts. They are also required to clarify how such prior negative exchanges, once they occur, are consolidated and affect the individual's response dispositions in future exchanges.

*Across-Episode Escalation.* The design of the observations and the coding scheme permitted the analysis of the relationships between negative episodes. In accord with a general escalation hypothesis, it was anticipated that the occurrence of an aggressive encounter would modify the threshold for the occurrence of another encounter. Specifically, it was expected that aggressive episodes would cluster in time.

This recurrence-in-time could be mediated by internal, dyadic, or contextual factors. At the individual level, the new negative episode could be promoted by the subject's lowered threshold for an impulsive, insulting act. This threshold might be influenced by the carry-over effects of preceding anger and emotional arousal, and/or the heightened intensity of expression. Alternatively, the individual could be viewed by other individuals as being in a provocative state, and his or her behaviors may be misinterpreted. At the dyadic level, the failure to resolve the preceding conflict could affect the next interchange between the same two individuals. Or, alternatively, new actors might be drawn into a fresh conflict to defend or otherwise support the initial victim. At the contextual level, the contextual factors that permitted the occurrence of the preceding conflict could still be operative so that other subsequent conflicts might be expected.

Insofar as data are available from the CLS observations, there is strong support for the proposition that negative, aggressive episodes cluster in time. There is a striking increase in the probability of a fresh conflict within the first minute following an earlier one, with the probability gradually diminishing to reach base line after 5 or 6 minutes. This across-episode effect is consistent with an earlier observational analysis of aggressive interchanges in a middle school setting. This time-based recurrence of aggressive episodes indicates that it might be productive to conduct observations over a sufficient time interval to identify the events that give rise to seemingly "spontaneous" aggressive provocations.

*A General Process?* Are the negative episodes distinctive to the aggressive risk subjects, or do the patterns apply to both risk and nonrisk persons? The question is an important one because it raises the issue of whether aggressive children operate according to different interchange principles than nonaggressive ones. Preliminary analyses of the patterns of exchange suggest that the risk and control subjects differ in the frequency of negative episodes but not in the pattern. When controlled for frequency, the pattern of an abrupt rise in intensity and then a diminution is consistently found. In this regard, the data are consistent with the "universal" assumption (i.e., that the syntax of negative interchanges in this setting apply to both aggressive and nonaggressive individuals, regardless of gender). It appears that the major difference among risk and control subjects lies in their propensity to initiate hostile and aggressive behavior, not in the dynamics and processes of interchange.

*Developmental Predictions.*   Recall there were reasonably high levels of agreement among aggressive episodes, concurrent teacher judgments of aggressive behavior, and peer nominations for conflict initiation (Cairns & Cairns, 1984). The finding of this correspondence appears to be at odds with the expectations that were offered by Cairns and Green (1979) on the different functions of direct observations and teacher–peer ratings.

In an earlier chapter it was argued that direct observations and ratings had different goals. Observations are designed to obtain veridical accounts of the individual's behaviors-in-context in the here and now. The observations thus are affected by such factors as (a) the dyadic partners with whom the subject interacts, (b) the contexts in which the observations occur, (c) the ephemeral states of the subject and those with whom he or she interacts, (d) the enduring characteristics and dispositions of the subjects, and (e) "errors" in measurement, including the characteristics of the observer and properties of the measurement instruments. Ratings and nominations are also influenced by multiple factors, but the goal of the judge (e.g., teacher, peer) is to abstract the properties of the individual from the contexts, relationships, and ephemeral events in which the individual is embedded. By virtue of the subjectivity of such judgments, there is usually more room for observer error, including biases of the judge and faulty reconstruction of past relationships and experiences.

On the basis of such issues of measurement, it was concluded that under the usual circumstances of application ratings should provide more efficient and stable measures of individual difference and developmental prediction than observations. Observations, on the other hand, were invaluable for the study of behavioral processes and functions. The preceding analyses of escalation, for example, have been obscured by judgments and ratings.

Certain conditions were specified by Cairns and Green (1979) where observations should be as effective as ratings in developmental prediction (or more effective). This would occur when reasonably large samples of social behavior were observed for each person across interactional partners, across contexts, and across time. The aggregated information across partners, context, and time should (a) diminish the distinctive contributions of these sources of variance and (b) increase the distinctive contributions of enduring dispositions in the individual. Accordingly, aggregated observations—if they reflect a reasonably heterogeneous database in terms of partners, contexts, and time—should provide reasonable predictors of subsequent stages. The CLS observation series provided such aggregated information.

In a preliminary analysis of prediction, a combined index of late adolescent and early maturity adjustment was computed for all subjects in the risk and control groups. Poor adjustment was determined as a composite score from five domains (school failure and dropout, arrests for delinquency and crime, serious acts of violence/assault, teenage pregnancy or marital failure, suicide or serious emotional disturbance). This adjustment index was computed for each subject. In three of the four gender–grade groups, the direct observations made in the fourth and seventh grades showed a robust relationship to the measure of adjustment 7 to 9 years later (i.e., post-high school graduation).[1] In this data set, the observations were as powerful in prediction as any other measure in adolescence.

## CONCLUDING COMMENTS

Escalation refers to interchanges whereby social actions become intensified through reciprocal feedback processes. When simply stated as an interactional concept, the concept suffers several flaws. Examination of the translation of the escalation hypothesis to the problems of aggression has identified shortcomings in the theoretical formulation and gaps in its validation. Perhaps the most damaging empirical result has been the finding that instances of the stepwise escalation in everyday conflicts are relatively infrequent, even when these conflict episodes have been identified in highly aggressive children and adolescents. As a result of this empirical audit, a question may be asked on whether the concept has outlived its usefulness for describing hostile interactions.

We believe that it would be a mistake to discard interactional concepts

---

[1]The one group that failed to show a strong relationship were fourth-grade females. The possible reasons for this difference are examined in a forthcoming paper.

because they were misapplied, overgeneralized, or too loosely formulated in the first place. The task of empirical research is to sharpen theoretical concepts, probe into their ambiguities, and determine where they apply and where they do not. Although most human conflicts do not escalate in intensity, some do, and these instances must be understood. Moreover, examination of the escalation concept has challenged theorists to become more precise about interchange dynamics and the multiple controls of social reciprocity.

One lesson is that a distinction should be drawn between explanations of (a) the establishment of interchange patterns and (b) the maintenance or recurrence of interchanges. The function of dyadic feedback in escalation seems to be most readily identified in the establishment of interchanges. This establishment-maintenance distinction is important because of the constraints that prior social learning experiences play in the facilitation and/or inhibition of escalation. In the settings of everyday life, it is unusual when "all things are equal." Prior associations establish conventions and hidden constraints.

A second lesson is that analyses of escalation can ill-afford to remain at the dyadic level. To understand the dynamics of interchange, one must bring into the picture the role of protective inhibitions and constraints, both internal and contextual. The properties of the individual, the social organization, and physical context figure importantly in whether or not escalation occurs, and the point at which it will be inhibited or facilitated. By the same token, it seems important to understand when these protective inhibitions—internal, contextual, dyadic—are not called into play.

The third and related lesson is that the developmental study of interactions can be invaluable. The goal would be to specify, in the life of persons—over contexts, relationships, and time—the conditions under which constraints on reciprocal escalation arise, and when and why they break down. Just as it is a mistake to remove dyadic processes from the person–context configurations in which they occur, investigations cannot afford to freeze interactions by a single snapshot of persons in one phase of development. The role of initiation in escalation underscores the need to look at the characteristics of the persons who provoke the interchange, and how these characteristics are modified in ontogeny. Similarly, the carry-over from one interchange sequence to another underscores the importance of the emotional states of the persons as well the structure of the context in supporting escalation. Developmental psychobiological investigations show that experiences across interchanges can become consolidated into personal dispositions. It seems reasonable to propose that parallel processes occur in human development.

We did not examine in this chapter the possibility that escalation can occur in positive directions as well as negative ones. Given the nature of reciprocity in relationships, there seems to be ample reason that kindly, thoughtful behaviors can elicit counter-responses of kindness and sensitivity. Although such reciprocal "prosocial" behaviors can be readily demonstrated (cf. reciprocal altruism), there has been little discussion of escalation processes in this context (Cairns, 1979; Trivers, 1971). The obstacles to the study of such interchange patterns are significant, due in part to problems in the assessment of prosocial behaviors. Nonetheless, the ability to enrich a relationship is at least as important as the ability to ignite it.

## ACKNOWLEDGMENTS

Preparation of this chapter was supported by NIMH to the CLS longitudinal project, codirected by Robert B. Cairns and Beverley D. Cairns.

Carlos Santoyo V. was supported by finds administered by the Universidad Nacional Autonoma de Mexico during his sabbatical year at the Social Development Laboratory, University of North Carolina at Chapel Hill.

Keith A. Holly was a Visiting Scholar at the Carolina Consortium on Human Development during a sabbatical leave from Point Loma Nazarene College.

## REFERENCES

Baldwin, J. M. (1902). *Social and ethical interpretations in mental development: A study in social psychology* (3rd ed.). New York: Macmillan. (Original Work published 1897)

Bell, R. Q. (1968). A reinterpretation of the direction of effects in studies of socialization. *Psychological Review, 75*, 81–95.

Brain, P. (1989). Aggression in mice as a model for behavioral evolution. In P. F. Brain, D. Mainardi, & S. Parmigiani (Eds.), *House mouse aggression: A model for understanding the evolution of social behavior* (pp. 1–30). London: Harwood Academic.

Cairns, R. B. (1966). Attachment behavior of mammals. *Psychological Review, 72*, 409–426.

Cairns, R. B. (1973). Fighting and punishment from a developmental perspective. In J. K. Cole & D. D. Jensen (Eds.), *Nebraska Symposium on Motivation* (Vol. 20, pp. 59–124). Lincoln: University of Nebraska Press.

Cairns, R. B. (1979). *Social development: The origins and plasticity of interchanges.* San Francisco: Freeman.

Cairns, R. B. (1986). Phenomena lost: Issues in the study of development. In J. Valsiner (Ed.), *The individual subject and scientific psychology* (pp. 97–112). New York: Plenum.

Cairns, R. B., & Cairns, B. D. (1984). Predicting aggressive patterns in girls and boys: A developmental study. *Aggressive Behavior, 10,* 227–242.

Cairns, R. B., Cairns, B. D., Neckerman, H. J., Ferguson, L. L., & Gariépy, J-L. (1989). Growth and aggression: I. Childhood to early adolescence. *Developmental Psychology, 25,* 320–330.

Cairns, R. B., Cairns, B. D. Neckerman, H. J., Gest, S., & Gariépy, J-L. (1988). Social networks and aggressive behavior: Peer support or peer rejection? *Developmental Psychology, 24,* 815–823.

Cairns, R. B., Gariépy, J-L., & Hood, K. E. (1990). Development, microevolution, and social behavior. *Psychological Review, 97,* 49–65.

Cairns, R. B., & Green, J. A. (1979). How to assess personality and social patterns: Ratings or observations? In R. B. Cairns (Ed.), *The analysis of social interaction: Methods, issues, and illustrations* (pp. 209–226). Hillsdale, NJ: Lawrence Erlbaum Associates.

Cairns, R. B., & Nakelski, J. S. (1970). On fighting in mice: Situational determinants of intragroup dyadic stimulation. *Psychonomic Science, 18,* 16–17.

Cairns, R. B., & Nakelski, J. S. (1971). On fighting in mice: Ontogenetic and experimental determinants. *Journal of Comparative and Physiological Psychology, 74,* 354–364.

Cairns, R. B., & Scholz, S. D. (1973). Fighting in mice: Dyadic escalation and what is learned. *Journal of Comparative and Physiological Psychology, 85,* 540–550.

Cairns, R. B., & Werboff, J. (1967). Behavior development in the dog: An interspecific analysis. *Science, 158,* 1070–1072.

Caspi, A., Elder, G. H., Jr., & Bem, D. (1987). Moving against the world: Life-course patterns of explosive children. *Developmental Psychology, 23,* 308–313.

Cottrell, L. S. (1942). The analysis of situational fields in social psychology. *American Sociological Review, 7,* 370–382.

Crowcroft, P. (1966). *Mice all over.* Chester Springs, PA: Dufour.

Green, J. A. (1978). Experiential determinants of postpartum aggression in mice. *Journal of Comparative and Physiological psychology, 92,* 1179–1187.

Hall, W. M., & Cairns, R. B. (1984) Aggressive behavior in children: An outcome of modeling or reciprocity? *Developmental Psychology, 20,* 739–745.

Hood, K. E., & Cairns, R. B. (1988). A developmental-genetic analysis of aggressive behavior in mice. II. Cross-sex inheritance. *Behavior Genetics, 18,* 605–619.

Kuo, Z.-Y. (1967). *The dynamics of behavioral development: An epigenetic view.* New York: Random House.

Lagerspetz, K. M. J., & Hautojärvi, S. (1967). The effect of prior aggressive or sexual arousal on subsequent aggressive or sexual reactions in male mice. *Scandinavian Journal of Psychology, 8,* 1–6.

Lewis, M. H., Devaud, L. L., Gariépy, J-L., Southerland, S. B., Mailman, R. B., & Cairns, R. B. (in press). Dopamine and social behavior in mice bred for high and low levels of aggression. *Brain Research Bulletin.*

Lorenz, K. (1966). *Why aggression?* New York: Harcourt Brace.

Patterson, G. R., & Cobb, J. A. (1971). A dyadic analysis of "aggressive" behaviors. In J. P. Hill (Ed.), *Minnesota Symposia on Child Psychology* (Vol. 5, pp. 72–129). Minneapolis: University of Minnesota Press.

Perrin, J. E. (1980) *Peer conflicts in female and male juvenile offenders.* Unpublished doctoral dissertation, University of North Carolina, Chapel Hill.

Raush, H. L. (1965) Interaction sequences. *Journal of Personality and Social Psychology, 2,* 487–499.

Schneirla, T. C. (1966). Behavioral development and comparative psychology. *Quarterly Review of Biology, 41,* 283–302.

Sears, R. R. (1951). A theoretical framework for personality and social behavior. *American Psychologist, 6,* 476–483.

Toch, H. (1969). *Violent men*. Chicago: Aldine.

Trivers, R. L. (1971). The evolution of reciprocal altruism. *Quarterly Review of Biology, 46,* 35–57.

Yarrow, M. R., & Waxler, C. Z. (1979). Observing interaction: A confrontation with methodology. In R. B. Cairns (Ed.), *The analysis of social interactions: Methods, issues, and illustrations*. Hillsdale, NJ: Lawrence Erlbaum Associates.

# PART IV

# Aggression Dynamics in Larger Social and Political Contexts: Game Theory Revisited

# CHAPTER 10

# The Dynamics of Riots: Escalation and Diffusion/ Contagion

John Bohstedt
*University of Tennessee*

## THE IMPORTANCE OF HISTORICAL CONTEXT

Riots are not emotional outbursts with universal characteristics across time and space. The very *forms* of riot vary significantly, from disciplined crowd take-overs of food markets, to ritual machine breaking by Luddites under masked leaders, to the dark saturnalia of American lynching and vigilantism, to rare revolutionary assaults on bastions of authority like the Bastille, to the alienated ghetto riots of the 1960s. Riots are complex forms of social/political behavior set in historical contexts comprising distinctive social networks, conflicts, and ideologies that create and equip the opposing collective actors and thus shape both the incidence and dynamics of riots. Social scientists have often been preoccupied with motivations for action, forgetting to ask whether people have the *means* to act and the *opportunity* to act on those motivations (Tilly, 1978). In turn, the opportunity to act is very much influenced by the actors' tactical calculations about the probable gains and costs of action, which incorporate estimates of their resources and attitudes as compared with those of their opponents. So a riot is a moment in a matrix of past relations, present calculations, and projections of the future. Within that moment, or sequence of moments, is a new frontier for research and analysis: the only partly calculable *dynamics* of riot. For whereas the social matrix of conditions and relationships may set limits and possibilities, the particular path of violence is the result of interaction—interaction between potential crowd members, and between rioters, their targets, would-be intermediaries, and the forces of "order."

The *dynamics* of riots, specifically diffusion and escalation, are not well understood. The diffusion of riots seems like the more familiar problem of how riots begin, with the added question of how a riot in Neighborhood A might influence the probability of a riot in Neighborhood B. The escalation of riots may be quite a different problem. Under some conditions, rioters' "normal" calculations about incentives and inhibitions might guide them throughout a riot. In other cases, once a riot begins it is a whole new ball game. Perhaps people seize the opportunity created by one set of conflicts to take actions on other grudges. Perhaps escalating *interaction* results in qualitative changes in riot behavior. Even the metaphors we use to think about diffusion and escalation may obscure clear thinking, for they tend to be analogies with physical or biological processes such as the growth of a fire, the spread of a contagious disease, or the rising of a fever, processes that are not directly driven by culture and intention, even if they are affected by cultural settings. There has not been a great deal of work on such questions, and this chapter suggests some avenues for further study.

Research on the *processes* of escalation and diffusion of riots has been scarce and difficult for two reasons.[1] First, most research on collective aggression, whether by experimental psychologists or sociologists, has been static rather than dynamic, based on correlations between inputs (prior conditions) and output (behavior) (McPhail, 1971; Snyder, 1979). Such statistical analyses and causal explanations are far simpler than those for interactive processes. Second, whereas escalation of more peaceful forms of contention and negotiation has been studied (Pruitt & Rubin, 1986), riots are too complex and dangerous to replicate in a laboratory. Rioters carry particular identities, group loyalties, values, and even "battle-tested" repertoires into action. Rioters and police forces have long, sometimes bitter, memories. Further, collective violence occurs at the frontiers of "legitimacy," on the boundary between politics and crime. Collective violence involves physical destruction of property and injury to "victims," whereas rioters run the risk of being hanged or shot. Such costs and risks (and potential real gains) obviously cannot be replicated in a laboratory.

History must be our laboratory. We must test theories about collective

---

[1]A related concept, *contagion*, has sometimes been used for the spread of excitement from one individual to another in a crowd. Classically, it implied a kind of mechanical imitation that is now discredited.

violence on actual historical episodes of riots. From all the varieties of collective violence—peasant revolts, race riots, election riots, lynchings, revolutionary insurrections, and so on—I have chosen two contrasting types as contexts in which to discuss theory: riots in industrializing England (1750–1850), especially food riots, and the American ghetto :iots of the 1960s. Both involve hundreds of incidents and a large literature. The first were customary modes of grass-roots politics, the latter, eruptions that shocked many Americans. By a riot, I mean simply crowd violence, hostile collective action by a group of about 50 or more people who physically assault persons or property or coerce someone to perform an action.[2] I first discuss the contours of riots in early modern England. I use that profile to review several theories about collective aggression and their implications about diffusion and escalation. I then turn to recent American riots and discuss work that has proceeded from "static" to dynamic analyses of diffusion and escalation through the effects of interaction, thresholds, and "contagion." Finally, I consider some recent work that takes whole national waves of protest as the events to be explained. In principle, this chapter focuses on escalation and aggression *after* rioting has begun, rather than the social tensions leading up to an outbreak of violence. In practice, that distinction is often impossible to maintain.

## ENGLAND 1750–1850: RIOTS AS CUSTOMARY GRASS-ROOTS POLITICS

In this century of transition, as modern forms of industry, urban society, and mass politics emerged, riots were so common as to be commonplace. Thousands of riots formed an important tradition of popular politics (Rudè, 1964; Stevenson, 1979, 1992; Tilly, 1979). Between 1790 and 1810, for instance, about 1, 000 riots occurred in England and Wales (population 9 million) without arousing fears of social or political collapse, despite the concurrent revolution in France (Bohstedt, 1983). The common people's survival was imperilled by a number of tangible threats that triggered riots—soaring food prices after bad harvests; military conscription that resembled legalized kidnapping; wage cuts or the replacement of skilled workers by machines or half-trained youths; the conversion of common land rights to private property. On the one hand, plebeians lacked votes or political parties, whereas sporadic labor

---

[2]I intend this definition to be objective, avoiding a priori analysis, such as assumptions that riots challenge norms or authorities.

"combinations" were hounded and suppressed. On the other hand, they often lived in small communities possessing both solidarity and patrons who might permit limited protest against targets within physical reach. Hence the common people often resorted to "collective bargaining by riot" (Hobsbawm, 1952), direct action to force "victims" to change course or to get the local magistrates to intervene. Riots manipulated the social and political system; they did not challenge it head on.

Most common were food riots. When harvests fell short once or twice each decade and merchants and farmers tripled their prices, crowds in hundreds of market places would force them to sell at the "just price." Rioters also intercepted grain shipments on the roads or rivers. In either case they typically paid for the grain rather than stealing it. Such behavior was guided by a popular ethos of a "moral economy" comprising traditional norms that gave priority to local subsistence over profits and trade and so legitimated local control of supplies and prices — by magistrates if possible, but by riots if necessary (Thompson, 1971). In the social context of England between 1760 and 1820, food riots were generally frequent, restrained, and successful in lowering food prices and shaking loose emergency charity relief from gentlemen and authorities (Bohstedt, 1983).

But this "community politics of riot" had different dynamics in different *kinds* of communities (Bohstedt, 1983). The disciplined bargaining by riot recently discovered and emphasized by historians was really typical of a particular kind of town: small, stable communities like Exeter (population 17, 000). Riots depended on social assets as much as social grievances. In such communities, dense social networks among the common people supported collective action but also restrained it in view of the vertical networks between magistrates and rioters, who knew each other well and had reciprocal claims on each other for loyalty, work, charity, and patronage. Such networks permitted communication and bargaining but also sanctioned limits to riotous violence by criminal punishment and loss of patronage. By contrast, in the large new industrial boomtowns like Manchester and Birmingham, rapid industrialization had swamped and dissolved such networks, the social skeleton that made riots coherent and restrained. There riots were more disorderly and violent. Rioters were more likely to seize food outright, to assault opponents, or to destroy property to punish or intimidate their targets.[3] Riots "escalated" beyond the conventional restraints, not

---

[3]The relationship between town size, growth rate, and occupations on the one hand and the degree of violence on the other hand is statistically significant ($x^2$) for 400 towns that had riots between 1790 and 1810 (Bohstedt, 1990).

merely because the anonymity of the larger towns reduced the risks of punishment for individual rioters. The absence of shared norms and relationships in these boomtowns made it impossible for rioters to bargain with magistrates over prices and supplies. So did geography: Neither magistrates nor rioters could reach the "guilty parties," profiteering food suppliers hundreds of miles away. The boomtown magistrates also lacked the supple resources of patronage and personal influence and so repressed riots more harshly, ordering cavalry charges and stiff jail sentences to try to protect the "freedom" of the markets on which their cities' precious—and distant—supplies depended. Still, on neither side was escalation unlimited: Rioters selected only food dealers as targets and did not burn buildings or kill victims, whereas magistrates made examples of only a few offenders.

In the long run, as industrialization and urbanization proceeded, more towns became like Manchester and fewer remained like Exeter, and so the tradition of rioting as a (grudgingly) "accepted" form of community politics died out (Bohstedt, 1983). By the middle of the nineteenth century, English towns and counties developed professional police forces to replace social control both by informal patronage and by potentially lethal military force. Police armed with nightsticks could control or disperse crowds with nonlethal force, and so riots could be suppressed without provocative bloodshed (Stevenson, 1977). By the time of World War I, riots had died away as a form of commonplace politics.

To summarize: (a) Most riots in early modern Europe were intimately related to "normal" political and social relationships and processes; they were not abrupt breaks with them (Tilly, 1979). If war is diplomacy by other means, riots were popular politics in the absence of other means of negotiation, a forceful kind of bargaining that reminded elites of their "paternalist" duties to the poor, and of the lower classes' capacity to inflict pain if they forgot (cf. Nieburg, 1969). (b) However, riots were no more homogeneous in form, motive, and dynamics than other kinds of politics like elections or legislation. By contrast to the pragmatic food riots just discussed, "pogrom" -type riots against ideological or ethnic enemies—by loyalists against radicals in the same period, by Protestants against Catholics or by Whites against Blacks in 19th-century England or America—had the essentially unlimited goal of annihilating the enemy. Like food riots, such ethnic battles might be rooted in established politics and beliefs, but they would have different "matrices" of influencing factors, hence different dynamics. (c) The element of convention in traditional small-town food riots marks them off from the riots of the 1960s that seemed to lack time-tested precedents.

## HISTORIANS' REACTIONS AGAINST EARLY
## THEORIES OF COLLECTIVE AGGRESSION

The history of riots has its own history. Our composite model of food riots as a goal-oriented form of bargaining was formed by dozens of studies between 1960 and 1985 in reaction against early social psychological theories about crowds. Marxist-humanist pioneers searching for the forefathers and mothers of modern labor movements and social historians creating an anthropology of the common people stressed the more or less rational character of riots as an antidote to the old primitive notion of the "group mind" associated with Gustave Le Bon. Le Bon's "mob psychology" views still regularly find voice in the uncritical "common sense" and political repulsion of lay observers like politicians and journalists. They reflect a recurrent intuition—that people lose individual identity and cognitive control in a crowd and submerge their identities in a bestial "group mind," summed up by Le Bon (1895/1960) as "the law of the mental unity of crowds" (p. 4). Le Bon claimed that in crowds people's cultivation and critical faculties were supplanted by savage instincts and "unconscious qualities." Ideas and impulses diffused within a crowd and across a continent by imitation, a form of "mental contagion," automatic and pathological (Nye, 1975). Such ideas seem to imply unlimited diffusion and escalation, rather than the particular dynamics just discussed.

Crowds inspire fear in many people, for they seem powerful and alien, all the more so when they are "other people" unlike the observer in class or ethnic group and thus in culture and "language" (cf. Harrison, 1988). The sources of Le Bon's ideas were not any systematic or empirical studies of acting crowds but rather his own fearful experience of violence during the Paris Commune and of a threatened demagogic coup in the 1880s against the Third Republic. He also relied heavily on Taine's conservative history of the French Revolution, which depicted the common people as criminal, savage, bloodthirsty "scum" (Merton, 1960; Nye, 1975).[4] In his zeal to denounce "the crowd mind," Le Bon barely bothered to distinguish between legislatures, rioting crowds, sidewalks of pedestrians, and so on. He systematized, although he did not test scientifically, widely shared bourgeois fears about crowds and about the new urban working class. By contrast with their own individualistic experience, such bourgeois observers interpreted popular

---

[4]The modern corrective to Taine is George Rudé's (1959) *Crowd in the French Revolution*, which painstakingly recovers the behavior and identities of the crowds from court records and eyewitness accounts, rather than from frightened aristocrats' memoirs. Two excellent critical reviews of "crowd" theory are Rule(1988) and McPhail (1991).

collective behavior as herdlike. But many workers lived most of their waking moments in public, in streets, cafes, and pubs outside their cramped living quarters, working and playing in groups, perhaps following customary rituals, and depending on neighborly mutual-aid networks for survival in illness or poverty and for support in collective protest. These ecological factors might help to explain their collective solidarity without assuming a "group mind" or loss of identity, for indeed social "memberships" were essential parts of their identity. The next "classic," Sigmund Freud's famous essay on "Group Psychology," was twice removed from first-hand evidence, for he simply based it on Le Bon's descriptions of crowds (Freud, 1921). Contemporary writers like Canetti (1960/1975) and Moscovici (1985) shared many of the same biases. One basic mistake is to assume that "the crowd" is a universal phenomenon possessed of common characteristics and dynamics wherever and whenever it occurs. Empirical studies of real crowds acting in specific situations have formed a more differentiated picture.

## LEADERSHIP

A notion related to the "crowd mind" is that leaders galvanize if they do not actually create crowds and so might account for the escalation of riots. Le Bon believed in suggestibility, a nonrational, automatic process akin to hypnosis that accounted for the relationship between leader and crowd (Nye, 1975). Freud suggested that crowds surrendered their will to a leader in a libidinal tie resembling both hypnosis and the infatuation of being in love. Crowd members then identified with each other on the basis of that shared emotional bond. Such erotic ties made crowds responsive to suggestion rather than reason; according to Moscovici (1985), they became a "passionate horde" (p. 275). However, even if they were testable, such notions are overgeneral; some leaders whip up, others restrain crowds (Bohstedt, 1983).

In the 1960s, psychologists studied the phenomenon of *risky shifts*. Individuals first chose from a list of solutions to dilemmas like marriage, career, or running for political office. After group discussion they seemed to choose "riskier" solutions. That suggested possible leadership influence from the "riskiest" member of the group, but further research revised the concept to that of *"extremities shifts,"* that is, group shifts toward the poles of either greater risk *or* caution. One theory about such shifts was that leaders served as models for groups because their "risky" behavior best expressed modal values shared by other group members (Pruitt, 1971). That suggested that rather than leaders creating crowds, leadership is a two-way process in which crowds follow leaders who best express their predispositions.[5] More recently, the "risky shift" experiments were repeated with groups asked to select actions in connection with social conflicts over the Vietnam war and civil rights. Again "risky shifts" were observed (Johnson, Stemler, & Hunter, 1977). Myers and Lamm (1976) concluded that the best explanation for "group polarization" (actually convergence) was that of cognitive learning of persuasive new arguments together with verbal rehearsal and commitment in discussions. Feinberg and Johnson's (1990) computer simulations suggested that group processes can achieve consensus, and that "escalating" agitators can move a crowd to a *somewhat* more radical action choice if, but only if, they begin by advocating positions already held by the crowd. Such focusing may explain the "keynoting" of crowd grievances in the escalation process described by John P. Spiegel and Joseph M. Firestone (later). McPhail (1991) recently argued that leadership provides focus, an essential ingredient in sustained collective action by large gatherings.

## FRUSTRATION–AGGRESSION

Another early paradigm—the deprivation–frustration–aggression syndrome—has been rejected in repeated studies by historians and other social scientists. There seems to be no regular correlation between the incidence or intensity of hardship on the one hand and the incidence of severity of violence on the other (Rule, 1988; Snyder, 1978). If anything, the relationship is inverse—poverty may disable collective action, which may require resources like social ties and stamina. For instance, English food rioters were not the transient, isolated poorest of the poor but instead were members of established social networks crucial for collective action. Nor did food riots cluster in places or times with the highest prices. No doubt food rioters were hungry, but they consulted more than their bellies, as suggested by their typical slogan, "We would rather be hanged than starved" (Bohstedt, 1983). The enforcement of market justice was as important a motivation as hunger, judging from the way

---

[5]Students constantly refer to the famous films like *Triumph of the Will* about the Nuremberg rally to illustrate the charisma of leaders like Hitler, forgetting that (a) the film is a work of art by Leni Riefenstahl meant to convey the mystical power of the Führer; (b) Hitler could play upon ancient social strains and symbols not hypnotic processes; (c) the rally itself was a carefully orchestrated emotional pageant that excluded conflicting cues; (d) the crowds were self-selected sympathizers; (e) they were cheering, not taking risky or harmful violent action.

they sometimes scattered grain in the streets to punish dealers (Thompson, 1971). Elsewhere, rather than protesting deprivation, collective violence has often been used to perpetuate dominance, by such groups as the Klu Klux Klan and lynch mobs. More generally, evidence has shown that frustration might lead not to aggression but to acquiescence, flight, or problem solving, whereas aggression might take place without frustration (Bandura, 1983; Berkowitz, 1989). Finally, frustration is notoriously hard to measure directly for acting crowds. Objective economic indicators beg the questions of how poor people perceive their poverty. History is full of classes of impoverished people who did not rebel. Were they complacent? Demoralized? Cowed? Absorbed in individual sauve qui peut survival strategies? Edward N. Muller and associates' work replaces the frustration–aggression nexus with expectancy–value theory: The strength of motivation to act is a result of the value of the object *times* the probability (expectancy) that action will attain it. Their research shows that, far more than deprivation, beliefs in the utility and legitimacy of political aggression explain participation in it (Muller, 1979; Muller & Opp, 1986). It seems likely that in the course of escalation and diffusion, both expectancy and value might change in response to feedback from initial stages of interaction.

## RATIONALIST APPROACHES TO COLLECTIVE AGGRESSION

Social psychological theory about aggression that best fits historians' empirical findings about traditional riots is Albert Bandura's (1986) *social cognitive* theory; *social* emphasizes the decisive relevance of context and interaction, past, present, and future; *cognitive* emphasizes conscious processing and choice. Bandura (1983) began with the observation that "Most aggressive activities . . . entail intricate skills that require extensive learning" (p. 4). Those "skills" or patterns of behavior are (a) learned by both direct *and* vicarious experience, (b) instigated by immediate triggers, but also (c) regulated by anticipated consequences. People learn far more by observation than they can possibly experience directly, and "observed outcomes influence behavior. . . . People can profit from the successes and mistakes of others" (p. 27). Instigating triggers may include both incentives such as opportunities and provocations like assaults, threats, or material deterioration. People do not automatically reproduce learned behavior when instigated. Rather, they choose to act or not, depending on their anticipation of "external" outcomes (gains, loses, or punishments) and their self-evaluation vis-á-vis personal goals and social norms.

Bandura (1983) rejected the traditional distinction between expressive and instrumental motivations, because all behavior is intended to produce desired results, whether material or emotional or relational. For instance, insults may provoke aggression: Bandura explained that unanswered insults might lead to future abuse and loss of status and self-esteem. In parallel fashion, a recent study suggests that, rather than material gain, many crimes are stimulated by an emotional calculus aimed at preventing humiliation or disastrous changes in relationships ("If I let her get away with that, life won't be worth living!") or at gaining status or the instant gratification of gamesmanship (Katz, 1988; and Zillmann, this volume). This may be a relevant element in urban ghetto riots triggered by humiliating police "brutality," although cumulative experience and additional context surely enter in.

Finally, various factors may disrupt the ordinary balance of incentives and inhibitions that regulate aggression. Normal inhibitions may be "disconnected" when "higher principles" or authorities urge inhumane acts. According to Bandura (1983), blaming the victim also disinhibits aggression, for antagonistic interactions between groups usually involve "a series of reciprocally escalative actions in which the victims are rarely faultless" (p. 33). The aggressor can always select one instance of defensive behavior by the adversary and blame it for the original instigation. Disinhibition may also be a gradual process in which lower levels of aggression are tolerated (internally and externally) that reduces inhibitions against a higher level.

Bandura's (1983) research has been most concerned with placing individual behavior in a rich analytic context. His discussions of collective aggression are not so helpful because they fail to take account of the contextual influences on social modeling:

> Symbolic modeling plays an especially significant role in the shaping and rapid spread of collective aggression. Social diffusion of new styles and tactics of aggression conforms to the generalized pattern of most other contagious activities: New behavior is introduced by a salient example; it spreads rapidly in a contagious fashion; and it then either stabilizes or is discarded depending on its functional value. (p. 8)

Somewhat more helpful was Bandura's (1973) observation that "modeled solutions to problems that achieve some measure of success are not only widely adopted by people facing similar difficulties, but tend to spread as well to other troublesome areas" (p. 104). Thus the civil rights movement's successful tactics spread to other campaigns, although urban rioting rose and fell in an apparent example of contagion despite lack of immediate success. Campus disorders in the Vietnam era gradually escalated from peaceful protests to trashing.

Bandura (1973) also noted that the threat of punishment or retaliation might deter low aggressors, but not high aggressors, who had probably had success in gaining objectives by force. Indeed, such groups as early modern coal miners, renowned as formidable rioters, may fit that analysis. Punishment might even contribute to escalation of aggression among such groups. It might also do so when initial conflicts or interactions raise questions about the legitimacy of norms or authorities. Bandura discussed the escalation of campus protest from initial demands to stalemate to moralistic rhetoric and sit-ins to the use of police to the discrediting of university administrations and/or the cessation of "normal" university life. Disciplinary punishments and police force both helped escalate conflicts from "external issues" to the legitimacy of university governance (Bandura, 1973). Contexts differed in regard to norms of conflict: In contrast to the riotous ghettoes, universities depicted themselves as special communities and encouraged conflict and debate "within reason," but administrative decisions were reached in undemocratic fashion. At Harvard in 1969, for instance, a minority of the Students for a Democratic Society occupied University Hall; their physical force escalated beyond accepted norms and so initially isolated them. The Harvard administration's use of suburban police to manhandle the occupiers revealed the hollowness of their rhetoric about community and debate, and so the conflict escalated to an emergent stage in which a majority of students and faculty sought a new equilibrium.

The leading student of frustration–aggression in violent political conflict has constructed a very valuable matrix that corrects the shortcomings of Bandura's discussion of collective action. Treating relative deprivation as the key motivation, Gurr (1970) found that whether and how much political violence occurs depends first on how far political violence is regarded as legitimate and useful, and second on the balance of physical and ideological resources between protestors and the regime. Using Gurr's model, if one replaces relative deprivation with motivations interpreted according to Bandura's social cognitive theory, one begins to have a concept of a social matrix in which learning, norms, and political probabilities affect collective violence. That is the direction taken by Muller's expectancy–value theory.

That matrix is placed in historical context by the *resource mobilization* approach to social movements and collective violence, most fully developed by Tilly. Psychological motivations including interests are only the beginning of the story. Many an impoverished peasant cannot act on his grievances, except perhaps suicidally. Rather, actors need *resources* to permit collective action. Such resources include organization (which Tilly defined as *common identity and unifying structure*), supporters, money, influence, and allies—assets that increase a group's leverage upon other holders of power, especially the state. The moment of collective action is shaped by *opportunity* that includes the balance of power, repression, which may be rising or falling, and new possibilities of either gains or losses. Tilly saw these factors at work within a polity or field of power, normally including a government and other power holders and challengers. Over the long run, that polity is reshaped by large processes like state centralization, industrialization, and urbanization that affect interests, opportunities, and capacities to mobilize. Finally, collective action generally follows inherited repertoires. Tilly's robust historical framework for Western society has informed studies of two centuries of riots in which purposeful collective actors have pursued their goals by conventional patterns of action in relation to changing norms, opportunities, restraints, and polities (Tilly, 1978, 1986).

These analytical approaches obviously shape our expectations about escalation and diffusion of riots. It is clear that collective violence does not necessarily imply that society has broken down or that social identities, resources, values, and relationships have been thrown overboard. Does diffusion take place when an example of "successful" violence (or a costly counterexample) persuades neighbors to recalculate their schedule of costs and benefits? As for escalation, if an initial outbreak of violence is unchallenged, does that suggest "the system" is now vulnerable to assault on other grounds? Or alternatively, if the police overreact harshly, does it create or increase grievances to the point where they overwhelm the ordinarily inhibiting costs of protest? At a national level, why does a wave of protest like the turbulent 1960s in the United States occur?

## DIFFUSION OF RIOTS IN HISTORICAL SETTINGS

If differences in community politics help to explain escalation, they may also explain diffusion. Studying the spread of rioting in Devonshire in 1766, 1975, and 1801, Bohstedt and Williams (1988) found that the "contagion" of food riot did not simply radiate out uniformly (i.e., by simple imitation) from a starting point. Given the widespread hardship of high prices, why did some towns riot and others not? The agencies of diffusion were, first, *example*: A neighboring community's success might enable townspeople to recalculate their own schedule of costs and benefits and thus decide on action. In a few cases there is direct evidence of news or rumor. One crowd even visited farmers in their neighborhood carrying a list of prices borrowed from their counterparts in another town. Second, *communication*: Riots clustered in districts that had denser population, but especially more roads and market towns. It was there that friction over food transactions and shipments occurred, and they also served as the "receivers" and "transmitters" of the riot model. They were also the bases of local militia units called Volunteers, who led food riots and seemed to have communicated with their comrades in the home defense network. Third, *facilitating social structures*: Some communities had horizontal networks among rioters and vertical networks between them and magistrates that facilitated successful, though coercive, "bargaining by riot" within mutually accepted limits. Other towns lacked these networks. Some hierarchical demonstration effect may also explain why the riots radiated out from the county's two main towns, Plymouth and Exeter. That was different from the diffusion of innovations, for riots had traditional precedents: Previous food crises had witnessed similar "epidemics" of rioting that left legacies of experience as valuable guides to tactics, costs, and benefits. Finally, the regional (county) authorities were also capable of escalating repression to bring the waves of rioting to an end in both 1795 and 1801 by unusual, "exemplary" hangings of rioters, whereas the local gentry "escalated" their efforts at raising subscriptions for emergency food relief. Clearly, the magistrates had a very practical understanding of the uses of both escalation and the force of example (Bohstedt, 1983)!

Bohstedt and Williams' contention that dense social networks enabled some communities to take up their neighbors' example of riot finds warrant in diffusion theory: Pinard (1971) summed up the key principle: "the higher the degree of social integration of potential adopters, the more likely and the sooner they will become actual adopters . . . on the other hand, near isolates tend to be the last to adopt an innovation" (p. 187). Oberschall (1973) reinforced the point: "Rapid mobilization does not occur through recruitment of large numbers of isolated and solitary individuals. It occurs as a result of recruiting blocs of people who are already highly organized and participants" (p. 125). McAdam (1982) argued that such networks of organizations within and between communities spread not only a model of action but also the "cognitive liberation" that underlies militant action, that is, both a sense of injustice directed at social conditions, and a confidence that action can bring change.

Two other careful studies of the diffusion of riots by the historical geographer Andrew Charlesworth (1979) also revealed the complexity of such diffusion and the inadequacy of simple mechanical or "false biological analogies" (p. ii). Comparing several series of riots by agricultural workers in early 19th-century England, Charlesworth (1983) found that their patterns of spread were significantly different, depending on the interaction of national political crises and local intervillage political networks. An initial set of agitations by the farmworkers in 1816 were weak, sporadic, and easily contained by the magistrates. That of 1822 was stronger but no axis of diffusion appeared. But the Swing riots of 1830 to 1831 by farm workers and allied villagers spread over much of southern England in strong waves of hundreds of episodes (Hobsbawm & Rudé, 1968). At first, as in 1822, protests spread slowly along local lines dictated by men's work schedules and geographical contacts. But once the national Reform crisis peaked in November, the protests accelerated, especially along the main London postal roads. Charlesworth believed that by 1830 those roads had become arteries for the spread of radical political ideas and agitators. The Revolutions of 1830 in France and Belgium also inspired hopes for change. Charlesworth believed the November crisis enabled village radicals to arouse protests in waves, and the Reform crisis also undermined the government's capacity to deploy troops.

Two other series of protests show different patterns. In 1839 to 1843 substantial farmers and/or their sons led the Rebecca Riots against turnpike toll gates, which spread slowly across parts of Wales, tied to the group cooperation and seasonal rhythms of farming and road use. The rough terrain and the intimacy of the rural communities prevented easy suppression. Initial successes led to protests over further grievances, but also rougher, more violent riots that turned the original leaders toward peaceful tactics (Jones, 1983). By contrast, in reaction to Louis Napoleon's coup against the Second French Republic in 1851, peasant uprisings spread almost instantaneously across the south of France. This was not spontaneous at all but resulted from the effective covert preparation by the underground network of radical Republican societies, ready to mobilize the villagers at a moment's notice (Charlesworth, 1983; Margadant, 1979). Likewise, some of the larger waves of labor protest in this period, by the West Country shearmen of 1802, the Lancashire handloom weavers of 1808, the Nottinghamshire Luddites of 1811–1812, and the Plug-Plot rioters of 1842, spread across districts by a combination of example and organized leadership, generally clandestine (Bohstedt, 1983; Mather, 1974; Randall, 1991; Thompson, 1968).

These waves of riots seem to correspond to Oberschall's (1980) theory that groups can reassess their positions and that this helps to account for the clustering of events in space and time. "A useful hypothesis is that diffusion occurs partly as a result of a reassessment by potential activists and participants and by authorities of the chances of success (P) and the costs of collective action(C), after the outcomes of similar collective action becomes [sic] known to them" (p. 52). And that will be especially true if the initial event takes place in a "pace-setter" place, like Paris for the continental revolutions of 1848, or Poland for 1989. Activists quickly seize the opportunity, knowing of their likely similarity to the proximate model, before authorities almost as quickly take action to strengthen their defenses.

## REDUCTION OF INHIBITIONS AND DEINDIVIDUATION

The conception of riots as episodes of rational political bargaining, and the corresponding social cognitive theory of aggression might be criticized on two grounds. First, riots are not occasions of "cool" learning like classrooms. Rather, they involve deeply felt emotional grievances and confrontations with powerful authorities that carry risk and danger. Indeed, acting in ambiguous situations beyond the guidance of routine is itself arousing (Lofland, 1985). Before inhibitions are overcome perhaps a threshold of anger must be reached. Zillmann suggested that cognitive control has a curvilinear relationship to arousal: At moderate levels of arousal, cognitive processing—interpretation of the situation— might still inhibit or control aggressive action, but at higher levels such control might be lost (Zillmann, 1983, this volume). It may be that conflicts such as food riots over divisible material goods are at the lower end of the curve of arousal, whereas pogrom-type riots involving group identity threats and clashes promote more visceral arousal and less cognitive control (cf. Oberschall, 1973). In any case, to emphasize the "rational" components of riots one need not exclude the emotional; other kinds of political behavior such as negotiations, legislatures' actions, and elections also may involve anger.

Second, other factors besides anger might tip the balance in which inhibitions normally restrain motivations. Modeling might lower avoidance (Wheeler, 1966; Wheeler & Caggiula, 1966). Or other contextual conditions or interactive feedback might disinhibit the norms that ordinarily and rationally restrain action. That could be a clue to escalation (Goldstein, Davis, & Herman, 1975). The erosion of cognitive control leading to escalation has been conceptualized best in the theory of *deindividuation* (Goldstein, Davis, Kernis, & Cohn, 1981). According to Zimbardo's formulation (1970), acting as a responsibly committed person is "individuated," whereas acting without responsibility implies deindividuation. *Conditions* such as anonymity, diffused responsibility in a group, arousal, novel situation, or altered consciousness change one's perceptions of self and others and release antisocial behavior that is intense, irrational, and not responsive to external feedback. *Escalation* might take place when the actor gets *absorbed in the action itself,* together with confederates, and ignores consequences so that the behavior enters a self-reinforcing spiral of unpredictable intensity. Such deindividuation of the subject is different from the *dehumanization* of victims that has facilitated lynching or genocide. Zimbardo's deindividuation is a restatement in scientifically testable terms of Le Bon's crowd theory (Diener, 1980).

Although intuitively attractive, deindividuation seemed at first to be an unprovable hypothesis. Bandura and his associates (1975) tested *internal* self-restraints on group aggression. They manipulated responsibility (diffused vs. individual) and dehumanization of victims. They found (a) dehumanization of the victim promoted the disinhibition and escalation of aggression more strongly than the diffusion of responsibility, for anonymity disinhibited mainly external restraints, whereas internal ones remained because individuals would know whether they had aggressed; (b) disinhibition did seem to lead to escalation, for it released mildly aggressive behavior, which then led to self-absolution that further reduced restraints and led to greater aggression. Diener insisted in a series of studies that the distinctive ingredient of deindividuation was the internal state of diminished self-evaluation, not the causal conditions nor the aggressive behavior. He found that, whereas diffused responsibility, cognitive justifications, and aggressive modeling disinhibited aggression, years of research had failed to link aggression to an internal state of deindividuation (Diener, 1977; Diener, Dineen, & Endresen, 1975). Anonymity might increase or decrease aggression, according to whom the actor was unknown—co-actors, victims, authorities, and so on (Diener, 1980). Physical arousal did seem to reduce self-consciousness and activate behavior but for individuals not groups, and the nature of that behavior would be shaped by situational cues (Diener, 1976).

Several years later Diener conceptualized a milder state of deindividuation consisting of a decrease in self-awareness brought about by arousal, absorption in intense group activity, and group cohesiveness that helped to block self-regulation according to long-term norms and consequences and to make individuals more receptive to situational stimuli. Such decreases could lead to antinormative behavior, such as eating mud or using silly language. Finally, escalation might occur slowly, as initial transgressions increased a person's toleration for greater transgressions (Diener, 1980). Although the behavior in these studies was individual and "foolish" rather than collective and aggressive, it suggested mechanisms of escalation in riots.

So far deindividuation, decreases in self-awareness and self-regulation, had been linked to antinormative but not aggressive behavior. Prentice-Dunn and Rogers (1980) provided that link. They found that anonymity, altered responsibility, and mild physical arousal produced deindividuation that (a) reduced self-awareness, (b) altered consciousness, and (c) permitted greater aggression, especially (d) in the presence of a high-aggressive model. Rogers and Prentice-Dunn (1981) found that decreased self-awareness lowered concern about others' disapproval, whereas group cohesiveness also increased aggression. They also found that when insulted aggressors reverted to older patterns of hostility toward Blacks, which they labeled regressive racism.

Finally, they (Prentice-Dunn & Rogers, 1982) distinguished between two different kinds of self-awareness. Accountability cues related to awareness of one's external reputation and liability to punishment, so that their reduction might lead to increased aggression, not through deindividuation but through recalculation of external costs and benefits. This might help to explain the spectrum of lesser-to-greater violence found in my studies of riots and community politics, for in the larger cities, despite the disorder, the rioters did not seem disoriented or unselective. Another set of cues, attentional cues, related to one's internal awareness of standards, and that might be reduced by outward redirection of attention, group cohesion, and physical arousal. The reduced cognitive mediation and increased reliance on environmental cues led to deindividuated behavior and enhanced aggression.

This model might help to explain the handful of the largest, exceptional, riots in industrializing England, in which both rioters' and peace-keepers' violence far exceeded the conventional limits observed in hundreds of ordinary food riots. For instance, the Gordon Riots of 1780 were the most destructive riots in English history. They were occasioned by a campaign led by the Protestant Association against the Catholic Relief Act of 1778, encouraged by successful riotous resistance to the measure in Scotland. After months of public mobilization, the Protestant Association led a demonstration of 60, 000 people to the doors of Parliament to present their petition for repeal of the Act. They jostled members of Parliament believed to be sympathetic to Catholics. Some then moved off to attack Catholic embassies and chapels, and then residential districts. For a week, London mobs attacked such Catholic targets, plus suspected sympathizers among the government or officials who tried to suppress the rioting. The climax was an attack on a huge Catholic-owned distillery and on the Bank of England. In all, 285 rioters were killed and 25 hanged, and damages ran into the tens of thousands of pounds (equivalent to millions of today's dollars) (Stevenson, 1979). Contemporaries reported that the skyline of the capital was in flames.

Why did this riot escalate to such violence? For two centuries, anti-Catholicism had nurtured visceral popular suspicions of Catholic conspiracies to subvert British liberties. More "rational" ingredients included the mobilization of the Protestant Association, the models of successful Scottish resistance, the eccentric but effective leadership of Lord George Gordon, and the expressed support of the London city government. In the initial rioting the targets and repertoires of action were selected, but the lack of forceful opposition, combined with the nearly unlimited objectives of ethnic abuse,[6] may have permitted a self-reinforcing escalation from the arousal and self-absorption of a week's action. Or so it appeared in the nightmarish peak of the violence, in the wild attack on Langdale's distillery, when the large establishment was in flames and rioters died trying to loot the building or to drink the flaming gin in the gutters. If evidence permitted, more analysis of the rioters' mentalities would be required to demonstrate that they were deindividuated. But also, from the fifth day of rioting, the military forces killed scores of rioters, and it seems worth asking whether that reflected a corresponding loss of cognitive control by the "forces of order" (cf. Bergesen, 1980).

## AMERICAN RIOTS OF THE 1960S

Riots' severity (and presumably their escalation) may require different explanations from their initial outbreak. That was the implication of the flood of research on the urban ghetto riots of the 1960s. These riots are a useful contrast to traditional food riots not only because the rules of riot changed but also because the data was better, or at least thicker. First I review studies of individual characteristics of rioters, and then studies of riot communities.

The paradigm tested most commonly in the research of the early 1970s was the deprivation–frustration–aggression explanation of riots that was also in harmony with the prevailing liberal "common sense." First, systematic studies showed that as individuals rioters were neither socially deviant nor unusually deprived, *compared to other ghetto residents.* Indeed, the predictions (really postdictions) of riot participation by postriot questionnaires in Watts could not strongly distinguish riot

---

[6]But the rioters did not kill any Catholics.

participants from nonparticipants (Moinat, Raine, Burbeck, & Davison, 1972). Because half the residents either participated or supported the riots, rioters could not be considered deviant or even distinctive personalities. (Apparently no studies have found systematic psychological differences between rioters and nonrioters.) They concluded that ghetto conditions, not individual characteristics, accounted for riots. However, myth and interpretation begin to form at street level from the moment of a riot, so that postriot questionnaires on participation and attitudes might reflect positive identifications with a riot by nonrioters and so obscure real behavioral differences. The Kerner Commission did find that, rather than the poorest of the poor, rioters tended more than nonrioters to be permanent residents of the riot cities, to have higher levels of education, and higher levels of social integration and political knowledge. In fact, postriot questionnaires found considerable militancy among Black residents in favor of aggressive action to secure civil and economic rights, and riots were not condemned as a means in that struggle. The wide support for that militant ideology in Black ghettoes "approaches normative proportions" (Caplan, 1970, p. 60; Tomlinson, 1970). Finally, McPhail (1971) analyzed dozens of studies that had assessed the relationships of individual deprivation to riot participation. He concluded that such relationships, whereas occasionally statistically significant, were never strong, and that therefore "there is considerable reason for rejecting the sociological and popular cliché that absolute or relative deprivation and the ensuing frustration or discontent is the root cause of rebellion" (p. 1064). However, to seek "*the* root cause" may be to pose the wrong question. The comparison of rioters with other ghetto residents may misspecify the problem: Because bosses, bankers, Brahmins, and baseball players were conspicuously absent from the crowds burning department stores, one can hardly avoid the inference that economic and political deprivation *contributed* to ghetto riots, probably as a necessary though not sufficient ingredient. It might be better to use a dichotomous variable for some threshold level of deprivation rather than expecting linear correlations between violence and incremental levels of deprivation, which are often measured indirectly or by aggregation, anyway. Above that threshold level of deprivation, a variety of behavioral outcomes might be possible, with the violent alternative resulting from interaction (Carter, 1990).

Parallel analyses of communities also failed to find *linear* correlations between deprivation and violence, either as to the outbreak or severity of riots. Spilerman (1970) found that riots' *locations* could not be statistically correlated with communities' structural attributes, including social disorganization, political alienation, or economic deprivation, but only with the size of their Black population, together with a location outside the South, where rioting seemed inhibited by low expectations of reform and harsh repression. He argued that riot readiness was grounded in an alienated mentality shared by Blacks across the country and created not by local factors but by television and the federal government's unfulfilled promises. According to Spilerman (1971), these factors led to "geographic" uniformity in the impact of frustrating stimuli" (p. 440). Spilerman (1970) rejected the Kerner Commission's (1968) suggestion that geographic contagion could account for clusters of riots touched off by the Newark and Detroit riots of 1967 (presumably via telephone contacts among acquaintances), and reiterated that the majority of riots in those states could be accounted for by the size of Black population in riot cities.

Morgan and Clark (1973) responded that the escalation and severity of riots, if not their initial outbreak, might be explained by the combination of large numbers of Blacks and the intensity of their grievances. Once a riot had broken out (for other reasons), deprivation of such things as jobs and housing would make more people more likely to participate and presumably contribute to escalation. (That connects with the mathematical contagion theory of Burbeck et al.; see later). But Spilerman (1976) criticized their methods and assembled statistics for 322 riots in 1967 and 1968, showing that measures of "deprivation" such as demographic change, poor plumbing, unresponsive local government, and poverty and inequality did not correlate with the degree of severity of the riots. Only the size of Black population and location outside the South did. Carter's (1990) recent reanalysis of the data found only weak and anomalous connections between Black grievances and intercity differences in riot severity.

Whereas any simple linear correlation between deprivation and violent propensities seemed discredited by Spilerman, other studies suggested more complex relationships between community attributes and collective action. Warren (1969) pointed out that neighborhoods were an important neglected middle level of social action between individual and community. His data indicated that, whereas alienated and isolated Detroit neighborhoods such as housing projects tended to recoil into withdrawal from riot activity, other neighborhoods with significant levels of informal social organization and ties to the larger community spawned both riotous and counter-riot *activism*. Carter (1986a) reanalyzed the riot–city argument and found that the severity of riots was best explained by a *curvilinear* relationship with economic and political deprivation. Riots were severest, not where Blacks were either very poor and repressed or very well-off but rather under intermediate conditions where moderate inequality and mixed political signals raised expectations and fostered mobilizations without satisfying them. These findings are consistent with historians' findings that protest is stronger from people with the right combination of relatively acute grievances and the resources to make them heard. In this case the size of Black population would be a critical resource. Carter also located significantly less propensity to riot in five more repressive Deep South states than in the arc of "Peripheral" South states from Arkansas and Texas to the District of Columbia. Even more interestingly, Carter (1986b) showed that the relationship between city factors and riots was not constant throughout the period 1964 to 1971. Rather the riots of April 1968 stood out as distinctly different from the periods of increasing and decreasing rioting before and after that "rupture." The earlier and later periods had curvilinear relationships to the community variables described earlier, whereas the rioting of April 1968 was related to a national expression of Blacks' outrage over the King assassination. That suggested not only different kinds of mechanisms for different kinds of escalation but also the value of analyzing the nation as a whole societal unit experiencing ebbs and peaks, including a "crescendo" phase sensitive to local factors, an "explosion" phase of national resonance, and a "decrescendo" phase once again localized. That concept of national escalation and deescalation has been developed more systematically in recent studies of "cycles of protest" (see following).

Lieske's *political development* hypothesis (1978) set the curvilinear relationship between "riot propensity" and community attributes in a longer trajectory. He argued that communities at different stages of sociopolitical development would have corresponding types of collective response to deprivations. In the poorest communities, Blacks would tend to be apathetic and socially quiescent. In communities with greater economic well-being but persistent social discrimination, Blacks might mobilize for social protest violence. At a higher level of economic prosperity and social organization, their demands might take shape in more specifically political violence. Finally, as economic and political participation increased in more responsive communities, violence would give way to organized nonviolent political activity. While his categories sorted out 119 communities into four types for cross-sectional (rather than dynamic) analysis, his argument suggests why the national level of violence rose and fell over time, and it also suggests parallels with Tilly's long-term framework for political development, and Bohstedt's more restricted spectrum of community politics.

## MEDIA AND CONTAGION

Ultimately, community attributes, whether optimum combinations of deprivation and political maturity or simply size of Black population and non-South location, can be only partial and not sufficient explanations of riots, for such factors did not change fast enough to explain why the riots took place in 1965 to 1968 and not, say, in 1960 to 1964. What might have triggered the riots? One popular explanation was televised models. But American social scientists tested the question of riot contagion via the media in the most puzzling fashion. Although two respected authorities made sweeping but unsupported claims of media contagion effects, the Kerner Commission cautiously downplayed inflammation by the media. Almost no social scientists took up the challenge of testing the claims that had been made; the opportunity for postriot surveys was missed. "Copycat riots" occasioned much more debate in Britain in the 1980s.

The Kerner Commission reported in 1968 chiefly on the riots of 1967. Charged by President Johnson to investigate media impact, their chief criticism was that the media had ignored the riots' underlying causes. Whereas the media had tried to balance their accounts of the disturbances, they had left an exaggerated impression of the scale and intensity of the disorders by using harried local officials' exaggerated estimates of damage and unsubstantiated headlines about sniping or carnage. Kerner concluded that if the media had reached some people who went out and rioted, they reached many more who did not. However, the Commission's local surveys found that reports of the Newark and Detroit riots were "prior incidents" contributing to two New Jersey and two Michigan riots, whereas reports and rumors about the Newark and Plainfield riots were *the* precipitating incidents in five New Jersey riots (Kerner, 1968). That was the evidence of contact disputed by Spilerman (see earlier).

Certainly, many police officers believed media coverage contributed to both the diffusion and escalation of riots (Lange, Baker, & Ball, 1969). But the most sophisticated claim about media contagion effects came from Morris Janowitz (1969) of the University of Chicago in his widely quoted history of Black rioting presented in the Kerner Commission staff study, *The History of Violence in America*. Janowitz argued that a combination of factors had contributed to the Black riots of the 1960s: the history of Black deprivation; migration to the north; changing policies and tactics of the police; political weakness in city governments; and the political climate of publicity and sympathy for Black claims, together with Blacks' growing sense of political efficacy due to the civil rights movement. He concluded that the riots were a largely unorganized parapolitical movement based on a shared consciousness of injustice.

Janowitz (1969) set contagion in the context of that synthesis. He concluded that "the impact of the mass media . . . has made a positive contribution to violence," through a "discernible but limited" effect on social values and the lowering of inhibitions (pp. 415, 437). The negative quantitative findings of the Kerner Commission had neglected the great impact of a relatively few telecasts of violence. Janowitz (1969) stated:

> detailed coverage of riots has had an effect on potential rioters . . . [through] a process of social learning. . . . Rioting is based on contagion, the process by which the mood and attitudes of those who are actually caught up in the riot are disseminated to a larger audience. . . . Television images serve to spread the contagion pattern throughout urban areas and the nation. Large audiences see the details of riots, the manner in which people participate in them, and especially the ferment associated with looting and obtaining commodities which was so much at the heart of riot behavior. . . . The media disseminate the rationalizations and symbols of identification used by the rioters. The mass media serve to reinforce and spread the feeling of consciousness among those who participate or sympathize with extremist actions, regardless of the actions' origins. . . . Knowledge of the riot would spread in any case, but immediate extensive and detailed coverage both speeds up the process and gives it a special reality. On balance, I would argue that these images serve to reinforce predispositions to participate and even to legitimate participation. To be able to generate mass media coverage, especially television coverage, becomes an element in the motivation of rioters. . . . In selected highbrow intellectual circles in the United States, a language of rationalization of violence has developed. The mass media serve to disseminate a popular version of such justification. The commentaries on television were filled with pseudosociological interpretations and the rioters themselves given ample opportunity to offer a set of suitable rationalizations. (pp. 440–441)

Singer's interviews with arrested Detroit rioters supported Janowitz's point that material highest in affective content was what people retained from television coverage: Those who recalled violent assaults on persons were more than twice the number who referred to materialistic looting (Singer, 1970).

In 1970, Spilerman suggested that television had contributed to a national mood of African–American alienation (aforementioned). In 1975, again without supporting evidence, Spilerman contended that disorders in ghettoes, campuses, and prisons were contagious when they provided behavioral models for persons with similar problems (Spilerman, 1975). In 1976, Spilerman echoed Janowitz's argument that television had created the national consciousness of Blacks—in the long run by publicizing the civil rights campaigns; in the short run by broadcasting vivid models of protest by riot against shared hardships. Spilerman (1976) asserted: "By conveying the intensity and emotion of a confrontation, television provided an essential mechanism for riot contagion. . . ." (p. 790). Spilerman concluded that such electronic, not geographic, contagion accounted for more than half the riots in 1967 and 1968, once normal inhibitions were broken down by the massively reported Newark riot of July 1967 and the King assassination of April 1968. But he presented no direct evidence that riots were spread by televised modeling.

Given such cogent and relevant hypotheses, it is astonishing that American social scientists did not test them. It is especially surprising given thousands of studies debating whether television models infected children with aggressive propensities (Geen, 1983; Signorielli & Gerbner, 1988). There are only a few other fragments of evidence on the relationship of communication processes to the American riots. A Detroit newspaper's survey of 360 Black residents found that 50% had learned of the riot from friends, another 30% from TV, another 19% from personal observation. Age, rather than the mode of communication, was more strongly associated with their participation in the riot (Slater & McCombs, 1969). However, Singer's (1970) study of Detroit suggested that many of those who passed on information about the Detroit riot of 1967 had originally gotten their information from television. In Miami a Black radio station's live broadcasts in the middle of a rock and roll program pinpointed the exact location of the origin of a riot and helped attract more people to the scene (Lange, et al., 1969). In 1967 Detroit television stations at first kept their crews away from rioting, honoring the concern of the state's Civil Rights Commission that coverage would only draw potential rioters to the scene (Riot beat, 1967). Martin Hayden (1968), editor of the *Detroit News*, wrote that the wire services exaggerated violence and conflict much more than local press; he concluded that the farther the observer was from the scene, the more his or her report exaggerated the violence. That relationship also held true for the English food riots of the 1790s. Likewise in contemporary England, a reporter (Clare, 1984), contrasted his soberer eyewitness account of the Brixton riot of 1981 with Scarman's (1981) exaggerated claim that only a "thin blue line" of police had defended society and the City against "the total collapse of law and order in the streets of an important part of the capital" (p. 74). Perhaps whereas, as argued earlier, the local matrix of sociopolitical relationships shapes the immediate incidence, form, and significance of riots, so also contagion, and perhaps escalation, operate at several levels of power and communication—affecting reactions not only among rioters but also by police and alarmed politicians and publics (for "crime wave" parallels, see Lofland, 1985).

Indeed, in England the claim that media coverage had contributed to "copycat" rioting aroused much more controversy, from the lurid headlines of the fiercely competitive London tabloids to Scarman's comments on the Brixton Riots of 1981. Scarman (1981), the Chairman of the Royal Commission investigating the riots of 1981, suggested that during the looting phase of the Brixton rioting, outsiders had been attracted by the publicity given the initial stages, and more generally that "it seems likely that there was a substantial 'copycat' element in many of the disorders that occurred during the summer, and that Brixton may have served in this respect as a model for others to follow" (p. 14). Scarman did not explain how the April riots in Brixton (South London) might have served as a model for July disturbances in Liverpool, Manchester, and Birmingham. It was only after the formidable and feared media critic, Mary Whitehouse, suggested on July 11 that television coverage helped to spread rioting that representatives of ITN-TV and BBC-TV conceded the possibility, whereas *The Times* of July 13 repeated the suggestion in its headline, "Copycat mobs in petrol bomb attacks on police," but none provided any evidence of imitation (Tumber, 1982). So seriously did some of the media take Scarman's calls for restraint that they did not report a number of urban disorders in 1982 (Benyon, 1984).[7] Commissioned by the British Film Institute, Tumber explicitly set out to assess the copycat effect by talking to media personnel, police and rioters. None felt that television had created such an effect. Rather, they agreed (Tumber, 1982), "wherever the rioters got their information it was not from television" (p. 46). Tumbler argued that television was much less important as a source of riot news for young people than the grapevine. The young "participants" on the streets of Brixton and Liverpool stoutly denied that imitation had contributed to the riots. But the most sophisticated critique of media contagion, by Graham Murdock of the University of Leicester, was equally skeptical of Scarman's simple assertions and Tumber's complete dismissal of television's impact on riots. Stronger evidence from a survey of local young men in the Birmingham riot district found they believed "copying of other areas" was second only to unemployment as a cause of the riot there in 1981. Fifty percent of them had first heard of the disturbances through the media, 31% through television (Murdock, 1984). According to Tumber (1982), one police official argued a more complex view, that a series of confrontations had shown Black people that they could take on the police, although another pointed out that "there was not a widespread breakout of looting and rioting across Britain as was reported" (p. 20). Both police and broadcasters said television reports were preferable to the rumors that might replace them. On balance,

---

[7]In 1985, serious riots in Birmingham were reported on television in very restrained terms with a voice over a still photograph (author's observation).

Murdock seemed right to insist that the *interaction* of riots and reporting must be recognized rather than evaluating media impact in simplistic either/or fashion (Murdock, 1984).

One analyst added a further suggestion: that social movements, operating outside "normal" political channels, partly depended on the media for their impact and recruitment (Molotch, 1979), and probably a parallel argument applies to the diffusion of riots. More generally, if social scientists would consider the *interaction* of context and dynamics, instead of the obsolete input–output approach, we might find that "electronic contagion" operates in *combination* with "receptive communities," along the lines of the Bohstedt–Williams study of food riots' diffusion. Initial modeling of riots in important communities like Watts or Detroit would create a "new ball game," a new schedule of instigations and inhibitions for potential rioters elsewhere.

Indeed, a new study (Waddington, Jones, & Critcher, 1989) suggests that interaction and context are connected by meanings. It analyzes the *flashpoint* of public violence, "a dramatic break in a pattern of interaction which might . . . explain why and where disorder broke out." In such episodes, "a pre-existent situation of tension or conflict [was] 'sparked off', to use a common metaphor, by an ostensibly trivial incident which became the catalyst for wide-spread disorder" (pp. 21, 1). Violence grew out of *interaction* when one adversary crossed the limits of what their adversaries would tolerate. But the limits of toleration, and the *meanings* ascribed to the adversaries' behavior *as signs* of intolerable insult or injury (the brick-bats thrown at the police, the beating of women protesters, the desecration of the flag), were created within a particular physical and tactical *situation* that defined possibilities of action, within a *pre-history* of similar incidents and relationships, within a *culture* of normative definitions which gave rise to expectations about rights, within a *political context* of previous conflict, and within *structural* distributions of economic and political power. Each set of factors from interaction to structure might increase the probability of violence without determining it. This complex but compact model of the connections via meanings between immediate interactions and background factors overcomes the defects of previous theories directed only at psychological or structural explanations.

## FROM INDIVIDUALS TO INTERACTIONS

Having discounted traditional emphases on the static characteristics of riot participants, McPhail (1971) argued that one must analyze riot dynamics. For how, he asked, could prior attributes account for the shifting strategies of rioters who switched behaviors on and off? McPhail built upon Turner and Killian's insight that the unanimity of collective action was illusory, and that such action actually comprised a variety of individual and collective actions (Turner & Killian, 1987). In this and subsequent studies, McPhail and associates suggested that *tactical* characteristics of rioters and communities would be more important that "structural" in explaining riots: rioters' availability in time and space, depending on their daily routines; the availability of gathering points; their participation in mobilization processes; and their interactions with other rioters, counter-rioters, and police (cf. Harrison, 1988). For instance, critical ingredients in the formation of a crowd of sports fans were "assembling instructions," which might be provided by precipitating incidents. Receiving and following such instructions partly depended on recipients' membership of the target group, their spatial availability, and transportation. Many studies of collective action showed that most people assembled and acted with small groups of family and friends, not as individuals; that because people in larger crowds would follow concerted cues, organizations would have significant effects; that for sports crowds the observation of violence neither served as a catharsis that drained the impulse to violence nor as a simple instigation to violence; and that police routinely controlled most gatherings by nonviolent instructions. Criticisms of overreaction and police riots in the 1960s had led to modifications of training and tactics that might well have reduced the number of precipitating incidents after 1970 (McPhail & Miller, 1973; McPhail & Wohlstein, 1983). McPhail is currently developing a "sociocybernetic theory of collective action" that sees people in gatherings continuously adjusting their behavior in response to feedback, so as to bring perceptual signals (of external reality) into line with reference signals (symbolizing their goals). Such reference signals must be shared by members of a gathering if they are to act in concert (McPhail, 1991). If one could capture the signals, this approach could depict the complex interactions of escalation and diffusion, but it seems likely that not only the behavior but also the reference signals are adjusted during a riot.

In pointing out the methodological flaws (overaggregation and cross-level inference) in a decade of inconclusive static input–output correlations, Snyder (1979) supported McPhail's emphasis on process rather than preconditions. He analyzed interactions between Black residents and police that served as signals to assemble, spatial and temporal conditions that facilitated assembly, and communication densities, and found that they markedly improved the prediction of riotous communities beyond Spilerman's measure of Black population size. Johnson and Feinberg's computer simulations demonstrated how crowd consensus could be achieved through milling and sorting processes that included interactions within and between the small groups of two or three in which people arrived at crowd scenes. They thus added the notion of a temporary emergent structure to Turner and Killian's concept of an emergent norm (Johnson & Feinberg, 1989). Obviously, consensus is not the same thing as action, but it seems that their work with heterogeneous distributions of predispositions to choose different actions might be fruitfully combined with Oliver and Marwell's demonstration of how early contributions of action affect later contributors (following).

Psychiatrist John P. Spiegel (1971), director of the Lemberg Center for the Study of Violence at Brandeis University, created a model of *transactions* leading to the escalation of violence. His model, or rather descriptive stages, implied that therapy that dispelled misunderstandings rather than politics was the antidote to violence. Preconditions included beliefs and value conflicts (without much specification of community conditions), poor communication, and the practice of undercontrol or overcontrol by police. A precipitating incident might bring crowds into the streets to begin milling. Police use of under or overcontrol might be decisive. If the crowd found leadership and "keynoting" (crystallization of their grievances by emergent leaders; [Turner & Killian, 1987]), it might "flip over" into a "Roman Holiday phase" of unrestrained violence, anarchic celebration, and expression of grievances. A fourth phase then might be siege or all-out "war" with little communication until authorities exerted their greater force. Spiegel's approach seemed to assume that collective violence was primarily expressive rather than goal directed. Firestone (1972), added mathematical formulae to Spiegel's model without conclusive results.

The emphasis on interaction, especially with police, was tested by Kritzer's study of data from 126 demonstrations to ascertain why some became violent. He (Kritzer, 1977) concluded that "exogenous variables [were] found to have little predictive power" and that "the outbreak of violence [at] protest demonstrations [was] the result of a dynamic process resulting from the interaction of police and protestors" (p. 630). Hence one could not explain that development without analyzing the behavior of both. But far more analysis has been devoted to rioters and communities than to police. To put it mildly, police forces have not generally operated as field-research stations for self-examination and publication of data. Partly for lack of information, studies have described police violence rather than explaining it. Marx found that excessive police violence had often escalated racial rioting by provoking Blacks or licensing White attacks. Marx (1970) stated that police officers' *unlawful* violence was "woven into a social fabric" of their own fear, frustrations, and social, ethnic, or political antagonisms (p. 51). Bergesen (1980) studied the escalation of police violence in connection with 91 deaths in the three biggest riots of the 1960s, Watts, Newark, and Detroit. He found that at most 9 (10%) of these victims might have been killed by civilians, and 14 by accidents. But 68 (75%) of the fatalities were inflicted by police and national guardsmen. He found that the pattern of police escalation culminated in the breakdown of organized control. Initial fatalities attributable to civilians and accidents were followed by shootings of looters (nearly two thirds of whom were running *from* the premises when they were shot), then shootings of persons in crowds and cars, then in homes and hotels, and finally killings of persons by police in personal attacks not connected with law enforcement ($N = 11$). Bergesen connected both the initial Black rioting and the reactive police riot to African-American political advance in the national arena at the expense of localized White ethnic groups. Newly proud Blacks initially resisted *ordinary, not excessive,* police actions, and in reaction, Whites reacted in escalating fashion to put them back in their places. Stark (1972) argued that the escalation of numerous police riots was due not to psychological processes such as loss of cognitive control or deindividuation but to socially developed patterns of behavior, identities, and beliefs, including policemen's *routine* use of excessive force, their isolated subculture, inadequate training in alternatives, choice of punitive tactics (perhaps accompanied by arousal) against enemies of the police, and a combination of disinhibitions: a monopoly on legitimate violence, departmental coverups, and public incredulity as to the magnitude of police violence. Midlarsky (1977) distinguished between large cities and smaller ones: In the larger ones measures of Black population size *times* police force size seemed decisive factors in outbreaks of riots, whereas in smaller cities diffusion by example seemed to explain more. Carter (1987) found a curvilinear relationship between police force size and the severity of riots, such that moderate use of police seemed to irritate without quelling rioting. Muller's (1985) cross-national analysis also found curvilinear relationships between moderate repression and greater political violence, concluding: "There seems to be truth in Machiavelli's dictum that a leader should either embrace or crush his opposition" (p.60). It seems clear that further research must consider not only the complex effects of police tactics but also police forces' significant contribution to escalation, as distinctive social groups rather than neutral instruments of the law, taking account of their social and political relationships and beliefs and the stage of their training, experience, equipment, and ethos.

## QUANTITATIVE ANALYSIS OF DIFFUSION
## OF RIOTING

Early work on "contagion" (diffusion) looked for mathematical patterns by application of Poisson distributions. Spilerman (1970) rejected slender indications of contagion radiating out from the Detroit and Newark riots in order to emphasize Black population size. Both Midlarsky (1970) and Li and Thompson (1975) found some contagion effect in the spread of military coups and developed formal models of the contagion process that were consistent with the observations. Midlarsky (1978) reexamined Spilerman's argument for the riots of 1966 and 1967, and found different effects and rates of spread of rioting in different segments of this period. For the majority of the period he found diffusion, that is, "the spread of a particular type of behavior through time and space as a result of the *cumulative impact* of a set of statistically independent events" (p. 1006; italics added). But for the intense period of the spread of rioting in July to August 1967, he argued for a hierarchical contagion effect from riots in the "large, visible cities" of Newark and Detroit, where police–community clashes set off rioting, to smaller cities that were instigated by contagion effects. Govea and West's study (1981) of contagion in Latin American rioting argued that different explanations were required for the outbreak of rioting and its subsequent spread. They followed Smelser's (1962) suggestion: "Once hostile outbursts begin . . . they become a sign that a fissure has opened in the social order, and the situation is now structurally conducive for the expression of hostility. As a result, a rash of hostile actions appear, many of them motivated by hostility unrelated to the conditions giving rise to the initial outburst" (p. 259). Govea and West compared rioting in Latin America with Poison distributions and "contagious Poissons." They analyzed the temporal distribution of riots in 14 Latin American countries for 60 quarter-year periods 1949 to 1963. Only in four countries did the temporal distribution of riots seem better fitted by a "contagious Poisson" (in which each event is assumed to increase the probability of subsequent events) than by a Poisson distribution (implying randomness). They called that fit *chronic contagion,* inferring that riots followed one another for imitative rather than instrumental reasons. In two other countries, whereas the overall temporal distribution did not fit the contagious Poisson distribution, brief periods of many riots were observed. Govea and West argued that such "acute contagion" seemed caused by political motivations rather than imitation. Although they did not attempt to explain much about their findings, their statistics, with those of Midlarsky, did raise the question of qualitatively different kinds of diffusion taking place in different periods.

A more promising approach analyzed contagion in relation to rational political calculation, learning, and interaction. Pitcher and associates (Pitcher, Hamblin, & Miller, 1978) set out to investigate the social contagion of collective violence as a process in which actors were instigated or inhibited by the information they received through time about the actions of others and their consequences. They rejected an earlier theory that outbreaks of violence were a case of diffusion of innovations that followed a logistic model of innovation. Drawing upon Bandura's and others' work, they theorized that imitative aggression occurs only when people *both* experience a threat in a conflict situation *and* observe a model aggressing against the threat successfully. They assumed that diffusion takes place by reports of successful aggression reported in the media, whereas inhibitions based on punishments will also probably accumulate, assuming organized police forces always have greater resources than rioters. Their model fit many of their data sets of "collective" violence,[8] but not the 1967 U. S. rioting, perhaps because the great publicity given to the Newark riot in July created a major discontinuity. They also found evidence of "nested" escalation in the Swing riots in England in 1830 and 1831; that is, *covert* forms of protest like arson began first and ended last, whereas large *overt* collective forms like wage meetings and riots marked a peak in the protest. A similar pattern could be observed in the Rebecca Riots in Wales in 1839 and 1842 and 1843, although social relations and political process were significantly different. Although led by village artisans, the Swing rioters were predominantly lowly farm laborers, and so their uprisings had some of the qualities and shock value of a servile revolt. After the authorities initially hesitated, they punished the rioters' limited actions with swift escalation of force and severe repression including many hangings and transportations to Australia. The Rebecca Riots against tollgates, however, were carried on at first by more independent farmers. After initial widespread success in getting concessions to their grievances, protest reached a peak in several atypically violent incidents and was then shifted toward peaceful mass meetings rather than rioting by a *combination* of factors: supporters' revulsion against the extreme violence; the rioters' success; the influx of troops; and the selective severity of sentences given violent offenders (Jones, 1989). The "mathematical" description of contagion in terms of time, events, and costs seems to require social weighting to take into account

---

[8]Including 10 studies of airplane hijacking, which is not collective action as used here.

rioters' and authorities' interactions, assessments, and inferences for further action.

## QUANTITATIVE THEORIES OF ESCALATION

Some of the earliest and best attempts to apply mathematical methods to the spread of rioting within a community came from a massive study of riot incidents in the Watts riot. Abudu, Raine, Burbeck, and Davison (1972) viewed rioting as neither carnival nor pathology but rather as a process of political communication that called for reforms, asserted Black potency as bargaining agents a la Nieburg, and aimed specifically at the main perceived oppressors of the Blacks—police, merchants, and White racists. They analyzed nearly 1, 800 riotous incidents and found four types of behavior—looting, setting fires, turning in false alarms, and throwing rocks. Pursuing their analysis through census tracts in Los Angeles, they found that rioting was neither localized nor random but related to "fertile ground" conditions including concentrations of Blacks, single males, unemployed, and people of at least eighth -grade education. This refined Spilerman's emphasis on the absolute number of Blacks as the key to riots.

The same authors analyzed patterns of temporal and spatial diffusion for 1, 850 events (Stark, Raine, Burbeck, & Davison, 1974). They found that different types of crowd actions clustered in different tracts, and especially arson and looting spread via different patterns and dynamics. So riot behavior was not monolithic, and diffusion was not mechanical and linear; indeed, in only 21% of the instances did rioting spread to a contiguous area. They concluded that diffusion was complex, although their method of presentation exaggerated this: If an event occurred at Fourth and Main Streets at 8 p.m., another 5 miles away at 8:05, and another at Sixth and Main Streets at 8:10, their linear path would show a wild zig-zag by strict chronological ordering, rather than the more commonsense proposition that the riot spread two blocks in 10 minutes. The temporal pattern they discovered was a clear daily cycle, with two thirds of the acts occurring between 8 p.m. and 4 a.m. (implicitly supporting McPhail's emphasis on rioters' availability) rather than events being spread across or accelerating through equivalent time periods. Successive days were also distinctively different and there were mini-riots within the larger process, so that there was no simple mechanical process of rise and decline.

Burbeck, Raine, and Stark (1978) continued their analysis in a more mathematical vein, assuming that riotous activity was analogous to a disease epidemic. The probability of the occurrence and the severity of an epidemic would depend on the size and density of the population at risk to be infected by a source. A reverse process of withdrawal would lead to the decline of the riot. They found temporal patterns in the Detroit and Washington riots of 1967 and 1968 similar to that in the Watts riot of 1965, which were consistent with their epidemic model, that is, the riot activity had a rather swift rise and a slow decline. This model has an emergent threshold property such that whether the precipitating event touched off a riot process depends on whether a sufficiently large number of susceptible individuals is available to be infected to riot. The puzzle was why apparently routine clashes with the police touched off riots at some times but not at others. Their explanation did not account for why the contagion went critical in 1965, 1967, or 1968 and not in 1964, assuming that neither susceptible population size nor interactions with police differed significantly. They did say that perhaps the threshold had been temporarily lowered in Watts by heat and smog, in Washington by the King assassination. That appears to be a rather large deus ex machina. Part of the problem is that they used a deterministic rather than a more intuitively plausible probabilistic model. In any event, they believed that such a contagion process resting upon the size of Black populations, rather than the distinctive characteristics of communities or individual rioters, could account for some of Spilerman's and McPhail's findings. It leaves open the question of why and how the susceptible people were susceptible, a more complex question than for infectious disease.

Sullivan (1977) offered a qualitative theory about the mechanisms by which such "contagion" might create a critical mass of rioters in a sequence of stages: First, precipitating events, like police–Black citizen episodes, are essentially random events, so that the likelihood of a riot is increased by the greater number of such contacts, and hence by the number of Blacks and the number of police in a community. As such a precipitating event draws a crowd, it becomes a critical mass when interaction and communication processes (rumor and milling) take place that inform and unify the originally diverse motives of crowd members into a collective definition of the situation, then emergent norms and identities. It is primarily the size and duration of the crowd, hence the "quantity" of such interaction, that increase the probability that any member's perceptions and behavior will be thus affected. Sullivan's concept is suggestive although he illustrated it only with the well-documented beginning of the Watts riot.

But why do some crowds go critical whereas other do not? One answer was Granovetter's (1978) influential argument on threshold behavior. Leaving out of account their preferences and norms, Granovetter focused on how individuals' behavior depended on what others did: "A person's threshold for joining a riot is defined here as the proportion of a group he would have to see join before he would do so" (p. 1422). A normal distribution of thresholds might contain one person who would have to see 1% of the crowd begin to riot, another 2%, another 3% and so on. Normal distributions of thresholds would occur in a population "where no strong tendencies of any kind exist to distort a distribution of preferences away from its regular variation around some central tendency" (p. 1427). But real distributions would probably vary a lot. In particular, the presence (or absence) of an actor with a particular threshold might provide (or not) a key link in an escalating curve of sequential decisions by different individuals to join the action and hence determine whether a riot escalated or died away. Moreover, the networks of friendship and other social influences might weight the participation thresholds—friends' participation (or not) might count twice as heavily as others'. In other words, escalation might be lumpy rather than smoothly linear (cf. Granovetter & Soong, 1983). Hence, very different behavioral outcomes might result from small differences in crowds, due to sampling variability rather than to background conditions. This would tend to support Spilerman's findings: Large Black populations provided more sampling trials, one of which might have the right configuration of thresholds for a riot to occur. So the key points in this line of analysis were the interdependence of decisions to participate and the heterogeneity of dispositions to act and also of crowd propensities.

Salert and Sprague (1980) proposed a mathemetical model of riot dynamics including rioter and police interaction and escalation. Drawing on Granovetter and Burbeck et al., they noted that after an initial triggering incident, a person becomes more likely to join through "contagion," increased contact with rioting, whereas fatigue processes might induce people to drop out. They introduced threshold effects (points "representing qualitative behavior changes") in two senses. First, because riots are volatile, there is a threshold of the number of rioters that determines whether or not the riot escalates beyond the initial level. Second, a threshold may determine whether or not an individual joins a riot, and that threshold varies for individuals. Given the first threshold effect, individual potential thresholds cannot be simply averaged out, so that interaction is crucial. Finally, there is a complex interaction between rioters and police such that the behavior of each *determines* that of the other. Salert and Sprague noted that after an initial moderate response to the riots of 1966, police forces reacted in divergent ways. Both undercontrol, which showed rioters they could "get away with it," and overcontrol, which provoked "defensive" escalation or prevented communication, seemed to increase rioting. So after an initial trial of levels, if the police "rationally" adjust their response to appropriate (although unpredictable and perhaps variable) levels, it will lead back to equilibrium. But if they go out of control due to training, fatigue, attitudes, or force levels, as in Stark's and Bergesen's police riots (aforementioned), probably only external political authority can restore control, as it did in Newark. Finally, after an initial outburst, riot contagion will be counteracted by fatigue, as people become hurt, tired, disillusioned, and responsive to police pressures. Fatigue also reflects people's reactions to "counter-rioters" and their established attitudes toward violence, the police, and the society. In short it is an immunization process, a negative contagion. So there are two sources of growth—inappropriate police repression and contagion—and two sources of decay—effective police repression and fatigue. Hence, *their model incorporates contagion, removal (by fatigue, repression, and immunization), thresholds, and police-rioter interaction.* They also recognize that different expectations are brought into a riot, including rioters' attitudes toward police, and policemen's attitudes toward rioting populations.

Whether police actions deter or escalate protest is still a puzzle. Resource mobilization theories tend to argue "repression works" by raising the costs of action, whereas deprivation arguments see repression as increasing frustration and aggression (Lichbach, 1987). Because Salert and Sprague's model tends toward equilibrium and hence zero violence, the police would be better advised to let fatigue operate, and so not to overreact but to adjust their response based on initial interactions. But this assumes that the police goal is to restore preexisting equilibrium. Because that equilibrium included the possibility of riot and challenge to police authority, the police might *wish* to "overreact" to strengthen inhibitions against violence, to vaccinate the community against riot. In August 1985 in Liverpool, England, unconfirmed but apparently reliable reports were that police forces had been caught off-guard and surrounded in their headquarters. Later that fall, police took the opportunity of another riot to reestablish their authority by engaging in a police riot to intimidate members of the neighborhood that had humiliated them earlier (author's observation). If this kind of police intimidation were simple and unchecked, it would approximate a police state, and that would probably be stable (Salert & Sprague, 1980). Besides that repressive option, Lichbach (1987) suggested an ameliorative option: in effect, if regimes consistently make concessions to nonviolent tactics and repress violent tactics, violence will decrease. That assumes that power holders will yield on the conflicts that may have provoked violence in the first place.

As long as police repression is near appropriate levels and does not incite further violence, the effects of fatigue and the costs imposed by repression will reduce violence. Salert and Sprague's graphs explore growth and decline of violence over 100 hours, for rioters, for police, with variations in thresholds, and at different rates of fatigue and immunization and police reaction. Their equations and the resulting graphs capture a great deal of complexity, but they conclude that it is still difficult to find a correlation between police action and riot intensity, so that chance may still play a part in riots. Chance, lack of complete information, and other accidents may shock the police–rioter system of interaction to produce large results and/or continuing violence. Killings may operate as a durable shock value. For instance, the acquittal in Tampa of four Miami policemen charged with the killing of a Black insurance agent touched off a riot 5 months after his death, because of a vigilant social process that kept it alive, together with a series of aggravating events (Ladner, Schwartz, Roker, & Titterud, 1981). Finally, it is worth noting that Salert and Sprague's curve of violence in individual riots (pp. 50, 51, and 92) resembles the shape of Sidney Tarrow's curve of protest cycles (see later): A rapid early rise to a rounded peak (suggesting the onset of deceleration), and then a declining slope about half as acute, maintaining a long tail of the onset of fatigue.[9]

## STRATEGIC INTERACTION

Granovetter's work on thresholds was an early step toward a *strategic* interaction theory, for it broke away from analysis of individual predispositions (even in sum) and recognized the *interdependence* of decisions to take action in a crowd. This approach has recognized that actors choose their actions not merely with regard to static quantities of discontent or resources on either side but with reference to the (dynamic) *range* of choices made by other players, including other rioters' decisions to act or not as well as responses of police repressors. Further, actors have goals, and the evolving *interaction* of actors changes their estimates of costs and probabilities of success, and hence their further participation choices. The speed and predictability of that interaction seem likely to be different for situations with little structure and

---

[9]However, social cataclysms can have very different temporal shapes. Rule and Tilly reconstructed the "unnatural history" of the French Revolution of 1830: The overthrow of the repressive regime *began*, rather than climaxed, a period of intense political ferment (Rule & Tilly, 1975). The same could be said of Russia in 1917.

precedent, like the ghetto riots of the 1960s, than for the highly conventionalized food riots of early modern England. Richard Berk suggested a "gaming" or strategic perspective from careful observation of a muted race riot in Baltimore: Militant White instigators were unable to persuade a crowd to attack Blacks, apparently due to serious reservations about violence and costs of fighting, and instead tensions were released in a limited, carnivalesque rock-throwing fight (Berk, 1972). His study of an antiwar street blockade at Northwestern University also revealed how a heterogeneous collection of people weighed alternatives, costs, and payoffs in relation to the actions of others as they chose varying, innovative, courses of action. Berk (1974) wrote: "What may distinguish crowds . . . [from other transitory groups such as audiences] is the common realization that each person's payoffs depend fundamentally on the actions of others at the scene" (p. 369).

Many of the strategic interaction theories began with a critique of Mancur Olson's "free rider problem." In a famous book mistitled *The Logic of Collective Action* (1965), Olson argued that collective action aiming at public goods to be enjoyed by all would be virtually impossible, for any "rational self-interested" individual would calculate that because his costs were non-negligible, and he could enjoy the good without paying the cost, the rational choice was the free ride—to let others make the effort. Where social movements did arise, they survived by providing their cadres with "selective" individual benefits, such as careers. Economists were impressed by the power and elegance of this argument, whereas to social historians it was tantamount to insisting that bumblebees could not possibly fly, and they continued to analyze the thousands of collective actions that regularly occurred in real life. Sociologists and political scientists took up the challenge of refining the explanations of why people acted in concert to struggle for collective goods despite the costs.

Fireman and Gamson (1979) and Ferree and Miller (1985) both attacked Olson's simplistic utilitarian individualism. Ferree and Miller pointed out that ideology helped define interests and justice, and ideologies were likely to be rooted in social networks. Of critical importance was whether people attributed their problems to individual failings or to the system, for only the latter was likely to lead to collective action. Fireman and Gamson argued that collective actions were based on solidarities, loyalties, and principles created "naturally" over long periods of shared experience, not during ad hoc mobilizations for a campaign. Mason (1984) argued that the reversal of racial discrimination by police and in education was a collective good that underlay the rioting of the 1960s. Only after such indignation had ignited collective rioting could individual material motives such as looting come into play.

Previous studies had shown that people engaged in collective action in groups of friends or family members, not as isolated individuals (Aveni, 1977; McPhail & Wohlstein, 1983). Drawing on studies by Chamberlin (1974) and Frohlich and Oppenheimer (1973), Mason showed that rioting was a rational choice of means to fight discrimination, because the larger the crowd, the greater the likelihood of success, and the smaller the individual cost. Klandermans (1984) applied expectancy-value theory to mobilization for collective action. Individual choices are based on estimates of costs and benefits, including the expectancy of success, and anticipations of others' views: Will enough people participate to make success likely, and how will *significant* others react to the individual's decision? Muller and Opp (1986) found that individuals in New York City and Hamburg might participate in rebellious action for collective goods when they perceived, *based on past experience*, that the whole group's cooperation might achieve success, and that individual participation would make a positive difference in that effort. In short, crowds change the "climate" in which their members make decisions. Acting crowds make it possible for people to exert power they could not wield as individuals. Crowds are more than simply the sum of their members.

Oliver, Marwell, and associates' studies based on computer simulations have significant implications for the dynamics of escalation (Marwell, Oliver, & Prahl, 1988; Oliver & Marwell, 1988; Oliver, Marwell, & Teixeira, 1985). They assumed that decisions to participate in collective action were interdependent—that individuals made decisions based on what others had contributed. Different collective actions had different "payoff schedules" or production functions, which were not linear, proportionate to increasing contributions, but most generally curvilinear. Some were decelerating, where early contributions achieved most effect, with later contributions having diminishing effects, as for instance in calls to City Hall to fix a pothole. But protest movements typically had accelerating payoff schedules—early payoffs were low, increasing only slowly until a threshold had been passed. Assuming groups of potential actors were very heterogeneous in the amounts of interest and resources they might contribute, a collective action might take place only if there were a small "critical mass" of individuals with unusually great interests and resources willing to pay the start-up costs until the less interested or resourceful contributors would be drawn in. That "critical mass" was more likely to exist, the more the population was (a) heterogeneous and (b) large. In most social groups the major contributors tended to be connected in social networks, and so together they could probably estimate that their contributions would be decisive and hence serve as bell-wethers for the group. Finally, social networks were critical in another way. Following Hardin's theory, the most effective way to overcome the free-rider problem was a contract that said individual contributions would not be called for until the total contribution reached the level necessary for success. Such a contract might be an implicit understanding based on traditional solidarities and conventions of participation, as in the traditions of food riot in the Devon towns, or in clan gatherings. Or it might be the work of organizers, especially those endowed with good networks. Such a contract might operate as a deliberate threshold of propensity to act. Allowing for differences between nonviolent collective actions and risky riots, further analysis might ask whether social factors might affect the critical escalation variables such as the differential distribution of threshold propensities to act, social networks, and the presence of "troublemakers" (i.e., escalators, effective organizers, etc.) across different social groups or communities.

## ESCALATION AND DIFFUSION IN THE NATIONAL POLITY: PROTEST CYCLES

Besides considering diffusion and escalation in terms of individual riots or communities, we might study escalation as a national process, with the national polity as the unit of study. The perspective that emerged in the 1980s to do this is the political process approach, which linked grass-roots political mobilization with changes in the larger political environment (Tarrow, 1988). This approach integrates the kind of historical contexts emphasized by Tilly and Bohstedt. In a national political process, both escalation and diffusion seem to result from protestors' strategies in response to changing opportunities, resources, perceptions, and costs and outcomes.

The concept of a "protest cycle" captures the dynamics of how protest activities in a national polity rise quickly to a peak and then peter out (Tarrow, 1988). Building in part on McAdam's (1982) work and resource mobilization theory, Tarrow and Klandermans (Klandermans, Kriesi, & Tarrow, 1988) emphasized "the social and political networks in which individuals and groups come together around common goals"; political opportunities; and the construction and diffusion of new frames of meanings as central to the process of mobilization (p. 3). These factors are likely to connect changes in the larger polity on the one hand to increasing decisions to participate on the other. Olzak showed strongly marked cycles of ethnic conflict correlated with immigration rates and economic hardship in the late nineteenth century United States. She found a wave-like diffusion in which conflicts spread rapidly across the country, reach a ceiling, and then decline in exhaustion (Olzak, 1987).

The fullest account of the escalation and diffusion of such a protest cycle comes from Tarrow's (1989) analysis of Italian protest between 1965 and 1973. For Tarrow, the dynamics of that cycle are driven by strategic political choices. Protest (collective disruptive action) begins among established organizations when structural political and economic change produces deep and visible grievances that have the potential to mobilize people in many social sectors. "Early risers" break the bounds of convention and demonstrate that protests are possible and/or that group esteem can be asserted.[10] Mobilization occurs as groups of people choose to express their grievances after reassessing probable gains and losses, as the costs of protest fall far below the probable gains, as for instance when they acquire new allies, new frames of meaning, or when the elites split. At that point a "social movement sector" emerges, that is, a field of ferment both inside and outside the established polity, with groups undertaking innovative mobilization in cooperation and competition. In fact, it is the cooperation and competition among groups that shapes the rise and fall of a protest cycle. Protest with a few common interpretative themes spreads throughout the society. As protest rises to a peak, innovators and groups devise new tactics and claims to win supporters. The cycle declines as protestors are exhausted, satisfied by partial reforms, or cowed by repression. Some of the former protest leaders go into political institutions, whereas others including new groups emerge on the extremes to try to exploit new political space by means of extreme claims and tactics including deliberate violence. Tarrow assumed protest can be both instrumental and expressive for it can achieve both the desired goals and also group cohesion and solidarity.

Some quantitative support for cycles of protest is implied by an 86-nation analysis by Lichbach and Gurr (1981). The extent of protest in 1 year strongly predicts the extent of protest in the next, but there is no such relationship from one 5-year period to the next, suggesting that short periods of protest do have distinct dynamics and contexts, perhaps structures of political opportunity, rather than manifesting persistent levels of ripeness for protest. Not surprisingly, extensive protest elicits strong repression, but protestors do not seem to be consistently deterred or instigated by past repression, moderate or severe.

---

[10]In other words, the "structure of political opportunities" (Eisinger, 1973) has changed; the political system has become more vulnerable to the pressures of dissatisfied groups.

The riots of the 1960s seem to fit into such a cycle of protest. McAdam (1982) developed the political process approach to explain the rise and decline of the (preriot) civil rights "insurgency" of the 1960s in terms of four *long-term* factors. First, the *structure of political opportunities*, factors external to Black social movements, changed between 1870 and 1954 to facilitate Black mobilization. The cotton economy collapsed, Blacks migrated from a tightly repressive rural south into northern and southern cities where they acquired the economic, social, and mental resources for action, and federal government policies became increasingly favorable. Second, these processes enabled the emergence of the *organizations*—Black churches, colleges, and National Association for the Advancement of Colored People (NAACP) chapters—that would provide the building blocks of the civil rights mobilization—members, leaders, communication networks, and a new sense of political efficacy. Third, *"cognitive liberation"* was a function of both urbanization and the increasing sense that change was possible, thanks in part to the increasing response of the federal government to Black claims between 1930 and 1954. The climatic *Brown v. Topeka Board of Education* (1954) ushered in a period of intense political mobilization. Success bred a success mentality, as well as resources in the form of members, media attention, and money. Finally, the *reactions of outside parties*—sympathetic donors, a reactive federal government, and White supremacists—both aided the civil rights movement's upswing and contributed to its decline.

McAdam demonstrated how these factors shaped the protest cycle of civil rights, and that cycle can certainly be extended to include the ghetto riots of 1964 to 1968. As Janowitz argued (earlier), it seems likely that the momentum and success of the civil rights campaign changed the "structure of political opportunities" and increased "cognitive liberation" so as to facilitate protest by riot. It is true that the civil rights movement was already beginning to experience tougher sledding after 1964, due to the beginning of White backlash, the onset of the Vietnam war, and the strategic shift from the south to the north, and from integration to radical social and economic demands less susceptible to direct action (McAdam, 1982). But one could speculate that its past success, aroused militancy, and then declining payoffs facilitated a shift to violent protest. Unlike the civil rights movement, the riots were a febrile one-shot outburst not underpinned by organizations. It is certainly easier to recover or infer strategic interaction and responses in social movements than in riots. Looting and burning could not long be tolerated by elites, as were the much less threatening food riots of Georgian England or the nonviolent civil rights campaign. Apart from the immediate gratification of redefining property norms by looting

(Quarantelli & Dynes, 1971), and the emotional gains from standing up to the police or attacking landlords and stores, the rioters of the 1960s could not immediately reach their targets as did the food rioters but had to depend on distant actors for remedial legislation.

So how were such outcomes related to the period of rioting? Piven and Cloward (1977) argued that *Poor People's Movements* gain their results from the disruption of mass defiance rather than permanent organization building that might actually be diversionary and counterproductive. Studies of the riots' impact on Black well-being and local and national policies have produced complex results summarized by Gurr (1980). Positive responses to the riots included local symbolic reassurances, increases in federal Aid to Families with Dependent Children, HUD grants, and Office of Economic Opportunity (OEO) programs. OEO was cut back in the 1970s under the more conservative Nixon regime. On the other side, police forces obtained federal funds from the new Law Enforcement Assistance Administration, but they were spent not only on arms but also on communication, training, and community relations. It is difficult to disentangle these effects from responses to the civil rights campaign, which included the Civil Rights Acts of 1964 and 1968, the Voting Rights Act of 1965, the Great Society programs, and rising numbers of Black elected officials. It does seem that Button's (1978) conclusions that the riots engendered first ameliorative reforms and later backlash repression helps to fit the riots into the cycle-of-protest theory. Moreover, if established power holders were both able and willing to respond to the riots with reform measures, it suggests that the riots were a realistic form of protest bargaining as Nieburg suggested: The riots' capacity to inflict pain helped keep Black grievances on the national agenda. "Bargaining" with such loosely structured protests requires some general systemic combination of concession and repression rather than a negotiated agreement (Oberschall, 1979).

The rioting stopped in 1968. In the short term, Kelly and Isaac (1984) argued that AFDC increased sharply enough during the rioting to contribute to its decline, although it is a little hard to see how that might restrain young Black males clashing with the police. Otherwise, the major reforms and backlashes were too long delayed to enter directly into the interactive processes of diffusion and escalation. But taken together, the political process and strategic interaction approaches would point to a major shift in the structure of political opportunities. Oberschall (1979) argued persuasively that the presidential campaign of 1968 was a turning point marked by the Wallace candidacy, the candidates' law and order emphases, and the Nixon victory. Given the heavy costs of the rioting for Blacks and the rising attention given to the Vietnam war, a realistic assessment of the political context of 1969 would certainly have suggested that riots would no longer win benefits commensurate with their costs.

## CONCLUSIONS

In the last 10 years analyses of riots have shifted increasingly in the direction of processes and interactions rather than the older tradition of correlating static preconditions or attributes with riot outbreaks or severity (Olzak, 1989). The dynamics of riot are obviously not mechanical, although patterns are observable. Diffusion through "contagion" is not a simple matter of imitation. Rather, modeling of "successful" action against similar problems does seem to enter into current actors' reassessments of their schedule of costs and benefits. But so do "structural" considerations based on people's experience, and so do factors arising out of interaction. Much more work could be done on the analysis of diffusion of rioting, keeping in mind Spilerman's, Carter's, and Midlarsky's findings that different phases of a cycle of protest may be operating according to different dynamics.

The most significant trend in recent research is to analyze how individual participation in collective action depends on the decisions and actions of others, both potential comrades and enemies. A number of studies have shown that people do not enter into collective actions as individuals but rather in small groups of friends and relatives, and associates from other forms of collective action. That finding needs to be tested in the ghetto riots of the 1960s. The theoretical work on thresholds from Granovetter through Salert and Sprague to Oliver and Marwell and Johnson and Feinberg seems promising, and one cannot help wondering if "chaos" theory might help to analyze the qualitative jumps in riot dynamics. McPhail's work on the constituent processes of gatherings and of action-in-concert is also promising. The emphasis on strategic interaction seems to fit the food riots of early modern Europe— it remains to be seen whether there is parallel evidence of articulate strategy in the ghetto riots of the 1960s. Were the post hoc "rationalizations" mentioned by Janowitz also voiced by rioters in action? Finally, much more work could be done on the police as social actors in riots not simply as neutral instruments of "order." Skolnick (1969) reminded us a long time ago that "Order, like violence, is politically defined" (p. 5).

Methodologically, a healthy trend is one away from the almost exclusive reliance on statistical analysis that characterized the 1970s toward a more balanced deployment of critical quantitative analysis together with hypothesis testing by other means including controlled comparative analysis. McAdam and Tarrow are two strong recent examples of such works. It is striking how scholars accepted Spilerman's statistical analysis and left unexamined his unsupported arguments about electronic contagion. To speak of historical contexts, structures of political opportunity, and national protest cycles necessarily involves some nonquantitative judgments. The analyses of interactions, for instance in the work of Carter (1986a, 1986b) and Tilly (1978), that turn up curvilinear relationships between circumstances and riot dynamics are another reminder of the complexity of the relationships. Finally, the analysis of outcomes is an underdeveloped area. It could be an important check on how "realistic" the goals of rioters are, particularly as we seem to have transcended old dichotomies between material and emotional, instrumental and expressive purposes.

## ACKNOWLEDGMENTS

I am grateful to Jeffrey H. Goldstein, Clark McCauley, and Susan Olzak for helpful references, and to Michael Potegal for expert editorial advice.

## REFERENCES

Abudu, M. J. G., Raine, W. J., Burbeck, S. L., & Davison, K. K. (1972). Black ghetto violence: A case study inquiry into the spatial pattern of four Los Angeles riot event-types. *Social Problems, 19*, 408–426.

Aveni, A. (1977). The not-so-lonely crowd: Friendship groups in collective behavior. *Sociometry, 40*, 96–99.

Bandura, A. (1973). *Aggression: A social learning analysis.* Englewood Cliffs, NJ: Prentice-Hall.

Bandura, A. (1983). Psychological mechanisms of aggression. In R. G. Geen & E. I. Donnerstein (Eds.), *Aggression: Theoretical and empirical reviews* (Vol. 1, pp. 1–40). New York: Academic.

Bandura, A. (1986). *Social foundations of thought and action.* Englewood Cliffs, NJ: Prentice-Hall.

Bandura, A., Underwood, B., & Fromson, M.E. (1975). Disinhibition of aggression through diffusion of responsibility and dehumanization of victims. *Journal of Research in Personality, 9*, 253–269.

Benyon, J. (1984). Scarman and after. In J. Benyon (Ed.), *Scarman and after: Essays reflecting on Lord Scarman's Report, the riots and their aftermath* (pp. 233–243). Oxford: Pergamon.

Bergesen, A. (1980). Official violence during the Watts, Newark, and Detroit race riots of the 1960s. In P. Lauderdale (Ed.), *A political analysis of deviance* (pp. 138–174). Minneapolis: University of Minnesota Press.

Berk, R. A. (1972). The emergence of muted behavior in crowd behavior: A case study of an almost race riot. In J. F. Short & M. E. Wolfgang (Eds.), *Collective violence* (pp. 309–328). Chicago: Aldine-Atherton.

Berk, R. A. (1974). A gaming approach to crowd behavior. *American Sociological Review, 39,* 355–373.

Berkowitz, L. (1989). Frustration-aggression hypothesis: Examination and reformulation. *Psychological Bulletin, 106,* 59–73.

Bohstedt, J. (1983). *Riots and community politics in England and Wales, 1790–1810.* Cambridge, MA: Harvard University Press.

Bohstedt, J. (1990). The myth of the feminine food riot: Women as proto-citizens in English community politics, 1790–1810. In H. B. Applewhite & D. G. Levy (Eds.), *Women and politics in the age of the democratic revolution* (pp. 21–60). Ann Arbor: University of Michigan Press.

Bohstedt, J., & Williams, D. E. (1988). The diffusion of riots: The patterns of 1766, 1795, and 1801 in Devonshire. *Journal of Interdisciplinary History, 19,* 1–24.

Brown v Topeka Board of Education, 347 U.S. 483 (1954).

Burbeck, S. L., Raine, W. J., & Stark, M. J. A. (1978). The dynamics of riot growth: An epidemiological approach. *Journal of Mathematical Sociology, 6,* 1–22.

Button, J. W. (1978). *Black violence: Political impact of the 1960s riots.* Princeton, NJ: Princeton University Press.

Canetti, E. (1975). *Crowds and power* (C. Stewart, Trans.). New York: Continuum. (Original work published 1960)

Caplan, N. (1970). The new ghetto man: A review of recent empirical studies. *Journal of Social Issues, 26,* 59–73.

Carter, G. L. (1986a). The 1960s Black riots revisited: City level explanations of their severity. *Sociological Inquiry, 56,* 210–228.

Carter, G. L. (1986b). In the narrows of the 1960s U. S. Black rioting. *Journal of Conflict Resolution, 30,* 115–127.

Carter, G. L. (1987). Local police force size and the severity of the 1960s Black rioting. *Journal of Conflict Resolution, 31,* 601–614.

Carter, G. L. (1990). Black attitudes and the 1960s Black riots: An aggregate-level analysis of the Kerner Commission's "15 cities" data. *Sociological Quarterly, 31,* 269–286.

Chamberlin, J. (1974). Provision of collective goods as a function of group size. *American Political Science Review, 68,* 707–716.

Charlesworth, A. (1979). *Social protest in a rural society: The spatial diffusion of the Captain Swing disturbances of 1830–1831* (Historical Geography Research Series, No. 1). Norwich: Geo Abstracts Ltd.

Charlesworth, A. (1983). The spatial diffusion of rural protest: An historical and comparative perspective of rural riots in nineteenth-century Britain. *Environment and Planning D: Society and Space, 1,* 251–263.

Clare, J. (1984). Eyewitness in Brixton. In J. Benyon (Ed.), *Scarman and after: Essays reflecting on Lord Scarman's report, the riots and their aftermath* (pp. 46–53). Oxford: Pergamon.

Diener, E. (1976). Effects of prior destructive behavior, anonymity, and group presence on deindividuation and aggression. *Journal of Personality and Social Psychology, 33,* 497–507.

Diener, E. (1977). Deindividuation: Causes and consequences. *Social Behavior and Personality, 5,* 143–155.

Diener, E. (1980). Deindividuation: the absence of self-awareness and self-regulation in group members. In P. B. Paulus (Ed.), *Psychology of group influence* (pp. 209–242). Hillsdale, NJ: Lawrence Erlbaum Associates.

Diener, E., Dineen, J., & Endresen, K. (1975). Effects of altered responsibility, cognitive set, and modeling on physical aggression and deindividuation. *Journal of Personality and Social Psychology, 31,* 328–337.

Eisinger, P. K. (1973). The conditions of protest behavior in American cities. *American Political Science Review, 67,* 11–28.

Feinberg, W. E., & Johnson, N. R. (1990). Radical leaders, moderate followers: Effects of alternative strategies on achieving consensus for action in simulated crowds. *Journal of Mathematical Sociology, 15,* 91–115.

Ferree, M. M., & Miller, F. D. (1985). Mobilization and meaning: Toward an integration of social psychological and resource perspectives on social movements. *Sociological Inquiry, 55,* 38–61.

Fireman, B., & Gamson, W. A. (1979). Utilitarian logic in the resource mobilization perspective. In M. N. Zald & J. D. McCarthy (Eds.), *The dynamics of social movements: Resource mobilization, social control, and tactics* (pp. 8–43). Cambridge, MA: Winthrop Publishers.

Firestone, J. M. (1972). Theory of the riot process. *American Behavioral Scientist, 15,* 859–882.

Freud, S. (1921). *Group psychology and analysis of the ego.* London: Hogarth Press.

Frohlich, N., & Oppenheimer, J. A. (1973). I get by with a little help from my friends. *World Politics, 23,* 104–120.

Geen, R. G. (1983). Aggression and television violence. In R. G. Geen & E. I. Donnerstein (Eds.), *Aggression: Theoretical and empirical reviews* (Vol. 2, pp. 103–126). New York: Academic.

Goldstein, J. H., Davis, R. W., & Herman, D. (1975). Escalation of aggression: Experimental studies. *Journal of Personality and Social Psychology, 31,* 162–170.

Goldstein, J. H., Davis, R. W., Kernis, M., & Cohn, E. S. (1981). Retarding the escalation of aggression. *Social Behavior and Personality, 9,* 65–70.

Govea, R. M., & West, G. T. (1981). Riot contagion in Latin America, 1949–1963. *Journal of Conflict Resolution, 25,* 349–368.

Granovetter, M. (1978). Threshold models of collective behavior. *American Journal of Sociology, 83,* 1420–1443.

Granovetter, M., & Soong, R. (1983). Threshold models of diffusion and collective violence. *Journal of Mathematical Sociology, 9,* 165–179.

Gurr, T. R. (1970). *Why men rebel.* Princeton, NJ: Princeton University Press.

Gurr, T. R. (1980). On the outcomes of violent conflict. In T. R. Gurr (Ed.), *Handbook of political conflict* (pp. 238–294). New York: The Free Press.

Harrison, M. (1988). *Crowds and history: Mass phenomena in English towns, 1790–1835.* Cambridge: Cambridge University Press.

Hayden, M. S. (1968). A view from Detroit. In C. U. Daly (Ed.), *The media and the cities* (pp. 55–64). Chicago: University of Chicago.

Hobsbawm, E. J. (1952). The machine breakers. *Past and Present, 1,* 57–70.

Hobsbawm, E. J., & Rudé, G. (1968). *Captain Swing.* New York: Pantheon.

Janowitz, M. (1969). Patterns of collective racial violence. In H. D. Graham & T. R. Gurr (Eds.), *Violence in America: Historical and comparative Perspectives* (pp. 412–444). New York: Bantam Books.

Johnson, N. R., & Feinberg, W. (1989). Crowd structure and process: Theoretical framework and computer simulation model. *Advances in Group Processes, 6,* 49–86.

Johnson, N. R., Stemler, J. G., & Hunter, D. (1977). Crowd behavior as 'risky shift': A laboratory experiment. *Sociometry, 40,* 183–187.

Jones, D. J. V. (1983). The Rebecca riots 1839–44. In Andrew Charlesworth (Ed.), *An Atlas of Rural Protest in Britain 1548–1900* (pp. 165–169). London: Croom Helm.

Jones, D. J. V. (1989). *Rebecca's children: A study of rural society, crime, and protest.* Oxford: Clarendon Press.

Katz, J. (1988). *Seductions of crime: Moral and sensual attractions in doing evil.* New York: Basic Books.

Kelly, W. R., & Isaac, L. (1984). The rise and fall of urban violence in the U.S.: 1948–1979. *Research in Social Movements, Conflict and Change, 7,* 203–233.

Kerner, O. (Chair). (1968). *Report of the national advisory commission on civil disorders.* New York: Bantam Books.

Klandermans, B. (1984). Mobilization and participation: Social psychological expansions of resource mobilization theory. *American Sociological Review, 49*, 583–600.

Klandermans, B., Kriesi, H., & Tarrow, S. (1988). *From structure to action: Comparing social movement research across cultures. International social movement research: A research annual* (Vol. 1). Greenwich, CT: JAI Press.

Kritzer, H. M. (1977). Political protest and political violence: A nonrecursive causal model. *Social Forces, 55*, 630–640.

Ladner, R. A., Schwartz, B. J., Roker, S. J., & Titterud, L. S. (1981). The Miami riots of 1980: Antecedent conditions, community responses and participant characteristics. *Research in Social Movements, Conflict and Change, 4*, 171–214.

Lange, D. L., Baker, R. K., & Ball, S. J. (1969). *Mass media and violence: A report to the national commission on the causes and prevention of violence.* Washington: U. S. Government Printing Office.

Le Bon, G. (1960). *The crowd: A study of the popular mind.* New York: Viking. (Original work published 1895)

Li, R. P. Y. & Thompson, W. R. (1975). The "coup contagion" hypothesis. *Journal of Conflict Resolution, 19*, 63–85.

Lichbach, M. I. & Gurr, T. R. (1981). The conflict process: A formal model. *Journal of Conflict Resolution, 25*, 3–29.

Lichbach, M. I. (1987). Deterrence or escalation? The puzzle of aggregate studies of repression and dissent. *Journal of Conflict Resolution, 31*, 266–297.

Lieske, J. A. (1978). The conditions of racial violence in American cities: A developmental synthesis. *American Political Science Review, 72*, 1324–1340.

Lofland, J. (1985). *Protest: studies of collective behavior and social movements.* New Brunswick: Transaction Books.

Margadant, T. (1979). *French peasants in revolt: The insurrection of 1851.* Princeton: Princeton University Press.

Marwell, G., Oliver, P. E., & Prahl, R. (1988). Social networks and collective action: A theory of the critical mass. III. *American Journal of Sociology, 94*, 502–534.

Marx, G. T. (1970). Civil disorder and the agents of social control. *Journal of Social Issues, 26*, 19–57.

Mason, D. (1984). Individual participation in collective racial violence: A rational choice synthesis. *American Political Science Review, 78*, 1040–1056.

Mather, F. C. (1974). The general strike of 1842: A study in leadership, organization and the threat of revolution during the plug plot disturbances. In R. Quinault & J. Stevenson (Eds.), *Popular protest and public order: Six studies in British history, 1790–1820* (pp. 115–140). London: George Allen & Unwin.

McAdam, D. (1982). *Political process and the development of Black insurgency, 1930–1970.* Chicago: University of Chicago Press.

McPhail, C. (1971). Civil disorder participation: A critical examination of recent research. *American Sociological Review, 36*, 1058–1073.

McPhail, C. (1991). *The myth of the madding crowd.* New York: Aldine de Gruyter.

McPhail, C., & Miller, D. (1973). The assembling process: A theoretical and empirical examination. *American Sociological Review, 38*, 721–735.

McPhail, C., & Wohlstein, R. T. (1983). Individual and collective behaviors within gatherings, demonstrations, and riots. *Annual Review of Sociology, 9*, 579–600.

Merton, R. K. (1960). Introduction. *The crowd: A study of the popular mind.* By G. Le Bon. New York: Viking.

Midlarsky, M. I. (1970). Mathematical models of instability and a theory of diffusion. *International Studies Quarterly, 14*, 60–84.

Midlarsky, M. I. (1977). Size effects and the diffusion of violence in American cities. *Papers of the Peace Society (International), 27*, 39–47.

Midlarsky, M. I. (1978). Analyzing diffusion and contagion effects: The urban disorders of the 1960s. *American Political Science Review, 72,* 996–1010.

Moinat, S. M., Raine, W. J., Burbeck, S. L., & Davison, K. K. (1972). Black ghetto residents as rioters. *Journal of Social Issues, 28,* 45–62.

Molotch, H. (1979). Media and movements. In M. N. Zald & J. D. McCarthy (Eds.), *The dynamics of social movements: Resource mobilization, social control and tactics* (pp. 71–93). Cambridge, MA: Winthrop Publishers.

Morgan, W. R., & Clark, T. N. (1973). The causes of racial disorders: A grievance-level explanation. *American Sociological Review, 38,* 611–624.

Moscovici, S. (1985). *The age of the crowd: A historical treatise on mass psychology,* trans. J. C. Whitehouse. Cambridge University Press and Editions de la Maison des Sciences de l'Homme.

Muller, E. N. (1979). *Aggressive political participation.* Princeton: Princeton University Press.

Muller, E. N. (1985). Income inequality, regime repressiveness, and political violence. *American Sociological Review, 50,* 47–61.

Muller, E. N. & Opp, K. (1986). Rational choice and rebellious collective action. *American Political Science Review, 80,* 471–487.

Murdock, G. (1984). Reporting the riots: Images and impact. In J. Benyon (Ed.), *Scarman and after: Essays reflecting on Lord Scarman's report, the riots and their aftermath* (pp. 73–95). Oxford: Pergamon.

Myers, D. G. & Lamm, H. (1976). The group polarization phenomenon. *Psychological Bulletin, 83,* 602–627.

Nieburg, H. L. (1969). *Political violence: The behavioral process.* New York: St. Martin's Press.

Nye, R. A. (1975). *The origins of crowd psychology: Gustave Le Bon and the crisis of mass democracy.* London: Sage Publications.

Oberschall, A. (1973). *Social conflict and social movements.* Englewood Cliffs, NJ: Prentice-Hall.

Oberschall, A. (1979). Protracted conflict. In M. N. Zald & J. D. McCarthy (Eds.), *The dynamics of social movements: Resource mobilization, social control and tactics* (pp. 45–70). Cambridge, MA: Winthrop Publishers.

Oberschall, A. (1980). Loosely structured collective conflict: A theory and an application. *Research in Social Movements, Conflicts and Change, 3,* 45–68.

Oliver, P. E., & Marwell, G. (1988). The paradox of group size in collective action: A theory of the critical mass. II. *American Sociological Review, 53,* 1–8.

Oliver, P. E., Marwell, G., & Teixeira, R. (1985). A theory of the critical mass. I: Interdependence, group heterogeneity, and the production of collective action. *American Journal of Sociology, 91,* 522–556.

Olson, M. (1965). *The logic of collective action.* Cambridge, MA: Harvard University Press.

Olzak, S. (1987). Causes of ethnic conflict and protest in urban America, 1877–1889. *Social Science Research, 16,* 185–210.

Olzak, S. (1989). Analysis of events in the study of collective action. *Annual Review of Sociology, 15,* 119–141.

Pinard, M. (1971). *The rise of a third party: A study in crisis politics.* Englewood Cliffs, NJ: Prentice-Hall.

Pitcher, B. L., Hamblin, R. L., & Miller, J. L. (1978). The diffusion of collective violence. *American Sociological Review, 43,* 23–35.

Piven, F. F., & Cloward, R. A. (1977). *Poor people's movements: Why they succeed.* New York: Vintage.

Prentice-Dunn, S., & Rogers, R. W. (1980). Effects of deindividuating situational cues and aggressive models on subjective deindividuation and aggression. *Journal of Personality and Social Psychology, 39,* 104–113.

Prentice-Dunn, S., & Rogers, R. W. (1982). Effects of public and private self awareness on deindividuation and aggression. *Journal of Personality and Social Psychology, 43,* 503–513.

Pruitt, D. G. (1971). Choice shifts in group discussion: An introductory review. *Journal of Personality and Social Psychology, 20 (Special issue on the risky shift,* D. G. Pruitt, Ed.), 339–360.

Pruitt, D. G., & Rubin, J. Z. (1986). *Social conflict: Escalation, stalemate, and settlement.* New York: Random House.

Quarantelli, E. L., & Dynes, R. R. (1971). Property norms and looting: Their patterns in community crises. In J. A. Geschwender (Ed.), *The Black revolt* (pp. 285–300). Englewood Cliffs, NJ: Prentice-Hall.

Randall, A. (1991). *Before the Luddites: Custom, community and machinery in the English woollen industry, 1776–1809.* Cambridge: Cambridge University Press.

The riot beat. (1967, August 14). *Newsweek, 70,* p. 78.

Rogers, R. W., & Prentice-Dunn, S. (1981). Deindividuated and anger-mediated interracial aggression: Unmasking regressive racism. *Journal of Personality and Social Psychology, 41,* 63–73.

Rudé, G. (1959). *The crowd in the French revolution.* London: Oxford University Press.

Rudé, G. (1964). *The crowd in history, 1730–1848.* New York: John Wiley & Sons.

Rule, J. B. (1988). *Theories of civil violence.* Berkeley: University of California Press.

Rule, J. B., & Tilly, C. (1975). Political process in revolutionary France, 1830–1832. In J. M. Merriman (Ed.), *1830 in France* (pp. 41–85). New York: New Viewpoints.

Salert, B., & Sprague, J. (1980). *The dynamics of riots.* Ann Arbor: Inter-university Consortium for Political and Social Research.

Scarman, The Rt. Hon. the Lord. (1981). *The Brixton disorders 10–12 April 1981.* London: H. M. Stationery Office.

Signorielli, N., & Gerbner, G. (1988). *Violence and terror in the mass media: An annotated bibliography.* New York: Greenwood.

Singer, B. D. (1970). Mass media and communication processes in the Detroit riot of 1967. *Public Opinion Quarterly, 34,* 236–245.

Skolnick, J. H. (1969). *The politics of protest.* New York: Ballantine Books.

Slater, J. W., & McCombs, M. P. (1969). Some aspects of broadcast news coverage and riot participation. *Journal of Broadcasting, 13,* 367–370.

Smelser, N. (1962). *Theory of collective behavior.* New York: Macmillan.

Snyder, D. (1978). Collective violence: A research agenda and some strategic considerations. *Journal of Conflict Resolution, 22,* 499–534.

Snyder, D. (1979). Collective violence processes: Implications for disaggregated theory and research. *Research in Social Movements, Conflict and Change, 2,* 35–61.

Spiegel, J. (1971). *Transactions: The interplay between individual, family, and society* (J. Papajohn, Ed.) New York: Science House.

Spilerman, S. (1970). The causes of racial disturbances: A comparison of alternative explanations. *American Sociological Review, 35,* 627–649.

Spilerman, S. (1971). The causes of racial disturbances: Tests of an explanation. *American Sociological Review, 36,* 427–442.

Spilerman, S. (1975). Forecasting social events. In K. C. Land & S. Spilerman (Eds.), *Social indicator models* (pp. 381–403). New York: Russell Sage Foundation.

Spilerman, S. (1976). Structural characteristics of cities and the severity of racial disorders. *American Sociological Review, 41,* 771–793.

Stark, M. J. A., Raine, W. J., Burbeck, S. L., & Davison, K. K. (1974). Some empirical patterns in a riot process. *American Sociological Review, 39,* 865–876.

Stark, R. (1972). *Police riots: Collective violence and law enforcement.* Belmont, CA: Wadsworth Publishing Co., Inc.

Stevenson, J. (1977). Social control and the prevention of riots in England, 1789–1829. In A. P. Donajgrodski (Ed.), *Social control in nineteenth century Britain* (pp. 27–50). London: Croom Helm.

Stevenson, J. (1979). *Popular disturbances in England, 1700–1870.* New York: Longman.

Stevenson, J. (1992). *Popular disturbances in England, 1700–1832* (2nd ed.). New York: Longman.

Sullivan, T. J. (1977). The "critical mass" in crowd behavior: Crowd size, contagion and the evolution of riots. *Humboldt Journal of Social Relations, 4,* 46–59.

Tarrow, S. (1988). National politics and collective action: Recent theory and research in western Europe and the United States. *Annual Review of Sociology, 14,* 421–440.

Tarrow, S. (1989). *Democracy and disorder: Protest and politics in Italy, 1965–1975.* New York: Oxford University Press.

Thompson, E. P. (1968). *The making of the English working class* (rev. ed.). Harmondsworth: Penguin.

Thompson, E. P. (1971). The moral economy of the English crowd in the eighteenth century. *Past and Present, 50,* 76–136.

Tilly, C. (1978). *From mobilization to revolution.* Reading, MA: Addison-Wesley.

Tilly, C. (1979). Collective violence in European perspective. In H. D. Graham & T. R. Gurr (Eds.), *Violence in America: Historical and comparative perspectives* (rev. ed.). Beverly Hills: Sage Publications.

Tilly, C. (1986). *The contentious French.* Cambridge, MA: Harvard University Press.

Tomlinson, T. M. (1970). Ideological foundations for Negro action: A comparative analysis of militant and non-militant views of the Los Angeles riot. *Journal of Social Issues, 26,* 93–119.

Tumber, H. (1982). *Television and the riots: A report for the Broadcasting Research Unit of the British Film Institute.* London: British Film Institute.

Turner, R. H., & Killian, L. M. (1987). *Collective behavior* (3rd ed.). Englewood Cliffs, NJ: Prentice-Hall.

Waddington, D., Jones, K., & Critcher, C. (1989). *Flashpoints: Studies in public disorder.* London: Routledge.

Warren, D. I. (1969). Neighborhood structure and riot behavior in Detroit: Some exploratory findings. *Social Problems, 16,* 464–484.

Wheeler, L. (1966). Toward a theory of behavioral contagion. *Psychological Review, 73,* 179–192.

Wheeler, L., & Caggiula, A. R. (1966). The contagion of aggression. *Journal of Experimental Social Psychology, 2,* 1–10.

Zillmann, D. (1983). Arousal and aggression. In R. G. Geen & E. I. Donnerstein (Eds.), *Aggression: Theoretical and empirical reviews, Vol. 1* (pp. 75–101). New York: Academic.

Zimbardo, P. G. (1970). The human choice: Individuation, reason, and order versus deindividuation, impulse and chaos. In W. J. Arnold & D. Levine (Eds.), *Nebraska symposium on motivation, 1969* (pp. 237–307). Lincoln, NB: University of Nebraska Press.

# CHAPTER 11

# Interstate Crisis Escalation and War

Russell J. Leng
*Middlebury College*

The term *crisis* has acquired so many different meanings in contemporary discourse, that a description of what is meant by an interstate crisis should be offered at the outset of this chapter. The type of dispute that I discuss can be labeled more precisely as a *militarized interstate crisis*, that is, a dispute between nation-states that reaches a level of severity at which participants on each side threaten, display, or use military force against those on the other side. In other words, these are disputes in which there is a significant threat of war.

## THE DYNAMICS OF CRISIS ESCALATION

Militarized interstate crises seem to escalate almost naturally, and there are good reasons for this. First, once a dispute crosses the threshold where one party has challenged the other with the threat of force, and the other resists the challenge, the stakes become high for both parties. Whatever interests may have led the parties to threaten the use of force—and states do not initiate such threats lightly—the threat of force itself dramatically raises the stakes in terms of each party's reputation for resolve. High stakes tend to encourage contentious bargaining and risk taking. By the same token, the high stakes reduce the probability that national leaders will find mutually beneficial solutions to the dispute.

The presence of threats to the security of both sides can turn the dispute into a zero-sum game.

The social context in which they take place also encourages interstate crises to escalate. Interstate crises are public, and the public expects its leaders to respond in a strong, even pugnacious, manner to threats from other states. In international politics, war leaders are venerated; appeasers are scorned. Moreover, the international system lacks the political and social constraints on contentious behavior that come from a centralized authority with a monopoly on the legitimate use of force, or from the sense of obligation to community order that can be found within well-integrated domestic systems. One reason why crises frequently escalate to war in the international system is because there is little to prevent them from doing so.

The most effective constraint on the escalation of interstate crises is prudential, that is, a recognition by statesmen of the costs and risks associated with provoking or attacking a powerful and highly motivated adversary. The difficulty comes in objectively and accurately estimating comparative power and motivation. In international conflicts, information is often ambiguous, particularly regarding the intentions of the other side. Moreover, when the information is ambiguous, the intentions of the adversary tend to be viewed as hostile (Pruitt, 1965, p. 100). This problem is exacerbated when states employ coercive bargaining tactics to demonstrate their resolve, that is, their willingness to accept the risk of war to achieve their objectives.

The conventional wisdom in international politics, which goes by the name of *deterrence theory*, is that effective crisis bargaining is based on exploiting the other party's fear of war. If that is the view of the parties on each side, the bargaining becomes, in Kahn's (1965) words, "a competition in risk-taking" (p. 15). By the same token, it is generally assumed that the best means of deterring the other side from the use of coercive tactics is through a firm demonstration of resolve in the form of deterrent threats. This is essentially the same process that one observes in the increasingly belligerent *displays* of animals described by Archer and Huntingford in this volume.

As more coercive tactics are employed and tensions mount, the stakes, in terms of each side's prestige and reputation for resolve, grow as well. This, in turn, encourages more contentious bargaining. At the same time, the coercive tactics encourage greater hostility. The hostility is expressed in the mood of the public, as well as in the actions of national leaders who must be responsive to public opinion. The relationship between the rise in political stakes with the escalation in conflict creates a situation that goes beyond the usual notion of entrapment

(Brockner & Rubin, 1985: pp. 121–125).[1] In an escalating crisis, the conflict escalates beyond the point at which its costs and risks can no longer be justified by the initial stakes, not just because so much already has been committed to the effort and there is the hope that success lies just around the corner, but because the political stakes now *are* much higher. Statesmen, not unlike the animals in escalating conflicts that are described by Archer and Huntingford in this volume, see the displays of coercive actions partly as a process of signaling and assessing relative strength and motivation, but, unlike the animal fights, the actions themselves raise the stakes.

An example of this phenomenon occurring over an extended period of time can be seen in the escalation of the U.S. commitment to the conflict in Vietnam in the 1960s. As the United States committed more and more troops to the war effort, the stakes, in terms of American credibility and prestige, grew. It was not just a matter of the "light at the end of the tunnel" syndrome, that is, the hope that just a few more resources might push the other side to the breaking point, but the sense that such an enormous commitment had raised the reputational stakes for the United States to the point where continuing to add to the commitment was perceived as justified. Thus, President Nixon found himself justifying continuing the commitment to the war on the basis of the preceding "commitments of four American presidents." To put it another way, the escalation can become a justification for continuing escalation.

The escalatory change is qualitative as well as quantitative. With the increase in the stakes, hostility, and distrust (Holsti, North, & Brody, 1968), the process itself increases the level of stress (Holsti, 1989), reduces perceived options (Lebow, 1981), and encourages zero-sum thinking. "If we are bled to death, England shall at least lose India," the German Kaiser is said to have muttered in desperation on the eve of World War I (Montegales & Shucking, 1924, p. 350). We can only speculate on the thoughts of Saddam Hussein on January 15, 1991.

Not all interstate crises escalate to war. Most crises, in fact, are effectively "managed" by controlling the escalatory process. The Cuban Missile crisis is frequently presented as a contrast to the pre-World War I crisis. President Kennedy, who read Barbara Tuchman's account of the

---

[1] In entrapment the actor expends more than would be justified by the original stakes because the perceived potential proximity of success encourages the actor to commit more and more resources, rather than cut his or her losses. A simple example would be that of a long distance caller whose call has been placed "on hold." The costs continue to grow as the caller waits, but the other party could come to the phone at any second. Hanging up and trying again incurs the higher initial costs of a long distance call. The possibility of imminent success encourages the continued commitment of resources.

pre-World War I crisis in *Guns of August,* is said to have been very conscious of the need to maintain an objective view of Soviet intentions. In fact, the United States and the Soviet Union engaged in four major nuclear confrontations in the post-World War II era,[2] all of which ended without bloodshed. The fear of the mutually disastrous consequences of nuclear war certainly had something to do with the management of these crises, but statesmen have been able effectively to manage many non-nuclear crises as well. The same European statesmen who went to war over a crisis in the Balkans in 1914 avoided war in the Bosnian crisis of 1908. What are the differences between those militarized interstate crises that escalate to war, and those that do not?

## UNITS OF ANALYSIS

In attempting to gain a better understanding of the dynamics of the escalatory process and how to control it, political scientists have focused most of their attention on one or more of four units of analysis. First, there is the question of crisis decisionmaking per se—the interaction between the dynamics of the evolving crisis and the foreign policy-making process within governments. In these studies, the unit of analysis is either the individual decisionmaker, or the national decision-making system. A third unit of analysis is the crisis itself. Analysts have examined and compared the attributes of crises, with particular attention to the process of escalation or de-escalation as the crises evolve toward stalemate, settlement, or war. Finally, a more microscopic approach examines the bargaining strategies and tactics of the parties to the dispute to consider their effects on the evolution of the crisis, and their relative effectiveness in obtaining the objectives sought by the participants. The discussion of findings that follow begins with research focusing on the decision-making process, then it moves to consider the dynamics of crisis escalation and de-escalation, before concluding with research focusing on crisis bargaining. But, before moving to a discussion of those findings, it might be helpful to describe briefly the major research approaches employed by political scientists working in this area.

---

[2]The crises were: Berlin, 1948–1949; Berlin, 1961; Cuba, 1962, and the Middle East "Alert" crisis of 1973.

## RESEARCH APPROACHES

Beyond speculative theorizing and the construction of imagined scenarios, research on crisis escalation can be classified into one of three categories: (a) qualitative case studies, (b) rational choice models, or (c) quantitative studies of historical data.

***Qualitative Case Studies.*** The case study continues to be one of the mainstays of research on interstate conflict. The approach consists essentially of a close qualitative examination of the available written record of the dispute, or disputes, of interest, informed by the insights of a scholar well versed in the politics and histories of the states being studied. The finished work may range from a richly detailed narrative account of a single crisis, to an attempt to draw generalizations by applying a highly structured conceptual framework to a number of cases, as in Snyder and Diesing's (1977) study of thirteen 20th-century crises. Case studies have played a major role in generating insights and hypotheses regarding crisis bargaining and decision-making. The detailed and contextually rich accounts provide a useful complement to the abstract models that have been developed by rational choice theorists, and the simplified models employed in quantitative studies. On the other hand, qualitative case studies lack the scientific attributes of random selection, operational definitions, and objective testing that are necessary for cumulative findings. Moreover, even in comparative studies, the number of cases considered is small, and the selection of the sample may be biased according to the particular interests or preconceptions of the researcher.

***Rational Choice Models: Game Theory.*** Rational choice models, with their spare, mathematical construction, are methodologically at the opposite pole from qualitative case studies. Richness of detail and nuance are sacrificed in favor of parsimony, mathematical elegance, and logical rigor. The dominant approach among rational choice theorists has been game theory, beginning with the suggestive models of conflict bargaining presented by Schelling (1960, 1966) in the 1960s, to more recent works by theorists like Brams (1985b), Zagare (1987), and Powell (1987).

Game theoretic models explore the logical consequences of alternative choices by goal-oriented, rational players in games of strategy, that is, situations in which each player's best course of action is dependent on the moves of the other player. The approach thus takes into account the interdependence of the parties to a dispute, while offering a parsimonious way to consider the consequences of their moves.

In normal form, the game appears as a payoff matrix of outcomes based on the intersection of the strategy choices of the two players, such as in the game of "Chicken"[3] depicted in Table 11.1.

In this game, each player must choose between two strategies: compromise or escalate. The numbers within the cells in Table 11.1 represent the ordinally ranked utilities for each of the players, with 4 representing the best outcome and 1 the worst outcome for each player. Traditionally, the moves are made simultaneously, with each player having complete knowledge of the preference orderings of the other side but being unaware of its strategy choice until it is made.[4] The outcome for the row player appears on the left, and that for column player appears on the right. Chicken has been depicted (Brams, 1985b) as the prototypical game for a nuclear crisis, as the mutually disastrous outcome (1, 1), if both sides choose strategies of Escalate, suggests. Even in this very simple form, Chicken suggests a paradox that appears in a nuclear crisis. Each player knows that choosing a strategy of Escalate runs the risk of disaster if the other player does the same. The reasonable choice appears to be to choose Compromise, to obtain your second best outcome (3), assuming that the other party also recognizes the mutual disaster of an (1, 1) outcome. Even if the other side does choose a strategy of Escalate, you are better off with your second-worst payoff (2) than with your worst (1). On the other hand, there is an element of temptation in this game. If you can count on the other party to be reasonable, that is, to choose a strategy of Compromise, why not choose Escalate and get your best outcome?

Suppose the rules were adjusted so that you could communicate with the other party. Then you could commit yourself to choose a strategy of Escalate. If the other party finds your commitment credible, then its only rational choice is to choose Compromise and allow you to receive your most preferred payoff (4). This would be an act of "brinkmanship," that

---

[3]The name of the game comes from the game of "Chicken" played by teenagers in the 1950s. Beginning at opposite starting points, each player drives a car down the center line of the road, directly at the other car. The first player to swerve is "chicken."

[4]Brams and Wittman (1981) developed a "theory of moves" for a sequential game, in which, after a simultaneous move to determine an initial outcome, or starting point, the players choose their moves in strictly alternating fashion; that is, either player may depart from the original outcome. If neither does so, the game ends there. If one player moves, then the other has the choice of moving or ending the game at the second outcome. If that player moves, that is, changes its strategy, then the other has the stay or move choice, and so on until the player with the choice or moving or staying decides to stay at a particular outcome. It is my view that the Brams–Wittman approach more nearly captures the dynamics of real world crisis bargaining.

**TABLE 11.1**
**Chicken Game**

|  |  | Column Player | |
|---|---|---|---|
|  |  | Compromise | Escalate |
| Row | Compromise | 3,3 | 2,4 |
| Player | Escalate | 4,2 | 1,1 |

is, threatening mutual disaster if the other did not yield. Of course, if each party commits itself to choose Escalate and neither is believed by the other, the outcome is (1, 1), a disaster for both sides. By varying the rules of play in Chicken[5] and other suggestive games, some remarkable insights into the logical consequences of what are outwardly simple choices can be derived, some of which are discussed among the findings presented below.

The limitations of game theory are a function of its strengths: its elegant simplicity and rationality. The decisionmaking of a large governmental organization, with its complex networks of influence, and far more subtle combinations of cooperative and coercive tactics, is a far cry from the usually strictly binary choices presented in game theory. Moreover, crisis decisionmaking is fraught with problems of ambiguous information, uncertainty regarding national priorities, and emotional reactions that can confound rational choice.

*Quantitative Studies: Content Analysis and Event-Data Research.* Quantitative research in international politics is relatively young, with most of the significant studies beginning in the 1960s. The first important quantitative study dealing with crisis behavior per se appeared in 1964, with the Stanford (North, Brody, & Holsti, 1964) study of the pre-World War I crisis. The Stanford researchers employed content analysis to analyze the stream of communications between members of the Triple Entente and Dual Alliance in an effort to measure the role of psychological and perceptual variables, particularly perceptions of hostility, in the escalation of that crisis. The Stanford study laid the groundwork for a number of new schemes designed to generate and code machine-readable data on internation conflict behavior in a simpler and more efficient manner.

The approach, which has been labeled *event-data research*, consists of extracting descriptions of the actions taken by states, or other international actors, from written records in the press and diplomatic histories

---

[5]See Brams (1985b) for a number of interesting variations relating Chicken to real-world nuclear crises, including some interesting variants of Chicken using sequential games.

and then coding these descriptions into machine-readable form for aggregate analyses along dimensions of interest, such as the escalation or de-escalation of hostile actions over the evolution of a crisis. The most ambitious of the early event-data projects was McClelland's (1968) World Event/Interaction Survey (WEIS), which began a day-to-day coding of all internation actions of sufficient salience to be reported by the *New York Times*. This writer's own research, the Behavioral Correlates of War (BCOW) project, has focused on the coding of events in a sample of 40 interstate crises occurring between 1816 and 1980. The BCOW project uses multiple sources and a fine-grained typology of state actions that allows for a detailed examination of the internation influence process, as well as time series analyses of the escalation and de-escalation of crises.

Event-data analysis offers the advantages of replicability and corrigibility that can be obtained only with operational research methods. Moreover, by dealing with large samples of real-world crises, it is possible for event-data researchers to test hypotheses in an objective manner that is not possible in qualitative case studies.

The approach, nonetheless, has attracted its share of critics. Most of the criticism centers around the validity question of the potential difference between the description of an action as it is reported—and available to the researcher—and the interpretation of the action by participants. Some critics have argued that the extraction of events from their historical context deprives them of their substantive meaning. A more common criticism is that, when event-data researchers deal with intergovernmental communications by working from the written record and then forcing each of these communications into a preset action category, they lose the subtle nuances that are a critical component of the crisis bargaining process.

Research efforts employing one or another of these three approaches—qualitative case studies, game theory, and event-data research—are the sources of the findings on crisis escalation discussed later. Each requires some degree of inference from a different context. Findings from one, or even several, qualitative case studies suggest caution in drawing generalizations. Game theoretical models require an obvious inferential leap to a far more complex real-world environment. Even the best of quantitative studies require some simplification of reality. The reader must make his or her own judgments regarding the length of the inferential leap required, but a degree of caution is appropriate in drawing conclusions in all cases.

The discussion of findings is divided into two parts. The first part considers attempts to describe and model the dynamics of escalation and de-escalation as crises evolve. The second part considers research on the bargaining strategies and tactics employed by the participants over the course of an interstate crisis.

## PATTERNS OF ESCALATION AND DE-ESCALATION

In 1965, the nuclear strategist, Herman Kahn, imagined a scenario of escalation to nuclear war that contained an escalation ladder of 44 rungs, beginning with an "ostensible crisis" and ending with a "spasm or insensate" nuclear war. Kahn (1965) stated that when the last rung is reached, "all the buttons are pressed and the decision-makers and their staffs go home – if they still have homes" (p. 50). Kahn worked within a *realpolitik* tradition that views the coercive bargaining that occurs within a crisis as a test of a government's resolve. The "competition in risk-taking" drives the crisis up the escalation ladder until one party is able to deter the other from reaching for the next rung, or war breaks out. Crisis bargaining is viewed as essentially coercive with the key to successful deterrence of the adversary dependent on credibility of one's willingness to accept a high risk of war, including nuclear war, to achieve national objectives. Thus, an already dangerous situation is complicated by the temptation to bluff. Here a useful comparison can be drawn to the recent debate in animal studies (see Archer & Huntingford, this volume) over whether the fight displays of animals are accurate representations of their willingness to attack, or bluffs. There is no doubt that nations sometimes do bluff. Unfortunately, as in a poker hand where the sky is the limit, bluffing against a determined opponent can increase the stakes to the point where the bluffer finds he or she no longer can afford to withdraw.

At about the same time that Kahn was working on his metaphorical escalation scenario, the Stanford researchers (North et. al., 1964) were completing their content analysis of the crisis preceding the First World War. North and his associates were drawn to the origins of World War I because the war that occurred in August of 1914 seemed both unwanted and avoidable. The researchers coded the physical and verbal actions exchanged between the Triple Entente and Dual Alliance from the day of the assassination of the Austrian Archduke Francis Ferdinand to the outbreak of war. A simple action–response model, mediated by the perceptions that each side held of its own actions and those of the other party, was employed to analyze the stream of events. The authors found that the decisionmaking that occurred in the crisis was far removed from the cool and careful calculations prescribed by *realpolitik*. In fact, as the crisis escalated, the participants – particularly those within the Dual Alliance–increasingly overestimated the hostility intended by the actions of the other side and reacted in accordance with their perceptions. This, the authors argued, fueled the conflict spiral that was observed in the escalating threats and counterthreats of the two sides. The key to understanding the escalatory process lay in mutual perceptions of hostility and, in this crisis at least, the relationship between perception and reality was pathological. The study was taken one step further by Holsti (1972), who found evidence that the misperception was a by-product the stress produced by crisis decisionmaking. Performing in a threatening situation, under severe time constraints and with little sleep, national policymakers become increasingly fatigued and pressured. The stress, Holsti (1972) argued, reduces the decisionmaker's attention span and reinforces cognitive rigidity.

In the 25 years since the original Stanford study there have been a wide range of findings, most often from qualitative case studies, indicating that crisis decisionmaking is a far from rational process, with numerous instances of serious misperception, intolerance for ambiguity, restricted search for alternative strategies, insensitivity to the other side's perspective, stereotypical thinking, and erratic behavior. Although not all of these studies relate the pathological behavior to stress, they suggest a strong link between a drop in cognitive performance and more belligerent, escalatory, policy decisions.[6]

These studies raise the issue of how "rational" policymaking can be in escalating crises. From a game theoretic perspective, rationality requires decisionmaking based on a conscious calculation of advantages in accordance with a logically consistent ranking of value priorities. At the very minimum, decisionmakers must be able to rank the perceived possible outcomes, to choose one over another.[7] But national decisionmakers are not always able, or willing, to choose between values that are of vital interest to the nation, or to themselves. Given the constraints that are endemic to national decisionmaking–incomplete and ambiguous information, difficulty in establishing priorities among competing values, and the politics of the decision-making process itself–rationality must be viewed in relative terms. Simon (1957, 1985) employed the notion of procedural or "bounded" rationality as an appropriate measuring rod in these situations. Simon (1985) described policymaking as "boundedly rational" if the policy is "adaptive within the constraints imposed both by the external situation and by the capacities of the decision-maker" (p. 294).

---

[6]A useful summary of these findings appears in Holsti (1989). For a contrary view, see Oneal (1988).

[7]For a fuller discussion of the rationality assumption in game theory, as well as a strong defense of the rational choice perspective, see Brams (1985a).

Simon's (1985) view of rationality has been adopted by scholars (see Oneal, 1988) who argued that, despite the stress created by decision making in interstate crises, the jury is still out with regard to its effects on the ability of decisionmakers to make rational choices. Perhaps the most prominent, and most controversial, proponent of this view is Buena de Mesquita (1981), who, in an empirical study of decisionmaking at the brink of war, claimed to have achieved a great deal of success in predicting national choices based on a straightforward *realpolitik* calculation of interests and capabilities. It is interesting to note that what conclusions one reaches on these questions seems to be related to the theoretical perspective of the researcher. Those political scientists who have adopted a more psychological perspective on crisis escalation tend to find evidence of pathological effects of crisis decisionmaking under stress; those who have invested their energies in rational choice models tend to find greater rationality in crisis decisionmaking.

Political scientists have been in greater agreement regarding the crucial phases of the escalation process itself. An interstate dispute is viewed as escalating to a militarized crisis when one party threatens the other with the use of force, and the threatened party resists the challenge with a counterthreat of force (Leng & Singer, 1988; Snyder & Diesing, 1977). Snyder and Diesing (1977), who conducted a qualitative comparative study of 13 crises occurring between 1898 and 1962, have labeled the period following the resistance to the challenge as the "confrontation" phase. During the confrontation phase, the crisis escalates rapidly as both parties rely on predominantly coercive bargaining techniques to demonstrate their resolve and to coerce the other into complying with their wishes. The authors argue that the crisis will continue to escalate until one or both parties decides that further coercive, or countercoercive, bargaining is futile. When that happens, the crisis will move into a "resolution" phase and end in compromise or capitulation by one side. Of course, the crisis could escalate to war in the confrontation phase and never reach the resolution phase, or it could remain stalemated, with no real resolution.

Whereas interstate crises do tend to escalate during the confrontation phase, event-data studies have yielded some interesting variations in the actions and interactions of the participants. In these studies, each of the coded actions of the participants is classified as cooperative or conflictive and weighted according to its intensity. Then the weighted actions are aggregated at daily or weekly intervals, to obtain frequency distributions exhibiting patterns of escalation and de-escalation. An effort to develop a typology of crises according to their behavioral characteristics was undertaken by Leng and Gochman (1982) and refined by Leng (1993). The current version of the typology classifies interstate crises along two behavioral dimensions: (a) the degree of

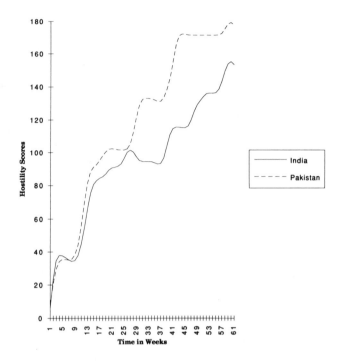

FIG. 11.1.   FIGHT: First Kashmir crisis, 1947.

reciprocity in the interactions of the disputants, that is, the extent to which their actions became more or less conflictive at the same times and to the same degree as the crisis evolves; and (b) the degree of escalation.[8] By employing dichotomous distinctions between high and low reciprocity and high and low escalation, the scheme yielded four behavioral types: a "Fight," which exhibits high scores on both dimensions; a "Stand-Off," with high reciprocity, but only moderate escalation; "Resistance, which exhibits low reciprocity, but high escalation; and a "Put-Down," which has low scores on both dimensions.

A good example of a "Fight" can be seen in Fig. 11.1, which presents a smoothed time series of hostility scores for the First Kashmir crisis, a territorial dispute between India and Pakistan, which erupted shortly after they achieved independence in 1947. As Fig. 11.1 illustrates, the

---

[8]The reciprocity measure combines two indicators: the distance between the two parties on the hostility measure, and the extent to which changes in the degree of hostility are moving in the same direction, at the same time, for the two parties. The measure of escalation combines the magnitude of hostility and the rate at which it is increasing or decreasing.

mix of cooperation and conflict for the two parties is remarkably similar in this rapidly escalating crisis. Had the crisis exhibited the same high degree of reciprocity but escalated only moderately, it would have been classified as a "Stand-Off." A typical "Stand-Off" pattern appears in the time series for the "Cod War" dispute between Britain and Iceland over fishing rights in 1975 and 1976, which appears in Fig. 11.2. The dispute began when Britain refused to accept a unilateral extension of its territorial limits. Icelandic forces harassed British fishermen, and the British responded with a naval show-of-force. As Fig. 11.2 illustrates, there was a good deal of reciprocity in the mix of cooperative and conflictive actions between the two sides, but the crisis never escalated beyond a number of minor military incidents. In a Stand-Off, neither party is willing to submit outright, yet the two sides manage to keep the dispute from escalating to a high level of conflict.

On the other hand, consider the precursor to the 1914 crisis, the 1908 Bosnian Crisis, which is depicted in Fig. 11.3. In this case the level of escalation is high, but the level of reciprocity is low. One reason for the low reciprocity score can be seen in the interesting "crossover" in the hostility levels of the two sides near the end of the crisis. This occurred when Germany entered the crisis on the side of her Austrian ally, thus encouraging Russia and Turkey to move to more cooperative bargaining strategies as the Austrians and Germans were becoming more belligerent. The label for this type of crisis is *Resistance*. It is interesting to compare this type with a *Put-Down*, in which the level of reciprocity is low but the level of escalation is only moderate, as in the case of the German *anschluss*, which united Austria with Germany in 1938 (Fig. 11.4). The escalation remains moderate because of the lack of serious Austrian resistance to Hitler's demand for the unification of the two Germanic states.

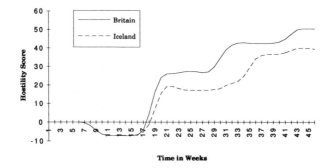

FIG. 11.2.  STAND-OFF: Cold War crisis, 1975–1976.

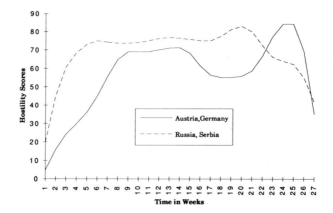

FIG. 11.3.   RESISTANCE: Bosnian crisis, 1908.

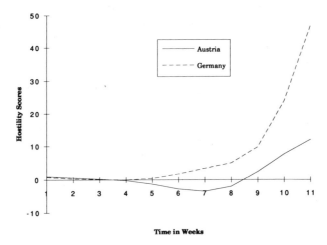

FIG. 11.4.   PUT-DOWN: Anschluss crisis, 1938.

An examination of 40 crises occurring between 1816 and 1980 (Leng, 1993) found that those crises ranking highest on both escalation and reciprocity (Fights) were the cases most likely to end in war. The second most war-prone type was the high escalation and low reciprocity "Resistance" category. If one compares these models with some models of crisis escalation appearing in the work of social psychologists, such as Pruitt and Rubin (1986), the escalatory process in a "Fight" closely resembles that of a classic "conflict spiral," in which the contentious actions of the two parties are highly reciprocal; whereas the escalatory process observed in the "Resistance" type resembles the "aggressor–defender" model, in which one party is responding defensively to the contentious initiatives of the other. In the Bosnian crisis, which is exhibited in Fig.11.3, there is a twist to the "aggressor–defender" model in that the tables are turned when Germany comes to the aid of Austria. Another interesting finding appears in the relationship between the degree of reciprocity exhibited in the actions of the two parties and compromise outcomes. Compromises occurred most frequently in low escalation, high reciprocity Stand-Offs, whereas crises falling into the low reciprocity Resistance and Put-Down categories were most likely to end either in war or in one side yielding to the demands of the other.

In addition to the question of the association between patterns of escalation and de-escalation and crisis outcomes, there is the question[9] of what induces the escalatory, or de-escalatory, patterns observed. The study (Leng, 1993) found that the degree of escalation was related to the security interests at stake for the two parties, and their optimism regarding success in war. Crises escalated more rapidly when vital interests (territorial integrity or political independence) were at stake and both sides were optimistic regarding their chances of winning at a reasonable cost should the crisis escalate to war. This is not surprising, because higher stakes and confidence in one's relative capabilities should increase the motivation to stand firm in humans and groups, just as they do in animals (see Archer & Huntingford, this volume).

One of the more intriguing descriptive findings that have emerged from event-data studies of crisis behavior is the overall high level of reciprocity in conflictive *and* cooperative actions (Leng & Wheeler, 1979) exhibited by the crisis adversaries. This finding becomes all the more interesting when one considers crisis bargaining at a more microscopic level.

## CRISIS BARGAINING AND ESCALATION

Research on crisis bargaining by students of international politics exhibits the tension between the competing perspectives represented by deterrence theorists, who view crises as games of strategy, based on rational choice, and those who view crisis decisionmaking as particularly prone to perceptual and psychological pathologies. Those taking

---

[9]The hostility measure is calculated by: (a) categorizing all actions as either cooperative or conflictive, (b) weighting each action according to the degree of cooperation or conflict, and (c) summing the positive (conflictive) and negative (cooperative) scores for each 7-day interval.

the former approach have directed their attention toward the techniques of manipulative bargaining, with a strong emphasis on building a credible demonstration of resolve through the use of commitments (see Schelling, 1960, 1966). Although these theorists do not assume that the most appropriate influence techniques are always coercive, their work has tended to view crisis bargaining from that perspective. Viewing crisis bargaining as a game of strategy, in which the object is to win in terms of one's own value preferences, and each player's best strategy is dependent on the choices of the other, neatly lends itself to the rational choice models of game theorists.

On the other hand, for those who view crisis escalation as a pathology, a more appropriate model is the *conflict spiral*. Escalation is seen as the consequence of increasingly coercive sequences of threats and counterthreats by two determined adversaries. Whether the reactions are prompted by a desire to retaliate or out of concern for security—to avoid the risk of appearing irresolute—the hypothesized consequences are the same: increased hostility, stress, and insecurity, with weakened perceptual and cognitive skills. For these researchers, the focus shifts away from manipulative influence strategies to psychologically generated responses. The prescriptive focus shifts too. The objective is not to best the adversary but to avoid the dangers of uncontrollable escalation.

The distinction that I have made between the two approaches is deliberately stark, to give the reader a sense of the paths over which political scientists approached the problem as systematic research began in earnest in the 1960s. It was not long, though, before researchers began to combine the two perspectives. Working from a deterrence perspective, George, Hall, and Simons (1971) completed a comparative qualitative study of three American foreign policy crises in the 1960s[10] and explored the tension between the use of a coercive bargaining strategy and the avoidance of war. The authors concluded that the cases suggested that eight conditions were necessary for the successful use of coercive bargaining techniques: (a) strong motivation on the part of the actor employing the techniques, (b) an advantage in motivation favoring that actor, (c) clarity of objectives, (d) a sense of urgency, (e) strong domestic support, (f) effective usable military options, (g) fear of escalation on the part of the adversary, and (h) clarity concerning the terms of a settlement. Comparable findings from case studies were reported by George and Smoke (1974) and Smoke (1977), who emphasized the critical role played by perception.

Game theorists, meanwhile, focused most of their attention on

---

[10]The crises were over Laos, Cuba, and Vietnam.

**TABLE 11.2**
**Prisoner's Dilemma**

|  |  | Column Player | |
|---|---|---|---|
|  |  | Compromise | Escalate |
| Row | Compromise | 3,3 | 1,4 |
| Player | Escalate | 4,1 | 2,2 |

nuclear crises, where an interesting paradox prevails. On the one hand, the mutually disastrous outcome for both sides, should the crisis escalate to nuclear war, encourages cautious bargaining. On the other hand, knowledge of the need for caution by the other party suggests to each player that the other's "provocation threshold" is quite high. This suggests that one might, in fact, take bigger risks than in those cases in which the decision to go to war would not have such a high probability of a total cataclysm. It also encourages bluffing, or "brinkmanship."

The prevailing model for nuclear crises is the game of "Chicken," described earlier, in which mutual escalation results in a disastrous outcome for both sides.[11] In non-nuclear crises, however, the appropriate model for evenly matched adversaries is Prisoner's Dilemma, a two-by-two game notorious for encouraging each player to choose a strategy of Escalate, even though the consequences of both choosing Escalate (2, 2) are worse than if both choose Compromise (3, 3).[12] The matrix for Prisoner's Dilemma appears in Table 11.2.

Political scientists have viewed this game as analogous to a crisis in which both parties perceive war as preferable to submission. Because each does not know which strategy the other will chose, it is in the best interest of each to choose Escalate over Compromise.[13] By choosing a strategy of Escalate, a player either receives its best outcome, or its second-worst outcome, whereas a strategy of Compromise yields either its second-best outcome, or its worst outcome. How does one encourage both players to choose Compromise so that each can achieve its second-best outcome, rather than choose Escalate and receive its second-

---

[11]Brams (1985b) provided a useful introduction to recent work on this question. Zagare (1987) presented an interesting argument to the effect that these games may be more appropriately modeled as Prisoner's Dilemma.

[12]Some analysts in the media described the Persian Gulf crisis as a game of Chicken; however, both of the adversaries—without using the terminology—did their best to indicate that they saw it as Prisoner's dilemma, that is, that they preferred war to submission.

[13]In game theoretic terms, Escalate is the *dominant* strategy for either player, that is, it yields a better payoff than Compromise regardless of which strategy the other player chooses.

worst outcome? There is no good answer if the game is played only once. But, if it is played for many repetitions, with each player seeing the outcome of each repetition, the situation becomes more interesting.

Axelrod (1984) sought an answer to the question through a computer tournament in which he invited contestants to submit their favorite strategy for playing repeated iterations of Prisoner's Dilemma. Each contestant submitted a computer program containing a strategy designed to compete for an extended series of plays against each of the other strategies submitted. The winning entry, which was submitted by the psychologist–mathematician, Anatol Rapoport, was to choose compromise on the first play of the game and employ a strict tit for tat strategy on every succeeding play, that is, to choose the strategy employed by the other player on the previous move. Axelrod (1984) speculated that the findings could be extended to a wide range of political bargaining situations containing the uncertainty and distrust found in Prisoner's Dilemma. He hypothesized that the overall success of Rapoport's tit for tat strategy was based on four features: (a) its niceness: the communication of a willingness to cooperate on the first move; (b) its firmness: the instant retaliation—on the next play of the game—for any defection by the opponent; (c) its forgiving nature—despite any earlier defections, any cooperative move by the other side is rewarded on the next play; and (d) its clarity—it should be easy for the other party to recognize the tit for tat strategy.

The model, in fact, does not fit interstate crisis bargaining very well. States do not make their moves simultaneously, but in action–reaction sequences; by definition, the first move in a crisis is never cooperative, and, without the cooperative first move, a strict tit for tat strategy will lock the players into an escalatory pattern of reciprocated coercive bargaining. Furthermore, Axelrod himself questioned the efficacy of the strategy in situations of high hostility, of the type exhibited in a militarized crisis. Nevertheless, there have been some intriguing results from empirical research on crisis bargaining suggesting that there might be something to Axelrod's initial conclusions.

As I noted before, there already was some evidence that the escalatory patterns of interstate crises were related to the tendency of states to reciprocate the actions of the other party (Leng & Wheeler, 1979; North et al., 1964). More importantly, about the same time that Axelrod's (1984) tournament results were being analyzed, Leng and Wheeler (1979) conducted an event-data study of 20 real-world interstate crises in which they found that states employing what they described as *reciprocating* influence strategies enjoyed more successes—diplomatic victories or compromises—than those employing escalating coercive, or *bullying*, bargaining strategies. This was true even when the opponent employed a bullying strategy. As Leng and Wheeler (1979) defined it, a reciprocating strategy does not require a cooperative opening move but allows cooperative initiatives later in the crisis. Otherwise it retains the essential features of tit for tat. Leng and Wheeler (1979) based their model of a reciprocating strategy on studies by social psychologists (Esser & Komorita, 1975) demonstrating the efficacy of a "firm-but-fair" approach to bargaining in interpersonal experiments. There are three essential components to the approach: (a) The party employing the reciprocating strategy does not initiate any belligerent moves that would threaten the security or prestige of the other party; (b) it demonstrates its firmness by immediately responding in kind to coercive actions by the other party; while (c) indicating its willingness to move toward a cooperative settlement through occasional cooperative initiatives. Thus it avoids provoking escalation of the conflict without appearing weak or irresolute. The findings from the Leng and Wheeler (1979) study were replicated in a study of extended deterrence by Huth (1988), and, most recently, in the study of crisis behavior described previously (Leng, 1933). The 1993 study indicated that the key to eliciting cooperation in real-world crises lay in mixing flexibility and firmness within single moves, through the use of carrot-and-stick initiatives and responses combining firmness in the face of attempts at coercion with an expressed willingness to negotiate. Moreover, successful statesmen were likely to offer cooperative initiatives, not at the outset of the crisis but only after they had exhibited their firmness in response to threats from the other side.

The study also indicated that statesmen were far more likely to employ reciprocating influence strategies when they found themselves defending, rather than challenging, the status quo. The choice makes sense when one considers the logic of an influence strategy based on exhibiting firmness in the face of threats, while avoiding the initiation of threatening moves and responding in kind to offers to cooperate. Reciprocating influence strategies clearly are better suited for deterrence than compellence. The United States chose a reciprocating strategy to defend its position in the face of Soviet threats during the "Alert" crisis in the Middle East in 1973, but it employed an escalating coercive "bullying" strategy in its attempt to compel Saddam Hussein to withdraw from Kuwait in the crisis preceding the Persian Gulf war in 1990–1991. Bullying strategies, however, have been found (Leng, 1993; Leng & Wheeler, 1979) to be highly associated with war outcomes.

The effectiveness of reciprocating strategies in deterrent situations challenges the conventional wisdom that the key to prevailing in a crisis lies in demonstrating the credibility of one's commitment to achieve national objectives by accepting a high risk of war. The findings also challenge the *realpolitik* view that accepting a high level of escalation, with its attendant pathologies and risks, is the only path to success in a militarized interstate crisis.


## ESCALATION IN RECURRING CRISES


What happens when rival states become engaged in recurrent crises? Real-world cases of the phenomenon are not hard to find: Israel and the Arabs, the United States and the former Soviet Union, Turkey and Greece, and India and Pakistan quickly come to mind. Common sense suggests that the success or failure of the bargaining strategy employed by a government in one crisis is likely to affect its choice of bargaining strategy in the next.

Jervis (1976, pp. 229–230) postulated that national policymakers tend to draw rather superficial lessons from history, and that they are likely to draw strong analogies from their experiences in previous disputes to guide their behavior in recurring conflicts. Jervis hypothesized that a tendency to see their own state's behavior as decisive encourages policymakers to consider unsuccessful outcomes as the result of ineffective bargaining; consequently, following a defeat, they are likely to switch bargaining strategies in the next encounter with the same adversary. On the other hand, Jervis (1976) argued, a successful outcome is likely to make policymakers insensitive to changes in the situation, so that they will tend to repeat the previously successful bargaining strategy in the next dispute rather than undertake the effort to devise a new strategy adjusted to changing circumstances (p. 280).

Working from these assumptions, I hypothesized that a *realpolitik* perspective on conflict bargaining encourages national policymakers to assume that, when bargaining strategies do fail, they do so because the government has not exhibited a sufficient demonstration of resolve (Leng, 1983 pp. 381–382). This view would encourage governments to respond to a diplomatic defeat in one crisis by adopting a more coercive bargaining strategy in the next crisis with the same adversary. I further hypothesized that a government that had been successful in the preceding encounter would repeat the same bargaining strategy in the next crisis *until* its adversary—the loser in the last dispute—adopted a more coercive strategy, in accordance with the first hypothesis. Once it did so, the previous winner, viewing the more coercive strategy as a challenge to *its* resolve, would move to a more coercive bargaining strategy as well. This led to the general proposition that, all other things being equal, unless the preceding crisis ended in a mutually satisfactory compromise, each succeeding crisis between the same pair of adversaries should escalate to a higher degree of conflict intensity. This prediction of coercion begetting coercion ran counter to the view of some students of crisis bargaining (Bell, 1971; McClelland, 1961), who argued that previous crisis experiences led policymakers to more effectively manage succeeding crises.

The question was investigated empirically through an events-data study of the behavior of six pairs of states,[14] who were engaged in three successive crises each, within a relatively short period. The *Realpolitik Experiential Learning* (REL) hypothesis of increased levels of coercion from one crisis to the next was supported by the findings, with the changes predicted by the hypothesis correct in 18 of the 24 cases. The study, of course, is based on a small sample of cases; moreover, however strongly the coercion begets coercion pattern is supported by the findings, the link between the observed actions and the putative motivations of the participant states is speculative. Still, the prominence of a *realpolitik* orientation to crisis bargaining, which places a heavy emphasis on the importance of demonstrating resolve when vital interests are at stake, provides a good deal of face validity to the REL hypothesis.

## CONCLUSION

A recurring theme in this chapter has been the tension between a *realpolitik* tradition that views crisis bargaining as a test of resolve and a perspective that suggests that the *realpolitik* approach itself contributes significantly to the pathologies that cause militarized interstate crises to escalate to war.

From a *realpolitik* perspective, the prudential management of interstate crises requires a careful weighing of costs and risks, and an accurate perception of the capability and motivation of the adversary. In a world of coolly calculating statesmen, such as that envisaged by deterrence theorists, successful crisis bargaining can be viewed as a contest in "perceived comparative resolve," in which a strategy of escalating coercive tactics is employed to convince the other party of a government's willingness to risk war to achieve national objectives.

---

[14]The pairs were: France and Germany, and Austria and Russia, in the period leading up to World War I, Britain and Germany during the interwar period, and India and Pakistan, Egypt and Israel, and the former Soviet Union and the United States in the post-World War II period.

Political scientists who have worked within the deterrence theory tradition have tended to direct their attention to rational choice models of crisis bargaining.

Those who reject the *realpolitik* approach tend to direct their attention to factors that drive crises to escalate out of control. The high stakes, reputational as well as strategic, public pressures for assertiveness, and the dynamics of the escalating conflict all exert pressure for these disputes to escalate. There also is a large body of research indicating that these problems are exacerbated significantly by perceptual and psychological problems endemic to crisis decisionmaking. The most provocative element of this research, however, is the conclusion that the coercive bargaining prescribed by deterrence theorists contributes significantly to crisis escalation, misperception, and intensified hostility. In fact, a number of case studies suggest that the effectiveness of an escalating coercive bargaining strategy is dependent on a high degree of asymmetry, in motivation as well as in usable military capability, favoring the party employing the coercive tactics. Important additional requirements are strong domestic support and fear of escalation on the part of the adversary. Otherwise, a strategy of escalating coercion is likely to lead to war.

The *realpolitik* approach to bargaining has been challenged by findings suggesting the efficacy of a *reciprocating*, or firm-but-flexible, bargaining strategy, which combines firmness in the face of threats with a demonstrated willingness to move to a cooperative solution. The "firm" component avoids direct threats to the immediate security of the other side. The "flexible" component represents a willingness to consider a negotiated solution. In its operational form, the technique combines occasional unilateral cooperative initiatives with tit for tat responses to influence attempts by the other party. My own research has indicated that this approach has been used effectively in a wide variety of crises.

Nevertheless, the view of international politics most widely accepted by national leaders continues to be *realpolitik*. Evidence of this was found in the study of recurring crises described earlier. There is more immediate evidence as well. In the recent crisis and war that occurred in the Persian Gulf, the leadership in both Iraq and the United States were guided by the prescriptions of *realpolitik*. The United States initially responded to the Iraqi invasion of Kuwait with a reciprocating strategy and then switched to an escalating coercive, or bullying, strategy in November when its troop commitment was raised to an offensive level and the Iraqis were presented with an ultimatum from the U.N. Security Council. The submit or fight choice was underlined by President Bush's public refusal to allow his adversary to save face. I wrote at the time

(Leng, 1990) that, based on my previous research on crisis behavior, this was a recipe for war.

Once they achieved control of Kuwait, the Iraqis adopted a reciprocating strategy in their bargaining with the United States. The threat to Saudi Arabia was reduced, and their behavior was directed toward maintaining the territorial gains in Kuwait, without provoking the United States into an attack. Based on the models of crises that I presented earlier, the United States–Iraq component of the Persian Gulf crisis fits the "Resistance" model, with the Iraqis in the position of attempting to defend the gains of their aggression in Kuwait from the U.S. challenge. Crises exhibiting this behavioral pattern are most likely to end either in the submission by one side to the demands of the other, or in war.

As the United States pressed the challenge, the stakes—in terms of each side's reputation for resolve, and the personal prestige of the leaders—escalated with the level of hostility and commitment; nevertheless, each party proceeded from the *realpolitik* assumption that the *other side* would decide that the outbreak of war would be counter to its interests. President Bush said that he "had a gut feeling" that Saddam Hussein ultimately would recognize that he only could lose in a military confrontation with the United States and its United Nations coalition partners, and that it would be more prudent to cut his losses.[15] Saddam Hussein is said to have been convinced that the United States would decide that the economic and strategic interests at stake were not worth the potential sacrifice in American lives. It appears that each side assumed an asymmetry in motivation in its favor.

During the course of the crisis, President Bush made frequent references to the Vietnam conflict and the lesson that he derived from that experience. I referred previously to Vietnam as an illustration of the interaction between escalatory tactics and rising stakes. The lesson that President Bush drew from the Vietnam conflict was that we fought the war "with one hand tied behind our back," that is, that we did not pursue the conflict with sufficient force. President Bush's view is consistent with our research on recurring crises, which suggests that national leaders are likely to interpret dispute outcomes, whether

---

[15]It has been argued by some that, by the end of October, President Bush was determined to go to war, and that the escalating coercive bargaining was directed toward that end. The comments of his closest advisors that have surfaced since the end of the war, however, are consistent in indicating that the President believed that the escalating coercion culminating in the ultimatum deadline offered the best prospect of achieving a dramatic diplomatic victory in a situation in which he assumed that a war would lead to incalculable consequences.

successes or failures, in *realpolitik* terms. Losses are viewed as the consequence of a failure to act with sufficient strength.

Even if we ignore the aggression against Kuwait and the other moral outrages committed by Saddam Hussein, his actions can be criticized on strictly pragmatic grounds from either a *realpolitik* or a psychological approach to crisis bargaining. On the one hand, he woefully misjudged Iraq's power and the motivation of his adversaries; on the other hand, his application of a reciprocating bargaining strategy was devoid of the demonstration of flexibility necessary to elicit cooperation from the other side. The only reasonable way out of the trap into which Saddam had led his country was through a face-saving retreat. His refusal to seek that exit is an inexcusable diplomatic failure. If one assumes that, for the United States, a diplomatic retreat by Iraq was preferable to the costs of war, then President Bush's public statements "no negotiations, no compromises, no attempts at face-saving," effectively eliminated that possibility. Bush created a situation in which the only way that Saddam Hussein could "cut his losses" was through cutting his throat.

Was there a face-saving way out for Iraq that would have avoided the deaths, human misery, and ecological disaster that the war produced? Certainly, there was nothing in the actions of participants to suggest that either side was interested in pursuing that option. Should aggressors ever be rewarded, even through so much as a face-saving line of retreat? How is the principle of not rewarding aggression weighed against the costs and risks of war? Those questions confront us today in Bosnia. The research that I have described in this chapter can help us understand why crises escalate to war and offer some suggestions on how to avoid having them do so, but it cannot tell us how to choose between war and compromise.

## REFERENCES

Axelrod, R. (1984). *The evolution of cooperation*. New York: Basic.

Bell, C. (1971). *The conventions of crisis: A study in diplomatic management*. London: Oxford University Press.

Brams, S. J. (1985a). *Rational politics: Decisions, Games, and strategy*. Washington, DC: CQ Press.

Brams, S. J. (1985b). *Superpower games: Applying game theory to superpower conflict*. New Haven, CT: Yale University Press.

Brams, S. J., & Wittman D. (1981). Nonmyopic equilibria in 22 games. *Conflict Management and Peace Science, 6*, 39–62.

Brockner, J., & Rubin, J. (1985). *The social psychology of conflict escalation and entrapment*. New York: Springer-Verlag.

Buena de Mesquita, Br. (1981). *The war trap*. New Haven, CT: Yale University Press.

Esser, J. K., & Komorita, S. S. (1975). Reciprocity and concession making in bargaining. *Journal of Abnormal and Social Psychology, 61*; 181–89.

George, A., Hall, D., & Simons, W. (1971). *The limits of coercive diplomacy*. Boston: Little, Brown.

George, A., & Smoke, R. (1974). *Deterrence in American foreign policy: Theory and practice*. New York: Columbia University Press.

Holsti, O. R. (1965). The 1914 case. *American Political Science Review, 59*, 365–378.

Holsti, O. R. (1972). *Crises, escalation, war*. Montreal: McGill-Queens University Press.

Holsti, O. R.(1989). Crisis decision making. In P. E. Tetlock, J. L. Husbands, R. Jervis, P. C. Stern, & C. Tilly (Eds.), *Behavior, society, and nuclear war* (Vol. 1, pp.8-84). New York: Oxford University Press.

Holsti, O. R., North, R., & Brody, R. (1968). Perception and action in the 1914 crisis. In J. D. Singer (Ed.), *Quantitative international politics* (pp. 123–158) New York: The Free Press.

Huth, P. W. (1988). *Deterrence and war*. New Haven, CT: Yale University Press.

Jervis, R. (1976). *Perception and misperception in international relations*. Princeton, NJ: Princeton University Press.

Kahn, H. (1965). *On escalation: Metaphors and scenarios*. New York: Praeger.

Lebow, R. N. (1981). *Between peace and war*. Baltimore: Johns Hopkins University Press.

Leng, R. J. (1983). When will they ever learn? Coercive bargaining in recurrent crises. *Journal of Conflict Resolution, 27*; 379–420.

Leng, R. J. (1990, December 13) Winning without war. *Christian Science Monitor*.

Leng, R. J. (1993). *Interstate crisis behavior, 1816–1980: Realism vs. reciprocity*. Cambridge: Cambridge University Press.

Leng, R. J., & Gochman, C S. (1982). Dangerous disputes: A study of conflict behavior and war. *American Journal of Political Science, 26*, 664–687.

Leng, R. J., & Singer, J. D. (1988). Militarized interstate crises: The BCOW typology and its applications. *International Studies Quarterly, 32*, 155–173.

Leng, R. J., & Wheeler, H. (1979). Influence strategies, success, and war. *Journal of Conflict Resolution, 23*; 571–591.

McClelland, C. A. (1961). The acute international crisis. *World Politics, 41*, 182–204.

McClelland, C. A. (1968). International interaction analysis: Basic research and some practical applications. *Technical Rep. No. 2: World Event/Interaction Survey*. Los Angeles: University of Southern California.

Montegales, M., & Shucking, W. (Eds.) (1924). *Outbreak of the World War, German documents collected by Karl Kautsky*. New York: Oxford University Press.

North, R. C., Brody, R., & Holsti, O. R. (1964). Some empirical data on the conflict spiral. *Papers, Peace Research Society (Int'l), 1*; 1–14.

Oneal, J. R. (1988). The rationality of decision making during international crises. *Polity, XX*; 598–622.

Powell, R. (1987). Crisis bargaining, escalation, and MAD. *American Political Science Review, 81*; 717–735.

Pruitt, D. G. (1965). Definition of the situation as a determinant of international action. In H. A. Kelman (Ed.), *International behavior* (pp. 391–432). New York: Holt, Rinehart & Winston.

Pruitt, D. G., & Rubin, J. Z. (1986). *Social conflict: Escalation, stalemate, and settlement*. New York: Random House.

Schelling, T. C. (1960). *Strategy of conflict.* Cambridge, MA: Harvard University Press.

Schelling, T. C. (1966). *Arms and influence.* New Haven, CT: Yale University Press.

Simon, H. A. (1957). *Models of man.* New York: Wiley.

Simon, H. A. (1985). Human nature in politics: The dialogue of psychology with political science. *American Political Science Review, 79.*

Smoke, R. (1977). *War: Controlling escalation.* Cambridge, MA: Harvard University Press.

Snyder, G. & Diesing, p. (1977). *Conflict among nations.* Princeton, NJ: Princeton University Press.

Zagare, F. (1987). *Dynamics of deterrence.* Chicago: University of Chicago Press.

# Author Index

# Subject Index

## A

Adrenocortical hormones, 18, 49 (*see* Autonomic)
Adrenomedullary hormones, 49, 61 (*see* Autonomic)
Aggression,
  aggression machine paradigm, 37–39, 146, 147, 203
  alcohol and, 64–65
  antisocial behavior and, 37, 39
  aversively motivated, 203–204
  cognitive dissonance and, 38–39
  cues for, 35–36, 37–39, 126–127 (*see also* Provokers)
  defensive, 91–92, 99
  developmental changes in,
    humans, 165 (*see also* Temper tantrums, changes with age)
    other animals, 229
  displacement of (*see* Redirection)
  emotionally reactive, 34–40, 65–67, 123–124, 129, 139, 146
  escalation of (*see* Escalation of aggression)
  genetics of, 232
  impulsive (*see* Emotionally reactive)

instrumental, 34–35, 40, 139
motivational characteristics of, 34–35, 52, 54, 66, 74–75, 89–90, 92, 95, 100–102
offensive, 91–92
proactive, 35, 139, 187 (*see also* Aggression, instrumental)
proneness, 34–37, 136, 150, 186, 211, 241 (*see also* Hostility)
redirection of, 88–89 (*see also* Priming)
reinforcement, 37, 52, 89–90, 118–119, 180–181, 185, 203
schedule induced, 74
scripts for, 214–215
self directed, 163–164
stimuli eliciting (*see* Provoker)
threshold for, 52, 85–86, 96, 98, 289–290, 292, 307, 323
Aggressive phenomenology, 141
Amygdala, 82, 87, 95–99, 102
  central nucleus, 94
  corticomedial (CMA), 79–82, 84, 90, 95, 103–104
  basolateral, 79, 97, 102, 103
Androgens, 17–18, 232
Anger, 36, 39, 45–48, 91–103, 157–172, 175–179, 181–182, 184–185, 187–189, 191, 201, 271